KNOWING
WOMEN

FEMINISM AND
KNOWLEDGE

This book is the first in a series of four published by Polity Press in association with The Open University. The complete list is:

Knowing Women: Feminism and Knowledge
edited by Helen Crowley and Susan Himmelweit

Defining Women: Social Institutions and Gender Divisions
edited by Linda McDowell and Rosemary Pringle

Inventing Women: Science, Technology and Gender
edited by Gill Kirkup and Laurie Smith Keller

Imagining Women: Cultural Representations and Gender
edited by Frances Bonner, Lizbeth Goodman, Richard Allen, Linda Janes and Catherine King

The books are one component of the Open University course *U207 Issues in Women's Studies*. Details of the course are available from the Central Enquiry Service, The Open University, PO Box 200, Milton Keynes MK7 2YZ. Telephone: 0908 653078

Acknowledgement

With many thanks to Veronica Beechey who conceived and initiated the project which became this book, but who through illness, unfortunately was unable to complete it.

The Open University U207 *Issues in Women's Studies* Course Production Team

Amanda Willett, Barbara Hodgson, Cathering King (Chair), Diana Gittins, Dinah Birch, Felicity Edholm, Fiona Harris, Frances Bonner, Gill Kirkup, Harry Dodd, Helen Crowley, Joan Mason, Judy Lown, Kathryn Woodward, Laurie Smith Keller, Linda Janes, Linda McDowell, Lizbeth Goodman, Maggie Riley, Maureen Adams, Meg Sheffield, Melanie Bayley, Randhir Auluck, Richard Allen, Rosemary Pringle, Siân Lewis, Susan Crosbie, Susan Himmelweit, Susan Khin Zaw, Tony Coulson, Veronica Beechey, Wendy Webster

External Assessor: Elizabeth Wilson, Professor of Policy Studies, Polytechnic of North London

Cover illustration by Christine Tacq

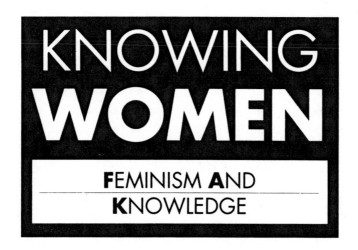

KNOWING WOMEN

FEMINISM AND
KNOWLEDGE

Edited by Helen Crowley and Susan Himmelweit

POLITY PRESS in association with  The Open University

Selection and editorial material copyright © 1992 The Open University

First published in the United Kingdom by Polity Press in association with
Blackwell Publishers Ltd and The Open University

Reprinted 2006, 2007

Polity Press
65 Bridge Street
Cambridge CB2 1UR, UK

Polity Press
350 Main Street
Malden, MA 02148, USA

Edited and designed by The Open University

ISBN: 978-0-7456-0975-1
ISBN: 978-0-7456-0976-8 (pbk)

A CIP catalogue record for this book is available from the British Library
and from the Library of Congress.

Typeset in Palatino on 10/12 pt
by Photo·graphics, Honiton, Devon
Printed and bound in Great Britain by
Marston Book Services Limited, Oxford

This book is printed on acid-free paper.

For further information on Polity, visit our website: www.polity.co.uk

CONTENTS

INTRODUCTION

This book is a contribution to the growing field that has, within the United Kingdom, become known as 'women's studies'. The accidental ambiguity in the field's name – whether it is what women study, or the study of women – is a fortuitous one for this book. For its purposely ambiguous title *Knowing Women*, which could mean either how we know about women or how we as women know, parallels the development of the field as a whole. 'Knowing women' no longer just means developing knowledge about women, in which women feature as the *objects* of knowledge. It also means understanding the subjective process whereby women understand, create and use knowledge. In other words, 'knowing women' now also involves understanding women as the *subjects* of knowledge, subjects both in the sense of being subject to and shaped by the social forces constituting particular forms of knowledge, and in the sense of intentionally creating and using new forms of knowledge to transform those social forces. It is this newer slant which justifies a whole volume on the topic.

Feminism as a political movement has, at every stage, produced a complementary academic interest in the study of women. In the initial stages of current feminism – in the late 1960s and early 1970s – the aim was to make women visible as objects of study. Existing studies had either ignored women altogether or homogenized them with men, subsuming them under the supposedly ungendered category of 'human-being'. Women as a gender were thus invisible, either because they were absent or because their gender was thought irrelevant. The task of feminist studies in those early stages was to render women visible, to claim equality for women as objects of knowledge.

This paralleled the feminist political project of creating equality for women, where that meant equality with the existing position of men, by the removal of those disadvantages currently associated with being a woman. However, this perspective failed to recognize that men's positions in society were just as gendered as women's. It was not only that women were disadvantaged by their gender, but that men were privileged by theirs; in a hierarchy it is, of course, impossible for everyone to be on the top. Similarly, in the theoretical project of making women count as equals, if women were to be rendered visible by measuring them against scales appropriate to men, all that could be shown was the ways in which women were either the same as or different from men, and little could be said about the structural interdependence of women's and men's characteristics.

Both the political project and the related academic one were based on an individualist philosophy in which the common humanity of women and men as rational, self-motivated individuals justified their equal treatment. However, the rational individual implicit in this picture of a shared humanity had some inherently 'masculine' characteristics and the picture was thus necessarily incomplete. For, even if men in our society were to behave as if they were such rational, self-seeking individuals, they could do so only because society also contains others – women – who do not behave in that way. For no society can continue in existence without its members being reproduced. But such unsexed, self-contained and self-seeking individuals could not reproduce themselves, nor would they altruistically choose to care for a dependent future generation. Real societies are thus structurally dependent on forms of behaviour which cannot be explained within the parameters of an individualist philosophy. And this implies that some difference between the sexes becomes a necessary additional assumption to support the very model upon which denials of the significance of sex are based.

Whether rational individualism provides an adequate model of the behaviour of individual men is not an issue here; what is at issue are its limitations as the basis of a theoretical model of society, and these become clear as soon as reproductive difference is recognized. Within the individualist model, women can only be discussed in terms of their failures (and occasional successes) to conform to this supposedly gender-free norm. In reality, however, the problem is that the norm itself comes from a model which is completely inappropriate to understanding a gendered, self-reproducing society.

A second, more theoretical stage in the development of women's studies, beginning in the 1970s, was the recognition that women's lives were centred around different issues from men's and that these needed to be studied if we were to gain an understanding of the way gender was structured in society. Thus areas that had not previously been theorized, such as the family, sexuality, interpersonal relations and other aspects of the private domain, all became objects worthy of theoretical analysis. This was an attempt to rectify the previous mode of studying women as substitute men. Women (and men) were to be studied not just in the masculine public domain, according to its criteria, but also in their own domain of the private. The recognition of the theoretical importance of those aspects of society around which much of women's lives and relations between the sexes turned, was supposed to correct the masculine bias of existing social theory with its concentration on the public domain of politics and economics.

Politically, this meant recognizing that women's position would be fundamentally improved only by a radical transformation of society in which the divisions between women's and men's arenas, between public and private, were transformed. Both these projects, the theoretical and the political, were extremely ambitious, for such a radical transformation of society would leave no aspect of it untouched. Similarly, the theoretical project of analysing previously untheorized parts of society involved a re-examination of all existing social theory, which had concentrated on the apparently separable, public, masculine aspects of society, ignoring their interdependence with the private domain. A new feminist social theory was sought which would be a totalizing theory, encompassing both public and private domains and showing not only their interdependence, but also the way in which the very separation between them was the product of a gender-divided society. In practice, of course, theory was more piecemeal than that and the study of housework or sexuality tended to be added on to existing theory, often sitting uncomfortably next to, rather than unseating, previously pre-eminent traditions.

By 1990 work on the project of developing such a totalizing feminist theory had largely been abandoned; whether this indicates a failure of ambition, or realism in the face of an inherently impossible task, remains an unresolved question. In the 1980s much academic feminist theory, along with similar trends in other branches of social theory, moved onto a different course. Rather than attempting to reconceptualize the whole world, a critique was developed of the aims of existing theory and its claims to objectivity. This critique, which formed part of what became known as 'post-modernism', took issue with two central tenets of Western Enlightenment thought: first, that underlying the particular forms that we observe there are essential general truths to be uncovered; and, second, that the role of theory is the pursuit of objective knowledge of such truths. Instead, post-modernism claims that the pursuit of totalizing theory is mistaken, for such theory is inevitably 'essentialist' in that it makes invalid generalizations, universalizing what should be seen as local and historically specific. It also argues that there are different vantage points from which the world can be seen, no one of which can make claim to have privileged insight into any objective truth. In this view, the subjective position from which theory is produced is just as relevant as its object.

Such post-modern arguments posed a new critical agenda for feminist theorizing. The false claims to objectivity of existing theory were to be debunked by showing how they masked masculine privilege and self-interest. And, at the same time, feminists were freed to construct their own theories without having to make any such claims for themselves, for the aim was no longer to arrive at some new universally valid objective truth which masculine bias had failed to uncover. Instead, the recognition that the standpoint of the subject – or producer – of knowledge cannot be divorced from the content of the knowledge produced left space, it was claimed, for the development of an autonomous feminist theory, rather than one developed in relation to existing men's theory.

And it opened up quite a different political project: not the pursuit of either equality for individuals or a degendered society, but of autonomy for women in which the criteria set by men need be of no relevance. Furthermore, knowledge developed along these lines itself becomes inherently political. For once a universal standard of objectivity is rejected, the only post-modernist test of feminist ideas becomes their political effectiveness. In this view, the production of knowledge becomes itself a political intervention.

Against this, other feminists argued that the post-modernist project can only be a critical one. It has value in uncovering the male-centredness of existing theory. But it goes too far, even to the point of undercutting the base upon which the whole feminist project stands. For, by rejecting as incoherent all universals and essentialisms, the very concept of women itself is undermined. Anti-feminists have used essentialist definitions of women to claim the inevitability of women's subordination, by arguing, for example, that women's current social position is a direct consequence of their reproductive capacities. A rejection of such anti-feminist essentialism does not, it was argued, entail a rejection of all essentialist notions of what it means to be a woman. Indeed, some such notion is implicit in any argument for feminism. Essentialisms that reduce the social to the biological and universalize particular forms of social relations between women and men do have to be challenged. But feminism could not and should not attempt to reject essentialism in itself.

According to this position, then, uncovering false universalisms remains a feminist tactic, but feminism can have a more constructive theoretical project too, one which can make greater claims for itself than the male-centred theories it criticized. This alternative 'feminist standpoint' argues that women, through their subordinate position in society and their experience of reproductive as well as productive labour, are able to develop a more objective viewpoint than men who have more restricted experience and have more to gain from hiding the truth. This standpoint, it should be noted, shares with post-modernism the view that what distinguishes feminist theory is that women are its subjects.

4

This shared claim, that it makes a difference who does the theorizing, forces us again to recognize that women are not just individual, rational members of an ungendered humanity. Here, however, that recognition leads to women being seen as holding a specifically gendered consciousness. This affects not only the way that they behave as objects of study, but also the way in which they as the subjects of knowledge understand themselves and the world. Feminist theory can no longer be defined only by its object of knowledge; indeed, a measure of the success of feminism has been the extent to which non-feminists have taken up theorizing about women and gender too. Rather, what is specific to feminist theory, according to both the post-modernist and the feminist standpoint view, is that it is carried out by women, that women are the knowing subjects of feminist theory.

The influence of such trends on academic feminism has been pervasive over the 1980s; whether they will remain so important in the '90s, we cannot at the moment tell. Despite post-modernism's current significance, there remain plenty of practitioners of earlier modes of studying of women and gender divisions. However, the questions post-modernism has posed for feminism, concerning what it means to be a woman and how this affects the way we theorize the world, are important not only to those feminists who are either sympathetic to or engaged in argument with post-modernism, but to all feminist research.

These questions have fundamentally influenced the structure of this book, which is organized around four themes: differences among women, the relation between sex and gender, the notion of subjectivity and the politics of identity.

DIFFERENCES AMONG WOMEN

The whole notion of feminist politics depends on women having some interests in common. But women are different: white, black, old, young, rich, poor, heterosexual, lesbian and so on. If women's difference from men gives them fundamentally different interests and theoretical approaches, is that not also true of differences between women? If the knowledge we seek is no longer to be seen as universal, but fundamentally imbued with the historical circumstances of its creation and therefore gendered, should it not also be seen as white or black, old or young etc.? Can anybody, then, speak for women as a whole? Black women, for example, have criticized white women for speaking as if the issues that concern them are universal feminist issues, arguing that white feminists can represent only the particular interests of one specific group of women in one specific set of historical circumstances. But can there be any such universal feminist issues? And does this question not also apply to knowledge about women? Must we reject the project of 'knowing women' at any level of generality, as the post-modernist critique of overarching theory would indicate, and instead see our project as one of simply learning what we can about all the different positions women find themselves in? If so, what remains of the political, or theoretical, project of feminism?

This issue – concerning the implications of differences among women for what it means to be a woman and for how we as women develop knowledge – forms the first theme of this book. It is taken up explicitly in Chapter 1 and Chapter 7. Chapter 1 poses the question of how feminist theory and politics can recognize diversity among women without divisiveness. This question can be seen as running throughout the book, but is then explicitly returned to in Chapter 7 which addresses the issue of how feminist politics and theory can develop ideas about identity and community which incorporate difference in a positive way.

THE RELATION BETWEEN SEX AND GENDER

Knowing what it means to be a woman, of necessity involves an understanding of the female body. Feminist theory, however, has always had an uneasy relationship with women's bodies, having been founded on the need to refute the traditional definition of women by their biology. Biology has most often been seen as the flag of the other side, used to justify existing social limitations on women. In order to escape such biologically determinist theories of what women can and cannot do, and distinguish the effects of society from those of nature, feminists adopted the distinction between 'sex' and 'gender'. According to this, gender refers to the differences between 'women' and 'men' which are socially constructed, whereas sex refers to the biological distinction between 'females' and 'males'.

One problem with this distinction is that it seems to imply, at least for an individual, that, whereas nearly everybody is defined as one sex or the other by their body, gender identity is a state of mind. However, there seems to be a logical contradiction in making this split between mind and body, for the experience of inhabiting a body of a particular sex must affect women's and men's sense of themselves. Indeed, we know it does, for why otherwise should gender be dichotomously divided as sex is, and individuals see their gender identity always in relation, even if not in a straightforward relation, to their sex?

Recently, both the logic and the utility of making an absolute distinction between sex and gender has been brought into question within feminism. This is in line with the critique of objectivity, a notion that also depends on a split between mind and body, for it is only disembodied thought which can be the arbiter of objective truth. If minds are never disembodied, the possibility at least arises that the body, as part of the subjective experience of the thinker, has real effects on the process of understanding. In that case, both sex and gender are relevant to what it means to be a woman.

This theme – the relation between sex and gender – is another that runs through this book. It is taken up most explicitly in Chapter 2 – Biology, society and the female body – which addresses the question of how feminist theory should approach the relation between biology and society, both in understanding individual development and in theorizing about society. It also arises in the subsequent two chapters where various ways of analysing sexuality are explored. These show that while sexuality cannot be reduced to reproductive biology, neither can it be related to gender in any straightforward way. Chapter 3 examines a variety of perspectives on sexuality, most of which focus on the way it is socially constructed, whereas Chapter 4 – Gender and mothering – looks specifically at theories which analyse sexuality in terms of the unconscious negotiation of sexual difference.

SUBJECTIVITY

A third theme in knowing what it is to be a woman is understanding where our sense of self – our subjectivity – comes from. 'Subjectivity' can be defined as that combination of conscious and unconscious thoughts and emotions that make up our sense of ourselves, our relation to the world and our ability to act in that world. Unlike the individualist notion of people as rational, self-motivated individuals in pursuit of their own clear and stable self-interest, the concept of subjectivity can capture both the notion of people as intentional subjects – actors in the world – and at the same time as subject to forces beyond their conscious control. For that reason, it has proved very useful to feminist theory, which has recognized that as women we behave in ways which we do not intend and are not always in our own interests. Such 'irrational' behaviour has been experienced by women as their own failure to make personal and emotional changes that politically and intellectually seem desirable. A need to understand why this happens, or how what is called a contradictory subjectivity is produced, led feminists to examine, among other accounts, psychoanalytic theories of the unconscious. Chapter 5 – Language and difference – introduces some of these theories in order to explore the contradictory nature of subjectivity.

Even though our subjectivity is, by definition, what we experience as most personal and most individual, our desires and expectations are acquired in a social context. Chapter 6 – Subjectivity and identity – critically examines theories which explore the relationship between the social and the unconscious processes that are involved in the creation of our subjectivities. This relation is an important one for feminism, for it may give the space needed to allow for change. For without some way of allowing the social to act upon the unconscious, women would be just as locked in to a subordinate position by the unconscious, according to psycho-analytic theory, as biological determinists would claim we are by our bodies.

THE POLITICS OF IDENTITY

A final theme is the question of identity – what it means for a woman to claim an identity as black, as white, as heterosexual, as lesbian and so on. Rather than being experienced as something purely imposed on one from outside, within feminism it has become a political act to choose an identity or indeed to accept a complex of identities. Differences between women and accusations of racism and heterosexism within the women's movement have made the politics of identity an important issue within feminism. Claiming an identity may be empowering, but it also excludes others. The notion of 'sisterhood' rested on such a claim to a shared identity as women, and this gave feminism power within and against a male-dominated world. But the recognition of differences among women shattered that notion of politics based on a single identity. Instead, the naming of differences became a way to claim a political identity, and at one level seemed to undermine the idea of women having any identity or politics in common.

Chapter 7 – Experience and the politics of identity – takes up these issues by using the analysis of the previous chapters to understand the shifting forces that shape our subjectivities and identities. The forces of racism, heterosexism and so on that shape the identities of black women and lesbians are shown to be equally implicated in the construction of white, heterosexual identities. All women are in that way shaped by all the forces that create divisions among women, and any effective feminism has to be able to recognize differences among women. Only by rejecting the illusion that any of us can lay claim to coherent, untainted identities can the diversity of women's experience be critically understood and incorporated into feminism.

Finally, Chapter 8 returns to some of the issues raised in this Introduction to look at the history and current state of feminist theorizing and, on a fairly optimistic note, points to the future.

The above summary of some of the themes of this book and the theoretical approaches taken in it may make it seem a somewhat daunting prospect. Inevitably, some of the theories that are examined are difficult and have to be presented in a language far removed from that in which feminist struggle is conducted outside academia. Many of those theories were developed initially by men, often men (such as Freud, Lacan and Foucault) unsympathetic or even downright hostile to feminism. Nevertheless, their theories are worth the effort needed to absorb them, for the critical uses of them made by feminism have been fruitful. We have chosen for this book articles which expound the theories from a feminist perspective, that is, which lay out critically those parts of any given theory which are needed to understand the ways in which they have been incorporated into feminist thought. We have not aimed to give an overview of any particular theoretical approach, be it psychoanalysis or post-structuralism; rather we have been guided in our choice of readings by the need to survey the current state of feminist knowledge and to do so as accessibly as possible. To this end we have used our own introductions to the chapters to explain why we see the particular theoretical approaches taken as important for feminism, and why, for us, they make the project of 'knowing women' a challenging and exciting one.

1
DISCRIMINATION, SUBORDINATION AND DIFFERENCE: FEMINIST PERSPECTIVES

All types of feminism are concerned with improving the lot of women. All are also committed to analysing women's present position and understanding its causes in order to improve it. However, within this common understanding of the importance of feminist knowledge, there is room for considerable disagreement. Such disagreement is not only about the means through which the position of women is improved, but also about what such improvements would be.

In particular, should the aim be to give women equal opportunities to compete on the same basis as men for the sought-after positions in society that are currently usually taken by men, hoping that women would thereby gain an equal share of the power, status and prizes that go with these positions? Or is it that the positions themselves need to be changed, not just the sex of the individuals who fill them? Must the very structure of society be changed, if women are to have the chance to lead more fulfilling lives? These questions are explored in the first two sections of this chapter, in the first of which – Discrimination and subordination – the differences between the two basic approaches are outlined, while the second looks at how ideology and socialization serve to maintain divisions between the sexes.

Or is the problem more about the ways in which men's and women's lives are currently valued, leaving whole areas of our work and our culture unrecognized and undervalued, in particular those concerning the nurturing side of life in which women predominate? If so, women should refuse to accept men's values which claim that their own activities are the important ones and need to build an alternative woman-centred culture of their own. The third section of this chapter, entitled An androgynous or a woman-centred society?, examines debates within feminism as to whether differences between the sexes should be minimized or revalued, with the following section, Motherhood and women's nature, looking specifically at how the two sides of this debate view women's capacity to bear children. In the fifth section, Gender difference and power, we examine two views that suggest that debates about differences between the sexes may be unresolvable, either because they miss the real issue of power between women and men or because the two perspectives are not so much alternatives but complementary to each other.

Finally, in the last section of this chapter, the issue of differences between women is examined to ask what the prospects are for building a feminism that can represent women as a whole, given the many differences that seem to divide us.

DISCRIMINATION AND SUBORDINATION

The current wave of feminism started in the 1960s with a focus on the lack of opportunities that women had to compete with men for jobs, power and status in the public world. At the same time, the American writer Betty Friedan pointed to how unsatisfying was the position to which women of her background were supposed to aspire, that of full-time housewife and mother:

> The problem lay buried, unspoken, for many years in the minds of American women. It was a strange stirring, a sense of dissatisfaction, a yearning that women suffered in the middle of the twentieth century in the United States. Each suburban wife struggled with it alone. As she made the beds, shopped for groceries, matched slipcover material, ate peanut butter sandwiches with her children, chauffeured Cub Scouts and Brownies, lay beside her husband at night – she was afraid to ask even of herself the silent question – 'Is this all?'
> (*Friedan, 1963, p. 15*)

Friedan's remedy was to improve women's access to the jobs and lifestyle that gave men the satisfaction and status denied to women trapped in the home. She was instrumental in setting up the National Organization of Women (NOW) to campaign for equal rights for women, by which was meant primarily legislative change to prevent women being discriminated against in the public world of work and politics on the grounds of sex. One of the most enduring campaigns of NOW was for an Equal Rights Amendment (ERA) to be added to the US constitution, a move which was finally defeated by the changing political tide which moved against feminism and other progressive movements in the 1980s.

Friedan and the National Organization of Women were what are known as 'liberal feminists'. They were liberal in that they worked within the framework of liberal democratic societies, sharing the belief that society can be improved by ensuring that the rights of individuals are safeguarded. Such a position argues that the key

problem for women is discrimination: in current society the view prevails that a women's sex disqualifies her from doing things that a man can do and this leads to decisions being taken which exclude women from traditionally male jobs and positions of power. In other words, sex is being used to discriminate between candidates, rather than the candidates' actual ability to do the job. Further, because of such practices, women are not given the chance to challenge the mistaken view upon which discrimination is based.

It was on such an analysis of the cause of women's unequal status in society that governmental legislation in the United Kingdom was proposed in 1975:

> The unequal status of women has not been perpetuated as the result of the deliberate determination by one half of the population to subject the other half to continued inequality. Its causes are complex and rooted deeply in tradition, custom and prejudice. Beyond the basic physiological differences between men and women lies a whole range of differences between individual men and individual women in all aspects of human ability. The differences within each sex far outweigh the differences between the sexes. But there is insufficient recognition that the variations of character and ability within each sex are greater and more significant than the differences between the sexes. Women are often treated as unequal because they are alleged to be inferior to men in certain respects, and

the consequences of their unequal treatment are then seen as evidence of their inferiority. Their unequal status has been caused less by conscious discrimination against women than by the stereotyped attitudes of both sexes about their respective roles. And many who make the important decisions about the treatment of women do not discriminate against them because of conscious personal prejudice but because of prejudices of which they are unaware, or the prejudices (real or assumed) which they ascribe to others – management, employees, customers or colleagues.

The unequal status of women is wasteful of the potential talents of half our population in a society which, more than ever before, needs to mobilize the skill and ability of all its citizens. Despite the major improvements which have occurred in women's status since the beginning of this century, the pattern of inequality is too pervasive and entrenched to be changed by the gradual process of voluntary initiative. It will not be changed by the mere passage of time. The movement towards equality for women requires the active support and intervention of Government itself. The Government is, therefore, resolved to introduce effective measures to discourage discriminatory conduct and to promote genuine equality of opportunity for both sexes.

(HMSO, 1974)

Note that, in this view, discrimination does not have to be conscious, but can occur through the existence of sexual stereotypes which assign women and men to particular sex-specific roles, so that women automatically appear not to have the characteristics required for positions with high status. The first piece of legislation enacted along these lines, the Sex Discrimination Act of 1975, widened the definition of discrimination further to include what has been termed 'indirect discrimination'. This means discriminating, not by sex directly, but by some other criterion, such as height, which is more likely to be satisfied by one sex than the other, in cases when it is not materially relevant to the performance of the job.

For liberal feminism, therefore, the task is to stamp out discrimination in its widest sense, including both unconscious and indirect discrimination. This would result in women being given the chance to show that they are as good as men in all the key positions in society currently denied to them. Of course, not all women may choose to compete with men for such positions, but they should be given the chance if they choose to do so. Similarly, men should not be prevented by discrimination from taking on women's traditional roles. Once discrimination is removed, it will be possible for women and men to be treated as individual human beings, with their own personal talents and preferences, no longer restricted in the opportunities available to them by stereotypical views of the capabilities and appropriate roles for each sex. Whether, should equality of opportunities be achieved, women and men would end up in equal numbers in all roles in society is not particularly important. A liberal feminist might believe that on average women are more likely to opt for certain roles or to be better at them than men. If this is the case, then women would predominate in certain roles and men in others. However, this would not be a problem, provided that the opportunities open to members of both sexes are the same and that all activities were equally valued.

This type of liberal feminism was very influential in the United States in the 1970s, where it tended to dominate the women's movement and influence the direction of feminist research. It also had a significant effect on the national political scene there. Indeed, the growth in the 1980s, of the 'New Right', with its emphasis on traditional family values and sex-roles, can be seen – at least in part – as a backlash against this type of feminism and the transformations that were taking place in women's lives.

By the late 1960s another strand of feminism was emerging on both sides of the Atlantic. Many of the women who became feminists at that time had been involved in other types of dissident politics, in particular working-class and community politics. Not being so much part of the political and intellectual mainstream as their US counterparts, they were more sceptical of those who argued that women's position could be improved just by using the law to challenge discrimination. They argued that a more fundamental overhaul of society was needed. Just giving women the opportunity to take on the high-status roles that men have traditionally held would not abolish status hierarchies themselves, nor would it improve the situation of the majority of women.

This argument is drawn from a similar one about the division between classes. In a society which depends upon the existence of different classes in order for its economy to be kept going, opening up more opportunities for social mobility between classes might improve the lot of some individuals, but cannot be the solution for everyone. This is because not everyone can be at the top, and the working class would still be needed to do the work on which the economy depends. The problem, therefore, is the existence of class divisions and the hierarchy between them, rather than just who takes which roles within it. By analogy, opening up the opportunities for women to take up roles traditionally restricted to men may benefit some women. But even when a woman becomes prime minister, this does not improve the position of most women, because the work women do, such as domestic labour and childcare, still has to be done.

This is how Alice Rossi put it, again in an American context, arguing against a liberal 'assimilation' model as a way of rectifying racial and sexual inequality in favour of what she calls the 'hybrid' model of social equality:

> The feminist-assimilation model has an implicit fallacy, however. No amount of entreaty will yield an equitable distribution of women and men in the top strata of business and professional occupations, for the simple reason that the life men have led in these strata has been possible only because their own wives were leading traditional lives as homemakers, doing double parent and household duty, and carrying the major burden of civic responsibilities. If it were not for their wives in the background, successful men in American society would have to be single or childless. This is why so many professional women complain privately that what they most need in life is a 'wife'!
>
> The assimilation model also makes an assumption that the institutional structure of American society developed over decades by predominantly white Protestant males, constitutes the best of all possible worlds. Whether the call is to blacks or to women to join white men in the mainstream of American society, both racial integration and a feminist ideology accept the structure of American society as it now exists. The assimilation model rejects the psychological theses of innate racial or sex differences implicit in most versions of the pluralist model, but it accepts the social institutions formed by the ascendant group. This is precisely the assumption numerous blacks, women and members of the younger generation have recently been questioning and rejecting.
>
> The hybrid model of equality rejects both traditional psychological assumptions and the institutional structure we have inherited. It anticipates a society in which the lives of men and of whites will be different, not only women and blacks. In fact, it might be that this hybrid model would involve greater change in the role of men than of women, because institutional changes it would require involve a restructuring to bring the world of jobs and politics closer to the fulfilment of individual human needs for both creativity and fellowship.
>
> (Rossi, 1969, pp. 183–4)

From this position, then, the question to be asked is how existing social institutions can be changed so that women and men can gain genuine equality, an equality which would require changes in the lives of both sexes, not just women's. Liberal solutions can only improve the access of a relatively small number of women to the prizes of existing society. However, if women as a whole are to be liberated, a fundamental transformation of the structure of society is needed, not just a different allocation of who does what. Such a restructuring would involve not only liberating women from their domestic and nurturing roles, but changing the goals of the public world of work and politics too. In this structural view, which focuses on the institutions of society and their effects on the people within them, the problem for women is not just that as individuals they face acts of discrimination, but that as a group they are boxed in and oppressed by the very structure of society, within which women's position is a subordinate one.

Of course, to say women's oppression is structural begs more questions than it answers. For the structures of oppression have to be explained. What are they based on? How did they originate? And how can they be changed? In the United Kingdom two main schools of feminism developed which shared this structural view of women's position, and thus talked about women as oppressed and/or subordinated. They differed, however, in their views as to what lay behind women's oppression and therefore in their strategies to overcome it. Socialist feminists saw the liberation of women as closely tied up with that of the working class, because they argued that the same (capitalist) structures of society that exploited the working class also oppressed women. Radical feminists, on the other hand, took the view that women's oppression had its own dynamic and was based principally on (patriarchal) relations of power between women as a group and men as a group.

Both these strands differed from liberal feminism in their strategies for change. They were sceptical of the extent to which legislation could improve the position of women, since discrimination was only a symptom of the underlying problem. Further, their structural view of women's subordination meant that all aspects of society were to be viewed as part of the same system and could not be seen as neutral instruments to be used by feminism. Thus, for example, the state, as part of the same system of oppression, was unlikely to produce legislation which really benefited women.

IDEOLOGY AND SOCIALIZATION

In these structural views of women's oppression, ideology has a particularly important contribution to make. An ideology is a set of ideas that a person holds in order to make sense of society and the position they find themself in within it. There are a vast range of ideologies concerning men's and women's place in society: for example, domestic ideology which identifies women particularly with the home and the complementary 'bread-winner' ideology by which men are supposed to provide financially for their families.

These ideologies are not the same, but they are obviously linked, and help each other make seeming sense of the world. Ideologies are social constructs, that is they are made in and by society and only make sense of the particular type of society which gave rise to them. Ideologies as part of society are not made or even chosen by individuals, but they influence us all and form the context in which we develop the specific ideas that we as individuals hold. Ideologies, since they make sense of existing society, tend to be supportive of the status quo and make existing power relations seem inevitable, serving thereby the interests of those with power. For that reason, feminists often talk of a dominant patriarchal ideology (in the singular) to mean the particular combination of linked ideas that seem to support women's subordination and make it seem natural.

Ideologies therefore encourage women and men to fit into the structures of society, into the particular positions allocated to each sex in any specific society. Anthropological studies document the wide variety of interpretations that different societies have of what it means to be a woman or a man. There is also considerable variation in sex-roles – the customary roles assigned to women and men – in different societies. Nearly all societies have, for example, some sexual division of labour so that certain tasks are carried out by women and others by men, but what these tasks are, and to which sex they are assigned, vary a great deal across different societies. For example, in the United Kingdom women are not considered strong enough to take on a number of jobs that involve carrying heavy weights; in most of the non-industrialized world, however, where water needs to be carried it tends to be women's work.

In psychology, the study of how children are reared to fulfil the expectations made of their sex – their socialization into sex-roles – had always been important, but feminism gave it a new focus. For feminism allowed the roles themselves to be questioned and showed the immense efforts that needed to be made to ensure that girls and boys grew up to take on the sexually-differentiated characteristics of women and men in our society. Rather than socialization into appropriate sex-roles being seen as a normal healthy process by which a natural state was arrived at, it became one fraught with difficulty – and sometimes resistance – in the pursuit of a socially constructed outcome.

Socialization theory can be used to explain how it is that women may seem to accede in their own oppression and show thereby why equal opportunities cannot be enough to create an equal society. For if women and men are socialized differently, they cannot then be expected to behave in the same way when offered the same opportunities. Women are therefore unlikely to fit exactly the roles for which men have been socialized, even if the material barriers to their doing so are removed. Thus, for example, an engineering firm which was determined not to discriminate against women in its appointment of its managing director will still be more likely to appoint a man; for women's socialization will have meant that they will have been less likely than men at every previous stage to have taken the steps necessary to put them in a position to apply for the job. The recognition that women's and men's lives are formed by the different experiences and expectations made of them allows for the possibility that current differences, rather than being assumed to be biological, can be shown to be due to socialization. Within this framework, understanding the different processes of socialization of women and men becomes an important task for feminist research.

The processes of socialization form part of the structure of society. Just as there are specific expectations made of women and men in every society, there are also social institutions – like the family, schools and culture more generally – through which these expectations are learned and shown to be appropriate. In a male-dominated society, men will be encouraged to develop the characteristics appropriate to a dominant group, women those appropriate to a subordinate group. This is how psychoanalyst Jean Baker Miller put it:

> Once a group is defined as inferior, the superiors tend to label it as defective or substandard in various ways. These labels accrete rapidly. Thus, blacks are described as less intelligent than whites, women are supposed to be ruled by emotion, and so on. In addition, the actions and words of the dominant group tend to be destructive of the subordinates. All historical evidence confirms this tendency. And, although they are much less obvious, there are destructive effects on the dominants as well . . .
>
> Dominant groups usually define one or more acceptable roles for the subordinate. Acceptable roles typically involve providing services that no dominant group wants to perform for itself (for example, cleaning up the dominant's waste products). Functions that a dominant group prefers to perform, on the other hand, are carefully guarded and closed to subordinates. Out of the total range of human possibilities, the activities most highly valued in any particular culture will tend to be enclosed within the domain of the dominant group; less valued functions are relegated to the subordinates.
>
> Subordinates are usually said to be unable to perform the preferred roles. Their incapacities are ascribed to innate defects or deficiencies of mind or body. They are therefore immutable;

no change or development is possible. It becomes difficult for dominants even to imagine that subordinates are capable of performing the preferred activities. More importantly, subordinates themselves can come to find it difficult to believe in their own ability. The myth of their inability to fulfil wider or more valued roles is challenged only when a drastic event disrupts the usual arrangements. Such disruptions usually arise from outside the relationship itself. For instance, in the emergency situation of World War II, inexperienced blacks and 'incompetent' women suddenly 'manned' the factories with great skill.

It follows that subordinates are described in terms of, and encouraged to develop, personal psychological characteristics that are pleasing to the dominant group. These characteristics form a certain familiar cluster: submissiveness, passivity, docility, dependency, lack of initiative, inability to act, to decide, to think, and the like. In general, this cluster includes qualities more characteristic of children than adults – immaturity, weakness and helplessness. If subordinates adopt these characteristics they are considered well adjusted.

However, when subordinates show the potential for, or even more dangerously have developed other characteristics – let us say intelligence, initiative, assertiveness – there is usually no room available within the dominant framework for acknowledgement of these characteristics. Such people will be defined as at least unusual, if not definitely abnormal. There will be no opportunities for the direct application of their abilities within the social arrangements. (How many blacks and women have pretended to be dumb!)

(*Miller, 1978, pp. 6–8*)

This poses an additional problem in transforming the position of women: current socialization prepares women only for their current roles in society, rather than for challenging them. How is change to happen if women are socialized into subordinate roles and thus are unlikely to believe in their own power to effect change? By some accounts, it would seem that socialization prepares us for existing sex-roles so effectively as to preclude the possibility of change.

Judith Bardwick, however, in the following extract, claims that change is already happening. She demonstrates this by looking at how concepts of healthy mental development with respect to sex-roles have changed since the 1950s:

Feminity and masculinity: changing perceptions

... All around us we see evidence of anxiety over gender identity. The changes we are witnessing today do not simply involve roles and responsibilities, but instead, invoke basic reformulations of what psychologically healthy women and men should be like. Sexual identity – the sense of knowing one is feminine or masculine and the certainty of what one's adult responsibilities are because of gender – has been an existential anchor for individuals and for society. We are undergoing a generally unrecognized but fundamentally revolutionary change because we no longer know what we ought to do or be as female or male, and we are no longer sure of what being an adult involves. This is reflected in the evolution of new ideas or criteria of mental health which are essentially the reverse of those we were certain of as few as ten years ago.

Historically, the great bulk of the relevant social science literature has been concerned with differences between the sexes. As professional interest in the psychology of women developed in association with the feminist movement, and as the role responsibilities of the sexes began converging, it became a scientific and political mandate to establish the existence of gender similarities. Psychologists and sociologists began to concentrate on the cultural, learned, and therefore arbitrary origin of sex differences. In this decade we can see this reversal both in the professional literature and the popular press. We emphasize the similarity of the sexes by demonstrating how they share in the distribution of any characteristic, by focusing on individualism, and by emphasizing how sex-roles are learned. The currently desirable implication is that no significant behavioural differences arise from biological differences. Implicit, although rarely articulated, is an attempt to refute our former sense that the sexes had different 'essential natures' which had to be gratified in different sorts of activities. We now focus more on the effects of learning on behaviour rather than on physiological explanations; we want to believe that human beings have infinite capacities to learn and therefore can become anything.

Psychological theories and therapies are always based on ideas of what healthy people are like and what they ought to be doing. They always involve judgements about what will make people happy or unhappy, fulfilled or constricted. Assessments about people's mental health also involve roles, the work people do, and responsibilities they have, because we do not evaluate 'health' in the abstract but in relation to how people measure up to what we expect them to do. The issue of roles also involves gender, since many roles have been assigned to one sex and essentially prohibited to the other.

Thus, basic concepts of psychological health are changing because our norms are changing, and 'normalcy' is always measured by criteria derived from the rules of society. Norms are based on consensus. They define the role choices, behaviours, and personality characteristics which are considered appropriate or normal. Norms are therefore powerful guides in directing people: they define goals, influence what we expect from others, and mould our self-definitions. Specific norms are blueprints which tell us how to achieve our adult identity.

[. . .]

We know that we are leaving a period of rigid gender norms. We are in a transition in which old and new, complementary and contradictory, concrete and vague norms coexist. When norms are stable, we do not notice them because we take them for granted. Now that they are changing, we are forced to examine them and analyse how they affect us. We are asking the most fundamental questions: What is feminine or masculine? What are the effects of physiological gender? How alike are the sexes?

Studies of psychological sex differences began in the early part of this century. The first work was very influenced by the theory of evolution. Evolutionary theory made biological and especially reproductive differences prominent, emphasized the genetic innateness of characteristics, and stimulated an overall focus on gender *differences* – with a concomitant blindness to *similarities*.

The scientific emphasis on differences reflected society's existing norms of appropriate characteristics for each sex, which had evolved so that the rules of behaviour for one sex were the literal reverse of those for the other. Women were defined essentially as tender mothers, men as assertive providers, and the responsibilities of both sexes were clearly delineated . . .

Masculinity–feminity tests

To the extent that female and male are defined by their differences, gender seems to be a variable divided into two parts: what one is, and what one is not. As masculine and feminine were seen as the opposite ends of the same parameter, it followed that the first tests psychologists devised to measure masculinity and feminity would emphasize sex differences. These tests were incapable of measuring similarities because they were composed only of items which females and males answer differently and because they were scored in such a way that a subject cannot have both feminine and masculine qualities. In addition, the healthiest people were supposed to score at either extreme of the distribution – women who scored as very feminine and men who tested as very masculine.

Until recently, then, psychologists measured sexual identity by how much one is like (or says one is like) the stereotype of one's sex and by how much one is different from the opposite sex's stereotype. The stereotyped characteristics describing feminine women include *passive, fragile, dependent, non-competitive, non-aggressive, intuitive, receptive, afraid to take risks, emotionally labile, supportive, maternal, empathic, having low pain tolerance, unambitious, sensitive to inner feelings and to responses from other people.* The comparable stereotype of masculine men is the *reverse* of that of women. Men are described as *aggressive, assertive, task-oriented, outwardly oriented, innovative, self-disciplined, stoic, active, objective, rational, unsentimental, confident, competent, courageous, analytic* and *emotionally controlled.* Since the tests included only questions that differentiate males from females, the gender differences that resulted were exaggerated, and could not be leavened by measures in which the sexes responded in the same way. These tests were, however, accurate reflections of the norms and assumptions used by laypeople and professionals alike.

It is very difficult to measure 'femininity' and 'masculinity' because the terms have several meanings . . .

In any event, if we just look at people it is obvious that masculinity and femininity are not opposite ends of a simple, unitary variable. Commonsense observation makes it clear that most people are more complicated and more variable than can be described by the stereotypic terms 'masculine' and 'feminine'. Furthermore, within the stereotyped descriptions we do not know how generalized the significant personality characteristics are. For example, are people who are very nurturant, nurturant all, most, or some of the time? Are they equally nurturant with everyone or are they more nurturant with the young, aged, or ill? Are they appropriately or inappropriately nurturant? Are they able to respond differently when the situation changes so that they are selectively empathic, warm, and protective – or independent, assertive, and active when that would be more appropriate? Are those who are high in nurturance necessarily low in assertiveness? Do people who have many feminine interests have few that are masculine? Are people who are conventional in their sex roles necessarily conventional in personality traits?

We really cannot answer any of these questions yet. More than that, we cannot know the answers until the measures we use allow people to be simultaneously nurturant and assertive, dependent and independent, feminine and masculine. We can only see what our measures allow us to see.

As feminism generated the awareness that psychologically healthy people were likely not to be one-dimensionally feminine or masculine, new tests were created. These tests are based, first, on the assumption that femininity and masculinity are not opposite ends of the same dimension, but are two independent dimensions so that anyone can be high or low on either. What we have called masculine or feminine qualities are therefore present in both men and women. The second new assumption is that people are complex rather than simple. Complexity refers to the idea that anyone can be simultaneously feminine and masculine. It also means that while people can be well aware of the simplistic gender stereotype and describe the sexes stereotypically, they may not have accepted that as the guideline for what they wanted to and have become. A third assumption is that androgynous people, those whose scores are high on both the feminine and masculine scales, have the highest levels of self-esteem. The last assumption is made because psychologists are moving toward the view that people function best if they have both feminine and masculine characteristics, and that people who cope well should feel good about themselves. This has been borne out by the research to date. In a study by Janet Spence, those who were high in both masculinity and femininity, and were therefore classified as androgynous, were highest in self-esteem, followed by those who scored high in masculinity and low in femininity. Those who scored low on both sets of characteristics were lowest in self-esteem. In an extension of the Spence study, which used college students, data from a sample of affluent adults had the same results. Women and men who scored high on both the feminine and masculine subscales had the highest self-esteem, and those with the lowest self-esteem scored low on both scales.

Older measures of masculinity and femininity were basically atheoretical and reflected a simple, static version of sex differences that paralleled the rigidly differentiated role choices of the 1950s. We are now in a period in which change in sex-roles is the major social movement. As people take on responsibilities historically associated with the opposite sex, and as they lead increasingly complex lives, they are encouraged by the demands of their tasks to develop characteristics traditionally associated with the other sex. While traditional roles have always required characteristics stereotypically excluded from the role – as housewives solve problems, innovate and make decisions, and even male executives hug their children and can be intuitive and emphathic – participation in non-traditional roles accelerates or increases the development of a complex personality.

Increasingly, psychologists and lay observers are making the judgement that people who score high on their own gender scale and low on the other are not psychologically healthy because their development is too confined. We are saying that such people have developed much too narrow a range of their own potential. This change in the criteria of mental health is occurring because our perceptions of the appropriate norms for each sex have changed so much, and because both sexes increasingly share roles. Because of these changes, by 1980 many more people will value both feminine and masculine qualities in themselves and in others than they did in 1950 to 1965.

Our new ideas about gender-related mental health are therefore reflections of changed reality, since healthy people are defined as those who effectively cope with what they have to do. Half the population of American women are employed; small families have become the new norm; men are looking for affirmation and security in their personal relationships. Obviously women and men are participating in areas previously assigned to the other sex and in which effective behaviour requires characteristics previously attributed to the other. Basically the new androgynous norm is a recognition of real changes. If well-adjusted people are those who come closest to cultural values, we can say that in the earlier period, those who were most extremely masculine or feminine may well have been the best adjusted, whereas today androgynous people conform most to new social norms and hence might be considered the best adjusted.

The androgynous concept of psychological health defines the ideal person as having a blend of interests, abilities and traits which are both expressive and instrumental. In an androgynous society people are not forced into roles or traits on the basis of gender. To the extent that roles are not assigned on the basis of sex and that society minimizes the importance of gender and emphasizes individual capacity for taking on any set of responsibilities, we will probably find that the interests and characters of most people do become androgynous. With more freedom and fewer rigid expectations, people will want to become secure enough to feel and act in the broadest range of imaginable experience. When sexual identity can be taken for granted, people are freed and able to take risks, even in areas where action once would have labelled them unwomanly or unmanly. In time, as the androgynous personality is recognized, gender could become irrelevant to the assignment of roles. Roles would depend overwhelmingly on individual characteristics.

(*Bardwick, 1980, pp. 153–9*)

AN ANDROGYNOUS OR A WOMAN-CENTRED SOCIETY?

At the end of the last extract, Judith Bardwick moves from discussing changes that have been occurring to looking at what might happen if we moved into an 'androgynous' society, where women and men were not assigned particular roles or expected to show particular character traits on the basis of their sex. In such a society she would expect people to become androgynous too: that as individuals they would vary, but that both women and men would combine the characteristics that are now considered stereotypically masculine and those that are considered feminine.

But is that sort of androgynous personality really so desirable or possible? Given the higher value put on the characteristics of masculinity, is it just demanding of women that they take on the previously valued psychological qualities of men, rather as liberal feminists demanded that women be given access to the jobs and positions of power of men? For the characteristics of femininity outlined by Bardwick are not highly valued in society; it is those of masculinity that are seen as more desirable for individuals and it is those same masculine traits that would help an individual of either sex achieve success in society. Indeed, as Bardwick showed, whereas a high degree of both masculine and feminine characteristics might lead to the greatest self-esteem, those high in masculine characteristics had a greater regard for themselves than those high in feminine ones. All this seems to be saying, then, is that an androgynous woman could be as good as a man.

Above all, this notion of androgyny fails to recognize that not only are the characteristics of masculinity and femininity it is supposed to combine opposed, they are produced in opposition to each other. This was the point Jean Baker Miller made in discussing the characteristics of masculinity and femininity in relation to each other as those of dominants and subordinates. Thus to talk of an androgynous personality as a combination of the two is to ignore the relations of domination and subordination which produced them both. As Janice Raymond wrote, 'the language and imagery of androgyny is the language of dominance and servitude combined. One would not put master and slave . . . together to define a free person' (Raymond, 1980, p. 161).

On these grounds, in the mid-1970s some radical feminists began to question whether feminism should be seeking to minimize the differences between women and men to build an androgynous society, and indeed whether the changes that had already happened were to the good. Instead it might be better to encourage women to recognize their own strengths and build a woman-centred society which acknowledges and values female qualities. Hester Eisenstein sees two phases of the debate within feminist theory, the first of which took place in the 1970s:

In this phase of the debate, the socially constructed differences between the sexes were judged to be the chief source of female oppression. In the main, feminist theory concentrated on establishing the distinction between sex and gender, and developed an analysis of sex roles as a mode of social control. Arguing for the reduction of the polarization between masculinity and feminity, it pointed, explicitly or implicitly, to the replacement of gender polarization with some form of androgyny.

But this was followed by a second phase of contemporary feminist theory, [characterized by] the rejection of androgyny and the adoption of a woman-centred perspective. The sex-roles analysis of the early 1970s was taken up and given wide circulation in the media and the academy, and had evoked a widespread but selective response in many quarters. As a result, women were being encouraged to overcome the defects of their feminine conditioning, and to seek to enter those areas of public life previously closed to them. The concomitant element of the radical feminist analysis, namely, the nature of the patriarchal structure that oppressed women, went virtually unmentioned. Women were to adapt themselves to the structure, rather than the other way around.

In part as a reaction to these developments, beginning in the mid-1970s the view of female differences from men began to change. Instead of being considered the source of women's oppression, these differences were now judged to contain the seeds of women's liberation. As outlined by the historian Gerda Lerner, the poet Adrienne Rich and others, the woman-centred perspective located specific virtues in the historical and psychological experience of women. Instead of seeking to minimize the polarization between masculine and feminine, it sought to isolate and to define those aspects of female experience that were potential sources of strength and power for women, and, more broadly, of a new blueprint for social change.

(*Eisenstein, 1984, pp. xi–xii*)

Jean Baker Miller is one of those who saw potential strengths in the psychological characteristics of women, even though, as we saw above, she recognized those characteristics as a product of subordination. She wanted women to develop a 'new psychology' which did not mean adding masculine characteristics to the weaknesses of femininity. Rather she saw the particular psychic development of women, in which their sense of self depends on their relations with others, as the basis for a new society in which both women and men would be more in touch with each other and show a more advanced approach to living and functioning:

Ties to others

Male society, by depriving women of the right to its major 'bounty' – that is, development according to the male model – overlooks the fact that women's development *is* proceeding, but on another basis. One central feature is that women stay with, build on, and develop in a context of attachment and affiliation with others. Indeed, women's sense of self becomes very much organized around being able to make and then to maintain affiliations and relationships. Eventually, for many women the threat of disruption of an affiliation is perceived not as just a loss of a relationship but as something closer to a total loss of self.

Such psychic structuring can lay the groundwork for many problems. Depression, for example, which is related to one's sense of the loss of affiliation with another(s), is much more common in women, although it certainly occurs in men.

What has not been recognized is that this psychic starting point contains the possibilities for an entirely different (and more advanced) approach to living and functioning – very different, that is, from the approach fostered by the dominant culture. In it, affiliation is valued as highly as, or more highly than, self-enhancement. Moreover, it allows for the emergence of the truth: that for everyone – men as well as women – individual development proceeds *only* by means of affiliation. At the present time, men are not as prepared to *know* this . . .

We all begin life deeply attached to the people around us. Men, or boys, are encouraged to move out of this state of existence – in which they and their fate are intimately intertwined in the lives and fate of other people. Women are encouraged to remain in this state but, as they grow, to transfer their attachment to a male figure.

Boys are rewarded for developing other aspects of themselves. These other factors – power or skills – gradually begin to displace some of the importance of affiliations and eventually to supersede them. There is no question that women develop and change too. In an inner way, however, the development does not displace the value accorded attachments to others. The suggestion here is that the parameters of the female's development are not the same as the male's and that the same terms do not apply. Women can be highly developed and still give great weight to affiliations.

Here again, women are geared all their lives to be the 'carriers' of the basic necessity for human communion. Men can go a long distance away from fully recognizing this need because women are so groomed to 'fill it in' for them. But there is another side: women are also more thoroughly prepared to move toward more advanced, more affiliative ways of living – and less wedded to the dangerous ways of the present.

[. . .]

A most basic social advance can emerge through women's outlook, through women putting forward women's concerns. Women have already begun to do so. Here, again, it is not a question of innate biological characteristics. It is a question of the kind of psychological structuring that is encompassed differentially by each sex at this time in our development as a society of human beings – and a question of who can offer the motivation and direction for moving on from here.

The central point here is that women's great desire for affiliation is both a fundamental strength, essential for social advance and at the same time the inevitable source of many of women's current problems. That is, while women have reached for and already found a psychic basis for a more advanced social existence, they are not able to act fully and directly on this valuable basis in a way that would allow it to flourish. Accordingly, they have not been able to cherish or even recognize this valuable strength. On the contrary, when women act on the basis of this underlying psychological motive, they are usually led into subservience. That is, the only forms of affiliation that have been available to women are subservient affiliations. In many instances, the search for affiliation can lead women to a situation that creates serious emotional problems. Many of these are then labelled neuroses and other such names.

But what is most important is to see that even so-called neuroses can, and most often do, contain within them the starting points, the searching for a more advanced form of existence. The problem has been that women have been seeking affiliations that are impossible to attain under the present arrangements, but in order to conduct the search women have been willing to sacrifice whole parts of themselves. And so women have concluded, as we so readily do, that we must be wrong or, in modern parlance, 'sick'.

(*Miller, 1978, pp. 87–93*)

MOTHERHOOD AND WOMEN'S NATURE

Motherhood has always posed a problem for feminism. Reproduction was the one area where all types of feminist analyses had to contend with an immutable difference between women and men: that women bear children and men do not. If this were to change, the very definition of the sexes would be in question. The androgynous view tends to minimize what motherhood entails. Of course women bear children, but in a more equal society women and men would develop equally the capacity and desire to care for them. Just like work in the public domain, parenting roles would be shared or allocated on the basis of individual choice rather than by sex. Indeed, as we shall see later in this book, shared parenting was seen by some feminists as a necessary step in the creation of the androgynous personality and a more equal society.

The alternative woman-centred perspective questioned this view of motherhood. One of the main voices in this debate was Adrienne Rich who, in her influential book *Of Woman Born*, first published in the United States in 1976, made a distinction between the 'experience' and the 'institution' of motherhood. In doing so, she took issue with what she saw as the contemporary view within feminism of motherhood as a limitation, preventing women from attempting to find self-realization in the public domain. For Rich, the institution of motherhood under patriarchy is indeed limiting and confining for women, but to adopt the view that it is motherhood itself that confines, and that women should therefore be freed as much as possible from it, is to adopt the view of a male-centred society. Rather the experience of motherhood should be seen as a resource, and woman's ability to bear children a source of strength out of which the possibility of change can arise. The following extract from the introduction to her book makes the point clear:

When I try to return to the body of the young woman of twenty-six, pregnant for the first time, who fled from the physical knowledge of her pregnancy and at the same time from her intellect and vocation, I realize that I was effectively alienated from my real body and my real spirit by the institution – not the fact – of motherhood. This institution – the foundation of human society as we know it – allowed me only certain views, certain expectations, whether embodied in the booklet in my obstetrician's waiting room, the novels I had read, my mother-in-law's approval, my memories of my own mother, the Sistine Madonna or she of the Michelangelo *Pietà*, the floating notion that a woman pregnant is a woman calm in her fulfilment or, simply, a woman waiting. Women have always been seen as waiting: waiting to be asked, waiting for our menses, in fear lest they do or do not come, waiting for men to come home from wars, or from work, waiting for children to grow up, or for the birth of a new child, or for menopause.

In my own pregnancy I dealt with this waiting, this female fate, by denying every active, powerful aspect of myself. I became dissociated both from my immediate, present, bodily experience and from my reading, thinking, writing life. Like a traveller in an airport where her plane is several hours delayed, who leafs through magazines she would never ordinarily read, surveys shops whose contents do not interest her, I committed myself to an outward serenity and a profound inner boredom. If boredom is simply a mask for anxiety, then I had learned, as a woman, to be supremely bored rather than to examine the anxiety underlying my Sistine tranquillity . . .

I have come to believe, as will be clear throughout this book, that female biology – the diffuse, intense sensuality radiating out from clitoris, breasts, uterus, vagina; the lunar cycles of menstruation; the gestation and fruition of life which can take place in the female body – has far more radical implications than we have yet come to appreciate. Patriarchal thought has limited female biology to its own narrow specifications. The feminist vision has recoiled from female biology for these reasons; it will, I believe, come to view our physicality as a resource, rather than a destiny. In order to live a fully human life we require not only *control* of our bodies (though control is a prerequisite); we must touch the unity and resonance of our physicality, our bond with the natural order, the corporeal ground of our intelligence.

The ancient, continuing envy, awe and dread of the male for the female capacity to create life has repeatedly taken the form of hatred for every other female aspect of creativity. Not only have women been told to stick to motherhood, but we have been told that our intellectual or aesthetic creations were inappropriate, inconsequential or scandalous, an attempt to become 'like men', or to escape from the 'real' tasks of adult womanhood: marriage and childbearing. To 'think like a man' has been both praise and prison for women trying to escape the body-trap. No wonder that many intellectual and creative women have insisted that they were 'human beings' first and women only incidentally, have minimized their physicality and their bonds with other women. The body has been made so problematic for women that it has often seemed easier to shrug it off and travel as a disembodied spirit.

But this reaction against the body is now coming into synthesis with new inquiries into the actual – as opposed to the culturally warped – power inherent in female biology, however we choose to use it, and by no means limited to the maternal function.

My own story ... is only one story. What I carried away in the end was a determination to heal – insofar as an individual woman can, and as much as possible with other women – the separation between mind and body; never again to lose myself both psychically and physically in that way. Slowly I came to understand the paradox contained in 'my' experience of motherhood; that, although different from many other women's experiences it was not unique; and that only in shedding the illusion of my uniqueness could I hope, as a woman, to have any authentic life at all.

(*Rich, 1976, pp. 38–40*)

Such a defence of female nature has, however, been criticized as being dangerously close to the traditional patriarchal view of women as defined by and absorbed in their role in biological reproduction. Further, once biology is appealed to as an essential basis for women's special understanding, then the differences between women and men seem to be fixed, and the only hope has to be for a cultural revaluation of female qualities, though it is not entirely clear how this is to be achieved. In the following extract, Lynne Segal argues that feminism has to strike a balance between defending what women are today and recognizing current characteristics as a potentially changeable product of women's subordination:

Feminist thought has always confronted intractable dilemmas in its own appraisal of women. Not only must it fight to end the subjection of women, and to eradicate the existing gender ideologies which endorse and maintain it, but it must fight to protect and respect women in their existing vulnerability and weakness. This means rejecting the cultural disparagement and insidiously false veneration of all that is 'female'. Asserting women's strength and value sits awkwardly beside an awareness that many of women's most distinctive experiences and perceptions are products of subordination.

There is, of course, nothing surprising about the observation that dignity and strength may emerge through subordination and weakness – along with inequality and diminished lives and possibilities. One of the first public declarations of British feminism, Mary Wollstonecraft's manifesto *A Vindication of The Rights of Woman*, published in 1792, portrayed women as emotionally and intellectually stunted by their lives as women and by the prevailing conceptions of true womanhood. But many suffragettes just over a century later elaborated similar conceptions of 'female nature' to insist upon the benefits of enfranchising the 'mothers' of the nation. Tactically, at least, it is clear that women can push for reforms, perhaps even most successfully, without any fundamental challenge to existing gender arrangements (that is, to the social relations between women and men) and the beliefs which maintain them. But the excitement of the feminism I once knew was precisely its promise that we *could* transform our own ideas of ourselves as women, hopefully keeping what was good in what we had learned from subordination, to create quite new relations between women and men, and between women and the world. We did not want to be like men; we wanted to be something new, and better.

Such talk of transformation and change is not found in the new idealized image of women in much contemporary feminism. Here is Susan Griffin:

> We [women] can read bodies with our hands, read the earth, find water, trace gravity's path. We know what grows and how to balance one thing against another ... and even if over our bodies they [men] have transformed this earth, we say, the truth is, to this day, women still dream.
>
> (*Griffin, 1984a, p. 175*)

It is true, of course; if we generalize, that women are in many situations warmer, more sensitive and more caring of others than men; women usually seem less aggressive and competitive than men. And men have always told us that we are. Renowned misogynists like Kingsley Amis find security and comfort in their patronizing belief that 'women are really much nicer than men. No wonder we like them' (quoted in Green, 1982). The image and reality of women's 'niceness', we can all agree, is connected with women's primary involvement with mothering and caring for others. But it is women's mothering and nurturing activities, and the social beliefs which support them, which are crucial to the maintenance of women's general subordination and economic dependence. While the virtues of maternal loving and caring are obvious, they have never been materially valued but instead applauded only with the hypocrisy of cheap sentiment. Might it not be, as some feminists once forcefully argued, that the reason men do not rear children in our society is not to do with any essential incapacity but because it provides little social prestige and little power?

Moreover, the virtues of maternal love can also be problematic. In our intensely individualistic, competitive, capitalist society, love and concern for others become inappropriate outside our very own small family groupings. Class privilege and racist exclusion are most frequently justified, by both women and men, in terms of the interests of one's own children. Narrowly focused on what often seems the threatened and precarious well-being of each individual child, maternal behaviour can be over-anxious and controlling, clinging and possessive. Children do become the self-enhancing surrogates for their parents' abandoned dreams. Within the context of male dominance, children may be the only reparation for a woman's more general frustrations and sense of powerlessness. Women's maternal selflessness can easily become a type of unconscious maternal selfishness, and an inability to allow children to develop caring relations with others.

The weight of responsibility for one's own children can mean a contraction of social vision, an envy and resentment of the welfare of others. So, for instance, while it may be true that women are more concerned about peace and a better world for their children (and, certainly, some women are organizing for peace at Greenham and in nuclear disarmament groups), this does not necessarily mean that women are any less nationalistic, racist or committed to class privilege than men. Women, in this sense, participate in the social world they share with men, however subordinate they are to men in their own group. An awareness of these contradictions was central to the feminist writing of the early seventies, when, for example, Juliet Mitchell assessed the effects of women's oppression within the family like this:

> It produces a tendency to small-mindedness, petty jealousy, irrational emotionality and random violence, dependency, competitive selfishness and possessiveness, passivity, a lack of vision and conservatism.
>
> (*Mitchell, 1971, p. 162*)

The suggestion that any such weaknesses are bound up with the objective conditions of women's mothering is disappearing from the contemporary celebration of female virtues and values.

Women and 'nature'

It is not so much the social realities of women's mothering which are stressed in today's popular feminism as the links between women's lives, women's bodies, and the natural order of things. The eco-feminism of the eighties, which overlaps with 'cultural' feminism and has been called a 'new wave' in feminism, suggests that women must and will liberate the Earth because they live more in harmony with 'nature'. Susan Griffin, introducing the British feminist ecology anthology *Reclaim the Earth* (Caldecott and Leland (eds), 1983), argued that 'those of us who are born female are often less severely alienated from nature than are most men.' It is woman's capacity for motherhood which is presented as connecting her with what Adrienne Rich calls the 'cosmic essence of womanhood', keeping women in touch with the essentially creative, nurturing and benign blueprint of nature.

It is a strange projection on to nature, of course, that nature is female; that it can be seen as gentle, sensual and nurturing rather than as brutal, ravaging and indifferent to individual life and survival. We have here an inversion of the sociobiology which is so popular on the right, where nature is 'male'. And bloody.

Such differing images of nature should not really surprise us, when, as anthropologists like Marilyn Strathern and others have pointed out, 'no single meaning can in fact be given to nature or culture in Western thought; there is no consistent dichotomy, only a matrix of contrasts' (Strathern, 1980, p. 177). In some of the symbols which we use to contrast nature and culture it is 'the male' which is seen as closer to nature: forceful, violent, animal-like and instinctive; 'the female' is the product of culture, tamed, domestic, civilized. In other symbolizations the dichotomy is reversed: 'the male' becomes the creator of culture, 'the female' becomes instinct and biology. Neither 'woman' nor 'man', then, is consistently connected with 'nature'.

The battles fought over the relation between nature and culture, between human biology and human society, are forever recurring. Each cultural period reworks the theme, and redefines the problem. Feminists have fought fiercely to demolish the significance given to the biological in determining the social inequalities between women and men, and the contrasts we draw between 'femininity' and 'masculinity'. But today some feminists, with equal passion, appear to have gone over to the opposite camp. Before puzzling over the place and significance of the biological in human behaviour, we can at least be clear that appeals to 'nature' as a guide to human action provide few secure reference points. Conceptions of the 'natural' have changed radically throughout human history. . .

Susan Griffin and Adrienne Rich, who both emphasize the significance of female biology, do recognize, though inconsistently, that the idea of 'nature' is culturally constructed, which for them means 'man-made'. However, they believe women must learn to trust their own biological 'instincts'. For Rich, this implies that women must 'think through the body' (1977, p. 39); for Griffin, that women must express 'what is still wild in us' (1984b, p. 217). Bodily states, with all their physiological complexities, are indeed a part of every move we make and every sensation we receive. Nevertheless, the biological/social divide is misleading since we can only experience, describe and understand these bodily states within specific social contexts, employing the cultural meaning available to us . . .

The feminist search for women's harmonious union with her bodily needs and functions may, however, fail to show how the social myths of a culture which reflects men's power in relation to women affect our experiences of our bodies. The female 'instincts' of Susan Griffin and Adrienne Rich, for example, just happen to express precisely what has been most central to traditional conceptions of womanhood within male-dominated culture over the last two hundred years. Should we not be a little more sceptical of an over-emphasis on the significance of 'female biology' where the woman's body is seen entirely in terms of sex and reproduction. Yet that is how Adrienne Rich depicts it for us:

> I have come to believe . . . that female biology – the diffuse, intense sensuality radiating out from the clitoris, breasts, uterus, vagina; the lunar cycles of menstruation; the gestation and fruition of life which can take place in the female body – has far more radical implications than we have yet come to appreciate.
>
> (1977, p. 39)

[. . .]

Before we race back to reaffirming ideas of the link between 'women' and 'nature', 'man' and 'machine', we should surely feel most troubled by their pivotal place in the gender ideology of male dominance. There they serve to rationalize women's exclusion from the pursuit of knowledge and from the exercise of power. And they combine sentimentality with contempt for the effects of this exclusion. Men have been seen as distanced from 'nature' because their power in the world has allowed them greater control over their own destinies and over the destinies of others, while the more restricted possibilities open to women have been justified and regulated through the ideology of 'biological necessity'.

(Segal, 1987, pp. 4–11)

GENDER DIFFERENCE AND POWER

Other feminist approaches argue that any focus on differences between the sexes is misplaced, whether it be to affirm or deny them, because the fundamental defining character of the relation between women and men is one of unequal power. As Catharine

McKinnon puts it: 'the social relation between the sexes is organized so that men may dominate and women must submit and this relation is sexual – in fact is sex. Men in particular, if not men alone, sexualize inequality, especially the inequality of the sexes' (1987, p. 3).

So for McKinnon this inequality of power is maintained through sexuality. We shall examine her views on sexuality in Chapter 3, for now what is more relevant is her insistence that a focus on difference between women and men obscures the fact that inequality comes first. She thinks mistaken:

> . . . the notion that gender is basically a difference rather than a hierarchy. To treat gender as a difference . . . means to treat it as a bipolar distinction, each pole of which is defined in contrast to the other by opposed intrinsic attributes. Beloved of left and right alike, constructing gender as a difference, termed simply the gender difference, obscures and legitimates the way gender is imposed by force. It hides that force behind a static description of gender as a biological or social or mythic or semantic partition, engraved or inscribed or inculcated by god, nature, society (agents unspecified), the unconscious, or the cosmos. The idea of gender difference helps keep the reality of male dominance in place.
>
> (ibid.)

So, to McKinnon, all the different explanations of the ways in which women and men are different serve to obscure the fact that the fundamental difference is not in the characteristics of women and men but in the positions they stand in relation to each other; the difference is that men have power and women have to submit. This is what she means when she says that the idea of gender difference helps to sustain male dominance and this is true however we try to explain gender difference. (Her long list covers many of the ways gender differences have been explained, many of which will be examined later in this book.) For her, gender is all about power. and differences between women and men are derived from that, rather than the other way round. The following extract states her position forcefully:

Gender

I wish I had been born a doormat, or a man.

(*Jean Harris, headmistress of Madeira School and convicted killer of Herman Tarnower, her former lover. She testified she had intended to kill herself instead.*)

Gender is an inequality of power, a social status based on who is permitted to do what to whom. Only derivatively is it a difference. Differences between the sexes do descriptively exist; being a doormat is definitely different from being a man. That these are a woman's realistic options, and that they are so limiting, calls into question the explanatory value and political agenda implicit in terming gender a difference. One is not socially permitted to be a woman and neither doormat nor man.

The differences we attribute to sex are lines inequality draws, not any kind of basis for it. Social and political inequality are, I think, basically indifferent to sameness and difference. Differences are inequality's post hoc excuse, its conclusory artefact, its outcome presented as its origin, the damage that is pointed to as the justification for doing the damage after the damage has been done, the distinctions that perception is socially organized to notice because inequality gives them consequences for social power. Distinctions of body or mind or behaviour are pointed to as cause rather than effect, without realizing that they are so deeply effect rather than cause that pointing to them at all is an effect.

Inequality comes first; differences come after. Inequality is substantive and identifies a disparity; difference is abstract and falsely symmetrical. If this is so, a discourse of gender difference serves as ideology to neutralize, rationalize and cover disparities of power, even as it appears to criticize them. Difference is the velvet glove on the iron fist of domination. This is as true when differences are affirmed as when they are denied, when their substance is applauded or when it is disparaged, when women are punished or they are protected in their name. A sex inequality is not a difference gone wrong, a lesson the law of sex discrimination has yet to learn. One of the most deceptive antifeminisms in society, scholarship, politics and law is the persistent treatment of gender as if it truly is a question of difference, rather than treating the gender difference as a construct of the difference gender makes.

(*McKinnon, 1987, pp. 8–9*)

Another approach sees the debate between those who would stress women's difference from men and those who look to the elimination of differences as part of a historical pattern. Similar debates have characterized previous phases of feminism. In the following piece the historian, Linda Gordon, emphasizes how both perspectives have formed part of the dynamic of feminism, that both strands are always present, though the emphasis on one or the other has varied according to context; in some contexts to assert differences between the sexes can be to capitulate to anti-feminism, in others to deny them is to deny the reality of women's position today. She herself is sceptical of the emphasis on difference, fearing that it has enabled women's studies to go off on its own (different) path without continuing to protest at women's exclusion from existing disciplines, and ignoring thereby the relations of male dominance and female resistance that give content to a feminist perspective:

Difference

In the 1980s, perhaps the dominant emphasis in women's studies scholarship has been on what is generally called 'difference'. I have severe reservations about this emphasis because I fear that 'difference' is becoming a substitute, an accommodating, affable, and even lazy substitute, for opposition.

A development of the single greatest theoretical contribution of second-wave feminism, the notion of gender *difference* is a code word that has now taken on two meanings. The primary meaning is that women have, according to discipline, a different voice, a different muse, a different psychology, a different experience of love, work, family and goal. To varying degrees, all the disciplines have been involved in demonstrating not only the existence of that difference in experience but also the difference that recognizing it makes in the whole picture.

'Difference' may be hegemonic today, but it is not without critics, and it has not always defined feminist work. Feminist scholarship has another edge, examining the imposition of difference – i.e. gender – as a squeezing of possibility, and protesting the exclusion and subordination of women in the name of our uniqueness. Different but equal may be the gender version of separate but equal. Indeed, the very notion of difference can function to obscure domination, to imply a neutral asymmetry . . .

If one uses the notion of 'difference' as an organizing principle, one can periodize the entire history of feminism in terms of the domination, in alternation, of an androgynous and a female-uniqueness view of women's subordination and liberation. The eighteenth- and early nineteenth-century Enlightenment feminists, religious *and* secular, tended toward an androgynous vision of the fundamental humanity of men and women; that is, they emphasized the artificial imposition of femininity upon women as part of a system subordinating, constricting and controlling them, with the result that 'women', as a historically created category, had had their capacities as well as their aspirations reduced. By contrast, the later nineteenth-century feminists tended toward a female moral superiority view. They applauded what was different in women, and while they were not always biologistic in their assumptions about how we became different, the process of differentiation was less interesting to them than the result: a world divided between a male principle of aggression and a female one of nurturance. Motherhood was for them the fundamental defining experience of womanhood.

In our second wave of feminism, a similar movement from androgyny to female uniqueness occurred. The early women's liberation movement, both radical and liberal, emphasized equal rights and equal access for women to previously male privilege. In the past decade, we have seen again a celebration of women's unique and superior qualities with, again, an emphasis on mothering as both source and ultimate expression of these qualities. But it is not as if an acute shift occurred from one perspective to another; rather, this duality persists continuously within feminism. Moreover, it can be described and evaluated according to one's point of view: one historian might see a conflict between libertarian opposition to gender and sentimental acceptance of a separate sphere for women; another might see it as male-stream abstract egalitarianism vs. the assertion of an alternate female value system. The implications of each perspective are also contextual. Denial of difference can mean inauthenticity, while assertion of difference can mean retreat from supporting women's transcendent aspirations. Put another way, love of difference can mean a retreat from anger at the limitation of possibility, while hatred of difference can mean self-hatred for women.

One of the worst things about the emphasis on difference is that it allows the development of new 'fields' and the adoption of new styles of critique that do not fundamentally challenge the structure of the disciplines. It does not force the reinterpretation of all existing interpretation on the basis of new evidence but instead creates, potentially, pockets of women's literature, women's psychology, women's morality, and so forth. That is not an argument against separate women's studies programmes; it is an argument about what should be the content of our women's studies.

. . . Neither do I like the segregation of women's history, its establishment, so to speak, as the description of a parallel course on which women ran through time. One main reason women do not, did not, keep to a separate track is, of course, the institution of heterosexuality. Institutionalized heterosexuality simultaneously helps to create gender and thus difference, and set limits on that difference. Lesbians and straight women alike, we are members and participants in all sorts of heterosexual institutions – economic, educational, cultural and commercial – which construct our identity, willy-nilly.

Women's history is not just different, it is critical; it is against men's history. One reason the discourse about difference matters so much is that through it, feminists debate the conceptions of domination and resistance. Both seem to me drained of their experience, of the ways in which they *matter* so much, when they are rephrased in terms of difference.

Another meaning of difference, which equally results from feminist debates about oppression and resistance, points to differences among women. It is directly related, and negatively so, to the first meaning of difference, for the emphasis on a *unique* female voice almost always becomes an assumption of a *homogeneous* female voice. Naturally, people get angry at arrogant uses of 'we'. The women's movement becomes several women's movements, both because new movements are stimulated by older ones and out of rage at the pretensions of some to speak for all – worse, at the replication of elitist patterns within our work and society. Thus, if the multiplicity and variety of feminist perspectives are a strength and a richness, they are also a reflection of inequality among women.

One response to this disunity has been a flowering of narratives of varieties of femaleness ... But too often these narratives do not criticize the generalizations ... made about femaleness, and instead confine themselves to the assertion, in a liberal relativist way, of variety. Indeed, by implication, they sometimes deny the legitimacy of generalization. Too often the response to Afro-American women's analyses, for example, is a tolerant acceptance of difference rather than an attempt to *integrate* that experience as part of our whole approach to the study of women.

(*Gordon, 1986, pp. 25–8*)

DIFFERENCES AMONG WOMEN: WHAT IS A 'WOMAN'?

The last extract raises another reason for disquiet about adopting a woman-centred perspective: not all women are the same or live in the same circumstances. In particular, the problems that women experience living in a male-dominated society are different for different women, and so therefore is their interest in change. We have already seen how the woman-centred perspective has been criticized for adopting a somewhat one-sided view of women, not that different from the traditional stereotype of women as mothers. If this is so, what other characteristics does this stereotype have? Is the woman white, for example, with the concerns and interests of white women in society today? Is she middle-class? Is she old or young? Is she heterosexual or lesbian? Or to put it another way, do women of different ethnic backgrounds, classes, ages and sexualities have enough in common that a single women-centred perspective can be advanced to represent them all?

This is not, of course, just a problem for those who would adopt a woman-centred perspective. Any feminist can be guilty of universalizing the perspective of the particular group from which she comes. Black women in particular have criticized white middle-class feminists for claiming to talk for women as a whole, for seeing their own position and the problems that face them as the most important ones for feminism, instead of recognizing that women in different positions, such as those having to fight racism, may have quite different problems. The family, for example, has been viewed differently in the writings of black and white feminists. Black feminists have frequently seen the family as a potential, even if problematic, support for women in a racist society, whereas white feminists have tended to see relations within the family as a fundamental cornerstone of women's oppression.

But to see black women as having a different perspective 'because of racism' is still to make it seem that white women, because they do not have this other problem to contend with, are in a position to lay down which are the purely feminist issues, to know the problems experienced as a result of being a woman rather than as a result of being anything else. The perspectives of other groups of women, while recognized, are seen as deviant and specific to their particular situations: of being black or of being working-class, for example. But women who are white are also affected in a racist society by their particular colour, by being treated as white and experiencing the privileges of being white. Similarly, middle-class women are affected by their particular class position. To encompass the diversity of women's positions, we have to recognize that different groups of women experience oppression in different ways and that the particular experience of sexism faced by white, middle-class women is no more definitional of women's oppression than any other.

We also have to recognize that however much we subdivide women, no group will be homogeneous. The perspectives of black women are just as varied as those of white women. The experience of racism, like that of sexism, does not define a single black woman's perspective, although it forms a common theme, differently experienced by different women.

In 1949 Simone de Beauvoir made a similar point about differences between women and men, when she accused men of seeing themselves as representing all humanity and women as different:

What is a woman?

To state the question is, to me, to suggest, at once, a preliminary answer. The fact that I ask it is in itself significant. A man would never set out to write a book on the peculiar situation of the human male. But if I wish to define myself, I must first of all say: 'I am a woman'; on this truth must be based all further discussion. A man never begins by presenting himself as an individual of a certain sex; it goes without saying that he is a man. The terms *masculine* and *feminine* are used symmetrically only as a matter of form, as on legal papers. In actuality the relation of the two sexes is not quite like that of two electrical poles, for man represents both the positive and the neutral, as is indicated by the common use of *man* to designate human beings in general; whereas woman represents only the negative, defined by limiting criteria, without reciprocity. In the midst of an abstract discussion it is vexing to hear a man say: 'You think thus and so because you are a woman'; but I know that my only defence is to reply: 'I think thus and so because it is true,' thereby removing my subjective self from the argument. It would be out of the question to reply: 'And you think the contrary because you are a man', for it is understood that the fact of being a man is no peculiarity. A man is in the right in being a man; it is the woman who is in the wrong. It amounts to this: just as for the ancients there was an absolute vertical with reference to which the oblique was defined, so there is an absolute human type, the masculine. Woman has ovaries, a uterus; these peculiarities imprison her in her subjectivity, circumscribe her within the limits of her own nature. It is often said that she thinks with her glands. Man superbly ignores the fact that his anatomy also includes glands, such as the testicles, and that they secrete hormones. He thinks of his body as a direct and normal connection with the world, which he believes he apprehends objectively, whereas he regards the body of woman as a hindrance, a prison, weighed down by everything peculiar to it. 'The female is a female by virtue of a certain *lack* of qualities,' said Aristotle, 'we should regard the female nature as afflicted with a natural defectiveness.' And St Thomas for his part pronounced woman to be an 'imperfect man', an 'incidental' being. This is symbolized in Genesis where Eve is depicted as made from what Bossuet called 'a supernumerary bone' of Adam.

Thus humanity is male and man defines woman not in herself but as relative to him; she is not regarded as an autonomous being. Michelet writes: 'Woman, the relative being . . .' And Benda is most positive in his *Rapport d'Uriel*: 'The body of man makes sense in itself quite apart from that of woman, whereas the latter seems wanting in significance by itself . . . Man can think of himself without woman. She cannot think of herself without man.' And she is simply what man decrees; thus she is called 'the sex', by which is meant that she appears essentially to the male as a sexual being. For him she is sex – absolute sex, no less. She is defined and differentiated with reference to man and not he with reference to her; she is the incidental, the inessential as opposed to the essential. He is the Subject, he is the Absolute – she is the Other.

(*de Beauvoir, 1953, pp. 14–16*)

Women, according to de Beauvoir, are seen as 'other' by men who claim that their perspective is that of humanity as a whole. Women are defined by their difference from men but this does not happen the other way round. The question for us here is whether some women have taken it on themselves to represent all women in a similar way to the way men have claimed to speak for all humanity. And have, consequently, the perspectives of all other groups of women been posed similarly as 'other'? If feminism has rightly been so aware of men's treatment of women in this way, it must take special care not to let the perspective of one (dominant) group of women falsely represent the interests of all women. In order to guard against this we have to find some way of recognizing differences between women, without posing any one group as the norm from which others deviate.

Although it was differences of race and class that brought these issues to the fore within feminism, other differences divide women too. Barbara Macdonald uses the same language as de Beauvoir to describe growing up to discover she was a lesbian: 'My life as the "other" had begun. I was not like anyone in my family. I was not like anyone in my school. I was not like anyone in my town' (Macdonald, 1984, p. 3); and later when she broke up with a lover: 'the experience of having the reality of your own life – your joy or your grief – unconfirmed by the reality around you is to know that you are the "other" and you must somehow chart your own course' (ibid., pp. 4–5). Macdonald is talking here about her treatment not only by society at large, but also by women in particular: her mother and her women friends. Although lesbians have always played an important part in the women's movement, lesbianism has sometimes been seen as an additional problem, which some women have to deal with, rather like a physical disability. Feminists have, however, been much slower to recognize and stop distancing themselves from the interests of older women and women with physical and mental disabilities: Jean Baker Miller would probably not use the term 'dumb' to mean stupid and 'sick' to mean misguided, as she does in the extracts quoted earlier, if she were writing today. The different voices of women with disabilities and those of older women are only now beginning to be given the recognition accorded to other differences among women.

But does recognizing difference leave any space for a shared women's perspective? How can we be sure that there is anything at all that women share across differences of race, sexuality, class, age etc.? Once we take account of the full implications of recognizing all the differences between women, what meaning can be given to talking 'as a woman'. Does it matter whether there is any essential notion of what being a woman is? Or would the rejection of any such essential notion of woman mean we must put paid to the idea of there being common women's interests, and therefore bring into question the whole project of feminism as a movement working to promote women's interests?

These are major questions concerning the meaning of what it is to be a woman, questions which run through this book. They were raised, but certainly not resolved, in the context of debates within the women's movement about differences between women and about racism in particular. We conclude this section with two readings addressing the issue of recognizing differences between women.

The first is by Audre Lorde, a black American lesbian feminist. She argues that it is not differences between women that divide us, rather it is the failure to recognize differences among equals that divides and weakens women. She does not, however, doubt that there are common interests which women share across such differences. The problem is an approach to difference which insists that it must involve domination and subordination, rather than equality. This leads to groups trying to root out differences among themselves in the name of unity, rather than recognizing that the problem is the way patterns of oppression have been internalized and used to divide us. In doing so, she points to the importance of understanding the forces that make for divisions in society and the way in which they affect us all.

The second reading consists of two extracts by Cynthia Rich, a white American writer who has written widely about the experiences of ageing and ageism in the women's movement. The first extract looks back with hindsight at what she thought about older women in 1974, when she first met Barbara, a woman twenty years older than herself with whom she subsequently developed a close relationship. It points to the difficulty of building unity among women if one refuses to recognize the strength of divisions between us, as she herself failed to recognize the importance of ageism. The second extract forms part of a review that Rich wrote of a study of women over seventy by a sociologist, Sarah Matthews. It looks at how old women who internalize the ageism of society compound their own isolation by fostering divisions among women.

Therefore both authors, although writing in different contexts, are stressing the same point – that if women are to transcend divisions between themselves, they need both to recognize what those divisions are and to know themselves.

Article 1.1
AGE, RACE, CLASS AND SEX: WOMEN REDEFINING DIFFERENCE

Audre Lorde

Much of Western European history conditions us to see human differences in simplistic opposition to each other: dominant/subordinate, good/bad, up/down, superior/inferior. In a society where the good is defined in terms of profit rather than in terms of human need, there must always be some group of people who, through systematized oppression, can be made to feel surplus, to occupy the place of the dehumanized inferior. Within this society, that group is made up of Black and Third World people, working-class people, older people and women.

As a forty-nine-year-old Black lesbian feminist socialist mother of two, including one boy, and a member of an inter-racial couple, I usually find myself a part of some group defined as other, deviant, inferior, or just plain wrong. Traditionally, in American society, it is the members of oppressed, objectified groups who are expected to stretch out and bridge the gap between the actualities of our lives and the consciousness of our oppressor. For in order to survive, those of us for whom oppression is as American as apple pie have always had to be watchers, to become familiar with the language and manners of the oppressor, even sometimes adopting them for some illusion of protection. Whenever the need for some pretence of communication arises, those who profit from our oppression call upon us to share our knowledge with them. In other words, it is the responsibility of the oppressed to teach the oppressors their mistakes. I am responsible for educating teachers who dismiss my children's culture in school. Black and Third World people are expected to educate white people as to our humanity. Women are expected to educate men. Lesbians and gay men are expected to educate the heterosexual world. The oppressors maintain their position and evade responsibility for their own actions. There is a constant drain of energy which might be better used in redefining ourselves and devising realistic scenarios for altering the present and constructing the future.

Institutionalized rejection of difference is an absolute necessity in a profit economy which needs outsiders as surplus people. As members of such an economy, we have *all* been programmed to respond to the human differences between us with fear and loathing and to handle that difference in one of three ways: ignore it, and if that is not possible, copy it if we think it is dominant, or destroy it if we think it is subordinate. But we have no patterns for relating across our human differences as equals. As a result, those differences have been misnamed and misused in the service of separation and confusion.

Certainly there are very real differences between us of race, age and sex. But it is not those differences between us that are separating us. It is rather our refusal to recognize those differences, and to examine the distortions which result from our misnaming them and their effects upon human behaviour and expectation.

Racism, the belief in the inherent superiority of one race over all others and thereby the right to dominance. Sexism, the belief in the inherent superiority of one sex over the other and thereby the right to dominance. Ageism. Heterosexism. Elitism. Classism.

It is a lifetime pursuit for each one of us to extract these distortions from our living at the same time as we recognize, reclaim and define those differences upon which they are imposed. For we have all been raised in a society where those distortions were endemic within our living. Too often, we pour the energy needed for recognizing and exploring difference into pretending those differences are insurmountable barriers, or that they do not exist at all. This results in a voluntary isolation, or false and treacherous connections. Either way, we do not develop tools for using human difference as a springboard for creative change within our lives. We speak not of human difference, but of human deviance.

Somewhere, on the edge of consciousness, there is what I call a *mythical norm*, which each one of us within our hearts knows 'that is not me'. In America, this norm is usually defined as white, thin, male, young, heterosexual, Christian, and financially secure. It is with this mythical norm that the trappings of power reside within this society. Those of us who stand outside that power often identify one way in which we are different, and we assume that to be the primary cause of all oppression, forgetting other distortions around difference, some of which we ourselves may be practising. By and large within the women's movement today, white women focus upon their oppression as women and ignore differences of race, sexual preference, class and age. There is a pretence to a homogeneity of experience covered by the word *sisterhood* that does not in fact exist.

Unacknowledged class differences rob women of each others' energy and creative insight. Recently a women's magazine collective made the decision for one issue to print only prose, saying poetry was a less 'rigorous' or 'serious' art form. Yet even the form our creativity takes is often a class issue. Of all the art forms, poetry is the most economical. It is the one which is the most secret, which requires the least physical labour, the least material, and the one which can be done between shifts, in the hospital pantry, on the subway, and on scraps of surplus paper. Over the last few years, writing a novel on tight finances, I came to appreciate the enormous differences in the material demands between poetry and prose. As we reclaim our literature, poetry has been the major voice of poor, working-class and Coloured women. A room of one's own may be a necessity for writing prose, but so are reams of paper, a typewriter, and plenty of time. The actual requirements to produce the visual arts also help determine, along class lines, whose art is whose. In this day of inflated prices for material, who are our sculptors, our painters, out photographers? When we speak of a broadly based women's culture, we need to be aware of the effect of class and economic differences on the supplies available for producing art.

As we move toward creating a society within which we can each flourish, ageism is another distortion of relationship which interferes without vision. By ignoring the past, we are encouraged to repeat its mistakes. The 'generation gap' is an important social tool for any repressive society. If the younger members of a community view the older members as contemptible or suspect or excess, they will never be able to join hands and examine the living memories of the community, nor ask the all-important question, 'Why?' This gives rise to a historical amnesia that keeps us working to invent the wheel every time we have to go to the store for bread.

We find ourselves having to repeat and re-learn the same old lessons over and over that our mothers did because we do not pass on what we have learned, or because we are unable to listen. For instance, how many times has this all been said before? For another, who would have believed that once again our daughters are allowing their bodies to be hampered and purgatoried by girdles and high heels and hobble skirts?

Ignoring the differences of race between women and the implications of those differences presents the most serious threat to the mobilization of women's joint power.

As white women ignore their built-in privilege of whiteness and define *woman* in terms of their own experience alone, then women of Colour become 'other', the outsider whose experience and tradition is too 'alien' to comprehend. An example of this is the signal absence of the experience of women of Colour as a resource for women's studies courses. The literature of women of Colour is seldom included in women's literature courses and almost never in other literature courses, nor in women's studies as a whole. All too often, the excuse given is that the literatures of women of Colour can only be taught by Coloured women, or that they are too difficult to understand, or that classes cannot 'get into' them because they come out of experiences that are 'too different'. I have heard this argument presented by white women of otherwise quite clear intelligence, women who seem to have no trouble at all teaching and reviewing work that comes out of the vastly different experiences of Shakespeare, Molière, Dostoyefsky and Aristophanes. Surely there must be some other explanation.

This is a very complex question, but I believe one of the reasons white women have such difficulty reading Black women's work is because of their reluctance to see Black women as women and different from themselves. To examine Black women's literature effectively requires that we be seen as whole people in our actual complexities – as individuals, as women, as human – rather than as one of those problematic but familiar stereotypes provided in this society in place of genuine images of Black women. And I believe this holds true for the literatures of other women of Colour who are not Black.

The literatures of all women of Colour recreate the textures of our lives, and many white women are heavily invested in ignoring the real differences. For as long as any difference between us means one of us must be inferior, then the recognition of any difference must be fraught with guilt. To allow women of Colour to step out of stereotypes is too guilt-provoking, for it threatens the complacency of those women who view oppression only in terms of sex.

Refusing to recognize difference makes it impossible to see the different problems and pitfalls facing us as women.

Thus, in a patriarchal power system where whiteskin privilege is a major prop, the entrapments used to neutralize Black women and white women are not the same. For example, it is easy for Black women to be used by the power structure against Black men, not because they are men, but because they are Black. Therefore, for Black women, it is necessary at all times to separate the needs of the oppressor from our own legitimate conflicts within our communities. This same problem does not exist for white women. Black women and men have shared racist oppression and still share it, although in different ways. Out of that shared oppression we have developed joint defences and joint vulnerabilities to each other that are not duplicated in the white community, with the exception of the relationship between Jewish women and Jewish men.

On the other hand, white women face the pitfall of being seduced into joining the oppressor under the pretence of sharing power. This possibility does not exist in the same way for women of Colour. The tokenism that is sometimes extended to us is not an invitation to join power; our racial 'otherness' is a visible reality that makes that quite clear. For white women there is a wider range of pretended choices and rewards for identifying with patriarchal power and its tools.

Today, with the defeat of ERA, the tightening economy, and increased conservatism, it is easier once again for white women to believe the dangerous fantasy that if you are good enough, pretty enough, sweet enough, quiet enough, teach the children to behave, hate the right people, and marry the right men, then you will be allowed to co-exist with patriarchy in relative peace, at least until a man needs your job or the neighbourhood rapist happens along. And true, unless one lives and loves in the trenches it is difficult to remember that the war against dehumanization is ceaseless.

But Black women and our children know the fabric of our lives is stitched with violence and with hatred, that there is no rest. We do not deal with it only on the picket lines, or in dark midnight alleys, or in the places where we dare to verbalize our resistance. For us, increasingly, violence weaves through the daily tissues of our living – in the supermarket, in the classroom, in the elevator, in the clinic and the schoolyard, from the plumber, the baker, the saleswoman, the bus driver, the bank teller, the waitress who does not serve us.

Some problems we share as women, some we do not. You fear your children will grow up to join the patriarchy and testify against you, we fear our children will be dragged from a car and shot down in the street, and you will turn your backs upon the reasons they are dying.

The threat of difference has been no less blinding to people of Colour. Those of us who are Black must see that the reality of our lives and our struggle does not make us immune to the errors of ignoring and misnaming difference. Within Black communities where racism is a living reality, differences among us often seem dangerous and suspect. The need for unity is often misnamed as a need for homogeneity, and a Black feminist vision mistaken for betrayal of our common interests as a people. Because of the continuous battle against racial erasure that Black women and Black men share, some Black women still refuse to recognize that we are also oppressed as women, and that sexual hostility against Black women is practised not only by the white racist society, but implemented within our Black communities as well. It is a disease striking the heart of Black nationhood, and silence will not make it disappear. Exacerbated by racism and the pressures of powerlessness, violence against Black women and children often becomes a standard without our communities, one by which manliness can be measured. But these woman-hating acts are rarely discussed as crimes against Black women.

As a group, women of Colour are the lowest paid wage-earners in America. We are the primary targets of abortion and sterilization abuse, here and abroad. In certain parts of Africa, small girls are still being sewed shut between their legs to keep them docile and for men's pleasure. This is known as female circumcision, and it is not a cultural affair as the late Jomo Kenyatta insisted, it is a crime against Black women.

Black women's literature is full of the pain of frequent assault, not only by a racist patriarchy, but also by Black men. Yet the necessity for and history of shared battle have made us, Black women, particularly vulnerable to the false accusation that anti-sexist is anti-Black. Meanwhile, woman-hating as a recourse of the powerless is sapping strength from Black communities, and our very lives. Rape is on the increase, reported and unreported, and rape is not aggressive sexuality, it is sexualized aggression. As Kalamu ya Salaam, a Black male writer points out, 'As long as male domination exists, rape will exist. Only women revolting and men made conscious of their responsibility to fight sexism can collectively stop rape' (1980).

Differences between ourselves as Black women are also being misnamed and used to separate us from one another. As a Black lesbian feminist comfortable with the many different ingredients of my identity, and a woman committed to racial and sexual freedom from oppression, I find I am constantly being encouraged to pluck out some one aspect of myself and present this as the meaningful whole, eclipsing or denying the other parts of self. But this is a destructive and fragmenting way to live. My fullest concentration of energy is available to me only when I integrate all the parts of who I am, openly, allowing power from particular sources of my living to flow back and forth freely through all my different selves, without the restrictions of externally imposed definition. Only then can I bring myself and my energies as a whole to the service of those struggles which I embrace as part of my living.

A fear of lesbians, or of being accused of being a lesbian, has led many Black women into testifying against themselves. It has led some of us into destructive alliances, and others into despair and isolation. In the white women's communities, heterosexism is sometimes a result of identifying with the white patriarchy, a rejection of that interdependence between women-identified women which allows the self to be, rather than to be used in the service of men. Sometimes it reflects a die-hard belief in the protective colouration of heterosexual relationships, sometimes a self-hate which all women have to fight against, taught us from birth.

Although elements of these attitudes exist for all women, there are particular resonances of heterosexism and homophobia among Black women. Despite the fact that woman-bonding has a long and honourable history in the African and African-American communities, and despite the knowledge and accomplishments of many strong and creative women-identified Black women in the political, social and cultural fields, heterosexual Black women often tend to ignore or discount the existence and work of Black lesbians. Part of this attitude has come from an understandable terror of Black male attack within the close confines of Black society, where the punishment for any female self-assertion is still to be accused of being a lesbian and therefore unworthy of the attention or support of the scarce Black male. But part of this need to misname and ignore Black lesbians comes from a very real fear that openly women-identified Black women who are no longer dependent upon men for their self-definition may well reorder our whole concept of social relationships.

Black women who once insisted that lesbianism was a white woman's problem now insist that Black lesbians are a threat to Black nationhood, are consorting with the enemy, are basically un-Black. These accusations, coming from the very women to whom we look for deep and real understanding, have served to keep many Black lesbians in hiding, caught between the racism of white women and the homophobia of their sisters. Often, their work has been ignored, trivialized or misnamed, as with the work of Angelina Grimke, Alice Dunbar-Nelson, Lorraine Hansberry. Yet women-bonded women have always been some part of the power of Black communities, from our unmarried aunts to the amazons of Dahomey.

And it is certainly not Black lesbians who are assaulting women and raping children and grandmothers on the streets of our communities.

Across this country, as in Boston during the spring of 1979 following the unsolved murders of twelve Black women, Black lesbians are spearheading movements against violence against Black women.

What are the particular details within each of our lives that can be scrutinized and altered to help bring about change? How do we redefine difference for all women? It is not our differences which separate women, but our reluctance to recognize those differences and to deal effectively with the distortions which have resulted from the ignoring and misnaming of those differences.

As a tool of social control, women have been encouraged to recognize only one area of human difference as legitimate, those differences which exist between women and men. And we have learned to deal across those differences with the urgency of all oppressed subordinates. All of us have had to learn to live or work or coexist with men, from our fathers on. We have recognized and negotiated these differences, even when this recognition only continued the old dominant/subordinate mode of human relationship, where the oppressed must recognize the masters' difference in order to survive.

But our future survival is predicated upon our ability to relate within equality. As women, we must root out internalized patterns of oppression within ourselves if we are to move beyond the most superficial aspects of social change. Now we must recognize differences among women who are our equals, neither inferior nor superior, and devise ways to use each others' difference to enrich our visions and our joint struggles.

The future of our earth may depend upon the ability of all women to identify and develop new definitions of power and new patterns of relating across difference. The old definitions have not served us, nor the earth that supports us. The old patterns, no matter how cleverly rearranged to imitate progress, still condemn us to cosmetically altered repetitions of the same old exchanges, the same old guilt, hatred, recrimination, lamentation and suspicion.

For we have, built into all of us, old blueprints of expectation and response, old structures of oppression, and these must be altered at the same time as we alter the living conditions which are a result of those structures. For the master's tools will never dismantle the master's house.

As Paulo Freire shows so well in *The Pedagogy of the Oppressed*, the true focus of revolutionary change is never merely the oppressive situations which we seek to escape, but that piece of the oppressor which is planted deep within each of us, and which knows only the oppressors' tactics, the oppressors' relationships.

Change means growth, and growth can be painful. But we sharpen self-definition by exposing the self in work and struggle together with those whom we define as different from ourselves, although sharing the same goals. For Black and white, old and young, lesbian and heterosexual women alike, this can mean new paths to our survival.

> We have chosen each other
> and the edge of each others battles
> the war is the same
> if we lose
> someday women's blood will congeal
> upon a dead planet
> if we win
> there is no telling
> we seek beyond history
> for a new and more possible meeting.

(From 'Outlines', unpublished poem.)

Article 1.2
AGEING, AGEISM AND FEMINIST AVOIDANCE

Cynthia Rich

But ageing is different. I have had what I believed were strong friendships with women in their sixties, seventies and eighties. But since they had not talked to me about ageing, I assumed that they had 'transcended' it. Their silence on the subject made it seem unimportant, and took away the shame, fear and guilt. I could have the illusion of the richness of difference without having to confront the reality of difference.

It does not occur to me, in 1974, that such an illusion is itself ageist – the short-cut of 'we are all women together', without wanting to hear out the pain of all that has divided us. Today, in 1983, I am not ashamed of that short-cut. It came out of ignorance, but also out of knowledge. It allowed me and other women to make a leap across the forces that throughout history have aligned women with men against other women, set daughter against mother, woman of colour against white woman, 'lady' against servant, Arab woman against Jew, Puerto Rican woman against Black, prostitute against housewife. We are indeed all women together – our hard work unpaid and unvalued; our thoughts silenced; subject everywhere to rape and battering; in poverty, poorer; in refugee camps, the last to eat. But it should have been obvious to me, even then, that we would need to redefine the path to unity: it would demand hard travelling through a maze of barriers erected to divide us. There can be no simple act of transcendence above those barriers.

But if, in 1974, I believe in transcending race, religion, culture in my feminist analysis, at least I have spent many years in the Civil Rights struggle, and I am a Jew. I do not want to pretend that racism or Jew-hating do not exist as crimes against humanity, as principal crimes of patriarchy.

'Ageism', however, is hardly a word in my vocabulary. It has something to do with job discrimination in middle age. And ageing itself I see as simply 'failing', a painful series of losses, an inevitable confrontation with the human condition. Since ending patriarchy will not change the course of physical deterioration and death, we had best spend our energies on what can and desperately needs to be changed. The special problems of the ageing woman – about which I have given little thought – are, I assume, only the accumulation of the problems of younger women throughout our lives. If we change the world for younger women, we change whatever can be changed for older women.

I do not know in 1974 what I know now, that old women everywhere in the world are the poorest of the poor, and in the United States are the single largest poverty group. Or that seven out of ten old people, and two-thirds of the people in our scandalous nursing 'homes', are women. Or that the population of the world is undergoing explosive change, so that every day more and more old women confront the world's indifference to them. Or that ageing is our 'failure' and our fear because it has been so defined.

I do not know that Barbara, in her depression, is turning her face towards what is painful as a source of self-knowledge and creativity, and that my attempts to cheer or divert her are telling her to block off that source.

Nor, at 41, do I believe, really believe, that I will ever grow old.

■ ■ ■

What *The Social World of Old Women* illuminates best is the enormous life energy that these women expend in trying to deal with the stigma of age. Without a history, without a literature, without a politic, they find it impossible to reconcile their sense of themselves – as real women, whose lives are ongoing – with the new, degrading ways in which they find themselves seen (or rendered unseen), or with their own lifelong training in ageism.

An important strategy for preserving their personhood against all odds becomes what Matthews calls 'information management'. In blunter terms, the old woman tries to pass. 'I don't think they know my age ... People don't think I'm as old as I am, so I don't go around blabbin' it.' Another old woman recommends 'taking on the qualities associated with youth. People will never think about your age. They'll just think how young you are.'

Passing – except as a consciously political tactic for carefully limited purposes – is one of the most serious threats to selfhood. We attempt, of course, to avoid the oppressor's hateful distortion of our identity and the real menace to our survival of his hatred. But meanwhile, our true identity, never acted out, can lose its substance, its meaning, even for ourselves. Denial to the outside world and relief at its success ('Very few people think of me as old as I am. They don't. People can't tell how old I am.') blurs into denial to self (I'm always surprised when I look down and see all that grey hair, because I don't feel grey-headed').

Given the hazards of passing and the fact that so many old people themselves have lived a lifetime of fear, contempt and patronizing of the old, it is easy to see why most old people 'share with other members of society the stereotypical view of old people' and also refuse to define themselves as old. Matthews suggests that 'flexibility in the definition (of age) is an advantage', but her book more strongly warns that 'you're as young as you think you are' is a deeply self-alienating defence. To be surprised, time after time, by my own grey hair on the hairdresser's floor is to be cut off from direct knowledge of my identity, from the adventure of my growth, from nature and her day-to-day processes at work in my own being. That surprise reflects my rejection, not simply of the stigma of age, but of the reality of age. It links me with my oppressor and divides me from myself. Grey hair is ugly, age is wrong; I cannot be that ugly and wrong. I cannot be the woman with grey hair.

It also divides me from other women. 'What occurs,' says Matthews, 'is that the old woman has one definition for other old people and one for herself.' That division can compound my isolation as well as rendering me politically impotent. If I see myself as young (interesting, intelligent, pleasant-looking, engaged with life) and see other women my age as old (dull, stupid, ugly, worthless), I will prefer friends younger than myself. But the younger woman sees me either as old (dull, stupid, ugly, worthless) or, as I see myself, as 'exceptional'. Exceptional, like passing, is a dangerous defence. It means that a single slip can trigger off 'old'.

2
BIOLOGY, SOCIETY AND THE FEMALE BODY

Feminism has always had some difficulty with biology. On the one hand, feminism was founded on the rejection of the idea that the positions accorded to women and men in current society are the inevitable result of biological differences between the sexes. On the other hand, feminism had to recognize that there are such differences and that they must have some effects.

SEX AND GENDER

The distinction between sex and gender was adopted initially to provide a way out of this difficulty. 'Sex' refers to a biological difference between human beings, occurring in many other species too, by which individuals can be sorted into 'females' and 'males' by differences in their chromosomes, genitals and reproductive functions. For most individuals these characteristics go together and so they can be unambiguously assigned to the female or male sex. A classification of this kind could be carried out by someone from a completely different society who, given the appropriate information, would be unlikely to make many mistakes.

In practice, however, we do not look at people's chromosomes, genitals or reproductive behaviour in order to tell their sex. We tend to use their clothes, their hairstyles, the way they walk and a whole host of other physical and behavioural characteristics which are not biologically given. And someone coming from another society is likely to make quite a few mistakes. In practice therefore it is a person's gender that we use to distinguish women and men. 'Gender' refers to the way, in a particular society, people are socially constructed to behave and experience themselves as 'women' or 'men'. Although all societies appear to treat women and men differently and thus have some notion of gender, what this consists of varies enormously from one society to another. In the United Kingdom, for example, women are not considered strong enough to take on a number of jobs that involve carrying heavy weights; in most of the underdeveloped world, however, where water needs to be carried it is usually women's work.

This separation of gender from sex allows all the processes that go into making us women or men to be questioned and, conceptually at least, those aspects of relations between the sexes that are 'merely' social constructs to be distinguished from those that really do depend on biological differences. Making such a conceptual distinction does not in itself, however, say anything about how we should understand the relation between sex and gender, nor how in practice we should analyse existing gender relations and assess the contributions of biology and society to the creation of gender.

BIOLOGY AND SOCIETY

Feminists have tended to stress the contribution of society, arguing that even if all hitherto existing societies have had some notion of gender, the variation between cultures in the tasks assigned to each gender shows that specific gender roles are not biologically given (Oakley, 1972). Such gender roles are therefore social constructs which could, given sufficient political will, be changed. Further, at an individual level, people's gender identities are not determined by their sex; cases in which children wrongly assigned to one sex at birth assumed their socially assigned gender identity rather than the one given by their biology can be cited as evidence of this (Money and Erhardt, 1972). This indicates that the existing psychological characteristics of men and women could be changed – indeed would be expected to change – along with changing gender roles in a de-gendered society. In this view gender roles are seen as totally socially constructed and individual development environmentally determined; even if biology had played a role in

'In practice, however, we do not look at people's chromosomes, genitals or reproductive behaviour in order to tell their sex.'

the past in getting to where we are now, it has no necessary role in the future.

Such social constructionism, or environmentalism, was the exact antithesis of the biological determinism popular among anti-feminists. According to this traditional view, our biology determines the way in which we as individuals develop both physically and psychologically, and this in turn determines which roles we are able and choose to play in society. In particular, males and females develop their respective masculine and feminine characteristics because they are biologically programmed to do so; the roles that are then available to each sex to play in society are based on those biologically given characteristics of the sexes. If cultural differences are noted in this view, they are dismissed as relatively insignificant. This is achieved by interpreting all behaviour within the cultural stereotypes of our society, so that, for example, whatever women do is seen as innate, nurturing behaviour but masculine roles as different from each other as hunting and share-dealing are taken as evidence for the universality of male aggression. Not only does this view attempt to defend the status quo by claiming change to be impossible and certainly unnatural, but, further, it refuses to recognize that change has already taken place historically, and fails to account for cross-cultural variation.

A popular intermediate conception of the relation between biology and society, adopted by both some feminists and some anti-feminists, is that biology provides certain fixed constraints within which society has a certain leeway and choices can be made. Thus the socio-biologist Edmund Wilson, not a noted feminist, can write:

> At birth the twig is already bent a little bit – what are we to make of that? It suggests that the universal existence of sexual division of labour is not entirely an accident of cultural evolution. But it also supports the conventional view that the enormous variation among societies in the degree of that division is due to cultural evolution. Demonstrating a slight biological component delineates the options that future societies may consciously select.
>
> (1980, p. 137)

And, in a similar vein, feminists have stressed that while only women may bear children, this leaves open to society all sorts of choices as to how they should subsequently be raised.

BIOLOGICAL CONSTRAINTS
AND SOCIAL CHANGE

All the above positions – from the social constructionist through to the biological determinist including more intermediate stances – seem to agree on one thing: that while what is social can be changed, biology is fixed. Indeed this belief might explain why feminist accounts tend not to explore the connection between biological sex and gender. One motive behind attempts to show how much of gender is socially constructed is precisely the belief that what is social can be challenged, but the biological is fixed and unchangeable.

However, to see biology as unchangeable does not accord with either common-sense or modern biological theory. At an individual level, it is clear that our biology can be changed by social and environmental factors, access to food and chances of exercise during childhood being obvious factors influencing physical and mental development. And at an evolutionary level, the biology of whole populations can change as the genetic characteristics of those who produce more children are passed on in greater proportion than the characteristics of those who have fewer offspring or die without having children. In any society the genetic characteristics of particularly favoured groups will become more prevalent as more of their children survive to reproduce themselves. Indeed, the extent of existing differentiation between the sexes may itself be influenced by society if women whose physical characteristics conform more to a feminine ideal, and similarly men who are more 'masculine', tend to have more children than those who conform less well to their gender stereotypes. If this is the case, then we have an example of gender determining sex rather than the other way round.

Further, a view of biology as immutable leaves out of account conscious attempts to change biological conditions. The whole development of technology can, after all, be seen as an attempt to overcome natural limitations. Some feminists have embraced the possibility of technological change as a way of overcoming the constraints of biology and the female body. Shulamith Firestone (1970) saw reproductive biology as the cause of women's oppression, and therefore viewed the development of artificial means of reproduction as the key to women's liberation. For her, as for biological determinists, existing relations between the sexes followed from biology. However, as a feminist, she rejected the conclusion that gender relations could not be changed, because she claimed that biological constraints could be overcome.

Biological constraints are not in practice unchangeable, indeed they may prove easier to change than social ones. Lynne Segal, whose critique of notions of women's essential nature was included in the previous chapter, puts it like this:

> The human body and its needs never reduce to some inevitable or natural process. In the Third World, for example, men outlive women; in the West these differential death rates are reversed. Human *society* has always mediated, controlled and adapted bodily needs. Food, erotic stimuli, etc. have symbolic meanings. Biological constraints, though undoubtedly real, may indeed be easier to alter than social or cultural constraints. So far, in human history, it has proved easy to invent bottles to replace breast feeding, but not to create the social conditions whereby men would take on the responsibility to bottle-feed their infants. All social conventions come to appear natural when in reality there are no inflexible and unchanging patterns, rhythms or relationships in which human development occurs. What is most essentially human is precisely that our lives, women's and men's, are *not* just determined by biological necessity but crucially also by human action and vision.
>
> (*Segal, 1987, pp. 10–11; emphasis in original*)

THE RELATION OF SEX TO GENDER

One problem with a social constructionist account of gender is that it does not allow us to analyse the experience of having sexed bodies. Such experience suggests that sex must have a bearing on gender. How else can one explain the fact that individuals are normally allocated to a gender on the basis of their sex, and that in all societies there are two genders just as there are two sexes?

Secondly, under current technological conditions, the fact that females can bear children and males cannot must ensure that in any society which successfully reproduces itself, men and women do some different things. In other words, the biological distinction of sex is something of which the organisation of society has to take account, just as it has to account for the satisfaction of the biological need for food. Biology cannot therefore be discounted in our view of what social possibilities are. A more logical way to take issue with the premise that sex determines gender is not therefore to claim that there is no relation between the two. Rather it needs to be recognized that the relation is a mediated one: in other words that gender does not follow immediately from sex but society in some sense 'makes' gender out of sex. The question, then, is how to give meaning to this notion of making gender out of sex.

Both the first two articles in this chapter propose ways to take account of society and biology in the creation of gender. Their views are not dissimilar but they explore their subject matters at different levels and use different terms to describe their approaches. Lynda

Birke gives a 'transformative' account of the process of individual development, whereas Alison Jagger argues that to consider these issues on a more social level we need to take a 'dialectical' approach. Both articles raise questions about the relation between sex and gender which will resurface in many places later in this book.

THE MIND/BODY DUALISM

Debates about the relations between sex and gender, and between nature and society, are similar, though not identical, to ones that have beset Western philosophy concerning the relation between the body and the mind. A 'dualistic' tradition stretching back to Plato, and put into its modern form by Descartes, has drawn a sharp division between the body and the mind, separating them into two distinct elements. Further, the two terms of the dualism are accorded different statuses: the mind constituting the individual's essential being compared with the arbitrary physical form that is the body. This dualistic view lies behind the liberal humanist espousal of women's rights: that a woman's body is different from a man's says nothing about her mind, and it is on the mind alone that any claim for human rights must be based. But the mind/body distinction can also be used to relegate women to an inferior status, for the body is seen as a fetter on the potential of the mind. If women are seen as being more controlled by their bodies, as closer to nature than men, then their minds do not have the same potential as men's and by this argument are not worthy of equal rights.

The distinction between society and nature can be seen to rest upon the same dualism. Society is what men and the mind have created, nature being the realm of women and the body. Placing too much emphasis on the distinction between sex and gender can be seen as partaking of the same rejection of nature and the body as that espoused by this dualistic tradition of Western philosophy. In arguing against Firestone's view that artificial reproduction would liberate women, Elisabeth Spelman writes:

> Undoubtedly, woman's body has been part of the source of our oppression in several senses. First pregnancy and childbirth have made women vulnerable, for a long time in the history of the species and even for a short time in the history of the most economically privileged of women. Second, woman has been portrayed as essentially a bodily being, and this image has been used to deny her full status as a human being wherever and whenever mental activity as over against bodily activity has been thought to be the most human activity of all. But is the way to avoid oppression to radically change the experience of childbirth through technology, as Firestone suggested, and insist that women *not* be seen as connected to

her body at all, that is, to insist that woman's 'essential self' just as man's lies in her mind, and not in her body? If so, then we are admitting tacitly that the men – from Plato on down – have been right all along, in insisting on a distinction between mind or soul and body, and insisting that mind is to be more valued than body. They have only been wrong in ungenerously denying women a place up there with them, among other minds. Women's liberation, on this view is just a much belated version of the men's liberation that took place centuries ago, when men figured out ways both to dissociate themselves from, and/or conquer, the natural world and that part of them – their bodies – which reminds them of their place on that natural world. And one would think, reading feminists as different as de Beauvoir, Friedan and Firestone, that indeed what women's liberation ultimately means is liberation from our bodies – both in fact, and in definition.

(Spelman, 1982, pp. 123–4)

She argues on this basis that many feminists too suffer from 'somatophobia', a fear of the body that is common to the Western philosophical tradition.

DISCOURSES OF THE BODY AND POWER

If we reject the notion that biology provides fixed constraints on social change, then it is important to analyse the way that society can itself influence biology. Besides more indirect effects through evolution or environmental conditions, there is also the direct intervention of society on the development of individual bodies: torture, mutilation and starvation are but a few of the forms in which social power can be inscribed on our bodies. However, power does not only involve physical force, it also operates through cultural practices, through the ideas that we hold as members of a society. The French theorist, Michel Foucault, analysed the way in which a society can exercise power through its discourses, that is the ways in which members of that society talk about things and give meaning to their experience. He argued that experience and knowledge do not exist outside the language in which they are talked about, so that discourses should not be seen as reflecting or representing anything that exists prior to them. Instead discourses actually create the experience of which they talk. Thus, for example, in the nineteenth century, medical discourse saw women in terms of their reproductive potential, talking about them as ruled by their wombs, creating thereby both the term hysteria (from the Greek for womb, hystera) and the condition itself. Thus, as the 'subjects' of this discourse, nineteenth-century women became, in some cases, literally hysterical. This was a form of power exercised by the medical establishment over the minds and bodies of women through a particular medical discourse constituting them as its subjects.

Power is exercised by the process through which any discourse constitutes its subjects. In particular, discourses of femininity always both constitute what it means to be a woman and in so doing control the behaviour of individual women, their subjects. Women are both the subject of such discourses and subjected to control by them. This is never a simple process, for the question of who is subjected by which combination of discourses needs to be explored, and at any particular time there are many competing discourses of femininity.

Foucault's discourse theory and the 'post-structuralist' methods of analysis which depend on it have become very influential within feminist studies. This is not surprising because a key question for feminism has always been to understand the ways in which women are subordinated which do not reduce to physical power. Although post-structuralism is examined in more depth later in this book, it is introduced here to examine the power inherent in discourses of the female body, how they have moulded and formed our experiences of our bodies and, through affecting our desires and behaviour, shaped those bodies themselves. Indeed, despite the way in which, being seen as part of biology, the body tends to be contrasted to the cultural constructs of society, it is, like everything else, experienced only through discourse. Our biological 'nature' is often talked about as if repressed or deformed by society. However, it is only through cultural practices, the discourses of society, that we have experience of anything that we might call our biology and, in particular, our bodies.

The final article of this chapter explores some of these discourses of the body, by exploring their effects in a pathological form, the syndrome anorexia nervosa, whose incidence has increased dramatically over the past twenty years. Susan Bordo sees its rise as very much bound up with changes in discourses of femininity and the position of women over this period. Central to her argument is the notion of the body, and particularly the female body, as the site of a power struggle. This is an issue which will come up again in the next chapter, which explores various accounts of sexuality.

Article 2.1
TRANSFORMING BIOLOGY

Lynda Birke

'Men are by nature of a more elevated mind than women', opined an Italian writer of the fifteenth century; women, he went on, 'are almost timid by nature, soft, slow, and therefore more useful when they sit still and watch over things. It is as though nature thus provided for our well-being, arranging for men to bring things home and for women to guard them' (Alberti, quoted in Sydie, 1987). He was not the first to invoke 'nature' to explain the existence of gender divisions; nor will he be the last – we are familiar enough with these statements today.

'Nature' means many things, but in the quotation it carries two important meanings. First, it was clearly intended to convey the message that this was how things *ought* to be; if it is men's natures to bring home the bacon, and in women's natures to cook it, then we should not try to defy nature. Secondly, it implies that that nature is *biological*, something inbuilt and fixed into our bodily selves.

Biological differences between people have often been invoked to explain any social divisions between them. Women's maternal instincts, for example, or their hormones have been given as reasons why domestic labour is predominantly done by women; thus, biologist David Barash claimed in 1977 that '. . . women have almost universally found themselves relegated to the nursery while men derive their greatest satisfaction from their jobs . . . such differences in male–female attachment to family versus vocation could derive in part from hormonal differences between the sexes' (Barash, 1977, p. 301).

Similar examples of biological arguments about women's behaviour and capabilities abound; they range from the notion that women should not be in positions of responsibility (managers, for example) because their 'raging (reproductive) hormones' render them incapable of making sensible decisions, to beliefs that something about women's biology – their genetic make-up, for example – ensures that they are not aggressive. By contrast, where biological determinism *is* applied to men, it is to argue that male dominance or aggression is irresistibly determined by biology. (Goldberg (1974) argued, for example, that patriarchy was inevitable because men's dominance was biologically ordained.)

Biological determinism, then, is a form of argument that can be applied equally to women and to men. But the symmetry ends there: what these examples have also in common is the tacit support they give to existing relations of power. It is male dominance and aggression, female passivity and domesticity, which are portrayed as biological. Women, in these stories, remain subordinated; they are victims of their biology in a way that men rarely are. One notable exception is the way that male sexuality is often portrayed as biological, inherent. Men, we are to believe, simply cannot help themselves when they rape woman; they are, in the words of one anti-feminist writer, 'victims of an impulse, which, left to itself is one of the most destructive of human urges' (Scruton, 1983). Men may be victims of this form of biological determinism, but the argument still justifies the victimization of women through rape. Men, it seems, cannot help themselves.

The biological factors that are held to blame are various, but those most often cited in relation to gender are *hormones* and, at a different level, *genes*. Hormones are chemicals produced within the body for particular functions. Women and men differ in the amounts they produce of the hormones involved in reproduction (the so-called sex hormones); 'raging hormones' refers to the idea that the changes in the amount of sex hormones produced by a woman's body during the menopause or the menstrual cycle will inevitably affect her behaviour.

By contrast, every cell of our bodies contains thousands of genes, arranged into chromosomes. The job of the genes in each cell is to make the proteins of which our bodies are made. Each of us inherits a slightly different assortment of genes from our parents, which is why we are all different. A few genes are different in women and men; so, the argument goes, these genes may be the cause of differences in men's and women's behaviour.

BIOLOGICAL BASES

Yet what does it mean to say that something about a person is 'biological'? And why should feminists object to these statements? When these arguments are made, they could mean simply that there are biological differences between, say, adult men and women. Few would deny that, and no one is likely to object to a statement that, for example, it is 'natural' for women to develop breasts at puberty, or that biology has something to do with it.

What is a source of concern to feminists, however, is the argument that something about a person's *behaviour* or *capabilities* is caused by some aspect of their biology. This argument implies that we cannot really expect to *change* something that is fundamentally biological. People who argue for biological determinism might admit that human learning and culture have a role to play, but only as an afterthought. If biology is the basis, they would claim, then it will tend to show through however much we try to change things through learning.

Thus biologist E.O. Wilson argued that 'even with identical education for men and women and equal access to all professions, men are likely to maintain disproportionate representation in political life, business and science' (Wilson, 1978). For Wilson, even if we could provide identical education, the basic biological imperatives would show through, ensuring that men predominated in the public domain.

Yet what are these imperatives? And how do they give rise to social divisions? The arguments start from the observation that there are biological differences between groups of people. Because there are slight genetic differences between human populations, biological arguments based on genetics were used in the 1970s, for instance, to explain alleged differences in intelligence between the Afro-American and white populations of the United States. Biological differences, not social conditions, were held to be responsible for black children's underachievement in American schools (see Rose, Kamin and Lewontin (1984) for criticism of this argument).

In relation to gender, of course, an important biological distinction lies in reproduction – the fact that it is women who bear children. This in turn, the argument goes, is responsible for social differences between women and men. Today, these arguments rarely say that women are subordinated because they possess particular bits of reproductive anatomy (a womb, say – although there was, for many centuries, a belief in Western culture that women's variable moods could be attributed to the fact that their wombs went wandering about the body!).

More commonly, such arguments rest on differences between women and men (such as differences in the amounts of sex hormones produced by each gender) that *depend* upon the fact of reproductive difference. So, for example, an obvious reproductive difference is that women carry foetuses within their body. Because of this, they produce more of the hormone progesterone, a hormone involved in maintaining pregnancy.

FEMINIST CRITICISMS

Feminism presupposes that we can change things, particularly existing structures of power; not surprisingly then, feminists are critical of any arguments suggesting that we cannot. One way in which feminists have countered biological determinism is to challenge the science on which these arguments appear to be based: it is often, quite simply, bad science – using poor statistics, for example, or experiments that did not take other possible explanations into account. For example, feminists were critical of claims that where children born with a hormonal disorder behave differently from other children, this was necessarily because of hormonal difference. (For example, females may – rarely – be born producing more androgens than normal: these hormones tend to have masculinizing effects.) If these children were known to differ, feminists pointed out, then their mothers might not have treated them in the same way as they would have treated other children, thus contributing to any differences in their behaviour (Fausto-Sterling, 1985).

A feminist response would emphasize the accumulating evidence indicating that gender divisions are created and socially reinforced in our society. To give one example in detail of the kinds of argument feminists criticize, a book was published in 1989 suggesting that many differences between men and women and their roles in society are caused by differences in the ways that their brains work (Moir and Jessel, 1989). The evidence for these differences is not well known, suggested the authors, because feminists and well-meaning liberals have suppressed it.

Feminist criticism of this can take many levels: first, contrary to the authors' claims, the evidence that there are fundamental differences in male and female humans' brains is, to say the least, poor (so, incidentally, is the evidence that anyone has suppressed findings about sex differences in the brain; on the contrary, newspaper reports of them have been plenty). Not only is the evidence poor, but it is often contradictory.

In a feminist article criticizing some of these allegations of brain differences between the sexes, Judith Genova (1989) looked at a number of scientific studies of sex differences in brain function. In 1979–80, some of these claimed that the left half of women's brains was more dominant (whereas for men it is the right half). The left half of the brain is, some scientists say, better at analytic and logical skills, while the right half is more intuitive and holistic. Yet it is women who are stereotypically supposed to be more intuitive, and men more analytic – exactly the opposite of the suggestion that women's brains are more dominant on the left side. 'What is so striking about these accounts', said Genova, 'is that the age-old tales of women being more intuitive and holistic, while men were thought to be more analytic and logical, are completely reversed. Somewhere, somehow the supposed special abilities of women and men have been switched.'

Genova speculated that the switch occurred just as male-dominated science was discovering that to do good science did not simply require logic; intuition was also essential. 'Once again men are viewed as natively equipped to do the truly inspired work', she commented. 'Women's cold, analytical, rational powers can only make them plodding amateurs in the creative game' (p. 213). So, the capabilities that are allegedly fixed into women's brains would seem to be the ones that are less highly valued; and if the evaluation changes, then so too must the tale of women's brains.

To examine the evidence in this way, and then to criticize the studies for their (often) poor methods and the assumptions they make, is the first plank of feminist criticism. The second is to point to the importance of social factors. So, one response to the book by Moir and Jessel is to say that, *even if* there are some differences in women's and men's brains, these cannot account for the extent of gender divisions. Anyone who doubts the importance of social values for gender should consider one of Moir and Jessel's examples: it is biological differences, they claim, that account for men's inability to load the dishwasher!

Criticism of methods, and emphasis on social factors – those have been the two major strands of the feminist critique of biological determinist arguments. I would add two others. First of all, such arguments accentuate the *dichotomy* between women and men, because the arguments are founded on reproduction. The fact of reproduction – bearing children – is dichotomous: only women do it. By contrast, the biological factors that are said to be determining gender in these arguments are rarely so dichotomous; all that differentiates women from men hormonally, for example, is the relative levels of particular hormones. So, gender stereotypes (usually dichotomous; these take the form, for instance, of women staying at home, while men wage war or go out to work) are caused by hormones (not particularly dichotomous) which is all because of reproductive differences (dichotomous) – or so the argument runs.

Another criticism to add is that biological determinism universalizes: it assumes, that is, that all women (or all men) are basically the same. Thus in the quote from Barash that I gave at the beginning, 'women have almost universally found themselves relegated to the nursery'. There are two problems with this universalizing. First, if we find something to be true in most – or even all – human cultures, it does not necessarily follow that the cause is biological. It *may* be – but it also may not; we would need to prove it so, rather than simply assuming that it is. Secondly, the 'universal woman' in these claims is not so universal after all.

She is basically white and middle-class. Biologically determinist arguments about women's 'natural' role in domestic labour, or men's role outside the home, are invariably describing a relationship between 'home' and 'work' that is fundamentally Western, white and middle-class. Yet, as Patricia Hill Collins notes, 'Black women's experiences and those of other women of Color have never fit this model' (1990, p. 47). Nor have those of poor, working-class women. Indeed, the biologically determinist arguments proposed by doctors in the nineteenth century, as arguments against women entering higher education, specifically *excluded* working-class women – for whom the allegations of weakness could hardly apply in a society happy to employ them for long hours in mines and factories (see Sayers, 1982). Today, similarly, biological determinism is more commonly applied where women are threatening to enter hitherto male domains; thus the idea that women were dominated by 'raging hormones' was used to argue against them becoming managers or the President of the United States (see Paige, 1973) – but not, of course, against them taking on the responsibilities of caring for children. The biologically determined woman is one who heeds her imperatives and does not try to enter the company boardroom. She also owns a dishwasher.

ADDING GENDER TO BIOLOGY?

Gender, feminists have consistently argued, is socially constructed, rather than biological. Gender, moreover, is something *adding onto* the biological base (that is, our sex, as male or female). We have used that argument, and the weight of evidence for the social construction of gender, as a basis for criticizing biological determinism. But there have been problems with this approach. By placing so much emphasis on social construction, feminists have been in danger of leaving the body outside our theorizing of gender. Minds may have gender; bodies have only sex.

This omission is not surprising. Western culture has for centuries tended to repudiate the body in favour of rational thought (see Jaggar, Article 2.2), while women have typically been defined in terms of their bodily functions. But it is problematic. In the first place, ideas of social construction cannot adequately acount for bodies that bleed, excrete, desire or hurt. Some feminist arguments propose that our ideas and experiences of (say) menstruation are socially constructed: see Sayers (1982). But it is stretching the argument to say that bleeding itself is socially constructed; few women would go that far.

Secondly, the dislike of the body that can be identified in some feminist thought can contribute to racism. As Elizabeth Spelman has argued, '. . . the idea that the work of the body and

71

for the body has no real part in human dignity has been part of racist as well as sexist ideology ... oppressive stereotypes ... have typically involved images of ... lives as determined by basic bodily functions ... and as given over to attending to the bodily functions of others ... Superior groups ... have better things to do with their lives' (Spelman, 1988, p. 127).

To repudiate the body within feminism, Spelman argues, is to deny the particular ways in which particular women are defined by characteristics of their bodies. Black women, she stresses, are not simply women: they are also black. It is this apparently biological characteristic that defines them within racist ideology (rather than the cultural characteristics by which Afro-Caribbean communities define themselves).

Denial of the body is part of a wider denial of ourselves *as* biological beings. There are many consequences of this in feminist thought; here, I want to consider two of these briefly before moving on to suggesting ways of thinking about biology without denying it.

The power of genes

One consequence of our uneasiness with biology is that we tend to forget that our biology can have some profound effects. Feminists have, rightly, been critical of arguments based on genetic determinism – the idea, for example, that men have genes that cause them to be aggressive, or that there are genes causing homosexuality. The main argument against the 'genes for aggression' idea is that there is no evidence that making a specific type of protein in a cell could cause something as complex as human social behaviour. Now while I think we have been right to reject such ideas, there is a danger that, in doing so, we lose sight of the fact that some genes do have very powerful effects on how our bodies work. It is, for example, only one or two genes that are involved in the production of haemoglobin, the substance responsible for carrying oxygen in the blood, around our bodies. If haemoglobin is inadequate (as in certain genetic diseases), then the supply of oxygen is inadequate – with profound effects on bodily function. (For example, the genetic disease thalassaemia results in abnormal blood cells.)

Animal bodies and human minds

A second problem with denying our biological selves has to do with the relationship between humans and animals. We know, of course, that we have some things in common with other animals: all female mammals, including women, produce milk with which to feed their young. But we usually draw the line when it comes to behaviour; human behaviour, it is generally assumed, is not really the concern of biology. Indeed, this is why biological determinism is a problem for feminism – we do assume that human (and specifically women's) behaviour is shaped by culture.

The behaviour of animals, by contrast, is included squarely within the domain of 'biology'. Everything about animals, that is, constitutes *their* biology, while only some things in feminist accounts (our anatomy or physiology) constitute ours. As far as behaviour is concerned, we thereby imply that we are not like other animals.

This distinction is not very satisfactory. Are we to assume that evolution has shaped our bodies, but not our minds, while shaping both bodies *and* minds for other species? This is simply another way of recasting the distinction (so prevalent in Western culture) between body and mind. Animals are basically bodies with little in the way of mind; we are minds busily denying that we have bodies.

Yet we cannot simultaneously hold two contrasting positions. If animals' behaviour *is* their biology, then we have to assume that the behaviour is caused directly by something inside the animal. If this was said about women, we would immediately cry foul and accuse someone of biological determinism. But if it is only animals, it is all right. Isn't it?

My short answer is no – I do not think that other mammals (at least) are mere puppets of their genes, any more than I think people are. But biologically determinist arguments always rely on drawing parallels between human and animal societies (Birke, 1991). So, as long as animals are wholly seen as 'biological', then the parallel will lead inevitably to seeing humans in the same way. An alternative way of drawing parallels would be to point to the extent to which individuals learn to be social – in both humans and other animals. This possibility is rarely considered, so we are left with either (a) accepting parallels based on biological determinism, or (b) denying any parallels or similarity at all.

Feminism, then, by accepting animals to be part of the biological domain, helps to contribute indirectly to the continuation of biological determinism – an uncomfortable thought. To get out of this impasse, we will need to question just how we use the whole idea of 'the biological' in feminist theory. But to do that, feminism will have to get beyond the knee-jerk reaction of denying it altogether.

SEX, GENDER AND DEVELOPMENT: BEYOND BIOLOGICAL BASES?

At the heart of a large body of feminist writing has been the distinction between biological sex and socially constructed gender. Sex, of course, being biological, does not rank highly in feminist accounts, which have concentrated on the determinants of gender (particularly in American and British writing).

That emphasis, however, has left the 'biological' (i.e. sex) unchallenged as, first, something that is relatively fixed and, secondly, something that comes first – the biological base *onto* which experience and the effects of the environment are added during our development as individuals. To see biology as coming first may be to acknowledge learning and the effects of the environment, but with biology imposing considerable *constraints* on what can be learned.

Recognizing that development is rather more complicated than that, biologists now emphasize the importance of 'interaction' between experience and internal physiology. In other words social experience is not simply added onto the biological base; it interacts with it. It is, of course, important that biologists are becoming more aware of a wider context for behavioural development, and are less willing to attribute everything to physiology or genes.

Yet it is not enough. Interaction, in this model, means the interaction between two or more separable variables, to produce an effect which can then be traced later in the individual's life (looking at how, say, genes interact with different levels of nutrition to produce differences in adult height; or, in Figure 2.1.1, how **A** and **B** interact to produce **C**).

In this diagram, **A** and **B** interact to produce an outcome, **C**. **A** could, for example, represent the genes, and **B** nutrition, both of which interact during childhood to produce the final height, **C**.

Figure 2.1.1

In this model, an individual's development becomes synonymous with moving along a path toward that final outcome (**C**). It is as though it unfolds, from **A** and **B**, to become **C**. But the individual still lacks agency, and takes no active part in its own developmental history: **C** cannot influence the interaction of **A** and **B**. It is as though the individual catches a bus along the path created by environment/heredity, rather than making its own path.

To move forward requires more than the simple interaction I have just outlined. We can do this by emphasizing that continuous and transformative change can occur throughout an individual's life (and not just before birth, when 'sex' is developing). That is, there is no actual outcome (**C**), but a continual process in which **A**, **B** and **C** all transform one another.

That seems quite abstract, so let me explain a bit further. When we think about biology changing during our lives, we tend to imagine the more obvious periods of change – bodily changes during puberty or the menopause, for example, or the early development of an embryo. Yet our biology at other times is not static; hormone secretion, for example, may change if we undergo stress or because we have taken a drug. It can change quite considerably with time of day. Scientific studies of animals, too, have shown that the individual's own behaviour (if it is being aggressive, for instance) can alter its own hormones. So, perhaps we should think of our biological processes not as fixed, but as themselves taking part in transformative change. And nor should we think of them as determining: for if what we do can change them, then we become active participants in that change.

I will illustrate the difference between determinist accounts and accounts that go some way toward acknowledging a more transformative process in development, by using an example from animals. The determinist story has it that sex differences in, say, rats are due to differences in their hormones, the underlying biology. But the story is complicated by the fact that mother rats behave differently towards male and female infants; infants, in turn, behave in ways that elicit specific reactions from mothers and from brothers and sisters (see Birke, 1986). If sex differences emerge out of all this, how much is due to hormones, and how much to those social interactions in the nest? And how important in this is the behaviour of the infant itself?

What this line of thought emphasizes is that what you are now – your biological body, your experiences – is a product of complex transformations between biology and experiences in your past. And those transformations happening now will affect any such transformations in the future. Biology, in this view, does have a role: but it is neither a base to build on, nor determining.

The most obvious reason why biologically determinist arguments have been so prevalent is that they justify existing social organization. A second reason is that biological arguments sometimes win on grounds of (apparent) common sense; it is nonsense to most people to suppose that everything we are is socially and ideologically constructed – as though we have no body. Feminist criticism based purely on arguing for social construction is likely to fall into the pit of appearing to lack common sense. To argue that biological bodies are indeed important components of what we are – but that their involvement is much more complicated and subtle than biological determinism would have us suppose – is a rather more sophisticated answer.

BEYOND FEMINIST CRITIQUES

To return to more explicitly feminist accounts, what feminism now needs is to move beyond the simple dichotomies of body/mind and sex/gender that are so pervasive. To do so means that we must seek ways of moving beyond the critiques of biological determinism (although we will have necessarily to continue to attack crass determinism wherever it occurs). Denying biological determinism, however, does not mean simply stressing social construction and thereby denying the body altogether: we have to find ways of bringing biological bodies back into our theorizing.

Ideas about development, too, must move beyond temporal dichotomies – first, the biology, then the social experience. Major theories of how our individual sense of gender develops assume that biological processes are largely irrelevant beyond the initial stages of determining sex; they also assume that gender identity is largely static after it has been acquired in early childhood. Yet bodies are social, too, and our experiences of, and engagement with, a gendered world is as *embodied* persons. Surely those bodies, and their (often messy) processes, must be part of any continuing construction of gender?

Developing a 'transformative' account (while admittedly much more difficult to think about than additive views) allows us to see bodies as part of the social context. It also – and importantly – helps us to move beyond the 'either/or' thinking that dominates Western culture. Additive viewpoints, by positing 'the social' as separate from 'the biological' simply reiterate that either/or thinking.

Domination and oppression of all kinds are grounded in 'either/or' thinking. Patricia Hill Collins has pointed out that:

> One must be either Black or white in such thought systems – persons of ambiguous racial and ethnic identity constantly battle with questions such as 'what are you, anyway?' This emphasis on quantification and categorization occurs in conjunction with the belief that either/or categories must be ranked. The search for certainty of this sort requires that one side of a dichotomy be privileged while its other is denigrated.
>
> (1990, p. 225)

Similarly, one must be either male or female in our society – hence the willingness of transsexuals to go through major surgery to become 'the other sex'.

In counterposing social construction to biological determinism, feminists initially tried to challenge the most obvious dichotomies that led to oppression – women *v.* men, black *v.* white. Sexism and racism, feminists insisted, were not that simple, and were constructed ideologically and economically. But that emphasis is itself founded on a dichotomy, between mind and the much denigrated body, and that, as Spelman argued, feeds into racism and sexism, too. There are undoubtedly powerful social divisions in our society; and feminists must insist that these are not caused by the biological attributes (sex, or colour of one's skin, for example) with which they are sometimes associated. But at the same time, feminists must also insist that we experience those divisions as embodied persons. Refusing to see our biology as primary and controlling is essential: human behaviour and social organization are not 'caused' by biology *or* by the social/cultural environment, and we are the puppets of neither. But we do have bodies.

Article 2.2
HUMAN BIOLOGY IN FEMINIST THEORY: SEXUAL EQUALITY RECONSIDERED

Alison M. Jaggar

... Feminists have always been suspicious of talk about biology – and their suspicion has good historical grounds. The Western philosophical tradition, which was the intellectual background against which modern feminism emerged, has always been marked by what E. V. Spelman calls a 'notable lack of enthusiasm for the human body'.[1] Within that tradition, Spelman reminds us, bodies have been seen as the source of epistemological uncertainty, mortality and lack of freedom, whereas minds have been seen as offering the possibility of certainty, immortality and freedom. On this view, our bodies are what humans share with the 'lesser' creatures, whereas our minds are supposedly what elevate us above them.

Of course, men as well as women have bodies, but women have been seen consistently as being connected with (or entangled in) their bodies in a more intimate way than men are with theirs. Even in the twentieth century, we find a pioneering feminist like Simone de Beauvoir accepting the view that 'the female, to a greater extent than the male, is the prey of the species'. Elaborating on de Beauvoir's view, Sherry Ortner (1974) points out that many of the areas and processes of the female body serve no apparent function for the health of the individual, but instead, in the performance of their specific organic functions, are sources of discomfort, pain, and even danger. Breasts are irrelevant to personal health; menstruation may be uncomfortable or painful and always involves bothersome procedures of cleansing and disposal; pregnancy and lactation involve depletion of women's own physical reserves for the sake of the offspring; and childbirth is painful and dangerous. Thus, women's bodies are thought to commit them to the biological reproduction of the species, and they are seen as closer to 'nature'. Men, on the other hand, are thought to express their creativity through the creation of 'culture'. The traditional Western view, therefore, is that women are more closely associated with nature and men with culture, women with the body and men with the mind.

This identification of men with the mind (and especially with reason, which holds a particularly exalted place in the Western philosophical tradition) has been used to justify male political dominance over women. Simultaneously, the identification of women with the body has been used as evidence that women are deficient in their ability to reason and consequently are not worthy of social and political equality with men.

LIBERAL FEMINISM

Organized feminism (as opposed to isolated acts of resistance by individual women) began in England in the seventeenth century. Women began to demand that the new liberal ideals of liberty, equality and democracy be extended to them as well as to men. Since it was generally accepted that men were entitled to these rights on the basis of their capacity to reason, feminists felt bound to show that women's capacity to reason was equal to that of men. This argument was pursued by Mary Wollstonecraft in the eighteenth century, by Harriet Taylor and J. S. Mill in the nineteenth century, and by Betty Friedan and many others in the twentieth century.

All these feminists accept the political theory and the underlying conception of human nature that constitute the basic conceptual framework of classical liberalism. According to the liberal conception of human nature, the essence of humanity consists in humans' special capacity for rationality. This is the specifically human capacity that constitutes the ground of the special moral worth of human beings and of their political rights. According to liberal theory, the physical or biological base of the human capacity to reason is theoretically and politically irrelevant. If Martians had a capacity to reason similar to our own, they would deserve to be treated with the same respect that we now accord to humans. Similarly with robots: whether they are made of 'hard' or 'soft' stuff is irrelevant to their moral and political status (Putnam, 1964). Of course, the same also applies to human beings: whether individuals are male or female is irrelevant to their equal rights to liberty and self-determination . . .

The liberal insistence on viewing people as 'abstract individuals', of no determinate age, race, sex or economic class, was extremely progressive in its time – and is progressive in many contexts even today. But it has its drawbacks. Its main drawback, of course, is that real human beings are not abstract individuals, but people who have lived different histories, who have different social relations with each other, and who have different capacities and different needs. Some, though probably not most, of these differences are linked with biological differences. To take an obvious example, the needs of physically disabled people are different from the needs of those who are not so disabled. We may say, if we like, that both groups have the same need for transportation, but this obscures the special arrangements that have to be made for physically different people. Similarly, I think it is also true that the special

79

features of women's biology, as we currently experience them, may mean that occasionally women's needs are different from men's. Most evidently, women's reproductive function may mean that women have special needs for pregnancy leave, maternity services, and arrangements for easy access to their nursing babies.

On a commonsense level, of course, everyone knows that women (and other groups) have these special needs. But the liberal insistence on 'formal' equality, which comes from viewing people as abstract individuals, makes it easy not only to ignore these special needs, but even to claim that satisfying them would amount to 'reverse discrimination' or giving special privileges to women. A good example of this is the 1976 US Supreme Court decision in the case of *Gilbert v. General Electric Co.* In this case, female employees of General Electric charged that the exclusion of pregnancy-related disabilities from their employer's disability plan constituted sex discrimination. The Supreme Court ruled that this was not so, in part because it argued that the exclusion of pregnancy was not in itself a gender-based discrimination but instead merely removed one physical condition from coverage. The justices counted as irrelevant the biological fact that this was a physical condition to which only women were subject!

In bringing up this example, I'm not suggesting that it poses a problem that cannot be resolved within the liberal tradition. The US Congress reversed the *Gilbert* decision in 1978, and even in the original judgement there were dissenting justices (namely, Brennan and Stevens) who took a more commonsense point of view. Nor am I saying that all or even most of women's social inequalities should be attributed to a neglect of certain features of female biology. But I do think that the assumption that the human essence consists entirely in its capacity for rationality diverts our attention away from the facts of human biology and in this way makes possible such absurdities.

Many people today see that it is absurd to refuse to take account of existing biological and other differences between women and men. Unfortunately, they often identify this ridiculous view as feminism, pure and simple.[2] As Iris Young has pointed out, however, feminism in fact is the conviction that women in our society constitute an oppressed group and that this oppression ought to be ended. It is not a defining tenet of feminism that everyone should be treated exactly alike. There are in fact many views on how social equality between the sexes ought to be achieved, and none of them requires that we should ignore existing differences between women and men (Young, 1981).

[. . .]

RADICAL FEMINISM

In the 1960s, with the emergence of the contemporary women's liberation movement, traditional political theory came under attack . . . The new and self-described radical feminists, by contrast, took the oppression of women as their central political and theoretical problem. They began to clarify the ways in which norms of gender, often invisible because so familiar, structure every aspect of contemporary society and subordinate women to men. Taking as their slogan 'The personal is political', they began to to develop a new political practice that included attempts to transform the family and sexual relations. Simultaneously, they began to develop a new political theory to provide an adequate description and explanation of women's subordination. The theoretical work of radical feminism contained a number of diverse strands, but two are especially interesting because of the way they conceptualize human biology.

Women's biology as the problem

In the late 1960s and early 1970s, several radical feminist theories located the source of women's subordination in female biology. There are several variants of this view, but the most interesting and plausible was put forward by Shulamith Firestone in *The Dialectic of Sex* (1970).

Firestone argues that the sexual division of labour has a biological basis. She claims that human reproductive biology has dictated a form of social organization that she calls 'the biological family'. This family is characterized by a child dependent on the mother and a women dependent on a man. In Firestone's view, this 'biological family' is the basic reproductive unit that has persisted in every society . . . The persistence of this unit is the result of two universal features of the human biological constitution: that women are physically weaker than men as a result of their reproductive physiology, and that infants are physically helpless relative to adults. These biological relationships necessitate certain social relationships if women and infants are to survive. Women must depend on men for physical survival, and infants must depend on adults, primarily on women, since human milk or a close substitute is one of an infant's basic needs. Although Firestone recognizes that biological imperatives are overlaid by social institutions that reinforce male dominance, she believes that the ultimate foundation of male dominance is human reproductive biology. Consequently, she argues that women can be liberated only by conquering human biology. In her view, this requires the development of, on the one hand, reliable contraceptive technology and, on the other hand, extra-uterine gestation or what is popularly called test-tube babies. Only these will make possible:

> The freeing of women from the tyranny of their reproductive biology by every means available, and the diffusion of the childbearing and childrearing role to the society as a whole, men as well as women.
>
> (*ibid.*, *p. 206*)

In Firestone's view, these technological developments would constitute the imposition of a set of consciously designed and deliberately chosen cultural practices onto a sphere of human life where the practices until now had been determined by human biology. Thus, they would be a victory over 'the Kingdom of Nature':

> (T)he 'natural' is not necessarily a 'human' value. Humanity has begun to outgrow nature: we can no longer justify the maintenance of a discriminatory sex class system on grounds of its origins in Nature.
>
> (*ibid.*, *pp. 9–10*)

In spite of the power and originality of Firestone's theory, it was never taken up by grass-roots American radical feminism. One of the several reasons for this undoubtedly lies in the fact that Firestone does not hold men responsible for the system of male dominance. Instead, in her theory it is female biology that is at fault and men appear as being ultimately women's protectors. Consequently, Firestone does not stress the need for a political struggle against male power, and her vision of the good society, as the full integration of women, men and children into all areas of life, is clearly a version of the androgynous ideal. This ideal has been under increasing attack by contemporary radical feminists and does not fit at all comfortably with the increasingly militant and separatist tendencies of the grass-roots radical feminist movement.

Women's biology as the solution

Since the early 1970s, radical feminists have become increasingly reluctant to locate the cause of women's subordination in anything about women themselves. For radical feminism, accounts which see the problem as lying either in women's psychology or in their biology are simply blaming the victim. They are further expressions of the misogyny that pervades contemporary society. In consequence, many recent radical feminist writings have tended to see the fault as lying in some flaw in *male* biology.

The belief that male biology is somehow to blame for women's subordination has been strengthened by feminist research during the 1970s, which has revealed that physical force plays a far larger part in controlling women than previously had been acknowledged . . . The recognition that women live continually under the threat of physical violence from men has led many radical feminists to the conviction that men are dangerously different from women and that this difference is grounded in male biology.

For some radical feminists, the main problem with male biology is simply that it is not female. At its most obvious, this has meant that men lack the special life-giving power that women possess in virtue of their capacity to become mothers. Except for a very few privileged women, however, being a mother has always involved caring for a child as well as giving birth to it; motherhood is associated conventionally with certain psychological qualities such as nurturance, warmth, emotional expressiveness, endurance and practical common sense. Most feminists have been at pains to argue that this association results simply from the social fact that mothers have always done child care. For some radical feminists, however, there is a biological as well as a social connection between women's manifestation of these psychological qualities and their biological ability to become mothers . . .

Problems with these versions of radical feminism

Neither of these versions of radical feminism offers an optimistic prospect for women's liberation. Firestone's version requires a technological solution to alter the biological basis of women's subordination; currently, however, control of technology is firmly in male hands, and radical feminism gives us no reason to suppose that men will voluntarily use this control to abolish rather than to increase their power over women. As for the view that women are superior biologically to men, this implies that if women are not to be dominated by men, they must either build societies entirely separate from those of men or else become the dominant sex themselves. These suggestions make fascinating science fiction but are impossible in practice.

Rather than looking for better solutions to the radical feminist problem, it is more fruitful to look critically at the definition of the problem itself. As defined by these radical feminists, the problem of women's subordination is a biological incompatibility between the sexes that makes it impossible for them to live together without one sex dominating the other. Obviously, radical feminists who accept this definition are accepting a form of biological determinism. Such a position is very unusual among advocates of social change because biological determinism is typically used to justify the existence of such social ills as racism, slavery, warfare, laziness, drug addiction, homophobia, rape, poverty, violence, corruption, political hierarchy and, of course, male dominance. Most feminist theorists have taken one of their major tasks to be precisely the revelation of the innumerable flaws in the many arguments that seek to justify male supremacy by arguing that it is determined biologically.

The trouble with attacking specific biological determinist arguments is, of course, that, no matter how decisive one's refutations may be, they always leave open the possibility that a new and more valid form of biological determinism may be invented. By using a dialectical approach, however, it is possible to develop an argument that tells against biological determinism in general by showing that it is incoherent . . .

THE SOCIAL DETERMINATION OF SEX DIFFERENCES

A dialectical conception of human biology sees human nature and the forms of human social organization as determined not by our biology alone but rather by a complex interplay between our biological constitution, our physical environment and our forms of social organization, including our level of technological development. The effect of each of these factors cannot be isolated because each affects and changes the others. In other words, the factors are not only related to each other but dialectically related. For instance, the physical environment does not set rigid limits to the organization of human social life; although the environment may impose certain constraints at any given time, organized human activity also affects the environment – by draining, damming, clearing, terracing, levelling, fertilizing or polluting. The humanly caused changes in the environment in turn allow for new forms of human social life, which in turn affect the environment in a new way, and so on. As we saw earlier, human biology, like the physical environment, is not just a pre-social given, remaining constant throughout the changes in human social life. Instead, it is a result as well as a cause of our system of social organization. This is as true of sex differences as of other aspects of human biology. Sex differences are in part socially determined both on the level of the individual and on the level of the species.

On the level of the individual, it is easy to see how a sexist society has different effects on the biological constitution of males and females. An obvious example is women's feet which, while no longer mutilated by foot-binding, are often still deformed by what used to be called winkle-picker shoes. In general women have been prevented from developing their capacities for physical speed and strength, and the effects of this prohibition can be seen simply by looking at women's bodies, particularly their upper bodies. The rate at which women's athletic records are being broken and the speed with which women's bodies have changed even over the past decade shows that in the past, social norms have limited the way in which women fulfilled their genetic potential, so that we have no idea of the extent of that potential.

Even the genetic potential that women and men inherit, however, is influenced by the social history of our species. For instance, a relatively advanced form of social organization was a prerequisite for the evolution of human reproductive biology as we know it. In the course of human evolution, the development of bipedalism narrowed the pelvis and reduced the size of the bony birth canal in women. Simultaneously, however, tool use selected for larger brain size and consequently for larger bony skulls in infants. This 'obstetrical dilemma' of large-headed infants and small birth canals was solved by the infants' being born at an earlier stage of development. But this solution was possible only because human social organization was developed sufficiently to support a long period of infant dependence.

Just as the process of human reproduction was a social as well as a biological development, so the fairly exaggerated sexual dimorphism that we see in contemporary industrial society may also have resulted, at least in part, from social factors. In some ethnic groups, there is little sexual differentiation between women and men. Women are as tall as men, have equally broad shoulders and breasts so small that it is often difficult to tell an individual's sex even from the front (Oakley, 1972, p. 30). The relatively smaller size of females in other ethnic groups is often due directly to the social fact that the nutrition of females is inferior because of their lower social status (ibid., p. 28). Differential feeding may also have resulted in selection for genetically shorter females, however, since taller women would have found it harder to survive on minimal food. Andrea Dworkin (1972) has suggested that even the sex distinction itself may be in part a social product because 'inter-sex' individuals were less likely to be preferred as marriage partners. These are some of the ways in which society produces genetically inherited sex differences and in which sex differences shape society.

The conclusion of this sort of reasoning is not simply that human biology and the forms of social life are more 'cultural' and less 'natural' than biological determinists suppose. It is rather that, where human nature is concerned, there is no line between nature and culture. Dorothy Dinnerstein puts it this way:

> The point is, humans are by nature unnatural. We do not yet walk 'naturally' on our hind legs, for example: such ills as fallen arches, lower back pain, and hernias testify that the body has not adapted itself completely to the upright posture. Yet this unnatural posture, forced on the unwilling body by the project of tool-using, is precisely what has made possible the development of important aspects of our 'nature': the hand and the brain, and the complex system of skills, language, and social arrangements which were both effects and causes of

hand and brain. Man-made and physiological structures have thus come to interpenetrate so thoroughly that to call a human project contrary to human biology is naive: we are what we have made ourselves, and we must continue to make ourselves as long as we exist at all.

(1970, pp. 21–2)

When this is understood, biological determinism becomes not so much false as incoherent. We cannot say that 'biology determines society', because we cannot identify a clear, non-social sense of 'biology' nor a clear, non-biological sense of 'society'. The thesis of biological determinism cannot be stated coherently.

SOME IMPLICATIONS OF THIS CONCEPTION OF HUMAN BIOLOGY FOR FEMINISM

1   A dialectical conception of human biology allows us to avoid not only biological determinism, but also the 'environmentalist' denial that human biology has any relevance at all. According to environmentalism, the human mind is more or less a blank slate that is inscribed by the individual's experiences in society. Various kinds of environmentalist theories attempt to explain human behaviour by describing the mechanism through which this inscription occurs. Whether or not environmentalism succeeds in answering this psychological question, however, it can give no insight into larger social questions, such as why certain messages rather than others are inscribed on the individual's 'slate', why society is organized in certain ways, or why, indeed, society exists at all. Moreover, it suggests, falsely, that all alternative ways of organizing future society are equally possible.

A dialectical materialist approach to human biology allows us to answer these sorts of questions by recognizing the obvious fact that our biological constitution does mean that we require food, air, sleep and so on. These requirements, together with our approximate size, strength, speed etc., have always been important influences on how we have organized our social life. What these requirements do not do, however, is set rigid limits on what is socially possible. Of course, human beings are a biological species and, of course, as such there is a biological basis for our abilities, limitations and needs. Human social organization must allow for the satisfaction of these needs by human abilities and in spite of human limitations. But human needs are flexible, and they are modified according to the means available for their satisfaction. And human abilities can be expanded, for example by technology, in order to overcome human limitations. For this reason, we can talk sensibly about human biology or human abilities, limitations and needs only within a particular social context. For this context determines the specific form taken by our biologically based abilities, limitations and needs, just as much or as little as our biological constitution in turn determines the specific form of our social organization. Human nature is both historical and biological, and the two aspects are inseparable.

2   A perhaps unexpected consequence of this dialectical conception of human biology is that it challenges the conceptual distinction between sex and gender that earlier feminists painstakingly established. As it is conceived ordinarily, sex is thought of as a fixed set of biological characteristics, whereas gender is construed as a set of variable social norms about the proper behaviour of sexed individuals. Yet if we acknowledge human biology, including human sex differences, as created partly by society, and if we acknowledge human society as responsive to human biology, then we lose the clarity of the distinction between sex and gender. As Ann Palmeri puts it, the original clarity of that distinction comes to seem 'a false clarity'. We see that there is a dialectical relation between sex and gender such that sex neither uniquely determines gender, as the biological determinists hold, nor is irrelevant to gender, as liberals and environmentalists believe. Instead, sex and gender create each other.

3   Given this dialectical conception of sex and gender, we can see that there is no simple answer to the question of whether women's subordination has a biological cause. Instead, we can see that the question itself is misleading, suggesting a linear model of causality that is quite inapplicable to this context. Women's biology is clearly relevant to the sexual division of labour in which their subordination is rooted, but it does not *cause* women's subordination because it is, in part, determined precisely by that subordination.

4   A further implication of the dialectical conception of human biology is that no social activity or form of social organization is any more 'natural' than any other. Male dominance is no more nor less natural than female dominance. It is not more or less natural for mothers than for fathers to rear children. Heterosexual intercourse is not more or less natural than other forms of sexual activity. Giving birth in a field is not more or less natural than giving birth in a hospital or even than providing an ovum for a test-tube baby. Some of these practices have a longer history and more ideological support than others, but none of them is determined by human biology or beyond the reach of conscious social control. Since both sexes are equally human, no sense can be given to the suggestion that women are closer to nature than are men. Going to war is neither more nor less natural than giving birth, and neither of these is more natural nor less than composing music or doing philosophy.

5   If nothing is natural, then the area of human social life that political theory has taken traditionally as its domain can now be seen to be too narrow. Traditional political theory has always made a distinction between the public and the private spheres of human

existence. Although the so-called public sphere has been variously defined, it has always excluded the areas of sexuality, childbearing, childrearing etc., which have been seen invariably as 'natural' or biologically determined. If this assumption of naturalness is false, however, then the distinction between the public and the private realm comes to seem philosophically arbitrary, without reason. When so much of women's lives are spent in the private sphere, moreover, it is not just irrational but sexist for political theory to ignore the work of human reproduction and to assume that women will carry on doing this work just as they have always done. Political theory must acknowledge explicitly that humans have a sex, that their sex is defined primarily by differences in reproductive physiology, that women bear children, that infant survival depends on human milk or a close substitute, and that human young require a long period of adult care ... Questions of sex, gender and procreation are virtually ignored by ... political theory. A dialectical materialist conception of sex differences, by contrast, allows us to reflect systematically and constructively on the political significance of human reproductive biology. It provides the conceptual foundations for bringing sexual, childbearing and childrearing practices within the domain of political theory and of conscious social control.

6   Although these practices have not been questioned by traditional political theory, they have begun to be explored by feminists, especially by the authors of feminist science fiction, such as Dorothy Bryant, Marge Piercy, Ursula Leguin and Sally Gearhart.[3] In her influential novel *Woman on the Edge of Time*, Piercy outlines her version of the good society. One of the most remarkable features of this society is that neither sex bears children, but both sexes, through hormone treatments, suckle them. On Piercy's view, the ability to bear and suckle children is not necessarily a disadvantage for women; on the contrary, this ability could become a power and a privilege. It is a privilege, moreover, that women will have to share with men in any society that is truly egalitarian. Thus Piercy envisions a situation where every baby has three social 'mothers' who may be male or female, and at least two of whom agree to breastfeed it. The point of this arrangement is not only to guard against sexual inequality. It is also to avoid feelings of reciprocal possessiveness and dependence that Piercy fears may be engendered by having children born to a single mother.

If these sorts of speculations seem bizarre or extravagant, I suggest that this appearance is an indication of the depth of our prejudices regarding the 'natural' basis of human social life. The truth is, no significant body of modern political theory reflects systematically on the apparent biological facts that every human being enters the world with a special biological connection to a single human male and, even more evidently, to a single human female. Yet that these apparent facts are of enormous social significance is obvious from the way that they are elaborated in every culture into a gender system that structures and, I believe, restricts not only our physical development but every other aspect of our lives. Feminist theory, perhaps influenced by recent developments in procreative technology, is now asserting that no biological facts are unalterable in principle and hence that there is no 'natural' basis for human social life. Monique Wittig writes:

> Our bodies as well as our minds are the product of [ideological] manipulation. We have been . . . distorted to such an extent that our deformed body is what they call 'natural', is what is supposed to exist as such before our oppression.
>
> *(1979, p. 70)*

It may be that full equality between the sexes requires the transformation not only of so-called sex roles or of gender norms, but of those biological aspects of human nature that we have thought of hitherto, in Firestone's words, as 'the sex distinction itself'.

Notes

1   On this topic, see also Spelman (1982).

2   See, for example, Wolgast (1980). Wolgast identifies feminism with the claim that women and men should be treated the same in all possible respects, and she then proceeds to attack this view, often with good arguments. Many ordinary people reject what they think of as feminism for reasons similar to Wolgast's.

3   Examples of feminist science fiction include the following:
Dorothy Bryant (1976) *The Kin of Ata are Waiting for You,* Berkeley, CA, and New York, Moon Books and Random House;
Charlotte Perkins Gilman (1979) *Herland: a lost feminist Utopian world,* New York, Pantheon (London, The Women's Press, 1979);
Marge Piercy (1976) *Woman on the Edge of Time,* New York, Fawcett (London, The Women's Press, 1978);
Sally Miller Gearheart (1979) *The Wanderground: stories of the hill women,* Watertown, MA, Persephone Press (London, The Women's Press);
Ursula LeGuin (1969) *The Left Hand of Darkness,* New York, Ace Books (new edn, London, Futura, 1981) and many others by this author.

Article 2.3
ANOREXIA NERVOSA: PSYCHOPATHOLOGY AS THE CRYSTALLIZATION OF CULTURE

Susan Bordo

Historians long ago began to write the history of the body. They have studied the body in the field of historical demography or pathology; they have considered it as the seat of needs and appetites, as the locus of physiological processes and metabolisms, as a target for the attacks of germs or viruses; they have shown to what extent historical processes were involved in what might seem to be the purely biological base of existence; and what place should be given in the history of society to biological "events" such as the circulation of bacilli, or the extension of the lifespan. But the body is also directly involved in a political field; power relations have an immediate hold upon it; they invest it, mark it, train it, torture it, force it to carry out tasks, to perform ceremonies, to emit signs.

Michel Foucault, Discipline and Punish

I believe in being the best I can be,
I believe in watching every calorie . . .

'Crystal Light' commercial

Psychopathology, as Jules Henry (1963) has said, 'is the final outcome of all that is wrong with a culture'. In no case is this more strikingly true than in the case of anorexia nervosa and bulimia,[1] barely known a century ago, yet reaching epidemic proportions today. Far from being the result of a superficial fashion phenomenon, these disorders reflect and call our attention to some of the central ills of our culture – from our historical heritage of disdain for the body, to our modern fear of loss of control over our futures, to the disquieting meaning of contemporary beauty ideals in an era of female presence and power.

Changes in the incidence of anorexia have been dramatic.[2] In 1945, when Ludwig Binswanger chronicled the now famous case of Ellen West, he was able to say that 'from a psychiatric point of view we are dealing here with something new, with a new symptom' (1958, p. 288). In 1973, Hilde Bruch, one of the pioneers in understanding and treating eating disorders, could still say that anorexia was 'rare indeed'. In 1984, it was estimated that as many as one in every 200–250 women between the ages of thirteen and twenty-two suffers from anorexia, and that anywhere from 12 to 33 per cent of college women control their weight through vomiting, diuretics and laxatives. The New York Center for the Study of Anorexia and Bulimia reports that in the first five months of 1984 it received 252 requests for treatment, compared with 30 requests received in all of 1980 (Smith, 1984, p. 28). Even allowing for increased social awareness of eating disorders and a greater willingness to report the illness, these statistics are startling and provocative. So, too, is the fact that 90 per cent of all anorexics are women . . . (Chernin, 1981, p. 63).

Anorexia nervosa is clearly . . . a multidetermined disorder, with familial, psychological and possibly biological factors inter- acting in varying combinations in different individuals to produce a final common pathway. Over the last several years, with growing evidence, not only of an overall increase in frequency of the disease, but of its higher incidence in certain populations,[3] attention has begun to turn, too, to cultural factors as significant in the pathogenesis of eating disorders. Until very recently, however, the most that one could expect in the way of cultural or social analysis, with very few exceptions,[4] was the (unavoidable) recognition that anorexia is related to the increasing emphasis that fashion has placed on slenderness over the last fifteen years. This, unfortunately, is only to replace one mystery with another, more profound mystery than the first.

What we need to ask is *why* our culture is so obsessed with keeping our bodies slim, tight and young that when 500 people were asked, in a recent poll, what they feared most in the world, 190 replied 'getting fat' (Chernin, 1981, pp. 36–7).[5] So, too, do we need to explore the fact that it is women who are most oppressed by what Kim Chernin calls 'the tyranny of slenderness'[6] and that this particular oppression is a post-1960s, post-feminist phenomenon. In the 1950s, by contrast, with women once again out of the factories and safely immured in the home, the dominant ideal of female beauty was exemplified by Marilyn Monroe – hardly your androgyn- ous, athletic, adolescent body type. At the peak of her popularity, Monroe was often described as 'femininity incarnate', 'femaleness embodied'; last term, a student of mine described her as 'a cow'. Is this merely a change in what size hips, breasts and waist are considered attractive, or has the very idea of incarnate femaleness come to have a different meaning, different associations, the capacity to stir up different fantasies and images for the culture of the 1980s? These are the sorts of questions that need to be addressed if we are to achieve a deep understanding of the current epidemic of eating disorders.

The central point of intellectual orientation for this paper is expressed in its subtitle. I take the psychopathologies that develop within a culture, far from being anomalies or aberrations, as characteristic expressions of that culture, as the crystallization, indeed, of much that is wrong with it . . . Anorexia appears . . . as a remarkably overdetermined *symptom* of some of the multifaceted and heterogeneous distresses of our age. Just as it functions in a variety of ways in the psychic economy of the anorexic individual, so a variety of cultural currents or streams converge in anorexia, find their perfect, precise expression in it.

I will call those streams or currents 'axes of continuity': *axes* because they meet or converge in the anorexic syndrome; *continuity* refers to the fact that when we place or locate anorexia on these axes, its family resemblances and connections with other phenomena emerge . . . The three axes that I will discuss in this paper (although they by no means exhaust the possibilities for cultural understanding of anorexia) are *the dualist axis, the control axis, and the gender/power axis.* [I choose these three primarily because they are where my exploration of the imagery, language and metaphor produced by anorexic women led me . . . The dualist axis serves to identify and articulate the basic body imagery of anorexia. The control axis is an exploration of the question 'Why now?' The gender/power axis continues this exploration, but focuses on the question 'Why women?']

Throughout my discussion, it will be assumed that the body, far from being some fundamentally stable, acultural constant to which we must *contrast* all culturally relative and institutional forms, is constantly 'in the grip', as Foucault puts it, of cultural practices. Not that this is a matter of cultural *repression* of the instinctual or natural body. Rather, there *is* no 'natural' body. Cultural practices, far from exerting their power *against* spontaneous needs, 'basic' pleasures or instincts, or 'fundamental' structures of body experience, are already and always inscribed, as Foucault has emphasized, 'on our bodies and their materiality, their forces, energies, sensations and pleasures' (1980b, p. 155). Our bodies, no less than anything else that is human, are constituted by culture.

The malleability of the body is often but not exclusively a matter of the body-as-experienced . . . rather than the physical body. For example, Foucault points to the medicalization of sexuality in the nineteenth century, which recast sex from a family matter into a private, dark, bodily secret that was appropriately investigated by doctors, psychiatrists, school educators etc. The constant probing and interrogation, Foucault argues, ferreted out, eroticized and solidified all sorts of sexual types and perversions, which people then experienced (although they hadn't originally) as defining their bodily possibilities and pleasures. The practice of the medical confessional, in other words, in its constant foraging for sexual secrets and hidden stories, actually *created* new sexual secrets – and eroticized the acts of interrogation and confession, too (ibid., pp. 47–8). Here, social practice changed people's *experience* of their bodies and their possibilities. Similarly, as we shall see, the practice of dieting – of saying 'no' to hunger – contributes to the anorexic's increasing sense of hunger as a dangerous eruption, which comes from some alien part of the self, and to a growing intoxication with controlling that eruption.

Although the malleability of the body is frequently a matter of the body-as-experienced, the *physical* body can also be an instrument and medium of power. Foucault gives the classic example of public torture during the ancien régime, through which 'the sovereign's power was literally and publicly inscribed on the criminal's body in a manner as controlled, scenic and well-attended as possible' (Dreyfus and Rabinow, 1983, p. 112). Similarly, the nineteenth-century corset appears, in addition to the actual physical incapacitation it caused the wearer, as a virtual emblem of the power of culture to impose its designs on the female body.

Indeed, women's bodies in general have historically been more vulnerable to extremes in both forms of cultural manipulation of the body. When we later turn to consider some aspects of the history of medicine and fashion, the social manipulation of the female body emerges as an absolutely central strategy in the maintenance of power relations between the sexes over the last hundred years. This historical understanding must deeply affect our understanding of anorexia, and of our contemporary preoccupation with slenderness.

This is *not* to say that I take what I am doing here to be the unearthing of a long-standing male conspiracy against women, or the fixing of blame on *any* particular participants in the play of social forces. In this, I once again follow Foucault, who reminds us that although a perfectly clear logic may characterize historical power relations, with perfectly decipherable aims and objectives, it is nonetheless 'often the case that no one was there to have invented' these aims and strategies, either through choice of individuals or through the rational game plan of some presiding 'headquarters' (Foucault, 1980b, p. 95). This does not mean that individuals do not *consciously* pursue goals that advance their own positions, and advance certain power positions in the process. But it does deny that in doing so, they are directing the overall movement of relations, or engineering their shape. They may not even know what that shape is. Nor does the fact that power relations involve the domination of particular groups – say, prisoners by guards, females by males, amateurs by experts – entail that the dominators are in control of the situation, or that the dominated do not sometimes advance and extend the situation themselves (Foucault, 1979, p. 26). Nowhere, as we shall see, is this more clear than in the case of anorexia.

THE DUALIST AXIS

I will begin with the most general and attenuated axis of continuity – the one that begins with Plato, winds its way to its most lurid expression in Augustine, and finally becomes metaphysically solidified and 'scientized' by Descartes. I am referring, of course, to our dualistic heritage: the view that human existence is bifurcated into two realms or substances – the bodily or material on the one hand, and the mental or spiritual on the other. Despite some fascinating historical variations, which I will not go into here, the basic imagery of dualism has remained fairly constant. Let me briefly describe its central features; they will turn out, as we will see, to constitute the basic body imagery of the anorexic.

First, the body is experienced as alien, as the not-self, the not-me. *It* is 'fastened and glued' to me, 'nailed' and 'riveted' to me, as Plato describes it . . .

Second, the body is experienced as *confinement* and *limitation*: a 'prison', a 'swamp', a 'cage', a 'fog' – all images that occur in Plato, Descartes and Augustine – from which the soul, will or mind struggles to escape. 'The enemy ['the madness of lust'] held my will in his power and from it he made a chain and shackled me', says Augustine. In all three, images of the soul being 'dragged' by the body are prominent. The body is 'heavy, ponderous', as Plato describes it; it exerts a downward pull.

Third, the body is the *enemy*, as Augustine explicitly describes it time and again, and as Plato and Descartes strongly suggest in their diatribes against the body as the source of obscurity and confusion in our thinking. 'A source of countless distractions by reason of the mere requirement of food', says Plato, 'liable also to diseases which overtake and impede us in the pursuit of truth: it fills us full of loves, and lusts, and fears, and fancies of all kinds, and endless foolery, and in very truth, as men say, takes away from us the power of thinking at all. Whence come wars, and fightings, and factions? Whence but from the body and the lusts of the body.'

Finally, whether as an impediment to reason or as the home of the 'slimy desires of the flesh' (as Augustine calls them), the body is the locus of all that threatens our attempts at *control*. It overtakes, it overwhelms, it erupts and disrupts. This situation, for the dualist, becomes an incitement to battle the unruly forces of the body, to show it who is boss; for as Plato says, 'Nature orders the soul to rule and govern and the body to obey and serve.' All three, Plato, Augustine and, most explicitly, Descartes provide instructions, rules or models of how to gain control over the body, with the ultimate aim of learning to live without it. That is: to achieve intellectual independence from the lure of its illusions, to become impervious to its distractions, and most importantly, to kill off its desires and hungers . . .

Dualism here appears as the offspring, the by-product, of the identification of the self with control, an identification that [lies] at the centre of Christianity's ethic of antisexuality. The attempt to subdue the spontaneities of the body in the interests of control only succeeds in constituting them as more alien, and more powerful, and thus more needful of control. The only way to win this no-win game is to go beyond control, is to kill off the body's spontaneities entirely. That is: to cease to *experience* our hungers and desires.

This is what many anorexics describe as their ultimate goal. '[I want] to reach the point,' as one put it, 'when I don't need to eat at all.' Kim Chernin recalls her surprise when, after fasting, her hunger returned: 'I realized [then] that my secret goal in dieting must have been the intention to kill off my appetite completely.'

It is not usually noted, in the popular literature on the subject, that anorexic women are as obsessed with *hunger* as they are with being slim. Far from losing her appetite, the typical anorexic is haunted by her appetite (in much the same way as Augustine describes being haunted by sexual desire) and is in constant dread of being overwhelmed by it. Many describe the dread of hunger – 'of not having control, of giving in to biological urge', – . . . as . . . 'the real obsession': 'I don't think the dread of becoming fat is the real . . . neurosis, but the constant desire for food . . . [H]unger, or the dread of hunger, pursues me all morning . . . Even when I am full, I am afraid of the coming hour in which hunger will start again.' . . . Bruch reports that her patients are often terrified by the prospect of taking just one bite of food, lest they never be able to stop (1973, p. 253) . . .

For these women, hunger is experienced as an alien invader, marching to the tune of its own seemingly arbitrary whims, disconnected from any normal self-regulating mechanisms. How could it be so connected? (For it is experienced as coming from an area *outside* the self.) One patient of Bruch's says she ate breakfsat because 'my stomach wanted it' (ibid. p. 270), expressing here the same sense of alienation from her hungers (and her physical self) that Augustine expresses when he speaks of his 'captor', 'the law of sin that was in my member'. Bruch notes that this 'basic delusion', as she calls it, 'of not owning the body and its sensations' is a typical symptom of all eating disorders . . . (ibid., p. 50)

Anorexia is not a philosophical attitude; it is a debilitating affliction. Yet quite often a highly conscious and articulate scheme of images and associations – one could go so far as to call it a metaphysics – is presented by these women. The scheme is strikingly Augustinian, with evocations of Plato. This is not to say, of course, that anorexics are followers of Plato or Augustine, but that in the anorexic's 'metaphysics' elements are made explicit, historically grounded in Plato and Augustine, that run deep in our culture. As Augustine often speaks of the 'two wills' within him, 'one the servant of the flesh, the other of the spirit', who 'between them tore my soul apart', so the anorexic describes a 'spiritual struggle', a 'contest between good and evil' (Liu, 1979, p. 141), often conceived explicitly as a battle between mind or will and appetite or body . . .

In this battle, thinness represents a triumph of the will over the body, and the thin body (that is, the nonbody) is associated with 'absolute purity, hyperintellectuality and transcendence of the flesh. My soul seemed to grow as my body waned; I felt like one of those early Christian saints who starved themselves in the desert sun. I felt invulnerable, clean and hard as the bones etched into my silhouette' (Woods, 1981, p. 242). Fat (i.e., becoming *all* body) is associated with the 'taint' of matter and flesh, 'wantonness' (Liu, 1979, p. 109), mental stupor and mental decay . . . Very often, sexuality is brought into this scheme of associations, and hunger and sexuality are psychically connected . . . Sexuality . . . is 'an abominable business' . . ., staying reed-thin is seen as a way of avoiding sexuality, by becoming 'androgynous' (Liu, 1979, p. 101) . . . '[T]he avoidance of any sexual encounter, a shrinking from all bodily contact,' according to Bruch, is characteristic (1979, p. 73).[7]

THE CONTROL AXIS

Having pointed to the axis of continuity from Plato to anorexia, we should feel cautioned against the impulse to regard anorexia as expressing entirely modern attitudes and fears. Disdain for the body, the conception of it as an alien force and impediment to the soul, is very old in our Greco-Christian traditions (although it has usually been expressed most forcefully by male philosophers and theologians rather than adolescent women!). But although dualism is as old as Plato, in many ways contemporary culture appears *more* obsessed than previous eras with the control of the unruly body. Looking now at contemporary American life, a second axis of continuity emerges on which to locate anorexia. I will call it the *control axis*.

The anorexic, typically, experiences her life as well as her hungers as being out of control. She is torn by conflicting and contradictory expectations and demands, wanting to shine in all areas of student life, confused about where to place most of her energies, what to focus on, as she develops into an adult. Characteristically, her parents expect a great deal of her in the way of individual achievement (as well as physical appearance, particularly her father), yet have made most important decisions for her (Bruch, 1979, p. 33). Usually, the anorexic syndrome emerges, *not* as a conscious decision to get as thin as possible, but as the result of her having begun a diet fairly casually, often at the suggestion of a parent, having succeeded splendidly in taking off five or ten pounds, and then having gotten *hooked* on the intoxicating feeling of accomplishment and control . . .

> The sense of accomplishment exhilarates me, spurs me to continue on and on. It provides a sense of purpose and shapes my life with distractions from insecurity . . . I shall become an expert [at losing weight] . . . The constant downward trend [of the scale] somehow comforts me, gives me visible proof that I can exert control. [. . . The diet] is the one sector of my life over which I and I alone wield total control.
>
> (*Liu, 1979, pp. 36, 46*)

The frustrations of starvation, the rigours of the constant exercise and physical activity in which anorexics engage, and the pain of the numerous physical complications of anorexia do not trouble the anorexic; indeed, her ability to ignore them is further proof to her of her mastery of her body. 'Energy, discipline, my own power will keep me going . . . Psychic fuel. I need nothing and no one else, and I will prove it . . . I will be master of my own body, if nothing else, I vow' (ibid., p. 123).

Surely we must recognize [here] a central modus operandi for the control of contemporary bourgeois anxiety. Consider compulsive jogging and marathon running, often despite shin-splints and other painful injuries, with intense agitation over missed days or not meeting goals for particular runs . . . Consider lawyer Mike Frankfurt, who runs ten miles every morning: '. . . To run with pain is the essence of life' (Smith, 1984, p. 29). Or the following excerpt from [a] student journal:

> When I run I am free . . . The pleasure is closing off my body – as if the incessant pounding of my legs is so total that the pain ceases to exist. There is no grace; no beauty in the running – there is the jarring reality of sneaker and pavement. Bright pain that shivers and splinters sending its white hot arrows into my stomach, my lung, but it cannot pierce my mind. I am on automatic pilot – there is no remembrance of pain, there is freedom – I am losing myself, peeling out of this heavy flesh . . . Power surges through me.

None of this is to dispute that the contemporary concern with fitness has nonpathological, non-dualist dimensions as well. Particularly for women, who have historically suffered from the ubiquity of rape and abuse, from the culturally instilled conviction of our own helplessness, and from lack of access to facilities and programs for rigorous physical training, the cultivation of strength, agility and confidence has a clearly positive dimension. Nor are the objective benefits of daily exercise and concern for nutrition in question here. My focus, rather, is on a subjective stance, increasingly more prominent over the last five years, which, although preoccupied with the body and deriving narcissistic enjoyment from its appearance, takes little pleasure in the *experience* of embodiment. Rather, the fundamental identification is with mind (or will), ideals of spiritual perfection, fantasies of absolute control. There is the same emphasis on will, purity and perfection: 'I've learned to be a stronger person with a more powerful will . . . pure concentration, energy and spirit.' 'I want to be as physically perfect as possible' . . . (Rosen, 1983, pp. 62, 14).

Most strikingly, there is the same emphasis on *control*, on feeling one's life to be fundamentally out of control, and on the feeling of accomplishment derived from total mastery of the body. That sense of mastery, like the anorexic's, appears derived from two sources. First, there is the reassurance that one can overcome all physical obstacles, push oneself to any extremes in pursuit of one's goals . . . Second, and most dramatic . . . is the thrill of being in total charge of the shape of one's body. 'What a fantasy, for your body to be changing! . . . I keep a picture in my mind as I work out of what I want to look like and what's happened to me already' (Rosen, 1983, p. 61). The technology of dictating to nature one's own chosen design for the body is at the centre of the bodybuilder's mania, as it is for the anorexic.

The sense of security derived from the attainment of this goal appears, first of all, as the pleasure of control and independence. 'Nowadays,' says Michael Sacks, associate professor of psychiatry at Cornell Medical College, 'people no longer feel they can control events outside themselves – how well they do in their jobs or in their personal relationships, for example – but they can control the food they eat and how far they can run. Abstinence, tests of endurance, are ways of proving their self-sufficiency.' In a culture, moreover, in which our continued survival is often at the mercy of 'specialists', machines, and sophisticated technology, the body takes on a special sort of vulnerability and dependency. We may live longer than ever before, but the circumstances surrounding illness and death may often be perceived as more alien, inscrutable and arbitrary than ever before.

Our contemporary body fetishism, however, expresses more than a fantasy of self-mastery in an increasingly unmanageable culture. It also reflects our alliance *with* culture against all reminders of the inevitable decay and death of the body. 'Everybody wants to live forever' is the refrain from the theme song of *Pumping Iron*. The most youth-worshipping of popular television shows, *Fame*, opens with a song that begins, 'I want to live forever'. And it is striking that although the anorexic may come very close to death (and 15% do indeed die), the dominant experience throughout the illness is of *invulnerability*.

The dream of immortality is, of course, nothing new. But what is unique to modernity is that the defeat of death has become a scientific fantasy rather than a philosophical or religious mythology. We no longer dream of eternal union with the gods; we build devices that can keep us alive indefinitely, and we work on keeping our bodies as smooth and muscular and elastic at forty as they were at eighteen. We even entertain dreams of halting the ageing process completely: 'Old age,' according to Durk Pearson and Sandy Shaw, authors of the popular *Life Extension*, 'is an unpleasant and unattractive affliction' (1982, p. 15). The megavitamin regime they prescribe is able, they claim, to prevent and even to *reverse* the mechanisms of ageing.

Finally, it may be that in cultures characterized by gross excesses in consumption, the 'will to conquer and subdue the body' . . . expresses an aesthetic or moral rebellion. Anorexics initially came from affluent families, and the current craze for long-distance running and fasting is largely a phenomenon of young, upwardly mobile professionals . . . To those who are starving *against* their wills, of course, starvation cannot function as an expression of the power of the will. At the same time, we should caution against viewing anorexia as a trendy illness of the elite. Rather, power-lessness is its most outstanding feature.

THE GENDER/POWER AXIS

Ninety per cent of all anorexics are women. We do not need, of course, to know that particular statistic to realize that the contemporary 'tyranny of slenderness' is far from gender neutral. Women are more obsessed with their bodies than men, less satisfied with them, and permitted less latitude with them by themselves, by men, and by the culture (Journard and Secord, 1955; Wooley *et al.*, 1979). In a 1984 *Glamour* poll of 33 000 women, 75% said that they thought they were 'too fat'. Yet by Metropolitan Life Insurance tables – themselves notoriously affected by cultural standards – only 25% of these women were heavier than the specified standards, and a full 30% were *below*. The anorexic's distorted image of her body – her inability to see it as anything but 'too fat' – while more extreme, is not radically discontinuous from fairly common female misperceptions.

Consider, too, actors like Nick Nolte and William Hurt, who are permitted a certain amount of softening, of thickening about the waist, while still retaining romantic lead status. Individual style, wit, the projection of intelligence, experience and effectiveness still go a long way for men, even in our fitness-obsessed culture. But no female can achieve the status of romantic or sexual ideal without the appropriate *body*. That body, if we use television commercials as a gauge, has become steadily leaner over the past ten years. What used to be acknowledged as extremes required of high-fashion models is now the dominant image that beckons to high school and college women. Over and over, extremely slender women students complain of hating their thighs or their stomachs (the anorexic's most dreaded danger spot); often, they express concern and anger over frequent teasing by their boyfriends: Janey, a former student, is 5'10" and weighs 132 pounds. Yet her boyfriend calls her 'Fatso' and 'Big Butt' and insists she should be 110 pounds because 'that's what Brooke Shields weighs.' . . .

[M]any anorexics talk of having a 'ghost' inside them or surrounding them, 'a dictator who dominates me', . . . 'a little man who objects when I eat' . . . The little ghost, the dictator, the 'other self' (as he is often described) is always male (Bruch, 1979). The anorexic's *other* self – the self of the uncontrollable appetites, the impurities and taints, the flabby will and tendency to mental torpor – is the body, as we have seen. But it is also (and here the anorexic's associations are surely in the mainstream of Western culture) the *female* self. These two selves are perceived as at constant war. But it is clear that it is the male side – with its associated values of greater spirituality, higher intellectuality, strength of will – that is being expressed and developed in the anorexic syndrome.

What is the meaning of these gender associations in the anorexic? I propose that there are two levels of meaning. One has to do with fear and disdain for traditional female *roles* and social limitations. The other has to do, more profoundly, with a deep fear of 'The Female', with all its more nightmarish archetypal associations: voracious hungers and sexual insatiability. Let us examine each of these levels in turn.

Adolescent anorexics express characteristic fears about growing up to be mature, sexually developed, potentially reproductive women. 'I have a deep fear,' says one, 'of having a womanly body, round and fully developed. I want to be tight and muscular and thin.' If only she could stay thin, says another, 'I would never have to deal with having a woman's body; like Peter Pan I could stay a child forever.' The choice of Peter Pan is telling here – what she means is, stay a *boy* forever . . .

In a characteristic scenario, anorexia will develop just at the beginning of puberty. Normal body changes are experienced by the anorexic, not surprisingly, as the takeover of the body by disgusting, womanish fat. 'I grab my breasts, pinching them until they hurt. If only I could eliminate them, cut them off if need be, to become as flat-chested as a child again' (Liu, 1979, p. 79). She is exultant when her periods stop (as they do in *all* cases of anorexia) . . .

Many anorexics appear to experience anxiety over falling into the lifestyle they associate with their mothers . . . One woman describes her feeling that she is 'full of my mother . . . she is in me even if she isn't there' in nearly the same breath as she complains of her continuous fear of being 'not human . . . of ceasing to exist'. . . Several of my students with eating disorders reported that their anorexia had developed after their families had dissuaded or forbidden them from embarking on a traditionally male career.

Here anorexia finds a true sister-phenomenon in the epidemic of female invalidism and 'hysteria' that swept through the middle and upper middle classes in the second half of the nineteenth century. It was a time that, in many ways, was very like our own, especially in the conflicting demands that women were newly confronting: the opening up of new possibilities, the continuing grip of the old expectations. On the one hand, the old pre-industrial order, with the father at the head of a self-contained family production unit, had given way to the dictatorship of the market, opening up new, non-domestic opportunities for working women; on the other, it also turned many of the most valued 'female' skills – textile and garment manufacture, food processing – out of the home and over to the factory system (Ehrenreich and English, 1979). In the new machine economy, the lives of middle-class women were far emptier than they had been before.

It was an era, too, that had been witnessing the first major feminist wave. In 1840, the World Anti-Slavery Conference had been held, at which the first feminists spoke loudly and long on the connections between the abolition of slavery and women's rights. 1848 saw the Seneca Falls Convention. In 1869, John Stuart Mill published his landmark work, 'On the Subjection of Women'. And in 1889, the Pankhursts formed the Women's Franchise League. But it was an era, too (and not unrelatedly, as I shall argue later) when the prevailing ideal of femininity was the delicate, affluent lady, unequipped for anything but the most sheltered doemstic life, totally dependent on her prosperous husband, providing a peaceful and comfortable haven for him each day after his return from the labours of the public sphere. In a now famous 1883 letter, Freud, criticizing John Stuart Mill, writes:

> It really is a still-born thought to send women into the struggle for existence exactly as men. If, for instance, I imagine my gentle sweet girl as a competitor it would only end in my telling her, as I did seventeen months ago, that I am fond of her and that I implore her to withdraw from the strife into the calm uncompetitive activity of my home.
>
> (in Jones, 1956, p. 193)

[. . .]

Freud never makes the connection . . . between the monotonous domestic lives these women were expected to lead after their schooling was completed, and the emergence of compulsive day-dreaming, hallucinations, dissociations and hysterical conversions.

[. . .]

So too for the anorexic. It is indeed essential to recognize in this illness a dimension of protest against the limitations of the ideal of female domesticity (the 'feminine mystique', as Betty Friedan called it) that reigned in America throughout the 1950s and early 1960s – the era when most of their mothers were starting homes and families. This was, we should recall, the era of the return to 'normalcy' following World War II, an era during which women had been fired en masse from the jobs they had held during the war and shamelessly propagandized back into the full-time job of wife and mother. It was an era, too, when the 'fuller figure', as Jane Russell now calls it, came into fashion once more, . . . that glamorized the voluptuous, large-breasted woman. This remained the prevailing fashion tyranny until the late 1960s and early 1970s.

But we must recognize that the anorexic's 'protest', like that of the classical hysterial symptom, is written on the bodies of anorexic women, and *not* embraced as a conscious politics, nor, indeed, does it reflect any social or political understanding at all. Moreover, the symptoms themselves function to preclude the emergence of such an understanding: the idée fixe – staying thin – becomes at its farthest extreme so powerful as to render any other ideas or life-projects meaningless . . .

Paradoxically – and often tragically – these pathologies of female 'protest' (and we must include agoraphobia here, as well as hysteria and anorexia) actually function as if in collusion with the cultural conditions that produced them. The same is true for more moderate expressions of the contemporary female obsession with slenderness. Women may feel themselves deeply attracted by the aura of freedom and independence suggested by the boyish body ideal of today. Yet, each hour, each minute that is spent in anxious pursuit of that ideal (for it does not come 'naturally' to most mature women) is *in fact* time and energy diverted from inner development and social achievement. As a feminist protest, the obsession with slenderness is hopelessly counterproductive.

It is important to recognize, too, that the anorexic is terrified and repelled, not only by the traditional female domestic role – which she associates with mental lassitude and weakness – but by a certain archetypal image of the female: as hungering, voracious, all-needing and all-wanting. It is this image that shapes and permeates her experience of her own hunger for food as insatiable and out-of-control, which makes her feel that if she takes just one bite, she won't be able to stop.

Let's explore this image. Let's break the tie with food and look at the metaphor. Hungering. Voracious. Extravagantly and excessively needful. Without restraint. Always wanting. Always wanting too much affection, reassurance, emotional and sexual contact and attention. This is how many women frequently experience themselves, and, indeed, how many men experience women. 'Please, please God, keep me from telephoning him,' prays the heroine in Dorothy Parker's classic 'The Telephone Call', experiencing her need for reassurance and contact as being as out of control and degrading as the anorexic experiences her desire for food. . . . One woman in my class provided a stunning insight into the connection between her perception of herself and the anxiety of the compulsive dieter: 'You know,' she said, 'the anorexic is always convinced she is taking up too much space, eating too much, wanting food too much. I've never felt that way, but I've often felt that I was *too much* – too much emotion, too much need, too loud and demanding, too much *there*, if you know what I mean.'[8]

The most extreme cultural expressions of the fear of woman-as-too-much – which almost always revolve around her sexuality – are strikingly full of eating and hungering metaphors. 'Of woman's unnatural, *insatiable* lust, what country, what village doth not complain?' queries Burton in *The Anatomy of Melancholy*. 'You are the true hiennas,' says Walter Charleton, 'that allure us with the fairness of your skins, and when folly hath brought us within your reach, you leap upon us and *devour* us' (quoted in Easlea, 1980, p. 242).

The mythology/ideology of the devouring, insatiable female (which, as we have seen, is the internalized image the anorexic has of her female self) tends historically to wax and wane. But not without rhyme or reason. In periods of gross environmental and social crisis, such as characterized the period of the witch-hunts in the fifteenth and sixteenth centuries, it appears to flourish (see Sanday, 1981, pp. 172–84). 'All witchcraft comes from carnal lust, which is in women *insatiable*,' say Kramer and Sprenger, authors of the official witch-hunters' handbook, *Malleus Malificarum*. For the sake of fulfilling the '*mouth* of the womb . . . [women] consort even with the devil' (quoted in Easlea, 1980, p. 8).

Anxiety over women's uncontrollable hungers appears to peak, as well, during periods when women are becoming independent and asserting themselves politically and socially. The second half of the nineteenth century saw a virtual 'flood' (as Peter Gay calls it) of artistic and literary images of the dark, dangerous and evil female: 'sharp-teethed, devouring' Sphinxes, Salomés and Delilahs, 'biting, tearing, murderous women'. 'No century,' claims Gay, 'depicted woman as vampire, as castrator, as killer, so consistently, so programmatically, and so nakedly as the nineteenth' (1984, pp. 197–201, 207). No century, too, was as obsessed with female sexuality and its medical control. Treatment for excessive 'sexual excitement' and masturbation included placing leeches on the womb (Chernin, 1981, p. 38), clitoridectomy, and removing of the ovaries (also recommended for 'troublesomeness, eating like a ploughman, erotic tendencies, persecution mania, and simple "cussedness"') (Ehrenreich and English, 1979, p. 124).

It is in the second half of the nineteenth century, too, despite a flurry of efforts by feminists and health reformers, that the stylized 'S-curve', which required a tighter corset than ever before, comes into fashion.[9] 'While the suffragettes were forcefully propelling all women toward legal and political emancipation, fashion and custom imprisoned her physically as she had never been before' (de Riencourt, 1974, p. 319).[10] Described by Thorstein Veblen as a 'mutilation, undergone for the purpose of lowering the subject's vitality and rendering her permanently and obviously unfit for work', the corset indeed did just that. In it, a woman could barely sit or stoop, was unable to move her feet more than six inches at a time, and had difficulty keeping herself from regular fainting fits. The connection was often drawn in popular magazines between enduring the tight corset and the exercise of self-restraint and control. The corset is 'an ever present monitor', says one 1878 advertisement, 'of a well-disciplined mind and well-regulated feelings.' Today, of course, we diet to achieve such control.

It is important to emphasize that, despite bizarre and grotesque examples of gross physical manipulation and external control (clitoridectomy, Chinese foot binding, the removal of bones from the rib cage in order to fit into the tight corset), such control plays a relatively minor role in the maintenance of gender power relations. For every historical image of the dangerous, aggressive woman, there is a corresponding fantasy – an ideal femininity, from which all threatening elements have been purged – that women have mutilated themselves *internally* to attain. In the Victorian era, at the same time as operations were being performed to control female sexuality, William Acton, Krafft-Ebing, and others were proclaiming the official scientific doctrine that women are naturally passive and 'not very much troubled with sexual feelings of any kind'. Corresponding to this male medical fantasy was the popular artistic and moral theme of woman-as-ministering-angel: sweet, gentle, domestic, without intensity or personal ambition of any sort. Peter Gay suggests, correctly, that these ideals must be understood as a reaction-formation to the era's 'pervasive sense of manhood in danger (1984, p. 197), and argues that few women actually fit the 'insipid goody' . . . image. What Gay forgets, however, is that most women *tried* – lower classes as well as middle were affected by the 'tenacious and all-pervasive' ideal of the perfect lady – and that many women did manage to achieve depressingly effective results.

On the gender/power axis the female body appears, then, as the unknowing medium of the historical ebbs and flows of the fear of woman-as-too-much. That, as we have seen, is how the anorexic experiences her female, bodily self: as voracious, wanton, needful of forceful control by her male will. Living in the tide of cultural backlash against the second major feminist wave, she is not alone in these images. Christopher Lasch, in *The Culture of Narcissism*, speaks of what he describes as 'the apparently aggressive overtures of sexually liberated women' that 'convey to many males the same message – that women are *voracious, insatiable,*' and call up 'early fantasies of a possessive, suffocating, *devouring* and castrating mother' (Lasch, 1979, p. 343; emphasis added).

Our contemporary beauty ideals, on the other hand, seem purged . . . 'of the power to conjure up memories of the past, of all that could remind us of a woman's mysterious power' (Chernin, 1981, p. 148). The ideal, rather, is an 'image of a woman in which she is not yet a woman': Darryl Hannah as the lanky, newborn mermaid in *Splash*; Lori Singer (appearing virtually anorexic) as the reckless, hyper-kinetic heroine of *Footloose*; The Charlie Girl; 'Cheryl Tiegs in shorts, Margaux Hemingway with her hair wet, Brooke Shields naked on an island' (Gaines and Butler, 1983, p. 63); the dozens of teenage women who appear in Coke commercials, in jeans commercials, in chewing-gum commercials.

The images suggest amused detachment, casual playfulness, flirtatiousness without demand, and lightness of touch. A refusal to take sex, death or politics too deadly seriously. A delightfully unconscious relationship to her body. The twentieth century has seen this sort of feminine ideal before, of course. When, in the 1920s, young women began to flatten their breasts, suck in their stomachs, bob their hair, and show off long, colt-like legs, they believed they were pursuing a new freedom and daring that demanded a carefree, boyish style.[11] If the traditional female hourglass suggested anything, it was confinement and immobility. Yet the flapper's freedom, as Mary McCarthy's and Dorothy Parker's short stories brilliantly reveal, was largely an illusion – as any obsessively cultivated sexual style must inevitably be. Although today's images may suggest androgynous independence, we need only consider who is on the receiving end of the imagery in order to confront the pitiful paradox involved.

Watching the commercials are thousands of anxiety-ridden women and adolescents (some of whom are likely the very ones appearing in the commercials) with anything *but* an unconscious relation to their bodies. They are involved in an absolutely contradictory state of affairs, a totally no-win game: caring desperately, passionately, obsessively about attaining an ideal of coolness, effortless confidence and casual freedom. Watching the commercials is a little girl, perhaps ten years old, whom I saw in Central Park, gazing raptly at her father, bursting with pride: 'Daddy, guess what? I lost two pounds!' And watching the commercials is the anorexic, who associates her relentless pursuit of thinness with power and control, but who in fact destroys her health and imprisons her imagination. She is surely the most startling and stark illustration of how cavalier power relations are with respect to the motivations and goals of individuals, yet how deeply they are etched on our bodies, and how well our bodies serve them.

Notes

1   Throughout this paper, the term 'anorexia' will be used to designate a general class of eating disorders within which intake-restricting (or abstinent) anorexia and bulimia/anorexia (characterized by alternating bouts of gorging and starving and/or gorging and vomiting) are distinct subtypes.

2   Although throughout history there have been scattered references to patients who sound as though they may have been suffering from self-starvation, the first medical description of anorexia as a discrete syndrome was made by W. W. Gull in an 1868 address at Oxford. Six years later, Gull began to use the term 'anorexia nervosa'; at the same time, E.D. Lesegue independently described the disorder (Garfinkel and Garner, 1982, pp. 58–91). Although cases have been recorded ever since then, researchers are in almost universal agreement that the evidence suggests a striking increase in frequency over the last twenty years.

3   Initially, anorexia was found to predominate among upper-class white families. There is, however, widespread evidence that this is now rapidly changing ... The disorder has become more equally distributed in recent years, touching populations (e.g. blacks and East Indians) previously unaffected, and all socio-economic levels (Garfinkel and Garner, 1982, pp. 102–3). There remains, however, the overwhelming disproportion of women to men (ibid., pp. 112–13).

4   Kim Chernin's book *The Obsession*, whose remarkable insights inspired my interest in anorexia, was the first outstanding exception to the lack of cultural understanding of eating disorders. Since the writing of this essay, Chernin's second book on eating disorders, *The Hungry Self* (1985) and Susie Orbach's *Hunger Strike* (1986) have appeared. Both contribute significantly to our cultural understanding of anorexia.

5   My use of the term 'culture' may seem overly homogenizing here, disrespectful of differences among ethnic groups, socio-economic groups, subcultures within American society, etc. It must

be stressed here that I am discussing ideology and images whose power is precisely the power to homogenize culture. Even in pre-mass media culture, we see this phenomenon: the nineteenth-century ideal of the 'perfect lady' tyrannized even those classes who couldn't afford to realize it. With television, of course, a massive deployment of images becomes possible, and there is no escape from the mass shaping of our fantasy lives. Although they may start among the wealthy and elite ('A woman can never be too wealthy or too thin'), media-promoted ideals of femininity and masculinity perniciously trickle down to everyone who owns a TV or can afford a junk magazine or is aware of billboards. Recent changes in the incidence of anorexia among lower-income groups (see note 3) bear this out.

6   Until very recently, this dimension was largely ignored or underemphasized, with a very few notable exceptions. Kim Chernin and Susie Orbach (*Fat is a Feminist Issue*) were ground-breakers in exploring the connections between eating disorders and images and ideals of femininity . . . Lately, there has been a veritable explosion of creative work, both theoretical and therapeutic, confronting the connections between eating disorders and the situation of women. Institutes such as The Women's Therapy Institute in New York have developed techniques of treatment that are specifically grounded in a feminist reconstruction of object-relations theory (see Eichenbaum and Orbach, 1983).

7   The same is not true of bulimic anorexics, who tend to be sexually active (Garfinkel and Garner, 1982, p. 41). Bulimic anorexics, as seems symbolized by the binge/purge cycle itself, stand in a somewhat more ambivalent relationship to their hungers than do abstinent anorexics.

8   This experience of oneself as 'too much' may be more or less emphatic, depending on variables such as race, religion, socio-economic class, sexual orientation etc. Eichenbaum and Orbach (1983) emphasize, however, how frequently their clinic patients, non-anorexic as well as anorexic, 'talk about their needs with contempt, humiliation, and shame. They feel exposed and childish, greedy and insatiable' (p. 49). Eichenbaum and Orbach trace such feelings, moreover, to infantile experiences that are characteristic of all female development, given a division of labour within which women are the emotional nurturers and physical caretakers of family life. Briefly (and this sketch cannot begin to do justice to their rich and complex analysis): mothers unwittingly communicate to their daughters that feminine needs are excessive, bad and must be contained. The mother will do this out of a sense that her daughter will have to learn this lesson in order to become properly socialized into the traditional female role of caring for others – of feeding others, rather than feeding the self – and also because of an

unconscious identification with her daughter, who reminds the mother of the 'hungry, needy little girl' in herself, denied and repressed through the mother's *own* 'education' in being female: 'Mother comes to be frightened by her daughter's free expression of her needs, and unconsciously acts toward her infant daughter in the same way she acts internally toward the little-girl part of herself. In some ways the little daughter becomes an external representation of that part of herself that she has come to dislike and deny. The complex of emotions that results from her own deprivation through childhood and adult life is both directed inward in the struggle to negate the little-girl part of herself and projected outward onto her daughter' (p. 44). Despite a real desire to be totally responsive toward her daughter's emotional needs, the mother's own anxiety limits her capacity to respond. The contradictory messages she sends out convey to the little girl 'the idea that to get love and approval she must show a particular side of herself. She must hide her emotional cravings, her disappointments and her angers, her fighting spirit. She comes to feel that there must be something wrong with what she needs and what she wants. This soon translates into feeling unworthy and hesitant about pursuing her impulses' (pp. 48–9). Once she has grown up, of course, these feelings are reinforced by cultural ideology, further social 'training' in femininity, and the likelihood that the men in her life will regard her as 'too much' as well, having been schooled by their own training in masculine detachment and autonomy.

(With boys, who do not stir up such intense identifications in the mother and whom she knows, moreover, will grow up into a world that will meet their emotional needs (i.e., the son will eventually grow up to be looked after by his future wife, well-trained in the feminine arts of care), mothers feel much less ambivalent about the satisfaction of needs, and behave much more consistently in their nurturing. Boys therefore grow up, according to Eichenbaum and Orbach, with an experience of their needs as legitimate, appropriate, worthy of fulfilment.)

The male experience of the 'woman-as-too-much' has been developmentally explored, as well, in Dorothy Dinnerstein's much-discussed *Mermaid and the Minotaur* (1970). Dinnerstein argues that it is the woman's capacity to call up memories of helpless infancy, primitive wishes of 'unqualified access' to the mother's body and the 'terrifying erotic independence of every baby's mother' (p. 62) that is responsible for the male fear of what he experiences as 'the uncontrollable erotic rhythms' of the woman. Female impulses, a reminder of the autonomy of the mother, always appear on some level as a threatening limitation against his own. This gives rise to a 'deep fantasy resentment' of female impulsivity (p. 59) and, on the cultural level, 'archetypal nightmare visions of the insatiable female' (p. 62).

9   It is significant that these efforts failed, in large part, because of their association with the women's rights movement. Trousers, such as those proposed by Amelia Bloomer, were considered a particular badge of depravity and aggressiveness, the *New York Herald* predicting that bloomer women would end up in 'lunatic asylums or perchance in the state prison' (Banner, 1983, p. 96).

10   The metaphorical dimension here is as striking as the functional, and it is a characteristic feature of female fashion: the dominant styles always decree, to one degree or another, that women *should not take up too much space*, that the territory we occupy should be limited. This is as true of cinch-belts as it is of foot-binding.

11   Some disquieting connections can be drawn, as well, between the anorexic and the flapper, who, according to Banner (1983) expressed her sensuality 'not through eroticism but through constant vibrant movement'. The quality that marked the sex appeal of the 1920s – the 'It' made famous by Clara Bow – was characterized by 'vivacity, fearlessness and a basic indifference to men' (p. 279), qualities high on the list of anorexic values.

3
SEXUALITY

Sexuality is an area that again raises the issue of how to understand the contributions of society and biology to our identities and our behaviour. Sexual practices involve our bodies, and some may result in human reproduction, so their study must involve some recognition of our biological make-up. Nevertheless, the sexual behaviour we engage in is subject to a large range of social controls; and the desires that give rise to that behaviour are seen by nearly all theories as influenced, to a greater or lesser extent, by social forces. To understand the collection of forms of behaviour and desires that come under the heading of 'sexuality' would therefore seem to involve a similar conceptual interplay of the biological and the social to that encountered when considering gender. The articles in the previous chapter recognized that biology and society were not two distinct influences which together made gender; rather gender itself, through the behaviour of people in a gendered world, had its own effects, influencing biology and society too.

That sexuality has effects is self-evident. Indeed, it often appears to have a dynamic of its own, in which sexual feelings seem to express our essential being in a variety of unpredictable ways, some of which may bear little relation to bodily sensation. Thus, although the term 'sexuality' would seem to delineate the area of our lives least amenable to rational analysis, the impact it has on all forms of social organization makes it an important area to study.

SEXUALITY, POWER AND LIBERATION

It is around sexuality that issues about power are raised in some of their most difficult forms. For it is frequently in their sexuality that women find that their feelings and actions seem to belie their aspirations for independence. Although an unfortunate number of women are kept in oppressive relationships by economic necessity or fear of physical violence, other such relationships persist for reasons which are less clear-cut and not reducible to material circumstances alone. There are forms of control operating in these, and thus presumably in other relationships too, which are not explicit, not fully understood but nevertheless powerful. Sexuality is an area in which fantasy plays an important part, and few women who have talked about it describe a fantasy world totally in accord with the desires that they would like to feel or, indeed, with prevailing expectations of what is sexually acceptable.

For some feminists, sexual relations between men and women are nothing but the acting out of gender inequality. In Chapter 1 we noted Catharine McKinnon's view that sexuality was the main process by which the inequality of power that defined the difference between men and women operated; this view is explored further in another extract from her work in this chapter. She argues that sexual access to women is one of the privileges of men as the dominant sex, and for them aggression against those without power is experienced as sexual pleasure. Women who enjoy sex in these circumstances are sexualizing their own subordination. Although this unequal relationship works at one level through mutual enjoyment, it is underpinned by the fear of sexual violence into which it turns when women step out of line. Indeed, living with the threat of violence is an inescapable attribute of being a woman and actual violence, she argues, is much more a part of normal sexual practice than we have been led to believe.

It is interesting that McKinnon, even though she places so much emphasis on the ultimate control of women by violence, still has to take account of the 'bewildering modes of female collaboration' in this system of sexual oppression. She recognizes that women's belief that they too experience sexual pleasure is an important element in their control. McKinnon implicitly exhorts women to avoid the trap of thinking that whatever we find sexually arousing must be empowering, for pleasure in heterosexual sex just gives us 'a stake in our own subordination'.

Although that notion of sexual liberation which McKinnon criticizes has brought many gains to women, modern feminists have always had an ambivalent attitude to it. On the one hand, they have worked to dismantle the 'double standard' whereby sexual expression is seen as an inevitable part of masculinity but is socially disapproved of in women. And, of course, feminists have fought hard for the development of the conditions which made sexual liberation possible: the freeing of heterosexual activity from unwanted pregnancies through the increased availability and safety of contraception and legal abortion. However, many feminists have suspected that such changes have been of more benefit to men than to women. Heterosexual intercourse still seems to be defined around the sexual needs of men, both in its physical practice and the ideology of conquest and competition that often goes with it.

THE STUDY OF FEMALE SEXUALITY

Already in the 1950s mass surveys of sexual practices challenged both the nineteenth-century view of sexuality as a male need to which women submitted and a Freudian view that healthy psychological development in women gave them a sexuality which was essentially passive and responsive to male sexual activity (Kinsey, 1953). Behind these surveys, and the detailed observation of sexual practices carried out in the 1960s, were the implicit assumptions that women's enjoyment of sex mattered and was not necessarily best achieved by the same practices which gave men most pleasure (Masters and Johnson, 1966). In particular, their empirical results seemed to indicate that women could achieve more and better orgasms from stimulation of their clitoris than from vaginal penetration. In recognizing this, two traditional assumptions were cast aside: that female sexuality was complementary to men's and that sexuality was 'naturally' centred around reproduction.

However, this research did retain two other assumptions that have proved difficult to dislodge: first, an essentialist view of sex, that the sexual drive is basically a natural one and, second, that whether this drive is satisfied depends on the right forms of physical stimulation. Many feminist writings on sexuality have taken the same approach, arguing that although it does not satisfy women's sexual needs, heterosexual intercourse has become the dominant sexual practice because patriarchal society inhibits women's natural sexuality by subordinating it to men's. But women can and should find preferable forms of sexual activity which they can either perform themselves or teach their partners to do – though they will probably find this easier if their sexual partners are women.

Lynne Segal, in the second article in this chapter, examines some of these feminist strategies and studies of sex. She criticizes those which focus only on the physical side of sexuality for reducing the sexual needs of women to finding the best way to get an orgasm and thus oversimplifying the question of sexual desire. She sees the patriarchal character of society being expressed not only in sexual practices but also in the formation of our sexual desires. Thus what women desire sexually is more than particular physical feelings, it is also particular emotional frameworks within which to experience them. It is this which makes sexuality such a difficult area, for what we desire may be to be *not* in control; it may be to be submissive or to be masochistic. This means that attempts to satisfy our sexual needs and attempts to make changes in our lives do not always sit easily together.

ESSENTIALISM VERSUS SOCIAL CONSTRUCTIONISM

The other assumption that these early feminist writings on sexuality shared with the research of the 1950s and '60s was that of a natural sex drive, which current sexual practices were failing to satisfy for women. In other words, while they recognized that sexual behaviour was socially constructed, and advocated that it should be changed, they saw sexual drive as a natural instinct – for both women and men. Segal takes issue with this too, rejecting 'any notion of sex as an innate or biological force' to argue that what is culturally and historically specific includes 'the ideas we hold about what is and what is not "sexual" or "erotic".' In doing so, she demonstrates a shift that has taken place in writings on sexuality, and not only among feminists, in the years since those early feminist texts were written.

This movement has been a movement away from essentialism, away from seeing everything about sexuality as naturally given, towards seeing more and more aspects of it as socially constructed. The final article by Carol Vance examines the different stages in this movement and the different degrees to which writers have taken a social constructionist position. The most radical social constructionist position is that of Foucault, who argued that the notion of 'sexuality' itself is a social construct. Though Vance is clearly sympathetic to this version of social construction, she recognizes that it also causes problems by leaving unclear what sexuality is – what it is we are studying and how it connects with anything to do with our bodies. What is the 'it', then, that is being socially constructed?

Foucault's position is one implication of his view, examined in the previous chapter, that everything about the body is constructed by culture and history. Indeed, it is in his *History of Sexuality* that this idea is given its most forceful expression. There he argues that Victorian discourses on sexuality, rather than controlling a natural given sexual instinct, actually produced the notion of sexuality as a distinct form of pleasure and that this became a central idiom of relations of power.

It is this which gets us back to the importance of the topic for feminism: the ways in which power operates through sexuality and the difficulties of challenging them. In search of an understanding of these difficulties, some feminists have turned to psychoanalysis, hoping to understand those unconscious processes which give rise to feelings that we cannot consciously explain. For this reason, the next two chapters of this book explore the writings of feminists on various psychoanalytic theories.

Article 3.1
SEXUALITY

Catharine McKinnon

They said, 'You are a savage and dangerous woman.' [I
said] 'I am speaking the truth. And the truth is savage
and dangerous.'

(*Nawal El Saadawi,* Woman at Point Zero *(1983), the story
of a prostitute*)

Since 1970, feminists have uncovered a vast amount of sexual abuse
of women by men. Rape, battery, sexual harassment, sexual abuse
of children, prostitution and pornography, seen for the first time in
their true scope and interconnectedness, form a distinctive pattern:
the power of men over women in society. These abuses are as
allowed de facto as they are prohibited de jure. Formal prohibition
has done little to alter their frequency; it has helped make it hard
to believe that they are so common. The reports that are believed
are treated as if the events and their victims are statistically deviant,
because the events they report have been branded as morally and
legally deviant. In fact, it is the woman who has not been sexually
abused who deviates.

The reason feminism uncovered this reality, its methodological
secret, is that feminism is built on believing women's accounts of
sexual use and abuse by men. The pervasiveness of male sexual
violence against women is therefore not denied, minimized,
trivialized, eroticized or excepted as marginal or episodic or placed
to one side while more important matters are discussed. The fact
that only 7.8 per cent of women in the United States have not been
sexually assaulted or harassed in their lifetime is not considered
inconsequential or isolated. The fact that sexual violation is a sexual
practice is faced. A new paradigm begins here, one that fits the
reality of the experience to be explained. All the ways in which
women are suppressed and subjected – restricted, intruded on,
violated, objectified – are recognized as what sex is for women and
as the meaning and content of femininity.

If this is done, sexuality itself is no longer unimplicated in
women's second-class status. Sexual violence can no longer be
categorized away as violence not sex. Women do not thrive on
violation, whether or not it is done through sex. But our rapists,
serial murderers ('I killed my mother for the same reason I've killed
all those other women. The reason was sex.'), and child molesters
('It's as natural for me to have sex with children the way it's natural

for some people to have sex with women.') enjoy their acts sexually and as men, to be redudant. It is sex *for them*. What is sex except that which is felt as sexual? When acts of dominance and submission, up to and including acts of violence, are experienced as sexually arousing, as sex itself, that is what they are. The mutual exclusivity of sex and violence is preserved in the face of this evidence by immunizing as 'sex' whatever causes a sexual response and by stigmatizing questioning it as repressive, knowing that what is thereby exempted includes humiliation and brutality and molestation and murder as well as rape by any definition. Violence is sex when it is practised as sex. If violation of the powerless is part of what is sexy about sex, as well as central in the meaning of male and female, the place of sexuality in gender and the place of gender in sexuality need to be looked at together.

When this is done, sexuality appears as the interactive dynamic of gender as an inequality. Stopped as an attribute of a person, sex inequality takes the form of gender; moving as a relation between people, it takes the form of sexuality. Gender emerges as the congealed form of the sexualization of inequality between men and women. So long as this is socially the case, the feelings or acts or desires of particular individuals notwithstanding, gender inequality will divide their society into two communities of interest. The male centrally features hierarchy of control. Aggression against those with less power is experienced as sexual pleasure, an entitlement of masculinity. For the female, subordination is sexualized, in the way that dominance is for the male, as pleasure as well as gender identity, as femininity. Dominance, principally by men, and submission, principally by women, will be the ruling code through which sexual pleasure is experienced. Sexism will be a political inequality that is sexually enjoyed, if unequally so.

Sexual abuse works as a form of terror in creating and maintaining this arrangement. It is a terror so perfectly motivated and systematically concerted that it never need be intentionally organized – an arrangement that, as long as it lasted, would seal the immortality of any totalitarianism. I have come to think that the unique effectiveness of terrorism, like that against Jews in Argentina, is that it is at once absolutely systematic and absolutely random: systematic because one group is its target and lives knowing it; random because there is no way of telling who is next on the list. Just to get through another day, women must spend an incredible amount of time, life and energy cowed, fearful and colonized, trying to figure out how not to be next on the list. Learning by osmosis what men want in a woman and trying to give it to them, women hope that being the wanted image will alter their odds. Paying attention to every detail of every incident of a woman's violation they can get their hands on, women attempt not to be her. The problem is, combining even a few circumstances, descriptions, conditions and details of acts of sexual abuse reveals that no woman has a chance. To be about to be raped is to be gender female in the process of going about life as usual. Some things do increase the odds, like being Black. One cannot live one's life attempting not to be a Black woman. As Black women well know, one cannot save it that way, either.

Because the inequality of the sexes is socially defined as the enjoyment of sexuality itself, gender inequality appears consensual. This helps explain the peculiar durability of male supremacy as a system of hegemony as well as its imperviousness to change once it exists. It also helps explain some of the otherwise more bewildering modes of female collaboration. The belief that whatever is sexually arousing is, ipso facto, empowering for women is revealed as a strategy in male rule. It may be worth considering that heterosexuality, the predominant social arrangement that fuses this sexuality of abuse and objectification with gender in intercourse, with attendant trauma, torture and dehumanization, organizes women's pleasure so as to give us a stake in our own subordination. It may even be that to be 'anti-sex', to be against this sex that is sex, is to refuse to affirm loyalty to this political system of inequality whose dynamic is male control and use and access to women – which would account for the stigma of the epithet.

Article 3.2
SENSUAL UNCERTAINTY, OR WHY THE CLITORIS IS NOT ENOUGH

Lynne Segal

> In this society the nearest any of us reach freedom,
> honesty and spontaneity with others is in bed with a
> lover or in the street hurling beer cans at the police.
>
> (*Letter to* The Leveller, *19 March–1 April, 1982*)

Some may question the anarchic 'freedom' we express through a riot in the streets, but most of us share the illusion that we are expressing something *natural, private and uniquely ourselves* in our sexual behaviour. And yet we are also, and women in particular, deluged from all sides with earnest and enthusiastic advice on how to enjoy this supposedly natural sexuality. Although some of the advice has been coming from within feminist writing, just how we follow its dictate towards adopting a positive and progressive attitude towards sexual pleasure remains both confusing and mysterious. I shall argue that much of the advice is misleading and inadequate, failing to identify the most significant problems.

Emerging as feminists from the end of the 1960s, many of us had experienced the increasing contradictions of 'sexual liberation'. Women, we had been told, were 'free now as never before', yet the . . . ubiquitous symbolism of male conquest and female submission, built into almost every image of heterosexuality, depicted a strange 'liberation' for women. And by the end of the 1960s many women were to recognize the male domination anchored in such a 'sexual liberation', as well as to express a deep dissatisfaction with the sexual experiences it had provided for them. When sexual expression and political liberation were believed to go firmly hand in hand – as ironically Mary Whitehouse and her opponents both agreed – women were largely excluded from that fraternal handshake.

But more available contraception, abortion law reform, and the general permissiveness of the 1960s had indeed raised women's expectations of sexual pleasure, or some sort of pleasure, even if we were disappointed more often than not. A desire for sexual freedom, to be active sexually outside of marriage, and a desire for more satisfactory heterosexual relationships were important reasons many women came to the women's liberation movement in the early 1970s. Sex and relationships with men were the focus of intense discussion. Most often it was full of resentment and frustration, yet at the same time there was optimism, and we were almost never without hope for some possible, much sought-after change. The early writings on sexuality were optimistic, whether describing possibilities for heterosexual or lesbian pleasure.

In the second half of the 1970s, however, much less was written about sexuality, and most of us rarely even discussed it within the women's movement. There were many reasons for this. First of all theoretical developments, even within socialist feminism, stressed that it was not just capitalism but a separate power-relation between men and women that maintained women's oppression. Connected to this, there was a growing tension between separatist and non-separatist feminist politics. More feminists came to support a strategy and tactics which eschewed any contact with men, as types of radical feminism grew which focused primarily on male behaviour, alongside a cultural feminism which celebrated the ways of women. And finally, the voluntarism and cheery optimism of much of our early writing on sexuality were shaken by a growing awareness of men's hostility and violence towards women. These factors all tended to silence discussion on heterosexuality. Heterosexual women were also attacked by separatist feminists not only as masochistic perpetuators of their own oppression (and unhappy in love many of us were), but as sharing in heterosexual privilege (which we did), and even as encouraging rapists and male violence. (Of course, we could as plausibly argue that heterosexual feminists might be expected to be rather actively discouraging rape and male violence towards women. But tactical and moralistic rhetoric is at issue here, not empirical assertion.) Soon it was not only feminist debate on heterosexuality – outside the prescription to reject it – but any more complex theoretical work on sexuality which became rare as attention focused on the dangers of male sexuality and the seeming inevitability of rape. Today that debate and theoretical work is hesitantly re-emerging, or at least some examination of the reasons for our silence. It's not easy to begin again.

Re-assessing our early writing on sexuality can perhaps suggest new directions. For I do think that the inadequacy of our early theorizing on sexuality fed into a growing uncertainty over the relationship between women's sexual experience and oppression. For example, most feminists had begun, as Pat Whiting was to argue in her 1972 article, by seeing women's sexual problems as stemming from their having 'accepted the male definition of their own sexuality, or at least pretended to' (p. 189). These definitions, she wrote, were now 'obsolete' as they did not correspond to reality. Women were therefore confused about their own sexual responses, and could not communicate their needs, so they remained sexually frustrated, which in turn led, she warned, to physical and mental disorders. Whiting attacked Freudian psychology, with its emphasis on the vaginal orgasm, as a 'disaster' for modern women, and a large part of women's sexual problems. The empiricist research of Masters and Johnson, by contrast, she saw as dedicated to liberating women's sexuality, suggesting that women had greater sexual potential than men. So Whiting was to conclude that: 'The research of Masters and Johnson indicates that widespread acceptance of female masturbation and learning to masturbate to orgasm in the post-puberty period would eliminate most of the female's sexual problems' (ibid., p. 209). Knowledge of women's 'sexual response' will show women 'where their male-inspired hang-ups end and their real sexual feelings begin' (ibid., p. 212).

That same year Angela Hamblin wrote of how women had been cut off 'from the inner core of their own sexuality' (1974, p. 87). Because women's sexuality had been, as of course it had, defined in male terms, feminists argued for some 'natural' or 'authentic' *female* sexuality, which we need to 'rediscover'. Quoting Susan Lydon in the USA, Hamblin saw Masters and Johnson as 'truly revolutionary and liberatory', moreover she claimed that 'when we reclaim our sexuality, we will have reclaimed our belief in ourselves as women' (ibid., p. 95). Though the American actress Viva was to compare the rejection of the vaginal orgasm with news of the birth of Christ, and Eva Figes to see modern women's discovery of the orgasm as another nail in the coffin of patriarchy, such proclamations were perhaps premature.

Masters and Johnson had become the authority on female sexuality, as feminists not surprisingly welcomed their critique of centuries of 'phallic fallacies'. Yet though feminists have been and still are greatly influenced by the theoretical perspectives of Masters and Johnson, these are, I believe, fundamentally flawed and misleading. It is easy, none the less, to understand the appeal of the empirical studies of sexologists over the last thirty years. They have begun to explode some aspects of the myths and moralisms surrounding human sexual behaviour, and in particular contributed to the long haul towards a positive assertion of female sexuality in contemporary western thought. They have not, however, represented as decisive a break with earlier conceptions of sexuality as most people have assumed.

The late nineteenth-century approach to sexuality, with its newly emerging 'science' of sexology – developed most systematically in the work of Krafft-Ebing – was to give sexuality a central position in human motivation. Indeed the very concept of sexuality, as some internal bodily desire, rather than as sex acts, only emerged at this time. (See, for example, Foucault and Sennett (1981).) Sexuality became a new but pressing 'problem', a dangerous, overpowering, biological urge, fortunately for civilization confined mainly to the male sex. From childhood masturbation – which was seen as linked to subsequent 'perversion', sex murder and madness – sexual behaviour was seen then as essentially destructive and anti-social. Freud's vast and elaborate theorization of sexuality from the turn of the century did introduce new and radical understandings of human sexual behaviour. No longer was sexuality to be located first of all in the norm of adult genital heterosexuality, from which all other manifestations deviated. It was to be seen instead in the variously located, continuously unfolding possibilities for physical sensuous gratification through auto-erotic and social encounters, from birth onwards. But the Freudian model also saw sexual desire as both central to human motivation and potentially dangerous, for both the individual and society. Mature female sexuality, because of women's lack of 'the phallus', was seen as attenuated – ideally passive, receptive and essentially responsive to male sexuality, as the girl abandoned her active clitoral sexuality to accept the phallus and vaginal orgasm.

So the 'revolutionary' appeal of the massive statistical surveys of sex behaviour by Alfred Kinsey and his co-workers in the 1950s, and of the elaborate anatomical and physiological recordings of sexual response by Masters and Johnson in the 1960s, was its reflection of a change in certain assumptions about sexual behaviour. The centrality of the sex drive in human behaviour remained, as well as its conceptualization as some sort of biological demand which needed to be satisfied, somewhat analogous to the drive for food or water. What was different from Krafft-Ebing or Freud was that both Kinsey and Masters and Johnson saw this pivotal sex drive as both healthy and good for society. They saw *mutual* enjoyment of sex as a basis for marital harmony, and sex as essentially harmless, if not beneficial, even in its 'deviant' expressions – outside marriage and in homosexual encounters. Both Kinsey and Masters and Johnson emphasized the similarity of male and female orgasmic potential, and stressed the necessary role of the clitoris in female orgasm; while Masters and Johnson stressed that women had a higher potential for orgasm and a more infinite variety of sexual response patterns than men.

Feminists and non-feminists alike have agreed that Masters and Johnson's work on female sexuality is both radical and progressive. Yet this is a strange state of affairs, when not only is their sexual therapy *always* geared to maintaining traditional marriage and the family, but it falls strictly within a behaviourist psychology which in other contexts most feminists and radicals have rejected as superficial, manipulative and misleading. This is because it looks at and attempts to modify individual behaviour in isolation from social relations. Human behaviour, on this view, has no cultural meaning, historical significance or even subjective importance, but is understood simply as physical response to physical stimulation. In this individualistic psychology sexual liberation is not about social relations or subjective experience, but about individual sensation. And sexual desire is understood not in terms of a person's relation to the object desired, but as some bodily state.

Indeed masturbation and auto-eroticism become the explicit paradigm of satisfactory sexual behaviour for Masters and Johnson, and always provide the model 'for any successful sexual experience'. Sexual behaviour is no longer seen, as in Freudian psychology, as a complex mixture of psychic longing, desire, anxiety, fear, hostility and repression built up over a lifetime of personal erotic encounters with others. Instead, it narrows down to become 'the effective stimulation for orgasm' – a straightforward physical event. And even this physical event is more or less the same for everybody on every occasion, never more or less significant, except that the orgasms in masturbation tend to be stronger and more multiple in women than those resulting from encounters with others.

When they venture at all from anatomical detail into acknowledging a psychological side to sexual arousal, Masters and Johnson provide only voluntaristic platitudes. Sexual arousal may be blocked by general negative attitudes either towards all sexuality or particular sexual acts (nothing interpersonal!) and the goal of sexual therapy is to replace these negative attitudes with positive ones. A person needs only anatomical information and the instruction to think positively, to 'correct' any lack of sexual pleasure. Sexual behaviour is seen as always malleable, and negative feelings of shame, disgust or hostility can always be replaced by favourable ones if the person really tries hard enough.

> When the partners in the sexually inadequate relationship see themselves as they have permitted the co-therapist to see them, when they can have their rationales for sexual failure and their prejudices, misconceptions and misunderstandings of natural sexual functioning explored with non-judgemental objectivity and explained in understandable terms with subjective comfort, a firm basis for mutual security in sexual pleasure is established.
>
> (Masters and Johnson, 1970, p. 62)

(We can only assume, I suppose, that Masters and Johnson must use slightly less pompous and stilted language when instructing subjects how to [reach] orgasm, than when describing this passage to victory!)

Most of the more recent popular feminist writing on sexuality, though now sparse, still remains heavily influenced by this crass and simplistic psychology of Masters and Johnson. In 1976 a series of articles appeared in Spare Rib by Eleanor Stephens presenting 'a feminist approach to female orgasm'. Based solidly on Masters and Johnson, masturbation is the route to sexual pleasure; orgasm the route to women's greater confidence and power in the world; and ignorance and superstition the obstacles in our way. Stephens sees everything in physical terms, 'every woman with a clitoris can become orgasmic given the right kind and amount of stimulation', though mysteriously, the physical becomes spiritual when we are told that for women to have orgasms is 'literally [for them] to learn to love themselves' (Stephens, 1975, p. 15). (Really? Even if my orgasm is dependent on my imagining myself tied up, beaten, degraded and fucked up the bum by a diseased rhinoceros? Presumably, since Stephens can recommend reading pornography to obtain a suitable 'mental attitude' for orgasm.)

Stephens draws upon the work of Lonnie Barbach in the USA, *For Yourself: the fulfilment of female sexuality*. Contrasting the good-natured, independent and strong orgasmic woman with the bitter, immature and sulky non-orgasmic woman, Barbach stresses, over and over again, the *unique* nature of each woman's 'very own' orgasm, 'each as unique as the woman herself' (1975, p. 19). That responses, again seen in purely physical terms, are quite so unique is surely surprising – the knee-jerk like none other! Whatever uniqueness attaches to sexual behaviour one might have expected to arise from the complex histories that have created our particular objects of desire, not the particular rub that ignites the clitoral nub.

No respecter of the power of unconscious mental processes, Barbach tells us that negative ideas of sexual repulsion or disgust 'may have been perceived unconsciously'. But looking at our genitals in the mirror will eliminate this (ibid., p. 53). Once we have studied our unique sexual response all sexual problems are solved. 'If you can have orgasms with one partner, you can probably have them with another ... No one "gives" you orgasms. You are in control' (ibid., p. 27). No one turns you on, you do it yourself? This goal of individual autonomy, applied to sexual encounters, seems to me remarkably odd, not to mention unerotic. How is it that in what is seen as our most intense and intimate connection, the other person slips into irrelevance? And Barbach's conclusion that 'After you find out what really turns you on, you can change your sexual practices to fit your responses' (ibid., p. 29) suggests we reign supreme in some solipsistic sexual universe where other people simply don't matter, or can be chosen at will.

[. . .]

The most ambitious study of female sexuality by a woman is the American *Hite Report* of 1976. Feminists welcomed it widely. The opening is promising, telling us that previous research has asked the wrong questions for the wrong reasons, and that what we need is a new theory of sexuality. I completely agree. But what we get, as Hite continues, is over 500 pages devoted to the same questions, asked for the same reasons, as Masters and Johnson – how do women reach orgasm? Her final section, offering a new theory of sexuality, is less than fifty pages and offers nothing new. She maintains the incorrigible optimism of contemporary sexology, which finds nothing problematic about sexuality, least of all our understanding of the meaning of the term. True to empiricist traditions, she makes no links between sexual experience and culture, not even between sex and gender – though she easily could, if only on the evidence she has collected.

Again, she does not acknowledge that there are any *unconscious* mental processes, and sees people as infinitely malleable: 'it is *we* who know what we want at any given time, and we who create sex in whatever image we want' (Hite, 1976, p. 434). And once we have learned to orgasm, as we should by now expect, we are becoming 'free'. 'Controlling your own stimulation symbolizes owning your own body, and is a very important step towards freedom' (ibid., p. 386).

Nowhere does Hite consider as a problem that women might *desire* sex where they can be passive, feel overpowered and *not* in control, though many women tell her this. Nor does she dwell on the problem that she is told that men still feel hostile to women, that there are still sexual double standards. Such observations are apparently trivial compared with what Hite sees as *the problem* – that girls are still kept in the dark about the clitoris. Yet some of us I suspect do manage to find our clitoris – even in the dark (especially in the dark). But more seriously, while knowledge of our genital organs can be important both for self-gratification and for seeking what we may want from sexual partners, Hite's attention to bodily reaction rather than social relations ignores what I see as critical in social relations – their connection to other relations of power, dependence, desire, hostility and fear. The message she has for us, and delivers as she tells us in her preface 'with great joy', is that 'You are free to explore and discover your own sexuality, to learn or unlearn anything you want, and to make physical relations with other people, of either sex, anything you like' (ibid., p. 528). Amen.

And finally, . . . the most recent feminist 'present' on sex [is] Anja Meulenbelt's *For Ourselves*, published in Britain in 1981 . . . The theme again: we must get in touch with our own needs (through masturbation) and then give ourselves what we want. Strangely, though within recent sexological fantasy not so strange at all, what we want, still seen entirely in terms of those bodily sensations we enjoy, turns out to correspond to 'feminist' aspirations. Our 'real needs', as Meulenbelt illustrates them, are all positive and progressive. They are about wanting equality in relationships, wanting to feel independent and in control. The good sensations are mostly unconnected to genital penetration, and above all they always create the basis for that happy 'love affair' we can have with ourselves ... [W]e can 'make' orgasms for ourselves – we can masturbate to orgasm and that even if we think we desire a *particular*, other person, we don't really need them for orgasm; nor do we need them for cuddles, which we can get quite easily from our feminist friends.

I am aware that books like the *Hite Report* and *For Ourselves* have been enjoyable and relevant for many women. Most importantly, they have encouraged us to be more assertive sexually, and to object to the male arrogance and insensitivity which sees sex in terms of penile performance. But though women have been strengthened by a stress on *women's* sexual pleasure, and knowledge of the dismal failure of many men to provide it, these books leave aside what is most complex and problematic about sexuality.

Sexual *desire*, for example, is rarely mentioned in *For Ourselves*. A very brief mention of sexual fantasy tells us that it can be fun, and that 'the images which surface in our fantasies will certainly change as our sexual relationships change' (Meulenbelt, 1981, p. 207). That is not my experience. And this new feminist sexuality, about loving ourselves and cuddling our friends, can become a new morality which does not in any way connect up with our erotic fantasies. However well-intentioned the gift, these books are no longer what I want. I think we deserve a more sophisticated analysis than they can provide.

What I do want to read and to hear is feminist reflection on sex which is less naïve, less prescriptively optimistic, and less individualistic. (You too *can* change your sexual life and fulfil all your own sexual wishes.) I think, on the contrary, it would be more helpful for us to understand why it is so very, very *hard* for us to change our erotic life, even when we do consciously desire to. We can consciously restrain or try to forget about our sexual desires – that may seem a sensible choice. But we cannot consciously change them at will. Since some of us do want to make the most of whatever sexual pleasure we can find, thoughtless Polyanna promises – 'The moon within your reach' – can deepen our frustration.

Sex is a problem. But this is neither because men are by *nature* sexually aggressive and coercive, nor because women have lost touch with their own natural sexuality which, rediscovered, would be wonderful. It is ironic that having exposed the myth of the 'liberated sexuality' of Lawrence, Miller and Mailer in the 1960s as little more than a homage to masculinity, some feminists seem in danger of coming up with a new version of the same myth. Transforming the myth into a naturally joyful, self-nourishing female sexuality may inspire some of us some of the time, but it also obscures much of the reality of much of our sex lives most of the time.

Sex is still a problem because whatever the current sexological steps to orgasmic happiness, at a more fundamental level many of the ideologies surrounding 'sex' have remained *unchanged* over the last hundred years. What we call sexual behaviour is still concealed from children, confined to a very special area of life, cut off from other activities, and acceptable only in certain types of relationship. It is still surrounded by taboos, shame, disgust and fear. Above all, sex remains the endorsement of gender. Language creates sex as the symbol of the male and the female. And whatever the questioning which is going on, and whatever the tolerance for 'deviance', sexuality is still seen in terms of its reproductive functioning, symbolized by a genital heterosexuality which men initiate and control. The culture of masculinity, rooted in male sexual assertion and domination, constructs heterosexuality as a symbol of male power over women. It fosters the use of male sexuality as a means of coercion of women. So the context for sexual development for everyone remains both repressive and deplorable, but for women in particular, subordinating and dangerous. That cannot be shrugged off, or rather overcome, with just an extra flick of the wrist – on the clitoris.

What might help us grapple with some of these problems is theoretical exploration by feminists of the links between sex and power, and sex and gender. And we need also to examine, rather than reinforce, the anxieties produced by the high valuation given to sex in our society, as that which most clearly expresses our true selves and identity, the place where we are most 'free' from social constraint. We need to understand why sexual behaviour is still largely secret and forbidden, despite its celebration in certain contexts. This would all entail looking at sexuality as it develops *through* social relations, and a genuine rejection of any notion of sex as an innate or biological force, either male or female. Anthropological and cultural studies indicate that human potential for physical pleasure – or anything else – is always mediated by society. Sexual behaviour is culturally and historically specific, including the ideas we hold about what is and is not 'sexual' or 'erotic'. While there is all sorts of evidence that people need physical comfort and physical contact (though no evidence for any overriding *exclusive* need for genital contact) there are an infinite variety of ways in which we may (hopefully) receive that contact.

Beginning here, as indeed some people do today, feminists might have more to say on the dynamics of women's sexual desire and how we strive for sexual pleasure even within deplorable constraints. Perhaps then we could touch upon, rather than ignore, women's actual sexual longings. We could explore how power is entangled with desire and pleasure in ways which may foster, disconnect from, or seek to redress more general relations of dominance and submission between men and women, one person and another.

In an illuminating study of mass-market romance, which feminists have rarely studied, Anne Snitow looks at the deep psychological structures to which they appeal. She sees them as 'accurate descriptions of certain selected elements of female consciousness' (1979, p. 143). These books, written by and for women, vibrate with 'phallic worship' of men – men as cruel, arrogant and threatening objects of enormous power and strength. The point of the romance, however, is for all this male power and strength to be ultimately, and despite all appearances to the contrary, laid at the feet of the swooning heroine.

Snitow sees the novels as women's pornography (or erotica, if you can maintain that fractured line), with all the contradictions of women's sexual desires in a sexist world. The titillation has little to do with any physical event. It is a 'social drama', and exists in the anticipation, anxiety, suspense and fear of waiting for the manifestation of – the impossible. The impossible longing is to be both helpless and in control, ravished and adored, powerless and yet supremely powerful. It's easy for feminists to see that the sexist imagery of the male sexual aggressor and passive heroine creates a sexual climate which condones rape and male coercion of women. Yet it also connects up with real romantic desire in a way which we cannot simply dismiss as a male plot.

Nowadays I never read these romances – just as I never look at porn – but I know they correspond to the impossible drama of my own sexual feelings. And these being the product of a social and shared, as well as a personal history, I suspect they are *far from* unique. As far back as I can remember, I have always spent substantial amounts of time in erotic daydreams. Once upon a time the object of desire in the daydreams was always a powerful woman (teacher or prefect) who was moved to comfort, stroke or cuddle me in response to my undeserved and humiliating suffering. Later the object of my desire, but also the one with whom I came to identify in the fantasy, was always a man. And I would have to invent circumstances for the most bizarre and impossible distortions of power-relations between the man and the woman (myself), but with me now more the object than the subject in the fantasy. The man whose feelings and behaviour I played out in the fantasy would be apparently totally powerful and the woman would be apparently totally powerless. But the impossible circumstances would mean that the man was really totally vulnerable and dependent on the woman, who was therefore *really* totally powerful. Yet it would be always important that in every way, to the woman and others, he would still *appear* all-powerful. In every fantasy, this power-ful/powerless man always ended up in a situation of having to make devoted reparation to the woman for some accidental abuse of his ambiguous power, for having caused her (me) some pain or injury.

I think these daydreams, despite their appearance, are in fact barely masochistic at all. But they do express a rather unhealthy admiration for the appearance of strength and power which I wish, by some means, to gain for myself. I think they do connect up with ambivalent feelings of desire for and hostility towards people I see as powerful. And this indeed can create sexual relationships which are ambivalently hostile and dependent, and therefore painful and unstable, as rejection becomes the proof of a person's superiority and hence desirability.

The fantasies which I have always needed to come to orgasm, by any methods, are for me far more tedious and obnoxious. In them I am always passive, objectified, humiliated and whatever abuse I can imagine to be happening at the time also contains the threat of even worse to follow. Since I avoid masochistic pornography, because it distresses and pains me, at the same time as titillating sexual desire, it is hard work to imagine this ever more hideous threat. I resent the content of the fantasies. And I resent the effort I have to make to produce them, and the disconnection which occurs with lovers who, at least recently, are most caring, gentle and as extensively physically stimulating as I could wish. Orgasm, as I said before, is simply not the problem. Part of the problem is that the magical impossibility of the daydream, of being all-powerful and powerless, cannot manifest itself in any actual sex life. Obviously!

What all this suggests to me, apart from the irrelevance of sexology to sexual desire, is that we must seek to understand how sexual desire comes to express such a variety of other social needs: needs which are irrational, unconscious and not easily understood and changed. Certainly until we attempt to understand what feeds our desire, prescriptions for change can seem repressive or irrelevant. I suspect that some of the emotional horror feminists and other women feel towards sexist pornography (which I share) is not simply that they think it encourages men to rape and objectify women (there is no evidence that they need pornography for that), but that it is obnoxious because it both degrades and titillates us. And that is *not* a connection which we like. It feels as though the connection is thrust upon us from outside, by pornography itself, which if removed would sever the connection. But it is not so unusual for feelings we dislike to seem to come from somewhere else, when in fact they are buried inside us as well as reflected in the social world which shaped them to begin with.

So when we talk as feminists about our efforts to understand and satisfy our sexual needs, and of the changes we are trying to make in our lives, it seems to me that these two goals may not flow together in the straightforward way feminists might hope and have suggested. The changes we might want to make may relate quite ambivalently to the needs our sexuality expresses. We may have to begin from accepting and attempting to understand what appears as a split between the social relations of equality and autonomy which we seek (and sometimes find) in our domestic and working lives, and the sources of our sexual desire. The satisfactions of the latter, however, do *not* determine the success of the former. Whatever the sexologists, feminist or otherwise, may claim, the relation between sexual desire and the achievement of power or autonomy in the world is very complex. For example, a recent study of the sexual activity of men in power has found that 'By far the most common service politicians demand from call-girls is to be beaten' (Janus *et al.*, 1976). This masochistic eroticism *accompanies* the achievement of and attachment to enormous power in the world – not its forfeiture.

It is because we cannot easily understand the nature of sexual desire that some feminists, and in different ways, have used psychoanalytic concepts which at least address the problem. They would suggest that it is not some straightforward need for physical gratification which motivates sexual behaviour and erotic desire, but rather, sexual desire is knotted through with all sorts of other emotional needs – to obtain approval and love, express hostility, dependence and domination, relieve anxiety, and repair deep-lying psychic wounds of rejection, humiliation and despair. Each of us has a particular history of psychic joys and misery, but we do share two crucial experiences – the dependency and relative powerlessness of childhood, and the overriding cultural significance attached to our biological sex from which we form a gender identity. The ambivalence of female sexuality and the prevalence of masochistic fantasy are hardly surprising in a cultural context where femininity defines weakness, and masculinity strength. Obtaining mythical strength and power through erotic fantasy (if not practice), even if it is as the weak gain power through the seduction of the strong, connects up with both what has been pleasurable in our experience of femininity as well as the pleasures of childhood recalled. As babies we have been the passive and powerless, but also powerfully demanding, recipients of enormous parental attention and, hopefully, physical gratification and love. One woman, writing in *Spare Rib* of her sexual relations with a man, confessed: 'I discovered that I didn't get any satisfaction from exciting him and what I wanted was to have things done to me.'

So, passivity and masochism in sex can, paradoxically, be demanding, self-centring and pleasurable. In her book, Maria Marcus describes how she always wants to see herself as 'the object' in sexual encounters, then she knows where she is. 'If a man looked at me I seemed to exist more clearly' (1981, p. 61). Marcus uncovers some of the contradictions of masochistic fantasies, where the 'masochist' is actually the consumer, the one receiving all the attention, to whom things are done. 'I am really the main character. I am the one who receives the right service to enable me to think I am nothing' (ibid., p. 123).

The problem with masochistic fantasy, I find, is *not at all* that it encourages real submissiveness, and most certainly *not* any desire for real pain, hurt or humiliation, but rather that, like any reliance on fantasy, it can make your sexual partner irrelevant, reducing sex to masturbation. I think it interferes with the feeling of personal connection, of being one with another, and therefore makes sex more rigid and less satisfactory (and orgasms less significant and cathartic!). I could feel, of course, that my masochistic fantasies provide me with an 'autonomous sexuality' – it is always me who is in control. But the problem is *I don't want to be*. I would like not to have to do all this work 'for myself'.

My masochistic fantasies seem to be unconnected to any attempt to rationalize actually existing personal power relations of heterosexuality – quite the contrary, in fact – though this is a common feminist interpretation of masochism: 'Perhaps fewer people would dream of being dominated if it weren't assumed that we ought to be underneath' (Meulenbelt, 1981, p. 106). They predated by over a decade any conscious experience of sex with men, and were first of all a part of sex play with girls and to accompany later sexual experience with women. Sexism and repressive attitudes to sex have certainly fed these fantasies. But on a more personal level I think they began as consolations for particular circumstances of a quite unusually extreme experience of loneliness in infancy and childhood, with the magical belief that somehow reparation should and would be made for suffering. I see them as, among other things, a way of making myself the centre of attention, when in fact I knew for certain that there was actually nobody there for me at all in reality. They express hostility and despair, mixed up with desire for attention and physical contact.

In describing her erotic passion for Sita, Kate Millett (1976) described similar sources of desire feeding her sexual excitement. 'How she knows me, rules me, masters me, plays me, pleasures me . . .' 'How I envy her everything.' 'How enormous my sense of inferiority', Sita is 'all-powerful'. Kate Millett's desire is triggered by envy, resentment, submission, and yes, hostility, she 'envies' and 'hates' Sita. And in this context, she can have truly thunderous orgasms! Sexual excitement is generated by, and in the service of, a multitude of needs, not all of them 'nice'. Whereas some feminists have claimed that the sex act for men serves as a kind of rape to express power, domination and hostility, we have usually written as though female sexuality is totally bland, devoid of any such emotions. I think it is wrong to see such emotions as present only in male sexuality and absent in female sexuality, or present in female sexuality only because of 'male definitions' of sexuality. I think it is also wrong not to see that men's sexuality as well expresses complex desires – for dependency, submission and forgiveness; of envy and fear of women; as well as the desire to dominate and control. Though of course it is hideously true that men's greater power in the world and the particular construction of masculinity both allow and *encourage* men to express domination and power through sex.

Anne Snitow, in another article (1980), looks at sex in recent women's novels. She shows them describing mainly women's disappointments, deprivations and difficulties in sexual relations (whether heterosexual or lesbian) through which women neverthe-less search for whatever pleasure they can find. Whatever our sexual preference, it would seem, our desires are imbued with both sexism, and all the socially structured anxieties, disturbances and humiliations that are generated endlessly throughout our lives under capitalism. Snitow writes 'Women have had to enjoy sex in ways that were destructive to them. Instead of calling this masochism, one might say that it has been life affirming for women to embrace sex even on painful terms, to find ways to enjoy sex in spite of sexism, *including their own*,' (ibid., p. 710).

I agree. And would argue that it is not necessarily orgasms that we are deprived of, but more likely any possible sexual scenarios for exploring and enjoying the contradictory tensions of erotic desire – dependence and strength, control and passivity, love and hate – in any playful, yet intense and pleasurable way. A possible scenario is hard to find when heterosexual relations are so fraught and bitter because of women's struggle against male oppression, while lesbian relations as well exist in reaction to, and against, our heterosexist, male-dominated erotic world. Anna Coote and Beatrix Campbell argue that what remains to be done in relation to sexuality 'is to explore the experience that lesbians and heterosexuals share and to build on this common ground a political understanding of sexuality' (1982, pp. 227–8). Again, I agree. But what they do *not* indicate is that what we 'share' is likely to involve all sorts of things we would rather avoid: masochism, self-objectification, domination, guilt, hostility and envy. We must accept and explore these censored emotions, and see how they might conflict with a now fashionably radical but somehow tritely optimistic vision of 'female eroticism, as something powerful and autonomous, which is shared by heterosexuals, lesbians and bisexuals' (ibid., p. 231), and transcends all those categories.

Feminists who are not separatists do engage with men. We engage with men politically, in fighting the oppression of class, race and other hierarchies, because we also to a certain extent share a common fate with particular men. We engage with men because of our personal histories – with fathers, brothers, sons, friends and yes, some of us engage with men sexually, because we desire them. The prescription that women should repress heterosexual desire to further the cause of feminism is one I believe to be strategically and morally wrong. Although our sexual pleasures are formed and deformed within the power relations of sexism and capitalism (as are all our pleasures), I do not conclude that we should give them up. But I would like to understand this formation in a way which increases my security, rather than exacerbates my doubts that I can accept and enjoy the tensions of erotic desire, even though I may as yet only very partially transform them from the sad and sorry state of their emergence into something closer to what our feminist hearts might consciously desire. At the same time, I agree with those who would like to see sex given a less privileged place in determining our 'unique identity'. What is wrong with our lives is perhaps not so much the lack of orgasms as our perpetual craving for that orgasm which can obliterate the isolation and emptiness we feel in the rest of our lives.

'I sometimes wonder if you are the right one for me to be submissive to.'

Article 3.3
SOCIAL CONSTRUCTION THEORY: PROBLEMS IN THE HISTORY OF SEXUALITY

Carole S. Vance

Social construction theory in the field of sexuality proposed an extremely outrageous idea. It suggested that one of the last remaining outposts of the 'natural' in our thinking was fluid and changeable, the product of human action and history rather than the invariant result of the body, biology or an innate sex drive.

Empirical and theoretical work on the history of sexuality has grown dramatically in the last twenty years, for which social construction approaches plus the invigorating questions raised by social movements like feminism and lesbian and gay liberation are largely responsible . . . Efforts to transform society inevitably raised questions about the past and the future, as they also called into question prevailing ideological frameworks for examining the 'facts' about sex and gender.

[. . .]

In the sometimes heated debates that have gone on about essentialism and social construction, the word 'essentialist', to some ears, sounds increasingly pejorative – a dirty word, a contemptuous put-down, a characterization of being hopelessly out of date. Yet we need to start this discussion by recognizing that we have all been brought up to think about sexuality in essentialist ways.

Essentialism can take several forms in the study of sexuality: a belief that human behaviour is 'natural', predetermined by genetic, biological or physiological mechanisms and thus not subject to change; or the notion that human behaviours which show some similarity in form are the same, an expression of an underlying human drive or tendency. Behaviours that share an outward similarity can be assumed to share an underlying essence and meaning.

The development of science and social science in Euro-America in the past century can be characterized by a general movement away from essentialist frameworks toward perspectives that, although called by various names, are constructionist. These new frameworks have challenged the 'natural' status of many domains, presenting the possibility of a truly *social* inquiry as well as suggesting that human actions have been and continue to be subject to historical forces and, thus, to change. Gender and sexuality have been the very last domains to have their natural, biologized status called into question. For all of us, essentialism was our first way of thinking about sexuality and still remains the hegemonic one in the culture.

UNHELPFUL CRITICISMS OF SOCIAL CONSTRUCTION THEORY

Some critics contend that social construction theory implies that sexual identity, or more to the point, lesbian and gay identity is somehow fictional, trivial, unimportant or not real, because it is socially constructed. The punch line 'it's *only* socially constructed' is a characteristic remark of these critics, revealing their belief that only biologically determined phenomena could have any significance in human social life. This is an odd position for historians and social scientists to take. Social construction approaches call attention to the paradox between the historically variable ways in which culture and society construct seemingly stable reality and experience: here, the ways in which the prevailing sexual system seems natural and inevitable to its natives, and for many individuals the expression of some deeply-felt essence. To explain how reality is constructed does not imply that it is not real for the persons living it – or trivial, unimportant or ephemeral, though it is also true that the insight of construction, when absorbed by the natives (that is, us) has the potential to subvert the natural status of the sexual system and cause us to question and rethink our experience of essential identity.

Other variants of this misreading suggest that individual sexual identity is easily changeable, much like a new outfit plucked from the closet at whim; that individuals have conscious control over sexual identity; and that large-scale cultural formations regarding sexuality are easily changed. Since social constructionists have said nothing of the kind, one is at first puzzled by the enormity of this misunderstanding, but the explanation for it is perhaps to be found in the special status of sex in our culture and our thought (Rubin, 1984).

An analogy from anthropology is useful here. It is commonplace for anthropologists to say that human behaviour is socially or culturally constructed, by which we mean that human behaviour is learned and not intrinsic or essentially determined. But to suggest that any feature of human life, for example, national or ethnic identity, is socially constructed is not to say that it is trivial. Nor is it to say that entire cultures can transform themselves overnight, or that individuals socialized in one cultural tradition can acculturate at whim to another.

This criticism of social construction confuses the individual level with the cultural level: that sexuality is constructed at the level of culture and history through complex interactions which we are now trying to understand does not mean that individuals have an open-ended ability to construct themselves, or to reconstruct themselves multiple times in adulthood. (This is not to deny individuals' experiences of sexual malleability and change, which are probably considerably more extensive than our cultural frames and our own biographical narratives admit.) The specialness of sex is highlighted by this comparison, since a quite ordinary and accepted insight about cultural construction in most areas of human life seems very difficult to understand without distortion when applied to sexuality. When we come to sex, our minds grind to a halt: normal distinctions become incomprehensible, and ordinary logic flies out the window.

DIFFERENT DEGREES OF SOCIAL CONSTRUCTION

The widespread use of social construction as a term and as a paradigm obscures the fact that constructionist writers have used this term in diverse ways. It is true that all reject transhistorical and transcultural definitions of sexuality and suggest instead that sexuality is mediated by historical and cultural factors. But . . . social construction spans a theoretical field of what might be constructed, ranging from sexual acts, sexual identities, sexual communities, the direction of sexual desire (object choice) to sexual impulse or sexuality itself.

At minimum, all social construction approaches adopt the view that physically identical sexual acts may have varying social significance and subjective meaning depending on how they are defined and understood in different cultures and historical periods. Because a sexual act does not carry with it a universal social meaning, it follows that the relationship between sexual acts and sexual identities is not a fixed one, and it is projected from the observer's time and place to others at great peril. Cultures provide widely different categories, schemata and labels for framing sexual and affective experiences. The relationship of sexual act and identity to sexual community is equally variable and complex. These distinctions, then, between sexual acts, identities and communities are widely employed by constructionist writers.

A further step in social construction theory posits that even the direction of sexual desire itself, for example, object choice or hetero/homosexuality, is not intrinsic or inherent in the individual but is constructed. Not all constructionists take this step; for some, the direction of desire and erotic interest are fixed, although the behavioural *form* this interest takes will be constructed by prevailing cultural frames, as will the subjective experience of the individual and the social significance attached to it by others.

The most radical form of constructionist theory[1] is willing to entertain the idea that there is no essential, undifferentiated sexual impulse, 'sex drive' or 'lust', which resides in the body due to physiological functioning and sensation. Sexual impulse itself is constructed by culture and history. In this case, an important constructionist question concerns the origins of these impulses, since they are no longer assumed to be intrinsic or, perhaps, even necessary. This position, of course, contrasts sharply with more middle-ground constructionist theory which implicitly accepts an inherent sexual impulse which is then constructed in terms of acts, identity, community, and object choice. The contrast between middle-ground and radical positions makes it evident that constructionists may well have arguments with each other, as well as with essentialists. Each degree of social construction points to different questions and assumptions, possibly to different methods, and perhaps to different answers.

[. . . A] review of social construction literature, which makes its first distinct appearance in the mid-1970s, as well as its forerunners in the 1960s, shows a gradual development of the ability to imagine that sexuality is constructed. The intellectual history of social construction is a complex one, and the moments offered here are for purposes of illustration, not comprehensive review.

Intellectual precursors to constructionist approaches, for example, include anthropologists doing cross-cultural work on sexuality in the 1960s. They assumed that culture encouraged or discouraged the expression of specific sexual acts and relationships. Oral-genital contact, for example, might be a part of normal heterosexuality in one group but taboo in another; female homosexuality might be severely punished in one tribe yet tolerated in another. However, these anthropologists accepted without question the existence of universal categories like heterosexual and homosexual, male and female sexuality, and sex drive. Culture shaped sexual expression and customs, but the basic material to work with – a kind of sexual Play Doh – was the same everywhere, a naturalized category and thus never open to investigation. Although we can recognize this work as a precursor to social construction theory, it clearly contains many essentialist elements.

The struggle to move away from essentialist and naturalizing ways of thinking about sexuality was a difficult one. Mary McIntosh's 1968 essay on the homosexual role appears to us as a landmark article, offering many suggestive insights about the historical construction of sexuality in England. But her observations vanished like pebbles in a pond, until they were engaged with by mid-1970s' writers, clearly motivated by the questions of feminism and gay liberation. An identifiably constructionist approach dates from this period, not before.

Early work in lesbian and gay history attempted to retrieve and revive documents (and lives) which had been lost or been made invisible. These lives were first conceived of as lesbian or gay, and the enterprise akin to a search for historical roots, an attempt to document the existence of gay people and experience. This was history against the grain, against the heterosexist narrative: in short, activist history and history as political work. To their credit, researchers who had started this enterprise from a firm point of fixed sexual categories began to consider other ways of looking at their material and more expansive questions to ask. Jonathan Katz's work is one example of this process, since his first book, *Gay American History* (1976), is very much in the 'gay ancestors' tradition. In the course of researching his second book, *Gay/Lesbian Almanac* (1983), he began to consider that sexual acts reported in American colonial documents from the seventeenth century, for example sodomy, might not be equivalent to contemporary homosexuality. Sodomy – then understood as any unnatural, non-reproductive sexual act – was a temptation and sin to which anyone, male or female, could fall victim, as to envy or theft. Although the documents amply show discovery and punishment, colonial society did not seem to conceive of a unique type of person – a homosexual – who engaged in these acts, nor did it provide a homosexual identity on a cultural level or anything resembling a homosexual subculture on a social level.

Katz's second book marks a sharp departure from the first, in that records or accounts that document same-sex emotional or sexual relations are not taken as evidence of 'gay' or 'lesbian' people, but are treated as jumping off points for a whole series of questions about the meanings of these acts to the people who engaged in them and to the culture and time in which they lived.

The intellectual development reflected in Katz's work is not unique to him, but appears in many others' as well. And from this work came an impressive willingness to imagine: had the category 'homosexual' or 'lesbian' always existed? And if not, what was its point of origin and the conditions for development? If identical physical acts had different subjective meanings, how was sexual meaning constructed? If sexual subcultures come into being, what leads to their formation? In these and other questions, they imagined what has become the foundation of lesbian and gay history.

The intellectual history of social construction is a complex one. The point of briefly noting a few moments in its history here is simply to illustrate that social construction theorists and writers differ in their willingness to imagine *what* was constructed. For us, their differences suggest that we should avoid using 'social construction' in such an undifferentiated way. As readers we should try to be clear about what each theorist or author imagines to be constructed. As writers and speakers, we should try to indicate more exactly what we mean by social construction in our own work.

THE INSTABILITY OF SEXUALITY AS A CATEGORY

Because they were tied to essentialist assumptions which posited biological and physiological factors as influential in determining the contours of sexuality, sexological and biomedical paradigms of sexuality nevertheless offered one advantage: sexuality enjoyed the status of a stable, ongoing and cohesive entity. The constructionist paradigm more flexibly admits variability in behaviour and motive over time and place. But to the extent that social construction theory grants that sexual acts, identities and even desire are mediated by cultural and historical factors, the object of study – sexuality – becomes evanescent and threatens to disappear. If sexuality is constructed differently at each time and place, can we use the term in a comparatively meaningful way? More to the point . . . have constructionists undermined their own categories? Is there an 'it' to study?

We have attempted to address the problem of false universalism by exercising more care in our terminology and conceptual categories: thus, in examining fellatio among Sambia adult men and teenage boys in the New Guinea highlands, it may be more appropriate to speak of 'same-sex' rather than 'homosexual' acts or relations. The first term attempts to describe sexual behaviour without assuming that its social and affective meaning is equivalent to that of contemporary society: New Guinea is not Amsterdam or Greenwich Village. This term and others like it encourage openness rather than premature closure in our thinking about the historical and cultural meaning of diverse sexual acts and identities. However, even with my care, I've already called these acts 'sexual'.

Here we may detect, despite genuine efforts toward conceptual and definitional openness, that even the new sex history has an ambivalent and more complex relationship to the idea of sexuality as a coherent category. Some social constructionists explicitly encourage the total deconstruction of the category of the sexual, for example, Foucault. Others have not taken this theoretical position, though it remains implicit in their work. For, if sexuality is constituted differently in different times and places, it follows that behaviours and relations seen as sexual by us (contemporary Euro-Americans) may not be by others, and vice versa.[2]

Questioning the very category of sexuality, however, proves difficult. A student of mine agreed that it would be incorrect to call Sambia male initiation rites involving fellatio between older men and younger boys 'homosexuality', but he was nevertheless convinced that this was experienced as a sexual act by those engaging in it. How did he know it was sexual, I asked? 'Their cosmology posits that young boys grow to adulthood only through the ingestion of semen,' he replied, 'but you don't see them eating it with a bowl and a spoon.' The move to question the category 'sexuality' remains counter-intuitive, therefore, and thus often results in an intellectual stance that can only be inconsistently or unconvincingly maintained. The attempt to deconstruct sexuality as a meaningful universal construct has also generated considerable backlash for reasons we will describe later.

Many other social constructionists assume, as perhaps it is easier to, that specific, core behaviours and physical relations are reliably understood as sexual, even though they occur in diverse cultures or historical periods. The knowledge or assumption that behaviour is indeed sexual serves as a guide to what must be studied of what might be safely ignored. To give up this assumption considerably widens the field of what might be the object of study, with both good and bad results. The often implicit assumptions about the sexual nature of physical acts or relations depend in turn on deeply embedded cultural frameworks that we use to think about the body.

THE ROLE OF THE BODY

Social construction's greatest strength lies in its violation of our folk knowledge and scientific ideologies that would frame sexuality as 'natural', determined by biology and the body. This violation makes it possible, indeed compels us to raise questions that a naturalizing discourse would obscure and hide. Social constructionists have been even-handed in this endeavour, dethroning the body in all fields – in heterosexual history as well as in lesbian and gay history. At first, we greeted this development with good cheer, happy to be rid of the historical legacy of nineteenth-century spermatic and ovarian economies, women's innate sexual passivity, and the endless quest to find the hormonal cause of homosexuality. Yet the virtue of social construction may also be its vice.

Has social construction theory, particularly variants which see 'sexual impulse', 'sex drive' or 'lust' as created, made no room for the body, its functions and physiology? As sexual subjects, how do we reconcile constructionist theory with the body's visceral reality and our own experience of it? If our theory of sexuality becomes increasingly disembodied, does it reach the point of implausibility, even for us? And if we wish to incorporate the body within social construction theory, can we do so without returning to essentialism and biological determinism?

Let me discuss these points more concretely by giving an example from my own work on female circumcision. [. . .I]t illuminates the difficulty of thinking about the relationship of sexuality to the body and has much to offer for other body issues.

Briefly, female circumcision[3] is an umbrella term for traditional customs carried out in various Middle Eastern and African countries. These customs involve the surgical alteration and removal of female genital tissue, usually performed by midwives and female kin. The procedures vary in severity and range from removing part or all of the clitoris (simple circumcision) to removing the labia (excision). In infibulation, the most radical form of surgery, the clitoris and labia are excised, and the vaginal opening is sutured to reduce its circumference, making heterosexual penetration impossible and thus guaranteeing virginity. These operations are done at different ages and for different reasons – to promote hygiene and fertility, to render women aesthetically more feminine and thus marriageable, and to promote virginity. It is important to understand that these procedures are widespread and in local terms thought to be required by religion or custom.[4]

In the past ten years, an intense conversation has developed between Western and Third-World feminists over these practices. It is not my goal here to thoroughly describe this debate, or to suggest, by examining Western views, that we enjoy a privileged vantage point or right to intervene. What interests me here is how we think about these practices and the body in less guarded moments.

First, we tend to think about the effect of these customs, particularly on sexual functioning. We draw on a physiological model of Masters and Johnson (1966), which places the clitoris at the centre of female sexual response and orgasm. We reason that removal of part or all of the clitoris interferes with orgasm, perhaps making it impossible. That is, we are universalizing a physiological finding made on American subjects without much thought.[5] Could Sudanese women's responses be different?

If we are willing to consider that sexual response is more than physiology, we might ask what is known about female sexual experience in these cultures. The answer is not clear cut, in part due to the small number of studies done and the difficulty of doing them. A Sudanese gynaecologist compared women with different degrees of circumcision in Khartoum, finding that women with milder degrees of circumcision reported orgasm whereas women with severe degrees did not (Shandall, 1967). But even this inquiry depends on eliciting a response to terms like 'orgasm', whose subjective meaning is what is at issue. A highly-educated Sudanese woman who had been infibulated mused on this problem during our conversation in New York. Familiar with the Masters and Johnson framework which would suggest orgasm was unlikely, she asked me if she had experienced an orgasm. But how could I know?, short of resorting to the clearly inappropriate American adage: 'if you have to ask, you haven't.' She struggled to navigate the boundaries of culture and language, saying that perhaps she did, since she enjoyed sex with her husband and found the experience pleasurable.

Our response is complicated: still tied to a physiological frame, we think about different degrees of tissue removed, the possible nerves remaining under the excised clitoris, the transferral of sexual response from one body zone to another. We strain to imagine a different scenario of pleasure, still plausible within our framework. Western feminists also think of what is familiar to us: women's accommodation to the lack of sexual pleasure and even active displeasure – rationalizations, protestations of satisfaction, low expectations. In viewing these customs, we oscillate between imagining the sexually familiar and the unfamiliar. Nor are we alone in our efforts to compare and contrast: another Sudanese woman familiar with Western culture found her situation far from unique. 'You circumcise women, too,' she said, 'but you do it through Freudian theory, not through surgery. You are not so different from us.'

If we give up physiological frames of thinking about circumcision and acknowledge that in these countries it is a culturally normative practice, we begin to entertain unsettling questions. Is female orgasm constructed? What are the conditions for it? Is it necessary? Is it a physiological potential, whose expression may be facilitated or curtailed? If curtailed, is that repression and injustice? Or is the construction of female orgasm open-ended, with no imperative for it to happen? Can sexual pleasure be constructed totally without orgasm for women? (And here I mean, can women in an entire culture experience sexual pleasure, though they rarely or never experience orgasm?, not the more customary question we might ask in our own culture: can a single sexual episode be pleasurable, even though the woman has not experienced orgasm? These are very different questions.)

By now, even social constructionists, particularly women, are disturbed and upset. Abandoning or even detaching from a physiological frame makes us feel – to the extent that we questioned this practice – that we are now losing ground to object to it. It points up the tendency, even among social constructionists, to defend sexuality and sexual pleasure in terms of an essential right and the functioning of the body. More importantly, the discomfort we experience as the body slips away, or threatens to, in this particular case suggests that we need to explore the limitations of sexual theory which has no room for the body. As we consider restoring the body to social construction theory, we wonder if it is possible to be a materialist without sliding into essentialism? Are there ways to integrate bodily sensation and function into a social construction frame, while still acknowledging that human experience of the body is always mediated by culture and subjectivity, and without elevating the body as determinative? The answer will not be found in a return to essentialism, whether frank or disguised, but in exploring more sensitive and imaginative ways of considering the body.

As difficult as these problems may be, social constructionists do not grapple with theoretical issues about degrees of social construction, the object of study, or the meaning of the body in a vacuum. The new sex history is indebted to feminism and gay liberation for many of its insights, for non-academic settings which nurtured this work during the early stages of its development when the university disapproved, and for its intellectual urgency. These popular political movements created an audience of activist and self-reflective individuals who very much wanted to know and to use the knowledge to inform their activism. I mention this because some of the problems in social construction theory, particularly the critical reaction to it in the last few years in lesbian and gay political circles, originate in the meaning of this theory to members of oppressed groups in the contemporary sexual hierarchy.[6]

THE SEXUAL SUBJECT'S DESIRE FOR HISTORY

A common motivation for fans of lesbian and gay history was a desire to reclaim the past and to insist on lesbian and gay visibility in every place and at every time. But the discoveries of the new sex historians have sometimes proved disturbing, as researchers gave up their initial certainty about the existence of 'gay people' and embarked on a more complicated discussion about the origins of gay identity in the seventeenth to nineteenth centuries. In these discussions, sexual acts could not be read as unproblematic indicators of homosexuality; and rather than an unchanging essence which defied legal and religious prohibitions, homosexuality increasingly came to be seen as a variable experience whose boundaries and subjectivity were shaped through complex negotiations between state institutions, individuals, and subcultures.

Variability, subjectivity, negotiation and change often violated the wish for a continuous history. If the point of gay history was to document an ancestry, a gay *Roots*, then for many activists this kind of gay history was frustrating, even a failure. The disappointment and anger at not being able to see oneself reflected in the mirror of history has fuelled some of the criticism of social construction theory in the belief that a more essentialist perspective would permit the development of group history and solidarity.

In addition, it is common for mainstream lesbian and gay political and lobbying groups in the United States to use essentialist argument and rhetoric in advancing their case. Lesbians and gays are deserving of civil rights, they say, much like women, ethnic and racial groups. This argument derives less from a self-conscious theoretical commitment to essentialism and more from the pervasiveness of essentialist frames in American culture, particularly in regard to race and ethnicity. In an ideological system that defines these groups as natural, real and organized according to relatively unchanging biological features, one obvious and powerful symbolic strategy is to claim an equal status for lesbians and gays. In this ideological and political context, it is to the advantage of all groups struggling for resources to stress not only group unity and historical privilege (buttressed by and documented through histories of the ancestors), but their status as an essential group to which members have no choice in belonging. Fundamentalists and conservatives are fond of ridiculing the analogy between gay rights and minority rights: minorities are 'real' groups to which members can't help but belong through their racial features, whereas no one has to be gay, if he or she simply refrains from sin and lust. Gays and lesbians do not constitute a natural group, right-wingers insist; they are just a bunch of perverts.

In such an arena, gay politicos and lobbyists find it helpful in the short run to respond with assertions about gays through the ages, to assert a claim to a natural group status, and to insist that being gay is an essential, inborn trait about which there is no choice. And, indeed, essentialist arguments about sexual identity can be extended to heterosexuals and used to good advantage: if sexual identity is inborn, or at least fixed by age three, then lesbian or gay schoolteachers pose no threat to students in terms of influencing their identity or development (in an undesirable way, the argument would seem to concede). By dint of repetition, ideas about gay essentialism were reinforced in the contemporary gay movement (though they were hardly unknown in American culture) and, more importantly, linked to group advancement, success and self-affirmation. Therefore, arguments which opposed or undercut essentialist rhetoric about gay identity were increasingly unfamiliar and heretical, even perceived as damaging to gay interests. Within the lesbian and gay community's internal discussions and self-education, the failure to make a distinction between politically expedient ways of framing an argument and more complex descriptions of social relations promoted an increasingly rigid adherence to essentialism as an effective weapon against persecution.

THE RELATIONSHIP OF MARGINAL GROUPS TO DECONSTRUCTION

In a similar vein, it is ironic to note that in the war of ideas against heterosexual hegemony, social construction theory has become most influential only in the intellectual circles of oppositional groups. Social construction theory may be the new orthodoxy in feminist, progressive and lesbian and gay history circles, but it has made a minimal impact on mainstream authorities and literatures in sexology and biomedicine. These groups continue their investigation and theorizing from the assumption that sexuality is essential. At most, the deviant status of homosexuality calls for inquiry into its etiology (whether hormonal, psychological or sociological), but the causes of heterosexuality have attracted little interest. In traditional sexual science, heterosexuality remains an unexamined and naturalized category, and little in popular culture causes heterosexuals to consider their sexual identity or its origins and history.

In contrast, the social constructionist framework common in lesbian and gay history has become disseminated to a larger lesbian and gay public. Some wonder whether this constructionist perspective is helpful. What are its implications? Why should lesbians and gays have a developed consciousness that their sexual identities have been 'constructed', when heterosexuals do not? Does this intellectual sophistication lead to a sense of group frailty instead of robustness? And does any history of construction inevitably pose the theoretical possibility of a future deconstruction, even disappearance, which is alarming and uncomfortable? . . .

The tension here is identical to a tension felt within feminism, which simultaneously holds two somewhat contradictory goals. One goal is to attack the gender system and its primacy in organizing social life, but the second goal is to defend women as a group. Defending women or advancing their interest (in equal pay, abortion rights or child care, for example) emphasizes their status as a special group with a unique collective interest, distinct from men, thus replaying and perhaps reinforcing the very gender dichotomy crucial to the system of gender oppression.

The same irresolvable tension exists within the lesbian and gay movement, which on the one hand attacks a naturalized system of sexual hierarchy which categorizes and stabilizes desires and privileges some over others, and on the other hand defends the interest of 'lesbian and gay people', which tends to reify identity and essential nature in a political process I've described. There is no solution here, since to abandon either goal for the other would be foolish. Real, live lesbians and gays need to be defended in an oppressive system, and the sexual hierarchy, which underlies that oppression, needs to be attacked on every level, particularly on the intellectual and conceptual levels where naturalized systems of domination draw so much of their energy. There is no easy solution here, but even an awareness of this tension can be helpful, since it powerfully contributes to the larger political and emotional climate in which social construction theory is received, and rightly so.

CONCLUSION

Social construction theory offered many radical possibilities in theorizing about sexuality. To take the next steps, we need to continue and deepen our discussion about its very real problems.

These problems will not be resolved through theoretical discussion alone, though such discussions offer clarification, but through the course of continued research and investigation.

To the extent social construction theory strives for uncertainty through questioning assumptions rather than seeking closure, we need to tolerate ambiguity and fluidity. The future is less closed than we feared, but perhaps more open than we hoped. All movements of sexual liberation, including lesbian and gay, are built on imagining: imagining that things could be different, other, better than they are. Social construction shares that imaginative impulse and thus is not a threat to the lesbian and gay movement, but very much of it.

Clearly, the tension between deconstructing systems of sexual hierarchy and defending lesbians and gays will be an ongoing one. In that case, we need to find a way to acknowledge more openly and respond more appropriately to the emotional responses social construction theory engenders, deeply felt responses about identity, community, solidarity, politics and survival – in short, our lives.

Notes

1   There is no suggestion that the most radical forms of social construction theory are necessarily the best, although the exercise of totally deconstructing one of the most essential categories, sexuality, often has an electrifying and energizing effects on one's thinking. Whether this degree of deconstruction can be plausibly maintained is another question, explored in a later section of this essay.

2   We have been sensitized to the dangers and limitations of imposing our categories and systems of meaning. The commitment to avoid ethnocentric readings of non-Western behaviour, however, encounters another problem: the tendency in cross-cultural literature to withhold and dismiss data about homosexuality, from combined motives of sexual reticence and homophobia. Similar problems occur in history. Knowing this, the alert reader is reluctant to accept the glib and formulaic dismissals that the behaviour in question does not constitute homosexuality, and instead leaps at suggestive evidence, treating data which can only be seen as clues as definitive evidence instead. We need to chart a course between these extremes.

3   Although 'female circumcision' is perhaps the most common Western term for these practices, many researchers in the field prefer the terms 'female genital surgery' or 'female genital operations'. Female circumcision too easily suggests an analogy to male circumcision, whereas the procedures performed on women are usually far more serious in terms of the degree of bodily tissue removed and in the physical and psychological consequences.

4   For more detailed description and discussion of female circumcision see El Dareer (1982) and Koso-Thomas (1987).

5   Constructionists might well question whether the sexual response among even American women should be viewed as a function of physiology.

6   For a discussion of the concept of sexual hierarchy see Rubin (1984, pp. 279–83).

Cover illustration from *Sex & Love* (edited by Sue Cartledge and Joanna Ryan)

4
GENDER AND MOTHERING

Early feminist discussion of sexuality, despite differing perspectives, nonetheless found a consensus in a shared hostility to Freudian theory. Freud's account of femininity was seen as part of the problem of women's position, rather than part of the solution. Much of this antipathy to Freud's ideas came from the United States where the psychoanalytic profession used its considerable cultural status to stress the need for women to conform to the dominant ideals of femininity. Being sexually appealing to men, finding a husband and having babies were advocated as the solution to women's discontents. True femininity was seen as the only antidote to 'penis envy' and as the way to women's fulfilment. Against this cosy prescription feminists objected that the social position of women was limited precisely by their position of dependence within the family, their role as mothers, and the way in which they were sexually objectified. They argued that it was women's social inferiority which produced a sense of inadequacy in women not – as some psychoanalysts would have it – an unconscious desire to be like men.

Many feminists continue to maintain the position that Freud's theory of the unconscious is not one that can be usefully employed by feminism. Others, however, turned to psychoanalytic theory because it provided a way of analysing sexual identity which seemed to have some bearing on the problems encountered in transforming the position of women. Attempts to change social attitudes about women in particular met with considerable resistance. Even amongst women committed to change it proved difficult to dislodge some of the emotional conventions of femininity. In consciousness-raising groups women discovered not only that their own attitudes were somewhat resistant to transformation, but also that their feelings about themselves were often at odds with their convictions about women. Intellectual and political commitment to sexual equality did not always translate into feeling equal. Political will was not enough to change emotional experience and it therefore seemed imperative to understand the tenacity of emotional self-perception.

Together these two developments within feminist politics made some women more receptive to psychoanalytic ideas because of the centrality Freud gave to the concept of the unconscious. What attracted feminists to Freud, despite his account of femininity, was his idea that the self was made up of unconscious desires as well as conscious intentions. Freud argued that our motivations are not just rational and self-interested, they are also unconscious and unrealistic. Unconscious desires are ones we refuse entry into our consciousness, precisely because they are unrealistic or threatening in some way. Nonetheless they continue to demand fulfilment, taking various guises which mask their origins in the unconscious, thereby distorting the fact that they have been banished from consciousness. The explanation as to why certain desires are repressed from consciousness and only able to re-enter consciousness in a disguised form was provided by the psychoanalytic account of sexuality. The story of psychosexual development – or how we come to acquire sexual desire for another – accounted for the split between conscious and unconscious mental processes, and provided the key to understanding why our sense of self should be divided into competing and even irreconcilable components.

THE UNCONSCIOUS

According to Freud, the unconscious was made up of those desires and wishes that arose out of the intense relationship of the child to its parents, particularly its mother. These desires are very powerful because they are both broad in outline (such as the desire to have the exclusive attention of the mother) and unmediated by a mature awareness of social reality. They become repressed (or held within the unconscious) precisely because they are so asocial and unrealistic, although this does not prevent them from trying to gain access to consciousness. It is only through becoming conscious that these wishes can be put into practice, and hence gain satisfaction. However, they are only accepted by consciousness if they are suitably disguised or if they can be expressed in socially acceptable ways. The idea of adult sexual relationships as monogamous and as guaranteeing to satisfy all the needs of both parties, for example, is one which can give expression to our unconscious desire to have the exclusive attention of a loved parent. This unconscious motive is one which gives an additional compulsion to seeking out certain kinds of relationships.

Freud gained access to the unconscious through focusing on particular mental phenomena such as dreams, slips of the tongue, forgetting and jokes. Dreams, he argued, were his royal road to the unconscious. In sleep our consciousness is withdrawn from reality or the external world, and the unconscious thought processes of our internal reality become uppermost in our thinking. In dreams unconscious desires are expressed as fulfilled, but they are also represented in such a way that they do not disturb sleep. In analysing dreams Freud discovered that the unconscious had its own kind of language, a particular mode of expression that allowed unconscious desires to become conscious. They could express themselves either through metaphor (through being like something else) or through metonomy (that is being associated with something else). Thus Freud argued that dream images either condensed a number of ideas into a particular image or that a particular symbol represented a displacement of ideas. The task of psychoanalysis was to analyse or translate the coded language of dreams in order to discover the unconscious desires they expressed. In other words, unconscious desires were knowable and we could gain an understanding of them through the process of analysis. However, in order to understand why ideas are repressed in the first place it is necessary to turn to Freud's account of sexuality.

THE STORY OF SEXUALITY

Freud argued that sexuality, initially at least, is made up of indiscriminate, infantile desires for pleasure. It is polymorphous in origin, which is to say that it has many modes of satisfaction because it emerges from sensations in different parts of the body which give pleasure. Moreover, pleasure can be achieved both actively and passively. It was this latter characteristic which led Freud to suggest that sexuality was bisexual in nature, as well as preoccupied with satisfaction rather than the person providing satisfaction. It is in the process of psychosexual development, that is the interrelated process of physical and psychological maturation, that sexuality becomes directed towards another person. However, although sexuality becomes object-directed as heterosexual or homosexual, it never loses its bisexual polymorphous qualities. Rather, apsects of our sexuality become repressed and barred from conscious acknowledgement, although the desire for their gratification remains within the unconscious and constitutes un-recognized demands upon our behaviour. Pleasure, however, can be achieved in an infinite variety of ways – some socially acceptable and others proscribed. Often the former are not always identified as sexual, making the sociological boundaries of sexuality difficult to draw. For example, conventionally sexuality is seen, rather reductively, in terms of heterosexual intercourse or even more narrowly in terms of reproductive heterosexuality. The much wider framework of psychoanalytic theory, however, allows us to identify a range of activities as expressing sexuality and giving rise to pleasure. These can include the feelings of power and control we experience driving a car, or the sense of security we derive from religious beliefs as well as the more obvious and unlimited physical pleasures of bodies. Freud argued that societies differed in how far they restricted sexual expression and he thought that European civilization was too severe a task-master of sexual pleasure, that it imposed too narrow cultural limits on forms of self-expression which in turn gave rise to psychological ill-health. The Victorians, Freud suggested, got the balance wrong, but he also argued that the contradiction between sexuality and society was an inevitable one and that society only existed through the repression of sexuality.

Freud argued that infantile desire for pleasure becomes controlled and structured in the process of acquiring sexual identity. This process of identity formation is contextualized by the infantile idea that the greatest form of pleasure for the child is to give the person it most loves and desires – that is, the mother – a baby. In other words, the very pinnacle of socially unstructured infantile desire is incestuous maternal reproductive sexuality. Such ideas about sexuality as infantile, polymorphously perverse and incestuous are certainly not easy to absorb on first encounter – and indeed Freud went so far as to suggest that if they initially did not offend and outrage, then their real import was not being considered. It is the infantile relationship to the primary love object of the mother which Freud suggests gives us the key to the nature of femininity and masculinity.

Freud's radically different conception of sexuality was, as we have said, to see it as – in the first instance – an infantile capacity for polymorphously perverse pleasure. This capacity has two sources: that derived from physical pleasure, for example when hunger is satisfied; and that derived from psychological pleasure, such as fantasies about the breast. Infancy for Freud was a period when the possibility of gaining pleasure was circumscribed by the nature of the maternal relationship. Initially the child experiences this as a symbiotic union rather than a relationship. Inevitably, however, the mother cannot always be present for the child and her absences gradually force upon the child a recognition of its dependence on – and separation from – the mother, as well as a recognition that she is the source of its pleasure. The inability to control her presence and therefore the satisfaction of its needs invokes the process of fantasy. If the child's needs are not immediately met, it can use its imagination to fantasize their satisfaction. Even when immediate needs are met, Freud argues, the child can gain pleasure through reproducing the experience of satisfaction in fantasy. It is at this point that sexuality becomes psychosexual and desire becomes something separate from need. It is at this point that the child begins to recognize that one way of controlling the presence of the mother is by acquiescing to her desires. In the infantile world of the child, the mother is what Freud called the primary love object, and is cast as an immensely powerful person for the child – a power Freud chose to call phallic – because of the way in which she controls the child's emotional, physical, pleasurable or displeasurable world. She is the one the child most desires because her presence and affection are the conditions of the child's pleasure.

In the ensuing process of physical and emotional development, the child's sense of self emerges along two axes: psychosexual and intellectual. In terms of psychosexuality the child learns that it can derive pleasure from both auto-eroticism and from becoming the person the mother wishes it to be. But also the child initiates an inquiry in to where it came from and this, Freud argued, is the very first intellectual project. Needless to say, it is an intellectual enquiry not governed by reason and logic but by sexual curiosity and infantile desire. The child establishes that babies come from people and, according to Freud, children develop their own theories about birth. The child, however, still lives in a sexually undifferentiated world and therefore does not discriminate between who can and cannot have babies. Both little girls and little boys assume that they can give the mother a baby and that they can have a baby for the mother. This implies that for children the assumption is that what the mother most desires is a child. It is the point at which children recognize that the sexes are differently implicated in reproductive sexuality, that they also finally recognize that their desire for exclusive access to the mother has to take second place to the more privileged access of the father. The father represents both the social rules of sexual access and the biological terms of reproductive sexuality. Even if no actual father is present, his presence is called up by the nature of reproduction.

This twofold recognition has different implications for girls and boys. Boys can retain their desire for the mother by transforming it into a desire for women. In this the boy is acknowledging that the father has prior access to the mother and that, if he challenges this, he may become castrated like a girl and thereby made into someone who cannot give the mother a child (that is someone who has no claims on the mother). The girl by contrast recognizes that she cannot give this privileged gift of a child to the mother, or indeed to other women. This profoundly affects the little girl's narcissistic sense of self and in surrendering the mother as her primary love object, she somewhat ambivalently transfers her affections to her father/all men as a way of getting a child and therefore becoming *like* the mother. These infantile desires for the mother become, at this crucial moment, repressed into the unconscious. This happens for different reasons for the little girl and the little boy. The girl represses her desire for the mother because for her the recognition that her homosexual relation to the mother can never be a reproductive one is too painful to acknowledge consciously. The boy represses his desire for the mother out of fear that he may become castrated if he challenges his father's superior power.

Thus both girls and boys depart from the world of non-differentiated infantile sexuality and the powerful and encompassing world of the mother. With very different psychological consequences, they accept the social rules of sexual access and the biological rules of reproductive sexuality. The differently threatening consequences of recognizing these truths are repressed and the social and cultural definitions of sexual difference accepted. Our infantile desires, although repressed and banned from consciousness, are never given up and our identities as gendered subjects are constantly threatened by unconscious desires to regain our repressed feminine and masculine selves as well as to re-enter the symbiotic union with the mother. Equally, our adherence to the normative terms of gender are an unconscious way of making sure that we are not threatened by the truth of those desires.

THE SIGNIFICANCE OF THE MOTHER

This chapter considers the particular variant of Freudian theory put forward by Nancy Chodorow in her theory of the reproduction of mothering. Chodorow's account derives from the object relations school of psychoanalysis which emphasizes the relational context of infantile development. Object relations theory rejects the ideas of an innate sexual drive as well as the idea that there are particular stages to psychological development arising out the child's physical development. Another central idea that is marginalized by this theoretical framework is that of the Oedipus complex and the role of sexual difference within it. For object relations theorists what is crucial in infantile development is the way in which the child builds up a sense of self, incorporating emotional 'objects' or parts of relationships, through which it is able to gain a sense of itself. In addition to taking into themselves aspects of other peoples' relationship to them, children can also project or externalize negative feelings which they do not wish to be responsible for. Projection and introjection are seen as the key mechanisms by which the child acquires a sense of its own identity.

What this framework makes central is the quality and type of relationship that constitutes the child's development. The emphasis of object relations theory is primarily social in that it stresses how the child integrates with, and develops through the primary emotional environment provided by the mother. As a framework it is necessarily preoccupied with the mother–child relationship and one criticism of this approach is that it marginalizes the psychic role and significance of the father. As you will see in the following chapter, there is a considerable divide between those feminists who adopt object relations theory and those who follow the much more classically Freudian account revised by Lacan. In the latter the crucial elements in the development of gendered subjectivity is the symbolic significance of the father and the role of language. Both

Lacanian and object relations theory attempt to incorporate the fundamentally social nature of the unconscious into social theory but with different consequences. Whereas the object relations approach is predominantly sociological, the Lacanian framework tends to stress the determining nature of the unconscious.

For Chodorow object relations theory allows her to incorporate questions concerning the social conditions of women's mothering, in particular the sexual division of labour, the prolonged absences of men from family life, and the very low status enjoyed by women and especially by mothers. If these material conditions were to alter, if men were to be more closely emotionally and nurturantly involved in childcare, and if women's identity included work as well as motherhood, then, she argues, the psychodynamics of gender would undoubtedly change.

The article by Joanna Ryan problematizes Chodorow's argument by rethinking her analysis of the mother–daughter relationship in terms of lesbian sexuality. She points to the way in which the women's movement created a positive cultural appreciation and validation of sexual relations between women. This allowed many heterosexual women to express their homosexuality. Given the complex nature of femininity due to its basis in the mother–daughter relationship, Ryan asks why Chodorow should see this relationship in exclusively heterosexual terms. That Chodorow does, illustrates a problem with her account of gender. This is that in using psychoanalytic theory to account for the nature of gender relations there is a tendency to analyse sexuality in normative heterosexual terms rather than as a contradictory composite of heterosexual and homosexual desires which are socially and psychically structured. Given the potentially powerful structure of desire that operates in relations between women it seems clear that feminist use of psychoanalytic theory to explain the reproduction of heterosexual gender relations is limiting it to an explanation of only half the story. Nor can psychoanalytic theory provide an explanation of heterosexuality as the dominant mode of sexual practice; it can only identify heterosexuality as one form of resolution of the Oedipus complex, but other paths may be taken and the choice is an individual one. In other words, although psychoanalytic theory has much to tell us of sexuality and the unconscious, it can only account for sexual identity theoretically via a retrospective analysis of the individual.

Article 4.1
THE PSYCHODYNAMICS OF THE FAMILY

Nancy Chodorow

Let us recall that we left the pubescent girl in a triangular situation and expressed the hope that later she would dissolve the sexually mixed triangle ... in favour of heterosexuality. This formulation was made for the sake of simplification. Actually, whether a constitutional bisexual factor contributes to the creation of such a triangle or not, this triangle can never be given up completely. The deepest and most ineradicable emotional relations with both parents share in its formation. It succeeds another relation, even older and more enduring – the relationship between mother and child, which every man or woman preserves from ... birth to ... death. It is erroneous to say that the little girl gives up her first mother relation in favour of the father. She only gradually draws him into the alliance, develops from the mother–child exclusiveness toward the triangular parent–child relation and continues the latter, just as she does the former, although in a weaker and less elemental form, all her life. Only the principal part changes; now the mother, now the father plays it. The ineradicability of affective constellations manifests itself in later repetitions.
Helene Deutsch, The Psychology of Women

A woman *is* her mother
That's the main thing
Ann Sexton, 'Housewife'

OEDIPAL ASYMMETRIES AND HETEROSEXUAL KNOTS

... According to psychoanalytic theory, heterosexual erotic orientation is a primary outcome of the Oedipus complex for both sexes. Boys and girls differ in this, however. Boys retain one primary love object throughout their boyhood. For this reason, the development of masculine heterosexual object choice is relatively continuous: 'In males the path of this development is straightforward, and the advance from the "phallic" phase does not take place in consequence of a complicated "wave of repression" but is based upon a ratification of that which already exists . . .' (Deutsch, 1925, p. 165). In theory, a boy resolves his Oedipus complex by repressing his attachment to his mother. He is therefore ready in adulthood to find a primary relationship with someone *like* his mother. When he does, the relationship is given meaning from its psychological reactivation of what was originally an intense and exclusive relationship – first an identity, then a 'dual-unity', finally a two-person relationship.

Things are not so simple for girls: 'Psychoanalytic research discovered at the very outset that the development of the infantile libido to the normal heterosexual object-choice is in women rendered difficult by certain peculiar circumstances' (Deutsch, 1925, p. 165). These 'peculiar circumstances' are universal facts of family organization. Because her first love object is a woman, a girl, in order to attain her proper heterosexual orientation, must transfer her primary object choice to her father and men. This creates asymmetry in the feminine and masculine Oedipus complex, and difficulties in the development of female sexuality, given heterosexuality as a development goal.

For girls, just as for boys, mothers are primary love objects. As a result, the structural inner object setting of female heterosexuality differs from that of males. When a girl's father does become an important primary person, it is in the context of a bisexual relational triangle. A girl's relation to him is emotionally in reaction to, interwoven and competing for primacy with, her relation to her mother. A girl usually turns to her father as an object of primary interest from the exclusivity of the relationship to her mother, but this libidinal turning to her father does not substitute for her attachment to her mother. Instead, a girl retains her pre-Oedipal tie to her mother (an intense tie involved with issues of primary identification, primary love, dependence and separation) and builds Oedipal attachments to both her mother and her father upon it. These attachments are characterized by eroticized demands for exclusivity, feelings of competition, and jealousy. She retains the internalized early relationship, including its implications for the nature of her definition of self, and internalizes these other relationships in addition to and not as replacements for it.

For girls, then, there is no absolute change of object, nor exclusive attachment to their fathers. Moreover, a father's behaviour and family role, and a girl's relationship to him, are crucial to the development of heterosexual orientation in her. But fathers are comparatively unavailable physically and emotionally. They are not present as much and are not primary caretakers, and their own training for masculinity may have led them to deny emotionality. Because of the father's lack of availability to his daughter, and because of the intensity of the mother–daughter relationship in which she participates, girls tend not to make a total transfer of affection to their fathers but to remain also involved with their mothers, and to oscillate emotionally between mother and father.

The implications of this are twofold. First, the nature of the heterosexual relationship differs for boys and girls. Most women emerge from their Oedipus complex orientated to their father and men as primary *erotic* objects, but it is clear that men tend to remain *emotionally* secondary, or at most emotionally equal, compared to the primacy and exclusivity of an Oedipal boy's emotional tie to his mother and women. Second, because the father is an additional important love object, who becomes important in the context of a relational triangle, the feminine inner object world is more complex than the masculine. This internal situation continues into adulthood and affects adult women's participation in relationships. Women, according to Deutsch, experience heterosexual relationships in a triangular context, in which men are not exclusive objects for them. The implication of her statement is confirmed by cross-cultural examination of family structure and relations between the sexes, which suggests that conjugal closeness is the exception and not the rule.

Because mother and father are not the same *kind* of parent, the nature and intensity of a child's relationship to them differ as does the relationship's degree of exclusiveness. Because children first experience the social and cognitive world as continuous with themselves and do not differentiate objects, their mother, as first caretaking figure, is not a separate person and has no separate interests. In addition, this lack of separateness is in the context of the infant's total dependence on its mother for physical and psychological survival. The internalized experience of self in the original mother-relation remains seductive and frightening: unity was bliss, yet meant the loss of self and absolute dependence. By contrast, a child has always differentiated itself from its father and known him as a separate person with separate interests. And the child has never been totally dependent on him. Her father has not posed the original narcissistic threat (the threat to basic ego integrity and boundaries) nor provided the original narcissistic unity (the original experience of oneness) to a girl. Oedipal love for the mother, then, contains both a threat to selfhood and a promise of primal unity which love for the father never does. A girl's love for her father and women's attachment to men reflect all aspects of these asymmetries.

Men cannot provide the kind of return to oneness that women can. Michael Balint argues that the return to the experience of primary love – the possibility of regressing to the infantile stage of a sense of oneness, no reality testing, and a tranquil sense of well-being in which all needs are satisfied – is a main goal of adult sexual relationships: 'This primary tendency, I shall be loved always, everywhere, in every way, my whole body, my whole being – without any criticism, without the slightest effort on my part – is the final aim of all erotic striving' (Balint, 1935, p. 50). He implies, though, that women can fulfil this need better than men, because a sexual relationship with a woman reproduces the early situation more completely and is more completely a return to the mother. Thus, males in coitus come nearest to the experience of re-fusion with the mother – 'The male comes nearest to achieving this regression during coitus: with his semen in reality, with his penis symbolically, with his whole self in phantasy' (Balint, 1956a, p. 141).

Women's participation here is dual. (Balint is presuming women's heterosexuality.) First, a woman identifies with the man penetrating her and thus experiences through identification refusion with a woman (mother). Second, she *becomes* the mother (phylogenetically the all-embracing sea, ontogenetically the womb). Thus, a woman in a heterosexual relationship cannot, like a man, recapture *as herself* her own experience of merging. She can do so only by identifying with someone who can, on the one hand, and by identifying with the person with whom she was merged on the other. The 'regressive restitution' (Balint's term) which coitus brings, then, is not complete for a woman in the way that it is for a man.

Freud (1931) speaks to the way that women seek to recapture their relationship with their mother in heterosexual relationships. He suggests that as women 'change object' from mother to father, the mother remains their primary internal object, so that they often impose on their relation to their father, and later to men, the issues which preoccupy them in their internal relation to their mother. They look in relations to men for gratifications that they want from a woman. Freud points to the common clinical discovery of a woman who has apparently taken her father as a model for her choice of husband, but whose marriage in fact repeats the conflicts and feelings of her relationship with her mother. For instance, a woman who remains ambivalently dependent on her mother, or preoccupied internally with the question of whether she is separate or not, is likely to transfer this stance and sense of self to a relationship with her husband. Or she may identify herself as a part-object of her male partner, as an extension of her father and men, rather than an extension of her mother and women.[1]

But children seek to escape from their mother as well as return to her. Fathers serve in part to break a daughter's primary unity with and dependence on her mother. For this and a number of other reasons, fathers and men are idealized (Chasseguet-Smirgel, 1964; Grunberger, 1964). A girl's father provides a last ditch escape from maternal omnipotence, so a girl cannot risk driving him away. At the same time, occupying a position of distance and ideological authority in the family, a father may be a remote figure, understood to a large extent through her mother's interpretation of his role. This makes the development of a relationship based on his real strengths and weaknesses difficult. Finally, the girl herself has not received the same kind of love from her mother as a boy has. Mothers experience daughters as one with themselves; their relationships to daughters are 'narcissistic', while those with their sons are more 'anaclitic'.

Thus, a daughter looks to her father for a sense of separateness and for the same confirmation of her specialness that her brother receives from her mother. She (and the woman she becomes) is willing to deny her father's limitations (and those of her lover or husband) as long as she feels loved. She is more able to do this because his distance means that she does not really know him. The relationship, then, because of the father's distance and importance to her, occurs largely as fantasy and idealization, and lacks the grounded reality which a boy's relation to his mother has.

These differences in the experience of self in relation to father and mother are reinforced by the different stages at which boys and girls are likely to enter the Oedipal situation. Girls remain longer in the pre-Oedipal relationship, enter the Oedipus situation later than boys, and their modes of Oedipal resolution differ. Bibring, Slater and John Whiting have suggested that in the absence of men, a mother sexualizes her relationship with her son early, so that 'Oedipal' issues of sexual attraction and connection, competition and jealousy, become fused with 'pre-Oedipal' issues of primary love and oneness. By contrast, since the girl's relationship to her father develops later, her sense of self is more firmly established. If Oedipal and pre-Oedipal issues are fused for her, this fusion is more likely to occur in relation to her mother, and not to her father. Because her sense of self is firmer, and because Oedipal love for her father is not so threatening, a girl does not 'resolve' her Oedipus complex to the same extent as a boy. This means that she grows up more concerned with both internalized and external object-relationships, while men tend to repress their Oedipal needs for love and relationship. At the same time, men often become intolerant and disparaging of those who can express needs for love, as they attempt to deny their own needs (Chasseguet-Smirgel, 1964; Grunberger, 1964).[2]

Men defend themselves against the threat posed by love, but needs for love do not disappear through repression. Their training for masculinity and repression of affective relational needs, and their primarily non-emotional and impersonal relationships in the public world make deep primary relationships with other men hard to come by.[3] Given this, it is not surprising that men tend to find themselves in heterosexual relationships.

These relationships to women derive a large part of their meaning and dynamics from the men's relation to their mothers.

But the maternal treatment described by Bibring, Slater and Whiting creates relational problems in sons. When a boy's mother has treated him as an extension of herself and at the same time as a sexual object, he learns to use his masculinity and possession of a penis as a narcissistic defence. In adulthood, he will look to relationships with women for narcissistic-phallic reassurance rather than for mutual affirmation and love. Because their sexualized pre-Oedipal attachment was encouraged, while their Oedipal-genital wishes were thwarted and threatened with punishment, men may defensively invest more exclusively in the instinctual gratifications to be gained in a sexual relationship in order to avoid risking rejection of love.

Women have not repressed affective needs. They still want love and narcissistic confirmation and may be willing to put up with limitations in their masculine lover or husband in exchange for evidence of caring and love. This can lead to the denial of more immediately felt aggressive and erotic drives. Chasseguet-Smirgel suggests that a strong sexuality requires the expression of aggressive, demanding impulses fused with erotic love impulses and idealization. To the extent that women feel conflict and fear punishmnent especially over all impulses they define as aggressive, their sexuality suffers.

As a result of the social organization of parenting, then, men operate on two levels in women's psyche. On one level, they are emotionally secondary and not exclusively loved – are not primary love objects like mothers. On another, they are idealized and experienced as needed, but are unable either to express their own emotional needs or respond to those of women. As Grunberger puts it, 'The tragedy of this situation is that the person who could give [a woman] this confirmation, her sexual partner, is precisely the one who, as we have just seen, has come to despise narcissistic needs in an effort to disengage himself from them (1964, p. 74).

[. . .]

Because women care for children, then, heterosexual symbiosis has a different 'meaning' for men and women. Freud originally noted that 'a man's love and a women's are a phase apart psychologically' (1933, p. 134). He and psychoanalytic thinkers after him point to ways in which women and men, though usually looking for intimacy with each other, do not fulfil each other's needs because of the social organization of parenting. Differences in female and male Oedipal experiences, all growing out of women's mothering, create this situation. Girls enter adulthood with a complex layering of affective ties and a rich, ongoing inner object world. Boys have a simpler Oedipal situation and more direct affective relationships, and this situation is repressed in a way that the girl's is not. The mother remains a primary internal object to the girl, so that heterosexual relationships are on the model of a non-exclusive, second relationship for her, whereas for the boy they recreate an exclusive, primary relationship.

As a result of being parented by a woman, both sexes look for a return to this emotional and physical union. A man achieves this directly through the heterosexual bond, which replicates the early mother–infant exclusivity. He is supported in this endeavour by women, who, through their own development, have remained open to relational needs, have retained an ongoing inner affective life, and have learned to deny the limitations of masculine lovers for both psychological and practical reasons.

Men both look for and fear exclusivity. Throughout their development, they have tended to repress their affective relational needs, and to develop ties based more on categorical and abstract role expectations, particularly with other males. They are likely to participate in an intimate heterosexual relationship with the ambivalence created by an intensity which one both wants and fears – demanding from women what men are at the same time afraid of receiving.

As a result of being parented by a woman and growing up heterosexual, women have different and more complex relational needs in which an exclusive relationship to a man is not enough. As noted previously, this is because women situate themselves psychologically as part of a relational triangle in which their father and men are emotionally secondary or, at most, equal to their mother and women. In addition, the relation to the man itself has difficulties. Idealization, growing out of a girl's relation to her father, involves denial of real feelings and to a certain extent an unreal relationship to men. The contradictions in women's heterosexual relationships, though, are due as much to men's problems with intimacy as to outcomes of early childhood relationships. Men grow up rejecting their own needs for love, and therefore find it difficult and threatening to meet women's emotional needs. As a result, they collude in maintaining distance from women.

THE CYCLE COMPLETED: MOTHERS AND CHILDREN

Families create children gendered, heterosexual, and ready to marry. But families organized around women's mothering and male dominance create incompatibilities in women's and men's relational needs. In particular, relationships to men are unlikely to provide for women satisfaction of the relational needs that their mothering by women and the social organization of gender have produced. The less men participate in the domestic sphere, and especially in parenting, the more this will be the case.

Women try to fulfil their need to be loved, try to complete the relational triangle, and try to re-experience the sense of dual unity they had with their mother, which the heterosexual relationship tends to fulfil for men. This situation daily reinforces what women first experienced developmentally and intrapsychically in relation to men. While they are likely to become and remain erotically heterosexual, they are encouraged both by men's difficulties with love and by their own relational history with their mothers to look elsewhere for love and emotional gratification.

One way that women fulfil these needs is through the creation and maintenance of important personal relations with other women. Cross-culturally, segregation by gender is the rule: women tend to have closer personal ties with each other than men have, and to spend more time in the company of women than they do with men. In our society, there is some sociological evidence that women's friendships are affectively richer than men's (Booth, 1972).[4] In other societies, and in most subcultures of our own, women remain involved with female relatives in adulthood.[5] Deutsch suggests further that adult female relationships sometimes express a woman's psychological participation in the relational triangle. Some women, she suggests, always need a woman rival in their relationship to a man; others need a best friend with whom they share all confidences about their heterosexual relationships. These relationships are one way of resolving and recreating the mother–daughter bond and are an expression of women's general relational capacities and definition of self in relationship.

However, deep affective relationships to women are hard to come by on a routine, daily, ongoing basis for many women. Lesbian relationships do tend to recreate mother–daughter emotions and connections (Deutsch, 1944; Wolff, 1971; Rich, 1976), but most women are heterosexual. This heterosexual preference and taboos against homosexuality, in addition to objective economic dependence on men, make the option of primary sexual bonds with other women unlikely – though more prevalent in recent years. In an earlier period, women tended to remain physically close to their own mother and sisters after marriage, and could find relationships with other women in their daily work and community. The development of industrial capitalism, however – and the increasingly physically isolated nuclear family it has produced – has made these primary relationships more rare and has turned women (and men) increasingly and exclusively to conjugal family relationships for emotional support and love.[6]

There is a second alternative, made all the more significant by the elimination of the first, which also builds both upon the nature of women's self-definition in a heterosexual relationship and upon the primary mother–child bond. As Deutsch makes clear, women's psyche consists in a layering of relational constellations. The pre-Oedipal mother–child relation and the Oedipal triangle have lasted until late in a woman's childhood, in fact throughout her development. To the extent that relations with a man gain significance for a woman, this experience is incomplete. Given the triangular situation and emotional asymmetry of her own parenting, a woman's relation to a man *requires* on the level of psychic structure a third person, since it was originally established in a triangle. A man's relation to women does not. His relation to his mother was originally established first as an identity, then as a dual unity, then as a two-person relationship, before his father ever entered the picture.

On the level of psychic structure, then, a child completes the relational triangle for a woman. Having a child, and experiencing her relation to a man in this context, enables her to reimpose intrapsychic relational structure on the social world, while at the same time resolving the generational component of her Oedipus complex as she takes a new place in the triangle – a maternal place in relation to her own child.

The mother–child relationship also recreates an even more basic relational constellation. The exclusive symbiotic mother–child relationship of a mother's own infancy reappears, a relationship which all people who have been mothered want basically to recreate. This contrasts to the situation of a man. A man often wants a child through his role-based, positional identification with his father, or his primary or personal identification with his mother. Similarly, a woman has been involved in relational identification processes with her mother, which include identifying with a mother who has come to stand to both sexes as someone with unique capacities for mothering. Yet on a less conscious, object-relational level, having a child recreates the desired mother–child exclusivity for a woman and interrupts it for a man, just as the man's father intruded into his relation to his mother.

[. . .]

For all these reasons, it seems psychologically logical to a woman to turn her marriage into a family, and to be more involved with these children (this child) than her husband. By doing so, she recreates for herself the exclusive intense primary unit which a heterosexual relationship tends to recreate for men. She recreates also her internalized asymmetrical relational triangle. These relational issues and needs predate and underlie her identifications, and come out of normal family structure regardless of explicit role training. Usually, however, this training intensifies their effects. In mothering, a woman acts also on her personal identification with a mother who parents and her own training for women's role.

This account indicates a larger structural issue regarding the way in which a woman's relation to her children recreates the psychic situation of the relationship to her mother. This relationship is recreated on two levels: most deeply and unconsciously, that of the primary mother–infant tie; and, upon this, the relationship of the bisexual triangle. Because the primary mother–infant unit is exclusive, and because oscillation in the bisexual triangle includes a constant pull back to the mother attachment, there may be a psychological contradiction for a woman between interest in and commitment to children and that to men. Insofar as a woman experiences her relationship to her child on the level of intrapsychic structure as exclusive, her relationship to a man may therefore be superfluous.

Freud points tentatively to this (to him, unwelcome) situation, in contrasting men's and women's object-love. In his essay 'On Narcissism' (1914), he claims that 'complete object-love of the attachment type is, properly speaking, characteristic of the male'. Women, by contrast, tend to love narcissistically – on one level, to want to be loved or to be largely self-sufficient; on another, to love someone as an extension of their self rather than a differentiated object. He implies here that the necessary mode of relating to infants is the normal way women love. Yet he also claims that women do attain true object-love, but only in relation to their children – who are both part of them and separate. Freud's stance here seems to be that of the excluded man viewing women's potential psychological self-sufficiency vis-à-vis *men*. This situation may be the basis of the early psychoanalytic claim that women are more narcissistic than men, since clinically it is clear that men have just as many and as serious problems of fundamental object-relatedness as do women.

[. . .]

On the level of the relational triangle also, there can be a contradiction between women's interest in children and in men. This is evident in Freud's suggestion that women oscillate psychologically between a pre-Oedipal and Oedipal stance (he says between periods of 'masculinity' and 'femininity') and that women's and men's love is a phase apart psychologically (that a woman is more likely to love her son than her husband). Deutsch points out that a man may or may not be psychologically necessary or desirable to the mother–child exclusivity. When she is oriented to the man, a woman's fantasy of having children is 'I want a child by him, *with him*'; when men are emotionally in the background, it is 'I want a *child*' (Deutsch, 1944, p. 205).

Women come to want and need primary relationships to children. These wants and needs result from wanting intense primary relationships, which men tend not to provide both because of their place in women's Oedipal constellation and because of their difficulties with intimacy. Women's desires for intense primary relationships tend not to be with other women, both because of internal and external taboos on homosexuality, and because of women's isolation from their primary female kin (especially mothers) and other women.

As they develop these wants and needs, women also develop the capacities for participating in parent–child relationships. They develop capacities for mothering. Because of the structural situation of parenting, women remain in a primary, pre-Oedipal relationship with their mother longer than men. They do not feel the need to repress or cut off the capacity for experiencing the primary identification and primary love which are the basis of parental empathy. Also, their development and Oedipal resolution do not require the ego defence against either regression or relation which characterizes masculine development. Women also tend to remain bound up in pre-Oedipal issues in relation to their own mother, so that they in fact have some unconscious investment in reactivating them. When they have a child, they are more liable than a man to do so. In each critical period of their child's development, the parent's own development conflicts and experiences of that period affect their attitudes and behaviour (Benedek, 1959). The pre-Oedipal relational stance, latent in women's normal relationship to the world and experience of self, is activated in their coming to care for an infant, encouraging their empathic identification with this infant which is the basis of maternal care.

Mothering, moreover, involves a double identification for women, both as mother *and* as child. The whole pre-Oedipal relationship has been internalized and perpetuated in a more ongoing way for women than for men. Women take both parts in it. Women have capacities for primary identification with their child through regression to primary love and empathy. Through their mother identification, they have ego capacities and the sense of responsibility which go into caring for children. In addition, women have an investment in mothering in order to make reparation to their own mother (or to get back at her). Throughout their development, moreover, women have been building layers of identification with their mothers upon the primary internalized mother–child relationship.[7]

Women develop capacities for mothering from their object-relational stance. This stance grows out of the special nature and length of their pre-Oedipal relationship to their mother; the non-absolute repression of Oedipal relationships; and their general ongoing mother–daughter preoccupation as they are growing up. It also develops because they have not formed the same defences against relationships as men. Related to this, they develop wants and needs to be mothers from their Oedipal experience and the contradictions in heterosexual love that result.

The *wants and needs* which lead women to become mothers put them in situations where their mothering *capacities* can be expressed. At the same time, women remain in conflict with their internal mother and often their real mother as well. The preoccupation with issues of separation and primary identification, the ability to recall their early relationship to their mother – precisely those capacities which enable mothering – are also those which may lead to over-identification and pseudo-empathy based on maternal projection rather than any real perception or understanding of their infant's needs. Similarly, the need for primary relationships becomes more prominent and weighted as relationships to other women become less possible and as father/husband absence grows. Though women come to mother, and to be mothers, the very capacities and commitments for mothering can be in contradiction one with the other and within themselves. Capacities which enable mothering are also precisely those which can make mothering problematic.

GENDER, PERSONALITY AND THE REPRODUCTION OF MOTHERING

In spite of the apparently close tie between women's capacities for childbearing and lactation on the one hand and their responsibilities for child care on the other, and in spite of the probable prehistoric convenience (and perhaps survival necessity) of a sexual division of labour in which women mothered, biology and instinct do not provide adequate explanations for how women come to mother. Women's mothering as a feature of social structure requires an explanation in terms of social structure. Conventional feminist and social psychological explanations for the genesis of gender roles – girls and boys are 'taught' appropriate behaviours and 'learn' appropriate feelings – are insufficient both empirically and methodologically to account for how women become mothers.

Methodologically, socialization theories rely inappropriately on individual intention. Ongoing social structures include the means for their own reproduction – in the regularized repetition of social processes, in the perpetuation of conditions which require members' participation, in the genesis of legitimating ideologies and institutions, and in the psychological as well as physical reproduction of people to perform necessary roles. Accounts of socialization help to explain the perpetuation of ideologies about gender roles. However, notions of appropriate behaviour, like coercion, cannot in themselves produce parenting. Psychological capacities and a particular object-relational stance are central and definitional to parenting in a way that they are not to many other roles and activities.

Women's mothering includes the capacities for its own reproduction. This reproduction consists in the production of women with, and men without, the particular psychological capacities and stance which go into primary parenting. Psychoanalytic theory provides us with a theory of social reproduction that explains major features of personality development and the development of psychic structure, and the differential development of gender personality in particular. Psychoanalysts argue that personality both results from and consists in the ways a child appropriates, internalizes and organizes early experiences in their family – from the fantasies they have, the defences they use, the ways they channel and redirect drives in this object-relational context. A person subsequently imposes this intrapsychic structure, and the fantasies, defences and relational modes and preoccupations which go with it, onto external social situations. This re-externalization (or mutual re-externalization) is a major constituting feature of social and interpersonal situations themselves.

Psychoanalysis, however, has not had an adequate theory of the reproduction of mothering. Because of the teleological assumption that anatomy is destiny, and that women's destiny includes primary parenting, the ontogenesis of women's mothering has been largely ignored, even while the genesis of a wide variety of related disturbances and problems has been accorded widespread clinical attention. Most psychoanalysts agree that the basis for parenting is laid for both genders in the early relationship to a primary caretaker. Beyond that, in order to explain why *women* mother, they tend to rely on vague notions of a girl's subsequent identification with her mother, which makes her and not her brother a primary parent, or on an unspecified and uninvestigated innate femaleness in girls, or on logical leaps from lactation or early vaginal sensations to caretaking abilities and commitments.

The psychoanalytic account of male and female development, when reinterpreted, gives us a developmental theory of the reproduction of women's mothering. Women's mothering reproduces itself through differing object-relational experiences and differing psychic outcomes in women and men. As a result of having been parented by a woman, women are more likely than men to seek to be mothers, that is, to relocate themselves in a primary mother–child relationship, to get gratification from the mothering relationship, and to have psychological and relational capacities for mothering.

The early relation to a primary caretaker provides in children of both genders both the basic capacity to participate in a relationship with the features of the early parent–child one, and the desire to create this intimacy. However, because women mother, the early experience and pre-Oedipal relationship differ for boys and girls. Girls retain more concern with early childhood issues in relation to their mother, and a sense of self involved with these issues. Their attachments therefore retain more pre-Oedipal aspects. The greater length and different nature of the pre-Oedipal experience, and their continuing preoccupation with the issues of this period, mean that women's sense of self is continuous with others and that they retain capacities for primary identification, both of which enable them to experience the empathy and lack of reality sense needed by a cared-for infant. In men, these qualities have been curtailed, both because they are early treated as an opposite by their mother and because their later attachment to her must be repressed. The relational basis for mothering is thus extended in women, and inhibited in men, who experience themselves as more separate and distinct from others.

The different structure of the feminine and masculine Oedipal triangle and process of Oedipal experience that results from women's mothering contributes further to gender personality differentiation and the reproduction of women's mothering. As a result of this experience, women's inner object world, and the affects and issues associated with it, are more actively sustained and more complex than men's. This means that women define and experience themselves relationally. Their heterosexual orientation is always in internal dialogue with both Oedipal and pre-Oedipal mother–child relational issues. Thus, women's heterosexuality is triangular and requires a third person – a child – for its structural and emotional completion. For men, by contrast, the heterosexual relationship alone recreates the early bond to their mother; a child interrupts it. Men, moreover, do not define themselves in relationship and have come to suppress relational capacities and repress relational needs. This prepares them to participate in the affect-denying world of alienated work, but not to fulfil women's needs for intimacy and primary relationships.

The Oedipus complex, as it emerges from the asymmetrical organization of parenting, secures a psychological taboo on parent–child incest and pushes boys and girls in the direction of extrafamilial heterosexual relationships. This is one step toward the reproduction of parenting. The creation and maintenance of the incest taboo and of heterosexuality in girls and boys are different, however. For boys, superego formation and identification with their father, rewarded by the superiority of masculinity, maintain the taboo on incest with their mother, while heterosexual orientation continues from their earliest love relation with her. For girls, creating them as heterosexual in the first place maintains the taboo. However, women's heterosexuality is not so exclusive as men's. This makes it easier for them to accept or seek a male substitute for their fathers. At the same time, in a male-dominant society, women's exclusive emotional heterosexuality is not so necessary, nor is her repression of love for her father. Men are more likely to initiate relationships, and women's economic dependence on men pushes them anyway into heterosexual marriage.

Male dominance in heterosexual couples and marriage solves the problem of women's lack of heterosexual commitment and lack of satisfaction by making women more reactive in the sexual bonding process. At the same time, contradictions in heterosexuality help to perpetuate families and parenting by ensuring that women will seek relations to children and will not find heterosexual relationships alone satisfactory. Thus, men's lack of emotional availability and women's less exclusive heterosexual commitment help ensure women's mothering.

Women's mothering, then, produces psychological self-definition and capacities appropriate to mothering in women, and curtails and inhibits these capacities and this self-definition in men. The early experience of being cared for by a woman produces a fundamental structure of expectations in women and men concerning mothers' lack of separate interests from their infants and total concern for their infants' welfare. Daughters grow up identifying with these mothers, about whom they have such expectations. This set of expectations is generalized to the assumption that women naturally take care of children of all ages and the belief that women's 'maternal' qualities can and should be extended to the non-mothering work that they do. All these results of women's mothering have ensured that women will mother infants and will take continuing responsibility for children.

The reproduction of women's mothering is the basis for the reproduction of women's location and responsibilities in the domestic sphere. This mothering, and its generalization to women's structural location in the domestic sphere, links the contemporary social organization of gender and social organization of production and contributes to the reproduction of each. That women mother is a fundamental organizational feature of the sex-gender system: it is basic to the sexual division of labour and generates a psychology and ideology of male dominance as well as an ideology about women's capacities and nature. Women, as wives and mothers, contribute as well to the daily and generational reproduction, both physical and psychological, of male workers and thus to the reproduction of capitalist production.

Women's mothering also reproduces the family as it is constituted in male-dominant society. The sexual and familial division of labour in which women mother creates a sexual division of psychic organization and orientation. It produces socially gendered women and men who enter into asymmetrical heterosexual relationships; it produces men who react to, fear and act superior to women, and who put most of their energies into the non-familial work world and do not parent. Finally, it produces women who turn their energies toward nurturing and caring for children – in turn reproducing the sexual and familial division of labour in which women mother.

Social reproduction is thus asymmetrical. Women in their domestic role reproduce men and children physically, psychologically and emotionally. Women in their domestic role as houseworkers reconstitute themselves physically on a daily basis and reproduce themselves as mothers, emotionally and psychologically, in the next generation. They thus contribute to the perpetuation of their own social roles and position in the hierarchy of gender.

Institutionalized features of family structure and the social relations of reproduction reproduce themselves. A psychoanalytic investigation shows that women's mothering capacities and commitments, and the general psychological capacities and wants which are the basis of women's emotional work, are built developmentally into feminine personality. Because women are themselves mothered by women, they grow up with the relational capacities and needs, and psychological definition of self-in-relationship, which commit them to mothering. Men, because they are mothered by women, do not. Women mother daughters who, when they become women, mother.

Notes

1   This is obviously only one side of the psychological matter. Chasseguet-Smirgel (1964), who points this out, notes that men also gain satisfaction and security from turning their all-powerful mother into a part-object attachment.

2   Chasseguet-Smirgel (1964) argues that what Freud and Brunswick (1940) call the boy's 'normal contempt' for women, and consider a standard outcome of the Oedipus complex, is a pathological and defensive reaction to the sense of inescapable maternal omnipotence rather than a direct outcome of gender differences.

3   Booth (1972) reports that women's friendships in our society are affectively richer than men's. Along the same lines, Mirra Komarovsky (1974) found that men students confided more in a special woman friend and that they maintained a front of strength with men. Moreover, those men felt at a disadvantage vis-à-vis their woman confidante, because she tended to have a number of other persons in whom she could confide.

4   This is a finding certainly confirmed by most writing from the men's liberation movement.

5   See, for cross-cultural confirmation, most ethnographies and also Rosaldo and Lamphere (1974). For contemporary capitalist society, see Booth (1972) and for concrete illustration see Bott (1957), Gans (1967), Komarovsky (1962), Stack (1974) and Young and Willmott (1957).

6   For a contemporary account of exactly this transition, see Young and Willmott (1957).

7   See Klein (1937). Barbara Deck (personal communication) pointed out to me that Klein's interpretation of a woman's participation in mothering is homologous to that described by Ferenczi (1924) and Balint (1956b) in coitus. A woman's gratification in mothering comes from identifying with her mothered infant. Similarly, she is both the receiving mother (womb) and identifies with the male penetrating her in coitus.

Panels from *Interim* by Mary Kelly, 1987

Article 4.2
PSYCHOANALYSIS AND WOMEN LOVING WOMEN

Joanna Ryan

I

In this chapter I want to look at some ways in which psychoanalysis can be helpful in understanding our sexuality. Clearly the scope of such a discussion is enormous, and I can only pick out some specific feminist uses of psychoanalysis and indicate the limits of these. I want to consider the central question of attraction in relation to the now widespread experience of change in sexual orientation from heterosexual to lesbian.

Our sexual relationships stand out in our lives as areas of felt irrationality, the focus of our strongest and most conflicting feelings. The phrase 'turned on', with its suggestions of switches and electricity, captures the seemingly absolute nature of attraction – how remote from conscious control our sexual feelings are, how forceful when they come, how total in their absence when they do not. There is often a tremendous difference in our feelings between people we feel sexual towards and those we don't, between lovers and friends, with little continuity between the two. This split, whilst experienced as quite natural, is itself part of the social formation of our sexuality, of the way in which it has been channelled, associated with some people and some emotions, and not with others. Sex is often written about as if it were an absolute and irreducible category of human experience, as if we knew without doubt what it is or isn't. But in fact this in itself is an assumption, a product of how our sexuality is formed and lived, that it should appear to have this discreteness from other forms of contact between people.

The notion of attraction has often been attacked as mystified and oppressive. There is a persisting tradition within libertarian and some feminist politics of trying to make sexual relationships less involuntary and exclusive, more rational. One means of doing this has been to blur the distinction between friends and lovers by substituting political sisters and comrades as sexual partners, in defiance of 'fancying'. Hence the sleeping rotas of some 1960s' communes, where the justification for sharing sex, if not the result, was the same as for other areas of domestic life: the creation of alternative structures which would allow different, less oppressive relationships to grow. Similarly now, there is a strong body of opinion that heterosexual women can decide to stop their sexual involvement with men and become, if not lesbian, at least more woman-identified. And some heterosexual feminists are insisting that men change their sexual inclinations, away from an obsessive focus on penetration and orgasm to one which accords more with what women might like or want. In all these instances sexuality is seen as subject to quite a degree of conscious control. The demand that it be so is posed not only as a challenge about who or what is attractive, but also about the nature of attraction itself. Does this have to remain a mysterious force in our lives?

Some people have been able to accommodate their sexuality in these ways, others have become confused, uncertain and often asexual, and yet others have remained stuck with familiar patterns of attraction and non-attraction, with varying degrees of guilt and compromise. Whilst we may disagree with the most voluntaristic politics as completely underestimating the strength, complexity and depth of our feelings, are we just to be stuck with old and mystified notions of attraction, or a complete collapse into the unconscious? What is the scope for understanding the sources of sexual attraction in a way that allows us some possibility of change and control in our lives and of opposition to prevailing norms, but which doesn't negate the reality of our emotions or result in untenable arrangements? One of the points at issue here is what does constitute the reality of our emotions. Are they as absolute and irreducible as it is often assumed? Or is the common assumption of their fixity another way in which we construct ourselves and are constructed?

We could view the process of sexual fetishism as only an extreme example of what happens 'normally'. There, the same objects or activities are needed over and over again for sexual excitement or release, with a consequent severe restriction in the kind of relationship involved (if any), and with a rigid lack of capacity for change. Parts of the body, specific acts or scenarios, clothes, etc. are substituted for whole persons, images for actual people. It is striking that massively more men than women are involved in fetishistic or 'perverse' practices of some kind – indeed most books on the subject really are about male sexuality (Stoller, 1975). And from a wider point of view the whole culture of compulsory heterosexuality seems fetishistic and suited primarily to male 'needs': women have to be of a certain shape, size, age and appearance in order to be desired; certain parts of the female body are at a premium as sexual stimuli, and certain repetitive patterns of behaviour (seductiveness, passivity) are required for the stereo-typically satisfying sexual act. The cultural imposition of norms and stereotypes of sexuality, and the hypervaluation of specific forms of attractiveness, represent an enormous restriction of our sexual potential and diversity. It excludes vast numbers of women from being seen as sexual at all, and elevates a few to impossible or untenable standards of attractiveness. With this comes a very specific oppression of women: a deep-seated self-hatred and dislike of our own bodies, a minefield of competitiveness with other women about appearance, all of which are surprisingly hard to eradicate even with the creation of alternative values and norms. It is within this context, as well as that of the immediate family, that our specific sexualities are formed.

The supposedly absolute nature of sexual attraction extends to common ideas of sexual orientation, the assumption that we have to be one or the other – homo- or heterosexual – and that there is an identity that is our real one, whatever our actual behaviour. It is clear that the construction of a discrete homosexual identity is a relatively recent development, for both sexes (McIntosh, 1968), and that this has necessitated the invention of a problematic third category, 'bisexual'. Although we cannot avoid using the terms involved (and often there are important reasons why, with a different valuation, we should do so), we should not adopt these categories uncritically, especially as regards the assumptions involved about sexual identity and attraction.

One of the major achievements of the women's movement has been its facilitation of sexual relationships between women. It is important that we try to understand this transformation, not only for its personal and political importance, but also because it can clarify our ideas about how sexuality is formed more generally. It certainly is not sufficient to see the process of change as only one of political choice, even though this may be a contributing factor. We have as well to look at the deeper emotional changes involved, and the basis on which our previous heterosexuality was constructed. Many psychological and psychoanalytic theories, including some feminist ones (Person, 1980), would predict that such an extensive change of sexual orientation as has occurred through the women's movement would not be possible or would only be 'superficial', and behaviourist attempts to condition adults (always, of course, into heterosexuality) have not been conspicuously successful.

The phrase most often used by feminists to describe this process is 'coming out'. Whilst this contains the suggestive imagery of blooming and flowering, and of needing the ground and the sun to do so, it also carries the implication, sometimes explicit sometimes not, of revealing previously hidden and unknown identities, our real or true selves. The enormous sense of self-discovery and self-realization that can accompany a long denied acknowledgement of sexual attraction to other women is not to be ignored or underrated: nor, even now, the courage required to do so. However, to describe this as the discovery of one's real identity begs too many questions about the processes involved and what was experienced beforehand. Not only does it imply a fixed (albeit hidden) identity of one or the other kind, it also is in danger of dismissing past engagement with heterosexuality as false consciousness, an unknowing or unwilling compliance, certainly not one's real self. For women with periods of substantial heterosexuality this problem is particularly acute: however painful and unsatisfactory these relationships may have been, they cannot be disowned. To do so is to deny a part of ourselves, the needs and hopes invested, however mistakenly, in such relationships, which may well carry over into present lesbian ones.

There is, though, a problem about how to describe the change involved, without it seeming chameleon-like and mysterious on the one hand, or excessively rational on the other. We need a way of sufficiently validating the enormous leap involved without losing all sense of continuity within ourselves. Whereas there *is* a complete discontinuity in lesbian and heterosexual existence in terms of social acceptability, discrimination and the possibilities for self-disclosure, with all that this means for any one woman, it does not have to be a political cop-out to consider the substantial continuities that do exist, at least for some women, in the primary emotions involved – love, dependency, jealousy, trust, for example.

Psychoanalysis as a whole does not have much to say about lesbianism that is unpejorative or illuminating, but it does contain a form of understanding that is at least adequate to the complexity of our sexual feelings, and which can contribute to our understanding of what is involved in such a change of sexual relationships.

II

Psychoanalysis is far from being one unified body of theory and practice, and since Freud it has developed into many distinct schools of thought. These developments have taken place in different ways: as a result of clinical and therapeutic practice in different settings, and through the introduction of new concepts and theoretical developments. The psychoanalysis that has been introduced into the women's movement represents two very different traditions and two very different sets of interest: Freudo–Lacanian theoretical writings about the construction of femininity and female identity, and the use of post-Kleinian, 'object-relations' theory in feminist therapy and writings about this. Here I shall consider some specific uses of object-relations theory, as it has been written about in the women's movement, without attempting to discuss the differences between the two approaches.

Feminist therapy has developed from quite pragmatic origins. It has had to tread a complex methodological and political path in understanding how what is social creates the individual, and what the limits of therapy are. It is no accident that feminist psychoanalytic therapy, as well as some more practical Marxist approaches (Hoggett and Holland, 1978), have turned to object-relations theory in attempting this. This branch of psychoanalysis, associated originally with Balint, Fairbairn, Guntrip and Winnicott, contains a decisive break with certain aspects of Freudian theory, with its inherent biologism, its notions of instinct and gratification, and its anatomically-based conceptions of sexuality. It contains a more inherently social view of psychological development, seeing individuals as formed in relation to, and seeking connection with, others. It replaces the notion of libidinal stages with an account of the gradual differentiation of the self, through the formation of internal 'objects' – reflections of our experience of real persons from earliest infancy which then form and structure our later relationships. I am not claiming that this school of thought is uncontentious for feminists – its perspective on mothering, for example, is very problematic – but feminist development of it has been extremely fruitful, particularly in its emphasis on the early mother–daughter relationship and the development of a sense of self within this.

Whilst disputing the Freudian notion of sexuality or libido as central to mental life, object-relations theory does not really contain a theory of sexuality as such. Instead sexuality is seen as stemming from the whole development of the personality rather than as determining it, and the goal of sexual activity is viewed as object rather than pleasure seeking. Recent feminist development of object relations theory contains as much of a theory of sexuality and sexual identity as is to be found in previous writings.

III

E.S. Person (1980) argues that sexuality expresses many aspects of personality and motivation, originating in both infantile and later experiences, and varying between individuals as to its role and importance in their lives. She also argues for the critical importance of early tactile experience in mediating the relationship between infant and caretaker, and assumes that later sexuality develops out of this early sensuality: 'Because sensual pleasure is the vehicle of object relations in the real world, sexuality expresses an enormous variety of motives, predominantly dependent or hostile, and the force of sexuality exists precisely because sexuality is linked to other motives.' In particular, because of the real dependence of a helpless child on a relatively powerful adult, 'it is unlikely that sexuality will ever be completely free of submission–dominance connotations.'

Chodorow (1978), in her far-reaching book, assumes that a main goal of adult sexuality is a return to a kind of 'oneness' or merging with the other. In this she is following Balint's notion of primary love and the attempts of adults to recapture it: 'This primary tendency, I shall be loved always, everywhere, in every way, my whole body, my whole being – without any criticism, without the slightest effort on my part – is the final aim of all erotic striving' (Balint, 1935). Sexual intercourse, according to Annie Reich, is the 'temporary relinquishment of the separating boundaries' (quoted in Balint, 1968), or, according to Alice Balint (1939), 'the situation in which the reciprocal interdependence as experienced in early childhood is recreated.' Eichenbaum and Orbach (1982) express a similar idea: 'Because adult sexuality echoes aspects of mother–infant pre-verbal sensuality in its very unique communication, sexuality and merger may stir up deeply resonant early physical experience before there was a definite sense of self and before language'.

Merging with another is also described in non-psychoanalytic writings, though more as a peak of sexual experience than a common occurrence, and not as an echo of childhood experience. The Hite investigation (1976) included questions on why sexual intercourse was important to women, and many of the answers referred not just to closeness and intimacy, but also to various forms of merging: 'complete contact', 'breaking down barriers between self and others', 'we are one', 'becoming one in love', 'ultimate human closeness where a person can express and understand more than the mind can conceive of'. (Other themes mentioned were: reassurance of being loved, becoming desirable, feeling like a woman, giving pleasure, feeling needed and special.) It is as well to remember that most sexual intercourse does not approximate to these descriptions of merging: feeling disconnected from oneself or the other person, ambivalent, alienated, or only in contact sporadically, are also frequent experiences which may well be accompanied by other forms of satisfaction and pleasure apart from merging (conquest, reassurance, for example).

The idea that adult sexual activity can stir up infantile feelings in adults is basic to any psychoanalytic approach. Whilst problematic in some ways (because it is not entirely clear what is meant or why it should happen), it does point to some common predicaments in sexual relationships. That infants first of all experience themselves as totally merged with their mother (or other primary person) and then gradually differentiate separating boundaries is now a common conception. The symbiosis of early infancy is very different for infant and mother. For the infant it is a reflection of its limited consciousness and actual total dependence, without regard for the mother as a separate person with her own interests. Mother-love, on the other hand, involves an often overwhelming sense of 'reality' as regards concern for the interests of the child, to an extent that can become self-loss.

The re-experiencing of infantile states in sexual relationships is described above as though it was a relatively safe and satisfying experience, if hard to achieve. In fact, this 'merging' can only be partial and temporary (whereas the infantile state is total and timeless), since we actually are adults and retain some awareness of this and our capacity to return to our adult state should we desire to do so. And frequently it is painful and full of conflict, partly because we cannot actually become infants, and partly because of all the unmet needs, defences and fantasies stimulated by just this possibility – the craving for obliteration that Lynne Segal [in Article 3.2] describes . . . [for example]. It seems it is the emotions associated with the infantile state that are stirred up so strongly rather than the state itself. The other person is felt as all-powerful, the self as needy, exposed and vulnerable (or sometimes the other way round). How acceptable such feelings are, how much trust or despair they evoke about being loved, depend on each person's history and current situation. Further, in adult–adult relationships we are also trying to be adults: both in reaction to our own child-like feelings of dependency and vulnerability, which may be too threatening, and also to care for the other person, both as adult and as child.

Despite these difficulties there are some interesting implications that have been drawn about this notion of merger. The first, described by Eichenbaum and Orbach (1982), is that sexual connection can bring with it a fear of loss of self, and that this is particularly acute for women given the difficulties they have with developing a secure and separate sense of self as children. They describe women as either overwhelmed by sexual merger or as unable to 'let go' emotionally and physically, both consequences of an unclear sense of self and the false boundaries developed to cope with it. They maintain that in order to let go fully, a defined sense of self is needed to return to, which thereby makes the experience not like an infantile state at all. Such fear of loss of self may keep women removed from sexual relations altogether or participating in them in a limited way: the result of either conscious or unconscious choices.

The implication that Chodorow (1978) draws is that heterosexual intercourse reproduces the infantile situation much more nearly for a man than for a woman, given the usual gender division of parenting: 'Men cannot provide the kind of return to oneness that women can.' Instead men come nearer to an experience of fusion with the mother in heterosexual sex than women can do, both because of the historic situation of female mothering and the fantasies and emotions associated with it, and also because of men's actual inabilities to be sensitive, caring and containing, to 'mother' in short. This creates an unequal situation in heterosexual relationships, where women can only recreate the experience of oneness at secondhand – either by identifying with the man's experience of fusion with her, or by becoming the mother to the man (child). Both are ways in which women can fail to experience either themselves as centre stage, or the great lack involved in this. The implication that Chodorow rather obviously does not draw is the absence of these particular structural inequalities from lesbian relationships, and the emotional possibilities that this opens out.

'Merging' is only one thread amongst many in sexual relationships. Loaded as it is with notions of caring and infancy, it does not convey anything very specifically erotic: for this we have to turn to discussions of sexual orientation.

IV

A strength of most psychoanalytic accounts is that they do not see a girl's pathway to heterosexuality as either straightforward or inevitable. Chodorow particularly, in that she is trying to break from all ideas of reproductive instinct or innate heterosexuality, emphasizes the complex and highly contingent developmental processes that are involved and how heterosexuality is never established without considerable pain and ambivalence, conscious and unconscious. Her focus, like much of psychoanalytic theory, is the so-called 'change of object' that girls have to effect in order to become heterosexual, given that their first and most powerful experience of love and physical care is with a woman, that is homosexual. To become heterosexual as an adult a girl has to transfer her primary affections to someone of a different sex, a boy only to a different member of the same sex. There are many different psychoanalytic versions of this transfer, but what is widely recognized is its problematic nature, and also how incompletely, at an internal level, it ever happens.

Chodorow sees the nature of a girl's early relationship with her mother as motivating her to look elsewhere for a primary person other than the mother, and argues that the roots of eventual heterosexuality lie in the early mother–daughter relationship. She describes in some detail what she thinks happens in this early relationship, drawing on both psychoanalytic and observational literature, and contrasting it with the mother–son relationship. She argues that mothers relate to their daughters with a greater sense of symbiosis and identification than they do to their sons, to the extent that daughters may be felt as extensions of or identical to the mother. Eichenbaum and Orbach, although they have a less overridingly functionalist account than Chodorow of the effects of social roles, also emphasize the importance of gender similarity in creating identification between mother and daughter. Both approaches concur in how this poses specific difficulties for girls in differentiating and separating themselves as individuals, and how these issues become connected to ones of loss of love and rejection.

Maternal identification does not guarantee that a daughter will feel adequately loved – quite the opposite is often the case, since, as Eichenbaum and Orbach describe, the identification is based on the culturally devalued attribute of femaleness and also mothers may perceive in their daughters, or project onto them, all the attributes of themselves that they least like (including their femaleness). Given the massive cultural preference for boys, it is hardly surprising that one common experience of women is of being inadquately loved and certainly less so than their brothers.

Chodorow adds to her account the tendency of mothers right from birth to sexualize their relationship with their sons but not with their daughters. Quite what this sexualization of mother–son relationships consists of is not so clear, although she describes how sons become emotional substitutes for relatively absent husbands. Nor is it clear why Chodorow is so categorical about the absence of any sexualization between mother and daughter. For one thing this differentiation assumes (which Chodorow acknowledges) the mother's exclusive heterosexuality and that this applies across the board to infants. Secondly it underplays any element of physical sensuality between mothers and daughters, which often, as Eichenbaum and Orbach point out, is an important aspect of women's memories of their mothers, but one which is largely ignored and devalued on all sides. They tend rather to emphasize the physical and erotic nature of the involvement of mothers with their daughters, but describe how this is curtailed, contained and cut off. The other aspect of sexualization between mother and daughter that they emphasize is not with the daughter as possible object of the mother's feelings, but as similar subject, in which a mother's feelings about herself, her body and sexuality in general are transmitted to a daughter with strong undercurrents of anxiety, approval and disapproval.

Chodorow argues that a girl's 'change of object' rests on these prior developments, and is motivated by a need to get away emotionally from the mother, a form of defence against even greater primary identification and dependence. The father or other parent-figure, regardless of gender or any other attribute, becomes a symbol of independence, of separation from the mother. 'The turn to the father . . . whatever its sexual meaning, also concerns emotional issues of self and other.' This underlines how non-gender processes (dependence, separation) become related to gender through the typical parenting practices of our society where women are primary and men secondary parents. As well, the girl's very love for her mother may be a problem for her; if she feels inadequately loved and not preferred, she may look for a kind of special love from her father she cannot get from her mother. And to this we may add, as do Eichenbaum and Orbach, and many writers before them, the girl's attempts to reject the inferiority and powerlessness of women, and acquire the power that men have in the world, as personified in her father.

Chodorow also describes the father's role in encouraging his daughter to look elsewhere than her mother to fulfil some of these needs, and, crucially for her account, describes this encouragement as 'sexualized in tone', which is where the father's gender is important. This allegedly consists in the father not only encouraging the girl in role-appropriate behaviour but also making her in some way an object of his sexual interest – encouraging flirtatious and seductive behaviour but not making himself actually available sexually (though of course this does happen much more often than is generally supposed). Eichenbaum and Orbach emphasize how mothers actively push their daughters in the direction of their fathers, or men in general, as sources of emotional involvement, but at the same time convey the disappointments and frustrations of such relationships.

Along with many other writers, Chodorow emphasizes that this 'turn to the father' is seldom absolute, girls remain strongly attached (internally if not externally) to their mothers, and fathers never become emotionally so dominant. The typically late and insubstantial role they actually play in a child's life may mean they are the target of much idealization and, as Eichenbaum and Orbach recount, bitterness.

In her account of adulthood Chodorow distinguishes three components: conscious heterosexual erotic orientation to men in general; heterosexual love or emotional attachment to a man with whom there is sexual involvement; and non-sexual emotional attachments; thus propounding a split between eroticism and emotional attachment. She views women as 'getting' the first from their fathers, who are seen as 'activating' genital sexuality but not the other two components because of their unavailability as satisfying love objects in most families. We are left with a view of women as pushed and pulled out of their original homosexual intimacy into an ambivalent and very incomplete heterosexuality, where men may be the exclusive and primary erotic objects but are for the most part emotionally secondary to women: 'a girl never gives up her mother as an internal and external love object, even if she does become heterosexual.'

Chodorow makes a girl's relationship to her father crucial to her eventual heterosexuality, albeit in the context of her prior relationship to her mother. She leaves undiscussed what happens if the father is not present, or does not behave in the way described. Her notion that fathers 'activate' genital sexuality is extremely problematic: it assumes a separate category of the sexual, defined in terms of eventual orientation, that comes only via the father. A girl's pre-existing sexuality, and erotic feelings between her and her mother, are unmentioned or denied. Despite her intention to avoid any form of biological determinism, Chodorow still invokes the 'broadening of innate sex drives' as one contributing factor in the girl's interest in her father, to fill this gap in her account.

What Chodorow leaves us with in terms of heterosexuality is a deep split between eroticism and emotional attachment, explicable in terms of the fact that sexuality is developed not in relation to the person with whom the deepest attachment is formed, but with one who is relatively unavailable for a close and caring relationship. Thus eroticism and emotional unavailability are closely connected, and men (for other reasons as well) are frequently extremely unsatisfactory love objects for women. Certainly this has been one of the collective realizations of the women's movement.

V

Chodorow provides us with a vivid account of the fertile emotional ground on which relationships between women can grow. Her account makes the attainment of heterosexuality seem at once inevitable and profoundly precarious, never achieved without major ambivalence and built upon primary feelings of attachment to women. Heterosexuality is seen to involve as much a rejection and denial of attachment to women, in the form of the mother, as a positive attachment to men. In this sense heterosexuality is a defence against homosexuality, at both a personal and a social level. The early need to separate and individuate from a primary parent figure, so often a woman, to attain some measure of independence and selfhood, interacts with the cultural disparagement of women and the hypervaluation of men as this is mediated both via the mother–daughter relationship, and in many other ways. The fear and shame that most women can experience about sexually loving other women is as much witness to the desire to do so as it is to the social stigma and personal cost involved.

What is extraordinary is that Chodorow does not herself consider the implications of her arguments for the possibility of sexual relationships between women – extraordinary because she is so insistent on the persistent importance of women in women's emotional lives, and the problematic and contradictory nature of sexual relationships with men. Her practical conclusions all concern the transforming of men to become primary parental figures and more satisfactory love objects for women, rather than the facilitation of lesbian relationships, which she virtually ignores. Her questionable account of the mother–daughter relationship as basically asexual (compared to father–daughter, or mother–son) supports this bias, given her overall framework in which sexuality is seen as 'coming from' one or other parental relationship. Though it can be very helpful to look at adult sexuality in terms of the sensual and erotic nature of particular parental relationships, and though the idea that some of these are more or differently sexualized than others has considerable meaning, we cannot let the whole understanding of where our sexuality 'comes from' rest on these ideas. To do so is to create an account that is too closed and too inevitable. Chodorow, despite her insistence on the complexity and ambivalence with which social roles are internalized via parent–child relationships, does not allow enough space for the mass of other influences that can shape sexuality (peer group pressure, the media, for example) particularly during adolescence and later. The contradictory nature of our expectations and experience which has often been the impetus for feminism; the fact that we do change from generation to generation and do not only reproduce our mothers' oppression, is as much in need of explanation as is the internalization of patriarchal ideology. What the women's movement has shown is how powerful later experiences can be, given the rich emotional ground that Chodorow describes. It has set out to counter the cultural disparagement of women, both as this exists in the world at large and within and between ourselves, and has thereby facilitated all kinds of relationship between women that would not have been possible before, both sexual and otherwise. It has also prompted an enormous re-evaluation of our mothers, and our relationships with them.

It has always been considered pejorative to consider lesbian relationships in terms of mother-love, and not surprisingly considering the use that has been made of this: the Freudo-medical stigmatizing of lesbianism as immature and hence only partially satisfactory and to be grown out of: and Wolff's (1971) ambivalent interpretation of lesbian relationships as basically 'incest' with the mother – ambivalent because incest is a pathologizing term, and because, despite her considerable empathy, she can only see lesbians as a stigmatized group with ultimately barren relationships. The imposition of heterosexuality is seen as its starkest: what men are allowed in terms of suitably displaced union with the mother is disallowed to women and made taboo. There has also been the argument amongst feminists that for too long women have been 'mother' to men – why should we now wish to be mothers to each other with all the connotations of powerlessness and dreaded omnipotence that this conveys? However, precisely such emotions are involved in our sexual relationships, as we have seen, and often they are even more overwhelming with women than with men, just because of where they 'come from'. Perhaps what we can do now is recognize the threads in our adult relationships that connect with our earliest homosexual affections without the necessity of defending ourselves against yet another invalidation of lesbian relationships, and without denying either the sexuality or the ambivalence involved.

Acknowledgements

I would like to thank Sheila Ernst, Sue Cartledge and Lynne Segal for many helpful comments.

5
LANGUAGE AND DIFFERENCE

Language has always been an area of concern for feminism. From the earliest days of the women's liberation movement, women took issue with the sexist language used to describe and address women in superficial and derogatory ways. They demanded to be called *women* and not dolly bird, bimbo, darling, slut or any of the other sexist terms in the vast, derisory vocabulary naming women. They also contested the language of intuitiveness, passivity and maternal instinct which conveyed the idea of women's essential nature. Feminists attempted to change the position of women by changing the language which defined them. In challenging the prevailing definitions of women and taking issue with the language of sexual stereotypes, a new space was created from which to understand women.

The knowledge about women that emerged from this seemed, initially at least, straightforward enough. Women had been negatively represented and their experience denied. But this seemingly incontrovertible truth about women and language was a deceptively simple one. It begged many questions, such as how we understand the process of representation, the relationship between language and experience, and why 'woman' so consistently signifies inferiority, as well as the negative of 'man'. These questions are explored in this chapter.

LANGUAGE AND DOMINATION

Feminist rejection of the dominant cultural meanings of femininity was initially greeted with a mixture of surprise and hostility. Women were told that in objecting to sexist language they lacked a sense of humour, that they took themselves too seriously, that they took offence where none was intended, and worst of all that their objections spoilt what was just a bit of harmless fun. Feminists, however, argued that they had no wish to be identified through the sexual banter and innuendo that seemed to define and socially delimit women to the status of sexual object.

In challenging the language of sexism, feminism created a new language with which to talk about the subordinate position of women. The term sexism itself was produced by feminism, as were sexual politics, oppression, sexual objectification, domination/subordination, male chauvinism and sisterhood. This critical language allowed women to distance themselves from sexist language and to attempt to create a more positive identity for women. The hope was that this would develop from a refusal to identify with the negative representations of femininity. Women would thus claim their status as persons, as people capable of self-definition, as subjects and not objects. This early confrontation with sexist language did have a significant cultural impact, and it is far less common today than twenty years ago to hear women referred to in sexualized and derogatory ways. Nonetheless the project of disengaging from, and transforming, the dominant meanings of feminity proved to be far more difficult than was initially thought.

Feminists soon recognized that the issues of language went beyond those of sexist conventions in modes of address and forms of expression. They found, within language, an underlying structure of bias against women. There are, for example, no words to describe a strong, independent woman although there are hundreds which refer to women in sexually derisory ways. This situation is, moreover, exactly reversed for men, so much so that the term 'man' itself signifies strength and independence. This imbalance between positive and negative ways of representing women is compounded by another discriminatory process in which gender-neutral terms are both devalued and sexualized when they refer to women: the word 'tramp', for example, has a sexual connotation if used in relation to a woman but simply means vagrant if applied to a man. Similarly the word 'professional' has a variety of interpretations depending on the gender to which it applies. Just think for a moment of the different meaning conveyed by 'He's a professional' and 'She's a professional'. When referring to men the expression is utterly unambiguous, but referring to women it conveys an ambiguity in which the sexual meaning is the more dominant. Even when the social context establishes the precise meaning as non sexual, the expression still reverberates with sexual innuendo. On the other hand when we refer to women professionals 'proper' it is often necessary to specify their gender as a form of qualification. We speak of *women* doctors or *female* surgeons because the assumption is that professional implies male. By contrast another gender-neutral term – prostitute – is implicitly seen as female so that it is necessary to say male prostitute to avoid the assumption that a woman is being referred to.

Much of the discrimination in language can be understood as an effect of who creates meaning. Men have long pronounced on linguistic rules and conventions, and women have long been excluded from those religious, educational and political institutions whose job it was to establish meaning and define social order. The term 'man' was originally a synonym for 'human being'; it has through time narrowed to mean 'adult male', but at the same time we are told (by men) that it continues to be a generic term referring to all humanity, even though the dominant usage clearly renders women invisible in the generic sense. Historically, men have had great power to define and give meaning to social reality, to order it according to their particular way of viewing the world. Consequently, the experience of women has been represented from a (male) position outside that experience. In her analysis of what she calls 'man-made language', Dale Spender (1980) argues that the 'politics of naming' is patriarchal, and that sexist and discriminatory language is the idiom of male power. Women experience themselves through the negative medium of a language which inferiorizes them. For Spender, women must appropriate their own power to define, at the same time as disengaging from the deeply entrenched consciousness of oppression and subordination.

THE SUBJECT OF EXPERIENCE

The difficulty with accounts such as Spender's which stress the linguistic power of men is that whilst they recognize the role of language in influencing consciousness, they fail to explore the way in which language articulates subjective as well as social meaning. Women may reject the sexist implications of being labelled attractive or desirable but at the same time experience pleasure in being seen in this way. Women may be unconsciously flattered by such identifications. Consciousness is not just about will-power, choice and rationality – the classic characteristics of 'the (male) individual' of liberal philosophy, it is also about pleasure and irrationality. To see language as simply communicating, in however distorted a manner, the experience of women, is to see experience as prior to language. But women are born into a pre-existing world of meaning which shapes their experience of femininity through defining, among other things, the meaning of sexual difference. This suggests that rather than language distorting women's *real* experience as women, it subjects us to particular kinds of experience through structuring and ordering reality. Although Spender's argument is a powerful one, its framework, in taking women's experience as given, acts as a brake to exploring further the interrelation of language and subjectivity.

DIFFERENCE AND SUBJECTIVITY

Other feminists have looked at the question of language and difference in terms of whether women and men acquire and use language differently. Numerous studies have shown that girls have a greater facility for language than boys and for a long time this was seen as an innate sexual characteristic. Against such biologically reductionist arguments, sociolinguists suggest that the gender pattern of language acquisition can be explained by the social environment provided by the mother, and the way she may (or may not) relate to girls and boys differently. Moreover, evidence suggests that there is a growing convergence in the language facility of girls and boys. One explanation of this could be changes in the way women relate to daughters and sons, as well as changes in the importance of mothering for women's identity. (This research echoes the work of Chodorow and her claims that women mother girls and boys differently, and that any changes in these practices would in turn affect the nature of masculinity and femininity.) This research suggests that the processes of gender and language acquisition intersect in ways that may have different consequences for girls and boys.

Another study of the different ways in which women and men use language was the research of Lakoff (1975) who found that, notwithstanding little girls' superior facility for language, *women were less authoritative than men* in their use of language, and lacked the conviction and seriousness that is conveyed in men's use of language. Considerable debate exists as to how we should best understand this difference, but clearly it implies that our use of language has emotional as well as semantic meaning. Other studies have shown, however, that this supposedly salient characteristic of diffidence in women's use of language does not appear in contexts where only women are present. In such situations it was found that women spoke as equals. This alerts us to the fact that women can occupy different positions in language – that there is more than one feminine 'I', more than one mode of identification – and that therefore any notion of an essential self is problematic.

The question of how and why women and men identify with language differently, and how this influences their respective relationships to the construction of social meaning, and to social and sexual power, is an extremely important one for feminism. The work of the French psychoanalyst Jacques Lacan is relevant here, because he argues that a conceptual grasp of sexual difference is a necessary precondition for a child to take up a subject position within language. For Lacan it is only when we recognize the symbolic significance of sexual difference that we fully acquire the facility to use language. Many of these issues are explored in the first article in this chapter. Rosalind Minsky's account of Lacanian psychoanalytic theory outlines this theoretical framework and suggests that it allows feminists to answer some of these questions. Lacan argues that social meaning and unconscious meaning intersect at the point when we accept our identity as gendered human beings. In bringing together the social and the psychoanalytic Lacan proposes a way out of the seemingly irreconcilable positions which understand either society as a product of the unconscious, or the unconscious as a product of society. In Lacanian theory both the psychoanalytic and the sociological are significant. It is this theoretical synthesis, Minsky suggests, which feminism must make use of, despite the fact that it presents us with uncomfortable problems about femininity and language.

Although Lacan rescues Freud's account of sexuality from biological determinism by stressing the importance of language in the formation of subjectivity, his account of the unconscious, the symbolic dimension of language, and the construction of meaning was certainly not formulated with any regard for the theoretical or political concerns of feminism. On the contrary, Lacan was even moved on occasion to echo the fatalistic and conservative views of Freud on the question of femininity. Neither were the attempts by feminists to revise or extend Lacanian theory greeted with any spirit of intellectual generosity by Lacan, and indeed some radical feminist psychoanalysts were summarily expelled from the Lacanian school for their feminist heresies. We should not however be dissuaded from considering the merits of Lacanian theory because of this antipathy to the concerns of feminism. Lacan has much to tell us about the meaning of sexuality and the sexuality of meaning, both of central importance to feminism. As you will see in the next chapter, Lacanian theory is not without its critics. What is most contested is that the meaning of femininity and masculinity is fixed in the unconscious.

The question of sexuality and the unconscious is considered from a completely different vantage point in the second article in this chapter. In reflecting on her diverse experience of psycho-analysis, Sarah Maguire shows how both social and unconscious identifications can mould and influence our sexuality. She discusses the kinds of sexual identifications feminism allowed and the different identifications that were invoked for her within the analytic relationship. She poses the question of sexual identity in an interesting and provocative way but without the fatalism of Lacan's account of femininity.

Her account is also concerned more specifically with the language of the unconscious, and how it is expressed through neurotic or hysterical symptoms, through slips of the tongue, or through resistances to certain ideas and relationships. She explains the complex and uncomfortable process of learning to translate the language of the unconscious and deal with the emotional reality it is articulating. She echoes Rosalind Minsky's view that knowledge which allows us to understand our sexuality and unconscious motivations is empowering of women. Sarah Maguire also agrees that in spite of the androcentric – or male-centred – tradition within psychoanalysis, it is important not to lose the insights it can bring to feminist knowledge and understanding.

The final article in this chapter looks at the language of visual representations of femininity, as critically portrayed in the work of the American artist Cindy Sherman. Her work challenges the idea of an essential femininity by showing that any woman – in this case the artist herself – can occupy all the disparate representations of femininity, precisely *because* there is no essence to womankind. What Sherman is saying is that our subjectivity is fragmented and contradictory, not unified and coherent in its essentials. Sexuality can be represented in many different guises, and how and why we choose to represent ourselves in particular ways is a complex question. Sarah Maguire investigated the unconscious dimension of this complexity. Clearly there are other considerations such as the dominant modes of representation and the power available to women to transgress or acquiesce to these. There is also the question of the desire to represent sexuality in certain ways and where we locate the source of that desire. These are questions which will be taken up further in Chapter 6.

Article 5.1
LACAN
Rosalind Minsky

What is new in Lacan's theory is his strikingly innovative and radical version of Freud's theories within the context of the discoveries of modern linguistics; these were unavailable to Freud, even though Lacan argues that most of these developments were latent within the broad sweep of Freud's work. However, before looking at what Lacan has to say about language, let's begin at the beginning with the very young baby and with Lacan's most accessible idea.

LANGUAGE AND CONSCIOUSNESS

As Freud first suggested, at the earliest stage of its life the baby is unable to distinguish between itself and other objects in the external world. The baby lacks a sense of self, any defined sense of a centre, and 'imagines' itself to exist in the objects in its environment. In this early period of total dependence on the mother as its main object, the baby lives in an undifferentiated and symbiotic relationship with the mother's body so that it never knows who is who, or who is dependent on whom.

Melanie Klein, a second generation Freudian, worked with very young children, and her work gives us some of the passionate flavour of this period when the baby seems to experience alternating states of love and hate. When it is full and satisfied by the mother, it experiences her and itself as good, psychically full and loves and idealizes her. When it feels frustrated and empty, it experiences itself as 'bad', and in danger of psychic disintegration. To overcome this danger to the survival of its fragile sense of self, the baby splits off its bad feelings and projects them onto its mother who is then experienced as attacking rather than as loving. The baby, like the adult who 'projects' in later life, is actually suffering from a paranoid fantasy: it feels itself under attack from its own externalized 'split-off' feelings of hatred and envy now embodied by the mother – its psychic 'other half'. As an adult, suddenly being angry with someone who is close to us when we are feeling very vulnerable harks back to this very early period of infancy. Being 'in love', and the sense of euphoria it produces, also refer back to the baby's earliest feelings of 'fullness' and love when it experienced the mother's breast as satisfying and fulfilling.

For Lacan this very early infant world is rather like a kind of soup of ingredients for a later identity: fantasies of love and hate circulating around the mother's body; fantasies of fragmentation, inchoate, inexpressible emotions and lack of boundaries; a world which for the baby seems to be an unpredictable mixture of heaven and hell, plentitude and emptiness. But into his hotbed of raw emotion and fantasy Lacan introduces the idea of the beginnings of a sense of identity – of being something separate from the mother. He uses the metaphor of a mirror to describe how the baby, at around the age of six months, first comes to perceive itself as a 'self' – through an integrated coherent image of itself in the mirror. The child who actually experiences itself as physically uncoordinated and overwhelmed by emotion and fantasies over which it has no control – in fact as 'all over the place' both physically and psychically – suddenly finds reflecting back from the mirror a highly satisfactory and seductive image of itself as a coherent whole – a thing with edges. At this moment the chaotic, unintelligible being the baby up to then experienced itself as, has been magically, mythically transformed into a unified whole. But, of course, the baby's idea of itself is still of a very blurred, undefined and imaginary kind: the mirror image of the baby both is and isn't the baby; at the same time the baby is both subject and object. But this experience is the baby's first encounter with a process of constructing itself – its identity – a sense of being centred on its own body, and Lacan argues that this taking of an identity from outside will form the basis of all its other identifications. The baby narcissistically arrives at some kind of sense of 'I' only by finding an 'I' reflected back by something outside itself and external – its (m)other.

So we first take on board an identity from outside ourselves – an 'image' of ourselves – yet one which we feel to be a part of who we are. We identify with something which looks like what we want to be, but something which is also alien and separate from us. The mirror image splits us into two. We 'misrecognize' ourselves in the alienated image of what we want to be because it denies the chaos we feel in our own being. Lacan calls this realm of images, of imaginary identifications, the 'Imaginary' – a world where our mother is the most available object, reflecting back to us the kind of image we want, which we misperceive and 'misrecognize' as ourselves. We are given a *sense* of identity but we think we are given an authentic identity. For Lacan, drawing on Freud's work on primary narcissism, the self, the ego, contains this narcissistic process which we use all our lives, by which we bolster our sense of ourselves with a fiction – a visual story we show ourselves – an illusion of self which depends on the view of ourselves we obtain from other people and objects throughout our life.

In many ways the Imaginary is Lacan's most 'human', most immediately accessible idea. We can see easily how the mother as the child's first contact with the external world, first 'other', gradually, if all goes well, mirrors to the child an image of itself with which it can identify and gain a coherent sense of an identity – who and what it is. The child perceives itself in the expression in the mother's gaze and voice, in the way she holds and touches it, in the quality of unspoken understanding and empathy she brings to her responses to the baby's needs, the way she communicates to the baby that it is lovable, full of potentiality and a person who gives joy and pleasure to the beholder. This is the first relationship in which we are given an image of ourself, an identity, a knowledge of who we are, a confidence that we exist and will continue to exist.

In the pre-Oedipal world of imaginary identifications, we are in a world inhabited by only two people, ourself and usually our mother. As the Oedipal drama approaches we see our mother increasingly as a whole person and fall deeply in love with her, whether we are a girl or boy. But the Oedipal moment finally arrives and brings a rupture, a dramatic intrusion of a third term, not just the father, but a father made terrifying by the child's fantasy of him as potentially destructive and castrating. The father represents something external intruding upon the child's idyll with the mother, the inevitable law against incest which prohibits both the small girl and boy from the fantasy that they can marry their mother as well as identify with her, that they and they alone can be the object of her desire instead of the father or anyone else. In recognizing the father for what he is – an insurmountable obstacle to the fulfilment of its passionate wishes – the child is brought into contact with the constraints of the wider external world, with the social dimension in which it must in future take up its place.

Up until the Oedipal crisis, the child has had fantasies that it is omnipotent, because the mother's response seemed to support this view. The intrusion of the father representing the law, society, language and culture beyond the body and presence of the mother shatters and ends the child's omnipotent fantasy of itself in a passionate love affair with the mother. The appearance of the father separates the child from its fantasies about her and drives its desire and the loss of its desire to be the exclusive partner of the mother, underground into the unconscious. This repression of the child's longing to have the mother for ever *creates* the unconscious. It also splits the newly created subject, now encapsulated within the social domain beyond the mother and child couple, into consciousness and the unconscious.

But at the same time that the child is transformed into a subject of language and history through its obedience to the law of the father, as well as becoming a split subject with an unconscious, it also becomes for Lacan a *gendered* subject. It is the ability to recognize sexual difference which allows the child to take on a sexual identity for the first time. The father (or the 'place of the father', the symbolic father) signifies this sexual difference by means of his association with the phallus. The phallus – a signifier of power within patriarchy – which is not to be conflated with the visible penis, although this is presumably what the child does, is the central term of Lacan's theory, and signifies to the child that there is a division between the sexes, and later that those who 'have' rather than 'lack' are privileged.

The child has probably been dimly aware of sexual difference before the onset of the Oedipal crisis. Once the crisis is in full swing, the sexual difference and the sexual identities based on it operate like a law, and the child is required to reorganize sexual difference to line up as a 'masculine' or 'feminine' identity in order for its socialization as a human subject to be completed. It is at this point that Lacan introduces his most original re-working of Freud's Oedipal drama through his introduction of the dimension of language.

To go back to the mirror phase in the imaginary pre-Oedipal period for a moment, the child contemplating itself in the mirror can be seen as something that bestows meaning – a kind of 'signifier' – and the image in the mirror as a kind of 'signified'. Both these terms derive from modern linguistic theory and the work of Saussure. The image of the child in the mirror is for the child apparently the meaning of itself – when it *felt* it had only a very chaotic, unbounded meaning before this moment. We can also see what Lacan calls 'the mirror phase' as a kind of metaphor: one item, the child, discovers a likeness of itself in something else, an 'other' (the reflection). This is really for Lacan how he sees everything that happens in the imaginary: objects repeatedly reflect themselves in a kind of sealed unit where there are no apparent differences or divisions, where everything is fluid. The mirror images in the 'Imaginary' are ones of fullness, wholeness, totality, complete identity. There is no separation or gap between the experience of the child and the world it inhabits. For Lacan this is the imaginary world of 'demand' where, through identification with the other, the self is actually annihilated while imagining itself complete and full because it is *completely* dependent on the mother. It is also the world where satisfaction is never entirely complete: the baby never feels that the mother's response to its demand is ever quite enough; there is always an element of dissatisfaction.

With the entry of the father onto the scene, the child is precipitated into a crisis. It has to recognize that identities can only come into being, as Saussure argued, as a result of the perception of *difference*. One term or subject only has meaning because it is different from other terms and other subjects, and excludes them. At the time when the small child is first discovering sexual difference it is also, highly significantly, acquiring language. And in the discovery of language the child unconsciously learns that a sign (in this case a word) only has meaning because it is different from other signs (words) and that signs always stand for, or represent, the absence of what they signify. The words in language stand in for objects, and in this sense operate like metaphors. We don't have to point to, or show, the actual objects to which we want to refer in order to refer to them, though when we don't speak a language that is exactly what we find ourselves having to do. And here we get to perhaps the central point in Lacan's theory. As the child learns about language standing in for objects in the world, it is also unconsciously learning about them in the psychic world of sexuality – in the discovery of sexual difference. The father, symbolized by the phallus, legislates to the child that it must take its place within a family which is defined by sexual difference, by exclusion (it cannot be its parents' lover) and by absence (it must give up its relationship with the mother). Its identity as a human subject capable of operating viably within the family and in society depends on its recognition that it is different from some people and the same as others. In its recognition of this pre-determined social fact, the child is enabled to move from a world of fantasy, into the world of language and the symbolic. The intrusion of the third term into the child's world turns out to be not only the father – the possessor of the phallus – but also, in Lacan's theory, the law of how we *perceive* the world, that is language and culture. In this way Lacan links the sexual psychic world with the social world – the dimension of language. The child recognizes the meaning of the phallus as a signifier (as something which bestows meaning although empty in itself) – as crucially the signifier of *difference* and at the same time the signifier of the *power* to break into the child's world with the mother and shatter it. Only this allows the child to enter into the rest of the chain of empty signifiers which bestow meaning – language.

For Lacan the phallus is a kind of 'pilot boat' signifier, whose meaning, if understood, allows the child access to all the other meanings signified in the same way in language. The recognition of the power of the phallic signifier within the context of the fear of castration – picked up and made significant by the undeniable visibility of the penis as the only mark of significant difference between the little girl and little boy – facilitates the acquisition of language by operating in the same symbolic way. The small child becomes a human subject capable of identifying with, seeing itself reflected in, the 'I' of language by means of this joint entry into language and at the same time sexual ordering and identity. ('He', 'him', 'she', 'her' are positions which pre-exist and lie in wait to receive the child when it 'steps into' language.) The child finds the idea of its gendered self awaiting it in language and can then identify with the sense of coherence and self it bestows, just as it did with the image in the mirror. But Lacan insists that there is a *misrecognition* in the perceived power of the phallus (Lacan always refers to the 'seeming' value of the phallus) and of the perceived identity within language which the child puts on almost like its symbolic clothes. The acquisition of language, Lacan reminds us, and the taking on of sexual difference are achieved only at a devastating price for the boy – symbolic castration by the father who retains the desired and desiring mother – and at the price of a catastrophe – the lack of what bestows identity and power, the negative – for the girl. Both children lose their sense of union with the mother's body – the object of what Lacan calls 'imaginary' desire – but the girl also loses all sense of the validity of her own body and being; since she lacks the legitimizing primary signifier, the phallus, she cannot be, become anything. And the pain of this loss of the mother and symbolic castration for the boy, and for the girl the loss of her mother and of any sense of potential as the representation of the 'lack', are repressed into the newly formed unconscious by both sexes at this moment of sexual division.

So the emergent human subject is created within an identity *split* between its conscious and unconscious. From then on the 'masculine' or 'feminine' child is inscribed into the empty world of absence and 'stand-ins' of language after the fullness of the imaginary relationship with the ever bodily present mother. But since this full, passionate world of imaginary desire with the mother has to be put aside and given up, language offers a kind of compensation, the best source of identification the child has yet had apart from the mother. By means of its entry into language the child can achieve some 'mastery' over its otherwise unbearable emotions of desire and loss of the loved object. It does this in order of meanings which, although they represent emptiness, absence and loss compared with those associated with the mother, also offer rationality, objectivity, coherence and meanings which the child perceives as fixed certainties – as linguistic pegs on which s/he can hang her/his identity. Through the reassuring anchorage of language and consciousness, the child can identify her/his self with the certainties of the meanings of the words s/he finds. So through language as a form of 'mastery' she or he can try to repress the pain of loss and division which is concealed and repressed into the unconscious. Language serves to cover the nakedness of painful experience with its rational, linguistic clothes. But the task of the little girl is to try to live out this unconscious 'lack' rather than 'presence' (of the phallus) *as if* they were her natural destiny. Lacan would argue that this destiny is entirely socially constructed, that because it is *so* easy to confuse the visible, physical penis with the phallus – the sign of power – as the most obvious sign of difference available to the child, the construction of 'femininity' can never be anything other than the 'lack', the 'not having'. This is what it takes to qualify for power and the assumption of a positive identity, and only a boy can do it.

So the child is excluded from the full, imaginary possession of the mother into what Lacan sees as the arid world of the symbolic – language. Language is empty because it is simply a never-ending chain of significance, whose words only have meanings as a result of the absence or loss of what they refer to (in the language of Linguistics, their referents) and which move in a linguistic chain of differentiated meanings which is potentially infinite; there is no ultimate meaning on which every meaning rests. One signifier implies another and so on until the end of time. The world of the mirror which, operated like a metaphor for identity, has been replaced by the metonymic world of language where meanings only imply other meanings.

Lacan fascinatingly ties the individual's repressed desire and yearning into the very stuff of language or discourse. Desire is seen by Lacan as the endless searching movement of one signifier to another in language. Like sexual difference, human language works through lack – the absence of the real subjects which signs designate. So, to take on the cloak of language is to become subject to desire. Language, says Lacan, 'is what hollows being into desire'. Language in a contradictory way, although it revolves around emptiness and absence, *articulates* the richness and fullness of the imaginary. We will never be able to find the ultimate meaning from which all meanings flow. In language we are permanently cut off from what Lacan calls *the real* – the inaccessible meanings which spill over from the fixed meanings of words – the excess, the inexpressible beyond the reach of signification which lies inviolate and out of reach of the symbolic order. Having lost access to the mother's body during the Oedipal crisis we are caught up in a constant search for substitutes (what Lacan called 'the object a') with which we try to paper over the cracks, plug the gaps at the core of our being, never able to regain the paradise of self-identity and self-completion which we fantasized with our mothers in the imaginary. To Lacan the phallus seems to offer the only possibility of grounding this endless longing and yearning for completion, the absolute guarantor of all meaning, the 'transcendental signifier', as he describes it. But this is in fact, as Lacan recognizes, not an object or reality, nor the actual male organ; it is an empty symbol, a sign which has the power to insert us into the phallic order of language, but which only gains any meaning from the fact that in patriarchal societies those who bear the sign of the phallus represented by the penis have the power to define all other meanings, and the material power to dominate women.

Lacan, as well as equating the structure of language with desire, the unending searching out of full satisfaction in terms of absolute meaning or truth, draws a crucial analogy between language and the unconscious. They are both structured by signifiers (signs that bestow meanings representing absence and loss) and the chain of signifiers only has meanings as a result of the absence or loss of that to which they refer. The system of meaning we call language, rather than representing certainty and coherence, is constantly shifting and changing its meanings depending on who is using a particular word and what she or he 'means' by using it. Like the meanings of the unconscious which we can try to grasp in dreams, slips of the tongue, jokes – all designated by Freud as the language of the unconscious – the meanings of language are never fixed and safe, although they may appear to be so. 'The unconscious', says Lacan enigmatically, 'is structured like a language.' It often looks as if, for Lacan, language – consciousness – *is* in fact the unconscious, but in a laundered, veiled form, through which we can see its actual content only in the slips and gaps and incoherences which 'poke' through it as we try to speak, or name, what we feel. Psychoanalysis and psychotherapy use language as the means to gaining direct access to the unconscious through making sense not of its coherences, but of its slippages, its excesses, its silences and gaps. And if we look hard at the articulations and desires for our lost mothers which language, according to Lacan, at bottom represents, we can see through the veil of apparent consciousness, the soft blurred outlines of what is really behind it – the unconscious – and the phallus, which *really* represents the loss and absence of the mother's desire.

In the unconscious there is a constant sliding and concealment of meaning like the confusing meanings we encounter in dreams. Lacan describes the unconscious as a 'sliding of the signified beneath the signifier' – as a constant dissolving and evaporation of meaning.

Quite clearly, if language and consciousness really reflected this turbulent, chaotic, enigmatic unconscious directly to us we would never be able to communicate with anyone. (It is because Lacan is trying to mirror his own theory in his writing, to uncover the unconscious in his own language, and avoid mastery, that much of his work is so unintelligible and lacking any clear exposition.) However, in conscious life, in the whole body of consciousness which is represented by the different disciplines, scientific and humanistic, we achieve some sense of ourselves as coherent and unified, *and* some sense of having created valuable bodies of knowledge which reflect this centredness. But Lacan says that all this is purely at the level of the 'imaginary ego' which is simply the tip of the iceberg of what psychoanalytic theory takes to be all that a human being is. In our language and knowledge, we have simply made yet another imaginary identification with an image of ourselves reflected back to us from words whose meanings are as illusory and fictitious as the identities we build on the basis of them. There is a radical split between what we really are and what we take ourselves to be in consciousness. When we say 'I will have another cup of coffee', the 'I' that is the subject of the sentence (known in linguistic theory as a 'shifter', that is the subject of the 'enunciation') is an immediately accessible and understandable point of reference. This 'I' 'veils' the shadow outlines of the precarious 'I' who is doing the speaking (the subject of the 'enunciating') from a self which can use the 'shifter' 'I' of the enunciation in any sentence s/he cares to invent. In the normal process of speaking and writing these two 'I's seem to refer to one unified self, but Lacan argues that this unity is still only of an imaginary kind. The subject of the enunciating – the actual person trying to communicate in language – is impossible to represent; there is no sign which can sum up my entire being, who I am. Most of what I am spills over like water from an overfilled cup, from the 'I' that appears in what I write or speak. Most of what I am can never be expressed in language. I cannot 'mean' and 'be' at the same time. To emphasize his total disagreement with Descartes' equation of consciousness and thinking with his being, Lacan re-writes the well-known 'I think therefore I am' as 'I am not where I think and I think where I am not'.

SEXUALITY

I want to move from Lacan's theory of language and consciousness to what this means for the child who enters language during the Oedipal crisis. According to Lacan, the price for the boy of being able to be a human subject, is for him to accept the loss of his mother and symbolic castration by the father implied by this, and contradictorily spend the rest of his life trying to justify his right to the power and value that the possession of the phallic signifier bequeaths to him. According to Lacan, he does this by making sure that he is always the object of desire for one or many women. To be unloved or undesired is to risk being reminded of the rejection by his mother and the symbolic castration by his father which ensued. In the case of the little girl, perceiving her total lack of what has apparent value and power – the 'thing to have' – she enters language entirely negatively. Quite clearly for Lacan, the girl is entering a symbolic order which has nothing to do with any signifier associated with her body. So the girl has to enter language and try to justify her existence as a full human subject in society, but as the one who lacks any crucial sign of difference, as the negative, the *not* having and therefore not *being* one. She can only get a phallus by 'being' the phallus for her future lovers, that is, being what the phallus needs and signifies – the object of desire for men through whom she can reach the phallus and have her own 'lack' filled. By doing this she then allows men to feel themselves as objects of her desire – the vital patriarchal requirement to bolster their sense of potency and phallic power. For Lacan, the absence of the penis in the woman only matters because it makes meaningful the father's prohibition on her desires for the mother; females appear retrospectively to have been castrated. She hasn't got what it seems to 'take', what is required to be her mother's lover, and – to add insult to injury – she hasn't got what is required to be an active, self-determining rational subject in life either.

However, in his very phallus-centred account of the coming into being of men and women in society (which may or may not accord with what we call reality), Lacan does ultimately pull at least the theoretical rug out from under the comparatively comfortable position of the boy, and later the man, in language and culture. Lacan makes it very clear that the phallus only *seems* to have value because it is the signifier which has the positive value within the powerful binary opposition of masculine and feminine. Its status is bogus. This, Lacan argues, opens the way to all the other binary oppositions which we use to categorize and falsely differentiate what we call reality (for example, light/dark, good/bad etc.). Lacan argues that the apparent power of the phallus is totally undermined and denied by the fact that it has been *symbolically castrated* by the father. So the boy's entry into language is based completely on what Lacan calls a hoax, an imposture which lies at the root of the division between 'masculinity' and 'femininity' and at the heart of phallocentric language and culture – at the very centre of the subject's being and therefore that of patriarchy.

I want at this point to try to clarify in more detail how Lacan sees the adult man and woman's relation to the phallus. The penis is elevated to the phallus within patriarchy on the basis that some do not have it, so that by its elevation half the human race will be excluded from what this elevation signifies, that is, from being human objects. The penis, a highly visible but arbitrary part of the male body, mainly used for urination and insemination, is valorized by the phallus which signifies power. By being veiled by the phallus, it instantly confers upon its owner the power to be a human subject. In the same way, within what Lacan calls the order of the symbolic, the unconscious is veiled by language and rationality. But what happens if we remove these veils? In the case of the phallic veil we see only a penis symbolically castrated by the father (the father was the object of desire for the mother, not the son). This is the meaning that has to be repressed into the unconscious at all costs and this repression is achieved by the veiling of the phallus. The only compensation for the Oedipal boy is that if as an adult he can make sure that he is the object of desire for another woman – a substitute for his lost mother – or other women, he can maintain the fantasy, the illusion, that he has never been symbolically castrated, that he is not lacking. This need of men – of the phallus – to be desired by women means that women *must* lack the phallus. They can only desire the phallus and therefore desire men if they want access to what they themselves lack. They can gain access through men, through whom they can fill their lack. So women's lack seems to be necessitated by men's need to shore up their sense of phallic power which cannot exist without being the object of desire, as they once fantasized that they were for their mothers. In this way women's lack and romantic love as the idea that each sex complements what the other does or does not possess, becomes a requirement for patriarchy, for bolstering up and supporting men's sense of themselves as powerful, active subjects. Without women's desire to get access to the phallus – what she lacks – through a kind of borrowing or taking of one in her relationships with men, male power and patriarchy collapse.

But the phallus also exists as the first signifier within language, where its power is also bogus. It therefore undermines the whole chain of signifiers which are based on this bogus power. The phallus, in being the first signifier the child confronts, because it comes to stand in for the absence and loss of the mother, also comes to represent the subject in language – the 'I' who experiences himself as active, whole and knowing. But because the power of the phallus conceals the unconscious repression of the symbolically castrated phallus, the power and meaning of the whole of language and man's place as subject within it is subverted and undermined.

To deny the symbolic is at one level for Lacan to deny one's humanity, however bogus the grounds on which it rests. To totally refuse to be 'subjected' within language and culture is to remain the prisoner of an undifferentiated existence with the mother where there can be nothing available to the adult but psychosis or madness. The acceptance of patriarchal language becomes the only condition of sanity for both sexes.

So, to summarize before looking in more detail at women's position in Lacan's theory. For Lacan, language, although appearing as something else, operates like a mirror in that it receives the post-Oedipal child exhausted by its loss and unsatisfied desire, whom it picks up and puts on its feet by constituting it as an apparently whole human being to itself and to other people who will recognize it as such and take it seriously. In this way, our identity is produced and structured by an order outside ourselves, language, something which pre-exists us like the rest of the social and historical and forces its impression on us rather like a jelly-mould. And as a result of bearing this impression, we are stamped with a coherent, stable identity to which we henceforth refer to ourselves, and to which we hope others will also refer. Ironically, we need to be recognized by others as what we are actually *not*. Tragically, this situation comes about because of the power invested in the phallus within patriarchy, which turns out, when unveiled, to be a hoax.

I want now to look at the position of adult women in Lacan's theory in more detail. Masculinity, for Lacan, rests on very shaky precarious foundations. Man is what Western philosophy now calls 'post-structuralist man', and although most men are unaware of it, most of the time they live, according to Lacan, within a massively repressed state of permanent post-structuralist crisis. But the essential point is that, in blissful ignorance of their unconscious, projected onto 'woman', they don't *know* that they are in crisis; they feel that they are potent active human subjects and as bearers of the phallic sign of power they manage to keep their heads metaphorically above water most of the time. But what is the position of Lacan's woman within patriarchy who lacks the crucial signifier of power and therefore can signify nothing? Lacan says that in this predicament, woman has no existence outside language, and even within language she can represent only the 'lack', the negative, 'not man', precisely what man must never be. She has no existence or destiny of her own. She exists in language only in relation to the male sign, as what man is not, as the negative end of the binary opposition: of masculinity/femininity. For Lacan, woman is the symptom of man – the symptom of male neurosis – a linguistic projection of men's own concealed loss and lack, his symbolic castration by his father. She is man's shadow, the one who carries the 'dark', repressed side of his nature, 'his lack'. As Toril Moi wrily puts it: 'Woman as defective becomes a defence against the thinking male subject's potential devastating insight into his own lack' (Moi, 1989, p. 195). Reduced to a projection or fantasy, woman as herself cannot exist. She is, as Lacan puts it, 'subjected only to become a passive receptacle of male fantasy, contradictorily, either denigrated as worthless, the male bad fantasy of himself – the witch-women or whore – or idealized and destined to become the Absolute Other, the site of all knowledge, wisdom and truth – the Madonna, the Wise Woman from the mountains, the unattainable Goddess.

Denigration of woman, says Lacan, is the precondition of man's belief in his own soul; without her to project on to he is nothing. In other words, without woman to hand as a foil, representing a place where he can unconsciously project everything of himself that he doesn't want to acknowledge, his weakness, his uncertainty, man would never have enough room to construct and believe in his own viability and goodness. Woman as nothing, as the site of man's unconscious in language, allows man in contrast to look like something – positive, potent and meaningful.

So how do women cope with their catastrophic predicament? Since 'woman' within patriarchy is constructed only with reference to the male sign, the phallus, her status as woman can only be as something for men, and therefore what Lacan calls a masquerade, a playing of the part man has assigned to her – the 'not man', 'not macho', in fact the complement to himself. So, according to Lacan, what society takes to be natural feminine behaviour is an acting out of the role of the patriarchal requirement of woman; it is a 'fitting into' the available representations of women through which men perceive and control them, for example, wife, mother, little girl, housewife, mother-in-law, baby doll, femme fatale, scarlet women, iron lady, shrinking violet, blue-stocking, bitch, bimbo. Woman can represent male fantasies but never herself. She can therefore never exist as subject within the patriarchal social order even in the bogus sense in which men can. In Lacan's post-structuralist world where no one has a genuine identity, woman represents a double lack – her own lack of a phallus, and as a projection of men, his 'lack', his symbolic castration by his father.

Building on Freud's concept of penis envy, and what he called secondary narcissism which can develop in the girl at the time of the Oedipal crisis, as a form of 'masculine protest' against accepting her lack, Lacan proposes the idea of masquerade. This is the way in which women 'package' themselves in response to the demands of male fantasy. They do this as a means of overcoming their 'lack'. In their desire for a phallus – for the power to be a human subject – they make their whole body and being over to attracting an 'other', through whom they think that they may become potent and whole. In this masquerade, determined entirely in relation to phallic desire, women effectively annihilate any possibility of a self of their own, becoming simply a receptacle for men. In fact, Lacan sees women's entire involvement with heterosexual activity as masquerade, as a participation in a phallic sexuality which has nothing to do with her or her body. In an attempt to find out what women really want, he develops the concept of 'jouissance' to suggest a form of sexual pleasure peculiar and specific to women. He describes her jouissance mysteriously as being 'something more – what escapes or is left over from the phallic function, and exceeds it.'

IMPLICATIONS FOR FEMINISM

Having described some of the main features of Lacan's theory, I want to look very briefly at some of their implications for feminism. A major problem is Lacan's positioning of women. If according to Lacan 'woman' within patriarchal societies has no position outside language, and within language she can represent only man's unconscious, his de-centredness, we are compelled to ask who is the 'I' or 'me' who speaks in language from a female body? Lacan's reply, as we have seen, is that she can only be woman in a masquerade, in a kind of psychical fancy dress. It is difficult to see how such a position for women within patriarchy can offer grounds for much optimism for feminists. It seems to condemn all women to being the unconscious symptom of men's hysteria, to being the symptom of male neurosis about their symbolic castration by their fathers, their fear of being 'feminine'. And Lacan's position on women is very uncompromising. He offers very little light at the end of the tunnel, no apparent means by which women can change their position, from negativity and powerlessness. However, feminists have taken issue with Lacan's theory of 'woman'. It doesn't equate with how many women feel, with women's experience of what they are or what they could become. Many of us don't feel totally disempowered within language or society. Lacan's theory seems to rule out all those positions for women which feminism and its practice has established. These positions have emphasized women as active, self-determining, conscious autonomous subjects who can and have united with other women to analyse their predicament within patriarchy and initiate both cultural and material change. The question is can we theorize this other way of being a woman within a Lacanian framework? Without a symbolic, Lacan argues, there can be no human subjectivity, only psychosis. Entry into language – intellectual mastery of unbearable emotion – is the *condition* of sanity.

There is a further problem for feminists around the issue of sexual difference and Lacan's category of 'woman'. It ignores the differences within each single woman – the complex interplay of different levels of experience. As Rosi Braidotti suggests, it leaves out 'questions such as how does the woman in me relate to the feminist in me, what are the possible tensions between being a feminist and being a woman, between politics and a sense of self, between subjectivity and identity, between sexuality as an institution and also as one of the pillars for one's sense of self?' (Braidotti, 1989, p. 94).

Lacan's work has been taken up with enthusiasm by French Feminists like Helen Cixous and Julia Kristeva. Cixous has used Lacan's insights and Derrida's deconstructive methods to enable her to analyse and pull apart. the binary, dualistic organization of language based on the primary opposition of sexual difference, the 'masculine' and 'feminine' first perceived by the child around the time of the Oedipal crisis. Kristeva seems to take the view that Lacan's view of 'woman' within patriarchy is probably justified although regrettable, but she has urged women in their practice to ally themselves with surrealism – with artists who want to turn consciousness inside out, to challenge the 'normal' values of intelligibility, rationality and coherence in their art, literature and music. She argues that artists like James Joyce, John Cage,

Stockhausen are like 'honorary' women in that they inhabit the same 'space' in culture, representing the free, unmastered ingredient of the human subject which spills over beyond the boundaries of conventional meanings, collapsing and sabotaging consciousness.

The problem is that although Kristeva has transformed Lacan's 'woman' into a positive critical category she has still left her divorced from her material, bodily existence and effectively left her outside politics. Rosi Braidotti wants to emphasize women as female subjects who are not disembodied entities but, rather, sexed beings with bodies. But she also wants, following Lacan, to see women as a joint biological–cultural entity in the future.

Margaret Whitford's re-reading of the French feminist Irigaray has also highlighted the need to use Lacan's insights into how 'masculinity' and 'femininity' are constructed within patriarchy without accepting his positioning of women as final. According to her reading, Irigaray sees the unsymbolized mother–daughter relationship (that is, the 'unspoken' relationship between mother and daughter before the onset of the male symbolic – language) as the primary cause of women's predicament. This is what hinders women from having any identity of their own in language so that they can never pose any threat to the male version of how things are. Irigaray dramatically describes women's position in the social as in a state of 'dereliction', abandoned by God outside the symbolic order and representing the residue or waste of language, leaving what Freud called their drives, their specific form of sexual desire without any possibility of representation. For Irigaray the problem of patriarchy is not a question of knowledge, as it is for Lacan, but a question of change. She sees all knowledge and science as the representation of male meaning and therefore about control, mastery and the domination of nature; women are seen as a part of that nature. The change that Irigaray argues women must work towards, is a move away from this control in language – what she called the 'male imaginary' – male fantasy, whatever the sex of the knower, be they man or woman.

Finally, there is the problem for feminists of Lacan's post-structuralism, his de-centring of subjectivity. At a time when feminists are trying to win acceptance for the idea that women too are subjects, the equals of men even if that means equal in a different way, Lacan is arguing that not only are women not subjects but that the subjects that men take themselves to be are fraudulent and based on a fallacy (phallusy). As far as Lacan is concerned, men beneath the veil of language, stripped of their rational categories, are still babies, polymorphously perverse (that is, driven by a variety of oral, anal and phallic aims like the pre-Oedipal child) and still living in the 'imaginary'. All this, however, is veiled from public, or social, view by means of language where it is projected onto women. This leaves feminists with an enormous problem. How can we affirm a female subjectivity at a time in our history when the whole of Western philosophy is challenging the very concept of subjectivity? If we have reached a theoretical position where *no one* can be a subject, where does this leave women who have never been subjects? What can women be if not a subject in this new situation? When women are trying to position women as the subject of another history, the 'I' of another path leading away from the symbiosis with the mother, it seems an irony that the intellecutal rug is being pulled from under us. Men may be de-centred, polymorphously perverse and lacking access to any authentic meaning beyond the pain of the loss of their mother. They may be possessed unconsciously by an incessant yearning to retrieve a paradise lost for which they can search endlessly in language but never find. However, the lived, material reality by which we, all of us, men and women, live, is that men have the power both materially and as the definers of what counts as reality even if they are at one level still babies. Ironically again 'the baby', 'the little girl' is one of the most frequent images men have projected onto women in Western culture (particularly since Rousseau) – woman as simple-minded, innocent, helpless 'little girl', 'baby doll', 'chick'; the list is endless. The question becomes, then, 'If men are babies, who, what are women – are they babies too but without the obscuring veil – or are they something else? If they are mothers – the creators – bearers of these perpetual but later disguised veiled babies (men) does this make *them* the *real* subjects (because the equivalent of symbolic castration has never happened to the womb)?! Perhaps we then have to ask 'Is this then the power that men envy and fear? Is Freud's penis envy simply a veiled, disguised inversion of womb envy?' Is it going too far to suggest that the whole of Western philosophy – all knowledge – might be about the concealment of this fact through the control first offered by the *visible* phallic signifier, the mastery of the terrible truth that men have had to tear themselves away from, differentiate themselves from – those who are the *real* subjects of history, those with whom they can never compete – their mothers? Is the future for men and women, and perhaps Western philosophy, man's acceptance and 'working through' of their envy of the mother, of their unconscious need to spoil and destroy all of her (woman's) potential *except* her ability to have babies? Perhaps womb envy is after all the basis for women's oppression within patriarchy. And if this were to be the case, how could we intervene and make it otherwise? In focusing on signification and the sexed human subject, Lacan's theory raises these kind of questions again.

'I wish I could do that.'

So where does Lacan's theory leave women? In response to Lacan's theory of language feminists have asked the question 'Can women be rational and articulate and still be feminists?' The answer surely has to be an emphatic 'yes'. Women have to use language as far as it is capable of communicating their own experience and where the existing categories and words don't accord with this, they have to use different ones, invent new styles of explanation, argue for new criteria for evidence which takes into account their specific experience and which may represent what they have previously been required to deny, their repressed feelings and emotions. Women can use language as it exists, where it suits them, and where it doesn't, change it – invent new forms, force it into new moulds. Women outside the symbolic – within the unintelligibility of the 'Imaginary' – is a dead end. Woman as madwoman cannot be any part of our agenda. Even if we don't define 'mad' in the same ways as patriarchy does, woman as 'hysteric' can get us nowhere because hysteria represents such a high level of precariousness of sexual identity that it sabotages anyone's ability to cope with the ordinary demands of survival, to be self-determining. Women, feminists especially, need to communicate intelligibly without being mystifying and difficult. We also need to be as rigorous as we possibly can so that we do not *delude* ourselves. We need to produce a form of knowledge different from the male version which often denies its unconscious content by means of the mastery offered by language and the projection of it onto women who then don't count.

Perhaps taking the most positive view of Lacan's ultimately extremely masterful theory, the single most important insight Lacan offers feminists is that we cannot achieve a language, a mode of knowledge, which is not bogus, without personal insight, however painful this may sometimes be. This is a new definition of rigour which goes beyond the intellectual, which includes emotional honesty about ourselves as well as intellectual honesty about the relationships between the rational categories we use to construct our theories. Perhaps feminism could be the first form of knowledge to argue that self-knowledge, insight into our unconscious, is the only way to produce knowledge which is not reducible to the mastery of unbearable emotion and makes no illusory claims to have mastered the world.

Article 5.2
SITTING UP AND LYING DOWN: EXPERIENCES OF PSYCHOTHERAPY AND PSYCHOANALYSIS

Sarah Maguire

For the first few weeks I couldn't take my duffle coat off. Every Friday I took the bus to Uxbridge then walked up the High Street to the Child Guidance Centre where I'd sit in the grimy, lino-floored waiting room until it was time to go upstairs for my 'session' with Mrs Z at 12.15.

The room she took me to was quite bare. There was a large battered wooden table and, at opposite sides of an old gas fire, two saggy chairs placed at an oblique angle. I knew that Mrs Z, a large, dark, bland woman with an American accent, was there to help me but I wasn't quite sure how. She didn't try to reassure me. She didn't ask me very many questions. Sometimes I'd not be able to say anything at all and we'd sit there for ages in total silence until she said it was time to stop, when I'd leave to catch the bus to school. Strangely, I think that it was these long silences that started to make me feel better: just being able to have someone as a witness to the enormous sadness I felt who didn't try to interfere. Gradually I started to realize that Mrs Z was on my side. After a while, I even took my duffel coat off (it had been painfuly hot the weeks I'd worn it) and I remember her saying that perhaps I'd been wearing it in order to hide how thin I was, which at first made me wish that I'd kept it on.

I was fourteen. I had the worst case of acne one of the endless dermatologists who examined me had ever seen (all his students were impressed and I only just avoided being admitted for observation). As a result I was being prescribed phenobarbitone – my GP having realized that my acne wasn't simply an adolescent inability to wash properly – so I spent most of those years asleep, a dumb, dead, dark sleep which was an enormous relief. I tried not to dream. My acne was the first visible sign that something was wrong, but no-one took that seriously and I had to endure endless teasing about being 'dirty'. It was strange. I knew that I was bitterly, deeply unhappy, but it was as though I wasn't quite sure how you were supposed to express it.

Then one day in the biology lab, sitting in the gloom behind the test-tubes and Bunsen burners, one of the other girls told me about her sister who was 'having a nervous breakdown' and had been taken into mental hospital. She told me that her sister had stopped talking, stopped eating and that she cried all the time. So that's what I did. I also began to have very frightening rages – like fits or hysterical outbursts – where I'd scream violently for a long time, attempt to hurt myself, pass out and then either refuse or be unable (it worried me that I wasn't sure how much 'pretending' was involved in this) to talk for some hours. Unsurprisingly, the first of these episodes occurred on my birthday, the one day of the year which I longed to be perfect, to feel entirely special, when my father had spoilt that by getting angry with me for some very minor reason.

Always a thin child, prodigiously fussy about food, I began to eat less and less. I became 'ill' and missed weeks, then months, of school. Eventually I was taken into hospital for tests as my GP suspected some sort of rare blood disease or viral infection. Apart from my weight (I was about five stone) they could find nothing the matter with me. This was in 1970, before anorexia became something obvious to look for.

My 'illness' went on for some time until my mother, who at that time was teaching so-called 'remedial' children in a Child Guidance Centre, talked to the visiting psychiatrist about me; she recognized the very obvious, and suggested that I was suffering from depression and in need of help. I was extremely fortunate in that the help I was offered did not consist of being hospitalized or having to take anti-depressants, rather I was referred to another Child Guidance Centre where they suggested I have psychotherapy.[1]

Although initially my sessions with Mrs Z baffled me, the desperation and misery I felt made me recognize that this was the only chance I had of getting better. And partly because of the work that my mother did and the mental illness that my aunt had endured (who had killed herself only a few years before – something that haunted and frightened me), the idea of psychiatrists and psychotherapy wasn't quite as alien as it might have been to other fourteen year-olds.

To be honest I find it very difficult to remember much from those sessions: it was so long ago and I've tried to forget the bleak misery of those years. Mrs Z was kind to me, though, I recognized that, even if I didn't fully understand what was going on, and I also sensed that she felt for me in some way, even though I'd picked up that the rules of the game precluded her from actually saying so. On one occasion I had a row with my nastily vindictive headmistress (she hated me because I was a wasted scholarship girl) who suggested that I should be on drugs and 'locked up' because my school-work was so bad. To further this end she then took it upon herself to write to my therapist to put her straight about me. Later I found out that Mrs Z had told my headmistress that my treatment was none of her business. So I knew that she cared about me.

The most important thing Mrs Z gave me was a vocabulary. She talked about how I needed 'space', about boundaries, about inside and outside – the topography of a Winnicottian – a topography which now I am able to think outside, and for which I am enormously grateful. I don't think she pushed me too hard, which was as well, given how fragile I must have been, rather she offered the security of simply being there for me. When I cut my hand very badly, which threw me into a serious crisis, she saw me three times a week until I was better. When I left school at seventeen and theoretically became ineligible for Child Guidance care, she continued to see me for another year. Neither did she pry too much: she knew I'd started having sex (I'd left home and started squatting in Notting Hill, entering a Sex-and-Drugs-and-Van Morrison phase), but she allowed me to be coy about it, so I didn't feel under pressure to 'confess' what I'd been up to.

A lot of people who've not had any therapy and who are resistant to the idea often use the argument that they can 'sort things out on their own', thinking that the therapeutic relationship simply consists in the therapist offering you theories and insights into odd behaviour. Therapists do produce such insights, but that's only a small aspect of what makes it into a healing process. What made me better was, quite simply, love: having someone there who would listen to me and tolerate my bad moods, my anger and my silences and who would not be hurt or shout at me or go away. Certainly she'd suggest that I was upset or behaving in particular ways because she was about to go on holiday, for example, but I wasn't made to feel that all of my private life was in thrall to my relationship with her. Not that the therapy was simply a weekly cosy chat – sometimes I really hated her and sometimes it was obvious that I was irritating her, too – but that it was more orientated to holding me together.

Finally, after four years, in the summer that I was eighteen, she left and went to live in Australia. At the time Mrs Z suggested that I have a full-scale analysis, but by that time I think I'd had enough and needed a break for things to settle, and she put no pressure on me to continue. I'd been working as a gardener for about a year by then and I can remember the long bus-ride of over an hour to my session after work, feeling pleasantly tired after weeding all day. It was very hot. She was wearing her white dress, which was always a good sign, and she seemed sad. At the end of the session she hugged me. We both cried.

■ ■ ■

At the age of twenty-five I began having a full-scale psychoanalysis under the auspices of The British Psycho-Analytical Society, one of the two main centres offering analysis in England. Since finishing my psychotherapy with Mrs Z seven years earlier I'd had a variable time: mostly functioning quite well, feeling happy and productive, but then going through some very difficult depressive phases which, on two occasions had necessitated me taking a variety of pretty powerful psychotropic drugs. When I was twenty-four I went through a particularly bad time and I ended up, on the advice of a friend of mine who was a psychiatrist, going to see a consultant psychiatrist at the Maudsley Hospital in South London for assessment. He was an enormously kind and perceptive man who felt that I was not suffering from an illness which could be helped with psychotropic drugs or any other form of physical treatment; that, rather, the best thing for me would be to have a full psychoanalysis, given the help I'd received from the psychotherapy when I was younger. So I began the arduous task of getting myself accepted for treatment.

In many respects it's simplest to say that psychoanalysis proper is psychotherapy writ large, as there's a great deal of continuity between the two – inevitably since therapy evolved as a less time-consuming and less expensive alternative to analysis. That said, despite the obvious similarities and shared theoretical premises, psychoanalysis is an unusually tough and upsetting form of treatment and my experience of it was very different from that of having psychotherapy when I was younger.

But both share the obvious ground-rules of the relationship between the client and therapist/analyst. As in psychotherapy the analyst will reveal as little about herself as possible. She will rarely ask questions and never make suggestions of ways in which the client can improve her life. There are two reasons for this lack of intervention: one is because the analyst talking about her own life would obstruct the transference relationship, which I'll talk about below; the second is because it would interfere with Freud's Basic Rule, the process known as Free Association.

In psychoanalysis (and in therapy, for that matter) your analyst will encourage you to say whatever comes into your mind. This might sound indulgently enticing, but it turns out to be both impossible and disturbing. Suddenly, you'll come up against a block: a gap in your memory, something you'd rather not talk about. Or you'll find yourself talking about a subject ostensibly far removed from the one you began with. The gaps, blocks, silences and reversals of speech are the stuff of analysis. They are all manifestations of resistance, resistance to unconscious material becoming verbalized and conscious. The analyst aims to keep fretting away at this resistance through interpreting the feelings which are behind these blocks.

Interpretation and resistance are aspects of analysis which often worry people who've never had the experience. How, they want to know, can you possibly disagree with your analyst when they'll interpret every argument with the tag, Resistance? Now, in fact, it's perfectly easy and possible to disagree with your analyst and for them to accept that you're right, that they happened to be on the wrong track. What happens when you are actively resisting an interpretation is that it has an enormous amount of affective content: you feel pity for their stupidity, or are hurt that they could imagine such a thing about you, or anger that they might dare to suggest something so implacably wrong. What they'll do then is to interpret those emotional reactions in turn, until what has been resisted and repressed becomes clear – which can take a considerable time, years perhaps, or can be the realization of a minute.

The Basic Rule, as I have said, is practised both in psychotherapy and psychoanalysis. However, this similarity is radically altered by the *structure* of the analytic session. Both because you have more sessions (in my case five times a week, as opposed to once weekly with my therapist) and – crucially – the room is arranged differently: instead of two people both sitting upright in chairs facing each other, the analyst has the only chair which is placed behind the head of the analysand as she lies supine on the analytic couch.

It is extraordinary how fascinated people are by the idea of the analyst's couch. Think of the thousands who have gazed at Freud's original, who have longed to lie down and be understood. Which is why it is both so fascinating and so frightening: lying down, surrendering to another, letting go, is something we only usually do when we're adults with those we desire. And they lie with us. Now the analyst demands that you must lie down in all that vulnerability with no-one to comfort and no-one to hold you. Moreover, the analyst is both placed in intrusive intimacy and simultaneously inaccessible: the earliest and most profound of human communications – that of facial gesture – is denied. Inevitably, the very structure of the analytic session, its *topos*, mimics the erotic, the confessional and the infantile. And inevitably, that leads to a powerfully charged set of emotional reactions structured around the forbidden and the tempting, triggering fears of passivity and abandonment, promising redemption and betrayal. Just lie there, in that thick silence, and sense all those longings and refusals rise up and darken the air. Not only those you consider 'personal' – your own private demons and lusts – but the complex weight of history, the social density attached to our versions of the child, the lover and the confessed.

These two structural differences which exist between therapy and analysis proper – frequency and furniture – have the effect of throwing the focus of the sessions profoundly onto unconscious, irrational areas. However wild and steamy a psychotherapeutic session may get, you can still check into another person's reality by *looking* at them, providing a constant reminder that they're not, in fact, your wicked stepmother, even if they seem to be behaving exactly like her. With analysis, reality checks go out of the window. It's you and your unconscious.

There's no getting away from the fact that psychoanalysis is a very bizarre way to carry on a relationship with someone. At first sight it seems highly improbable as a way of helping someone with emotional difficulties. But the way that analysis works is through what is called the transference relationship. What happens when you're stuck in a room every day with someone you don't know at all, whose face you can't see and who says nothing whatsoever is that you project your own ideas of what the analyst is thinking and feeling onto her. You might think, for example, that a protracted silence means that your analyst hates talking to you. Or that she's giving you a lot of loving space to feel without having to speak. Either response will derive directly from what such silences meant to you when you were small and how you best learned to deal with them. Thus what 'in fact' the analyst's reasons for her silence may be (and she could simply be thinking about her dinner) are irrelevant. What you need to understand is what your reaction *means*, not whether it's empirically true or not. Through making conscious the fact that certain kinds of reactions which you take to be inevitable could in effect have a history and a set of purposes, you're given a chance to understand and alter those feelings which may have constricted and embittered your life.

But it's very tough. Tough because analysis isn't about understanding your difficulties but, by reliving those painful feelings, beginning to change them. And the reliving is as agonizing and disturbing as it is essential. This means that analysis is highly unsuitable for anyone who's still in a great deal of distress because it does stir you up enormously. As a result the British Psycho-Analytical Society make the acceptance process for their clients (they call us 'patients') very difficult indeed. If you can survive the scrutiny, you can survive the analysis.

■ ■ ■

I met my analyst for the first time one afternoon when I had an appointment with her at her consulting room in order that we might arrange our sessions. It was a clear spring day at the beginning of May. I was feeling cheerful and confident about starting the analysis, optimistic that I'd learn a lot and change a great deal. My analyst had a room in a large, late Victorian house off the Finchley Road in north-west London, where they all seem to gather, Freud having made his home a couple of miles away in posher Hampstead. A nice, white, solidly middle-class area, perfectly appropriate for the eminently bourgeois task of scrutinizing one's doubts and mores.

I was very nervous, despite the confidence. I stood on the porch and rang the bell for the top flat. I was asked to go up. We met on the stairs, my analyst coming half-way down to meet me. She was nervous, too. And very young. And far too small. And Spanish. I was terrified. How on earth was someone this fragile and this foreign going to cope with me, with my dangerous rages, my baffling complexities, my dazzling intelligence? Surely, I was far too important, far too difficult, to be assigned to someone as clearly insignificant as this woman was?

She led me into a small, blue room. One window looked out over a garden I never saw. There was a formica table, a hard-backed chair, a couch I tried not to look at and, behind the head of that, a more comfortable armchair next to the window. No carpet (dark-blue linoleum), no pictures, no books, no flowers.

I hovered on the edge of the hard-backed chair; she sat in her armchair and we talked about dates and times. Nothing went in. After a while she suggested I write down the times of our daily sessions. So I did. But I knew that I could have absolutely nothing to do with this woman. That she couldn't possibly be my analyst. Not that I said so to her. So I tried to be polite and to get out as quickly as possible with the least amount of fuss.

The sessions were to start the following week. I had a final appointment to see my consultant psychiatrist at the Maudsley so I decided to tell him I couldn't see her. I expected him to be his usual kind and patient self, that he would rescue me from this awful woman. But he didn't. All he suggested was that I had another appointment with a doctor I'd seen before for referral who was both a consultant psychiatrist and a psychoanalyst. She was more sympathetic, but she clearly recognized my aversion to my analyst for the transference reaction it was and gently suggested that I try working with her for a while, promising that if things really did go badly that I could see her again and that the Society would deal with matters if the analytic relationship really didn't work out.

Most analytic relationships start off with some kind of 'honeymoon' period: the client feels grateful at having someone to listen to her and invests the analyst with all sorts of 'good parent' feelings, so that the analyst becomes the wise, caring parent none of us ever had. This positive phase then can act as a buffer when more difficult aspects of the transference manifest themselves: however horrible, cruel and depriving the analyst seems to be, some faint memory of a good analyst will remain. In my case, of course, I started out with hate, fear and hostility and, although, over the years, I came to be rather fond of my analyst, I never felt that close to her, or 'fell in love' with her as many analysands do. That would have been far too frightening.

So there I was on a Monday afternoon at the beginning of May in a small blue room with a small foreign analyst feeling hostile but pretending to be good. As there was nowhere else to be but on the couch (the other chair had vanished) I sat, awkwardly, on that, in profile to Dr T. Lying down was out of the question – the first session at least (after a while I got to like the security and privacy it offered).

It took me some time to recognize that one of the main reasons for my disliking Dr T was because she was foreign, because of my racism.[2] After all, political activity had led me to believe that I was anti-racist – so being confronted with fears of foreignness came as something of a shock. But what one believes consciously and what one feels unconsciously are two entirely different things, as psychoanalysis is only too keen to point out to you. What I'd wanted to bury was the extraordinary weight 'the foreign' had in my life: my first parents were Irish, but I was adopted and brought up by an English Methodist mother and a second-generation Irish Catholic father. Throughout my childhood I was painfully aware that I was *wrong*: I looked wrong – as all adopted children do (hence the skin diseases) – simply because I was in fact *foreign* myself.

I soon discovered that my hating Dr T because she wasn't up to coping with my fascinating difficulties was a mistake. This woman was tough. I got away with nothing. My most devious strategies (and I can't fail to pride myself on the twisted quality of their deviousness) were cooly unmasked. Damn. Cool was the term though. My god she was cool. And very formal. Not a hair out of place. Neat, proper suits. It is, of course, possible that, when not being an analyst, my analyst was a raver. But I think not. Humour was not one of her stronger points, though she did have a sweet smile.

Of course, we had the usual fights, most of which, inevitably, were structured around the analytic parameters: money and time. They set these things up and you do your best to reassert your shamed self-esteem by fighting back. Lateness is a familiar weapon, but they've got you there: it's your session you're missing and you don't get extra at the end, even if London Transport is unemphatically to blame. (It was fascinating how, when I was late 'on purpose', even if I wasn't really conscious of the fact, I always felt cross and guilty; whereas, when I had truly been thwarted by the 31 bus, nothing difficult came up.) Holidays were a bigger issue. (Who'd be an analyst?: two weeks for Christmas, two for Easter and the month of August are all you're allowed; for that matter, who'd be an analysand? Though in my time I was too poor to afford holidays anyway.) However much I pretended I cared not a whit for my analyst's absence, my moods and dreams indicated strictly to the contrary. And, despite myself, I always felt better on her return.

Money we had more of a direct battle about. The Society will charge you what you can afford, once they've decided that you're a suitable case for treatment. But behind that 'what you can afford' premise lies all kinds of mess, avarice and vitriol. Analysis being a supremely bourgeois phenomenon, it is couched in the values of the bourgeoisie, the cardinal value of that caste being that everything has its price, that unless you suffer, you can't enjoy. Now, I was getting my analysis entirely for nothing, being the recipient of an NHS-funded place. Having fully appreciated four years of psychotherapy absolutely free in my youth, this obsession about cash struck me as, well, an obsession – but not, for once, one of my making. So we fought. And I continued to assert that not paying in cash for my sessions didn't mean that I failed to appreciate the service, and that it was costing me enough as it was in bus fares. So we left that one, after a while.

Let me warn you what an arduous, tedious and painful experience analysis is. I have done some difficult things in my life but nothing comes anywhere near this one for sheer unpleasantness. It is the essence of unpleasantness because all the poisonous, vile sides of your personality – the mean, selfish, spiteful parts we all usually hide relatively well – are laid out and sifted through, day after day. Like everyone else, I had theories about my depression and misery which all pointed to mistreatment during childhood. I was a victim. I was adopted: brutally snatched away from the person I loved most in the world and, what is more, adopted by a woman unfit for the task. My mother is, shall we say, disturbed: complete with a battery of hysterical symptoms (food and skin diseases) and a range of highly effective phobias which prevent her from travelling. My father failed to protect me from her often violent mood swings (her chronically manic-depressive sister committed suicide when I was eleven), being effectively dominated by them for some years. Neither of them were model heterosexuals. So my victim-credentials were firmly intact. And waiting to be shattered. This is really the most difficult thing about analysis: suddenly you are confronted with the fact that not only were you mistreated but you misbehaved back. For a while I went through a period of enormous guilt and grief about how simply vile I was, what a pretence all this nice, good, polite behaviour was. So much hate. But after a time, after the viciousness and the self-loathing have started to diminish, a certain tolerance sets in. I know that I was a difficult, angry, spiteful child at times, that I can be those things now, but it's a matter of taking responsibility for those feelings, recognizing that they are true, that I can be like that, and that I was being cruel for a reason.

Which also means relinquishing all those highly pleasant feelings of destructiveness: being the vilest person in the world is little different from being chief victim. Both are fantasies of omnipotence. What tames them is that the potent feelings of hate and destruction fail to have any impact on your analyst. There you are, having relived exploding pus-filled fantasies of violent hatred – and your analyst smiles at you and says 'goodbye'. And there she is the next day. So your violent fantasies become explicable as not at all out of the ordinary. Understandable. And sometimes dull.

Both historically and theoretically psychoanalysis has an intimate connection with the figure of the female hysteric. One of the main conclusions Freud came to about hysterics was that they were unhappy with the constraints of femininity, that at the root of the problem was an unquenchable desire to be bisexual: both in terms of sexual object and sexual identity. My 'presenting problem' as they call it, in seeking psychoanalytic help was one of chronic depression. But what triggered off the depression were 'gender difficulties'.

■ ■ ■

I wrote the section above, on my experiences of psychotherapy some weeks earlier than this part and sent them to my editor for comments. One of the things she said was that the piece lacked a 'gender perspective'. Which it does. Read it again and you'll see it could have been written by anyone. My instant response to her comment was that I didn't have a gender perspective when I was an adolescent. Which I didn't. All I knew was that I hated girls. I hated being at the stuffy all-girls' school I attended because they made me so miserable, because I didn't fit in, because I felt constrained to be someone I clearly wasn't, nor ever would be.

Yet whilst my conscious feelings were that I hated girls, I was also passionately in love with one of the older girls at school for some years. At the time no-one knew about this as I sensed that there was something profoundly wrong with what I felt. One of the more terrifying moments in my adolescence, which I referred to in the first part, was when I'd been taken in to hospital for tests because I was so thin. Lying on a trolley in the corridor after the tests, a nurse came up to me and said that they didn't think there was anything physically wrong with me. She then picked up my painfully thin wrist and said 'I know what's the matter with you – you're in love, aren't you?' 'My god', I thought, 'they can tell!' But they couldn't. I was so concerned to hide these feelings that, in four years of psychotherapy, I managed not to confess my inappropriate desires to my therapist. I never talked to Mrs Z about the person I was most affected by. Which is some feat of repression.

I left school early, when I was seventeen, and my life changed radically. I began working in an all-male environment as an apprentice gardener where, for the first time, I felt able to be female in a positive way, whilst doing something which definitely was not feminine. When I left home and started squatting in Notting Hill at about the same time I began having casual-ish (heterosexual) sex, because everyone else did and I liked it. Nothing too serious occurred until I had a tempestuous relationship with a man in Dublin which broke my heart and ended in great pain and tragedy. I loved him more than anyone else in my life. And he vanished. About three months later I began my first lesbian affair. Three days later I was covered in psoriasis.

The psoriasis was my first, spectacular hysterical symptom. It developed the first time when I was about five and seemed to occur as a result of my mother being cruel to me. One of the most difficult things about my relationship with my mother was her extreme mood swings which I was unable to predict. One minute we'd be playing together, the next she'd be screaming hysterically, would rush off and lock herself in the bedroom – leaving me to deal with my father's terrible rages. He couldn't stand my mother behaving like that, so in his frustration he took it out on me. I developed psoriasis as a result of a burn on my back, a medical impossibility. My mother had been playing a game with me in which she was pulling me across the floor by my ankles. Suddenly my back began to burn and I started screaming. But she wouldn't stop. From the huge sore that resulted, the psoriasis seemed to spring. It went after a few years of miserable treatment with coal-tar lotion which made me stink so that other children refused to play with me. Then nothing until I was nineteen.

For the following six years I continued to try to be a lesbian. I was heavily involved in the women's movement at this time and the congruence between what was seen as sexually correct and politically desirable meant that any deviation from the lesbian norm was frequently looked on with scorn and hostility by certain separatist feminists. Despite the nightmare that some of my relationships with women had become, one of the things that worried me most about having analysis was that of having my sexuality 'taken away' from me, of becoming dull and normal, with a desire to bring up 2.4 children in Carshalton with a husband in banking.

For six years before entering analysis I had relationships with women. A few months later I had stopped.

There is no doubt that my lesbian relationships had been the cause of enormous distress. I knew that. But I also very fiercely resisted the notion that homosexuality was sick. And the last thing I wanted, before I began the analysis, was to be 'cured' of loving women. Neither was that what happened. Nor, I am convinced, was that what my analyst set out to do – simply because the analytic situation in itself militates against any direct form of intervention on the analyst's part which might lead to the client's behaviour modification. They make no suggestions. They make no judgements. They try their utmost to be as neutral as possible by rigidly concealing their own prejudices and desires. All of this is eminently plausible if you think of psychoanalysts and their analysands as being atomized individuals, extraneous to society and history.

A significant part of depression, hysteria, schizophrenia – or any other form of mental distress – is that the disturbed person is unable to function socially. I couldn't work. I couldn't have relationships that made me feel stable and fulfilled. Sometimes I couldn't even leave the house. So part of any form of therapy – from behaviour modification to Lacanian analysis – is aimed at making you able to feel socially at ease, free to interact with whom you choose and work as productively as you desire. As a result, when you enter into analysis you meet a social order: the analyst, like the rest of us, is embedded in a web of social, historical and political relationships, all of which have informed her training and practice. And just as the seemingly objective scientific stance of psychoanalysis masks a determined ideological position, so the aloofness of the analyst conceals a set of deeply held values. (That such an aloofness may be therapeutically effective is beside the point.) The analyst may not say – or even believe – that homosexuality is sick, but she operates within a set of social relations, just as we all do, which are predicated upon versions of human sexuality which do not regard the homosexual as a creature to be emulated.

What I *felt* when I was in analysis was an overwhelming desire to be 'good', to conform, to be properly feminine – I grew my hair, I shaved my legs, I started to wear make-up, I began to be heterosexual – all because *I wanted my analyst to like me*. And also because those were the things I assumed my analyst did (and I had no direct way of knowing apart from the very rich range of sexual signifiers I picked up from her dress sense and her deportment: very neat, never trousers) and *I wanted to be like her*. It is difficult both to convey and to overestimate the pull of such desires. They are, of course, exactly the feelings we have as children in relation to our parents. Failing to conform is hard work, otherwise more of us would do it. Which is how analysis may seem to 'cure' homosexuality. Being good, for me, seemed to indicate being properly feminine and heterosexual, desires which inevitably have lessened as I've grown more distant from my analysis.

In other words, it is naive to suggest that the transference relationship, the core of psychoanalytic treatment, is constructed on the model of a 'neutral' analyst confronting the patient. However little the analyst may in fact say about herself, her beliefs, her desires, the client *knows* an enormous degree about her. Analysts are not interchangeable cyphers. But this said, it's enormously difficult to draw a clear barrier between the unconscious and consciousness, between irrational psychic reality and rational real reality. Neither can exist on their own. To say that psychoanalysis made me straight is a clearly inadequate and untrue assertion. But to imagine that someone who was largely heterosexual before being analysed might end up gay is stretching the bounds of possibility. I feel enormously ambivalent about the change in sexual orientation which I experienced in analysis: politically, it troubles me; practically, I know that I'm happier. Think about it.

Whilst the aspect of the transference relationship which shifted my sexual orientation was something about which I remained unaware at the time, the real struggle in my analysis was with the violent negative transference which manifested itself at the beginning, as I mentioned above. Along with the obvious racist elements, this hostility revealed itself to be largely the fear of an adopted child about not being looked after by the right person. Of course, I constructed all sort of water-tight, rational reasons for my not liking Dr T: because she was cool, prim and proper, I argued to myself, she was someone I'd never get on with in 'real' life; thus, the analytic relationship was doomed from the start. Whether we would have hated each other in a different situation might well have been true. Or might not. What was at issue was that I'd constructed another 'victim' myth: they'd given me the 'wrong' analyst; that had been my story at the beginning and I was sticking to it. Liking Dr T would have been a threat to my victim role. It would also have opened me up to the unbearable pain of her disappearing – which is partly why I left a few months before the agreed period of three years was up.

My hostility to Dr T of course had very little to do with what she might be like as a 'real' person (though there's no doubt I'd picked up and elaborated upon some of the signifiers of her personality through her dress and voice etc.). Instead, it had far more connection with my absolute refusal to accept that maybe I'd had the *right* adoptive parents, that they'd been good for me in lots of ways, that I wouldn't be as cheerful, confident and creative as I can be on good days had it not been for their love. Now, that challenge to my omnipotence I still have problems with.

It must be tough being an analyst. All that arrogance. Imagine, first thing on a Monday morning, having to tell someone who's just fallen in love for the first time in years, that they're only really interested in this ideal person because they represent the analyst. That when they make love, it's you they're really being intimate with. Imagine it. Imagine having to say that when someone leaves or begins a job, moves house, loses their purse, has an accident, defrosts the fridge, makes a sculpture, breaks the television, goes deaf in one ear, or drinks a whole bottle of Laphroaig in an evening – that they're doing all these things because of how they feel about you. And conversely, imagine having to sit there and take their ludicrous fantasies about what a cruel, manipulative, sexually voracious, breathtakingly successful human being you are – and not say one word. It is absurd, isn't it? And yet not. Because we're dealing with two different sorts of reality: the quotidian stuff we all stumble about in and psychic reality, unconscious reality which, as we know from our dreams, pays scant regard for how things are supposed to be. And once you're in analysis proper, there's no doubt that psychic reality comes to play a dominant part in your life, just as it does when something traumatic happens – someone dies or you fall in love – when life very similarly seems to be slightly out of kilter, determined by forces which are not at all obvious. Just as in those states you'll notice that you do a lot of inexplicable things so, when you're in analysis, lots of small incidents occur which, behind their seemingly banal façade, lurk all sorts of irrational bogeys.

When we stop to think about it, we know that we always do things 'for a reason', rarely (if ever) for their surface appeal; that certain pleasures and terrors have a complex history which it is possible to tease out. What psychoanalysis aims to unpack is what those other reasons might be. Now obviously this unpacking only becomes necessary if the avoidance of or attraction towards certain objects, people and situations becomes limiting or crippling in some way: having a strong dislike of cabbage – whatever the reason – has little relevance to the conduct of anyone's life unless it is a significant factor, say, in a major eating disorder.

Psychoanalysis is about making patterns out of details. One of the things I've noticed since I stopped analysis over six years ago is the way in which I'm able to continue finding those patterns on my own. Prior to the analysis I'd fall into deep depression or indulge in behaviour that made me anxious, and not really know why. Now when something goes wrong (or when it goes right) I can usually work out some sort of reason. That doesn't mean that I can necessarily 'undo' what's going on, but it does considerably lower the frequently accompanying anxiety, anxiety so often being about 'nameless dread'. And if you do know something at times there are ways of beginning consciously to change behaviour.

When I started writing this piece, for example, it all seemed to be going quite well. I wanted to write about my analysis, I realized, rather a lot. As time went on I found a remarkable variety of distractions, from sex to shopping to sleeping, and spent days and days 'doing nothing'. Now this is an all-too-common writers' complaint: most of us will do absolutely anything at all to avoid writing until the very last minute, then stay up all the night before the deadline, glowering at the word-processor (this is the afternoon before that night). Sometimes it seems like nothing more complex than sheer indolence (although I've always suspected indolence not to be a simple phenomenon). Other times it is clearly depressive behaviour. It certainly was for me in this case. Once I worked out why I'd been engaging in 'displacement activities' with such devotion, and recognized that I was in fact feeling dreadful, I started to begin to be able to write again.

The trouble with writing is the trouble with psychoanalysis: you don't ever loftily *analyse* what you're dealing with, you *feel* it. Otherwise you couldn't write. So writing about my analysis was a bit like having it again: initial enthusiasm; hostility; misery; understanding; resolution; work. Pleasure.

In an ideal world I should have stayed in analysis for longer, I suppose. I stuck it out for nearly three years, five times a week, but I left because I had the opportunity to go to university and, at twenty-seven, I didn't want to wait. My analyst, of course, insisted that I was going to university because I wanted to leave the analysis, which was clearly partly true, and clearly partly untrue. Writing this has stirred up a lot of 'unfinished' cross feelings, which makes me think that I did leave too early, that she was right: going to university was an 'excuse', a form of resistance; I'd had enough and I wanted to go back to the pleasures of non-good, neurotic behaviour. (One of the blissful things about stopping analysis is that, whatever you're up to, at least you know you won't have to get up at some ungodly hour and talk about it).

What is unequivocally true is that, had I not had analysis, I would not have been able to go to university. I was a mess before I started and suspect that I might have continued to be a mess – unless fate had intervened to an extraordinary degree and we can never really count on fate. My analysis changed my life. It gave me my life. It's clear that I wouldn't be here writing this article about psychoanalysis had I not experienced it. I also suspect that, without it, I might not be here at all.

Notes

1   The psychotherapy I am about to describe is based on the theories of D.W. Winnicott which is very common in this country as a form of therapy for children and adults. His approach is summarized in Davis and Wallbridge (1983). By far the best account of psychoanalysis, psychotherapy and other forms of therapy can be found in Joel Kovel (1978). Kovel, however, fails to deal with Kleinian psychoanalysis, the form I experienced when I was older, as it is little practised in the USA. There are significant theoretical

differences between the Kleinian and Freudian approaches though not in terms of the way that the analysis itself is practised. An introduction to Melanie Klein can be found in Segal (1979). Introductions to Freud are a waste of time as he did it so well himself. In terms of analytic practice read 'Transference' and 'Analytic therapy' in his *Introductory Lectures on Psychoanalysis* (Volume 26, 1963) and Volume 1 of *The Pelican Freud Library* (1973).

During my involvement with the 'anti-psychiatry' movement in Notting Hill in the early 1970s (based on the work on R.D. Laing and David Cooper, fuelled by the '60s counter-culture), I also experienced a baffling variety of group therapies, then later some individual feminist therapy at The Women's Therapy Centre in London, all of which were exercises in social skills rather than life-changing challenges.

2   See Joel Kovel's *White Racism: a psychohistory* (1988) for a psychoanalytic account of racism.

Article 5.3
IMAGES OF 'WOMAN': THE PHOTOGRAPHY OF CINDY SHERMAN

Judith Williamson

When I rummage through my wardrobe in the morning I am not merely faced with a choice of what to wear. I am faced with a choice of images: the difference between a smart suit and a pair of overalls, a leather skirt and a cotton frock, is not just one of fabric and style, but one of identity. You know perfectly well that you will be seen differently for the whole day, depending on what you put on; you will appear as a particular kind of woman with one particular identity *which excludes others*. The black leather skirt rather rules out girlish innocence, oily overalls tend to exclude sophistication, ditto smart suit and radical feminism. Often I have wished I could put them all on together, or appear simultaneously in every possible outfit, just to say, Fuck you, for thinking any one of these is *me*. But also, See, I can be all of them.

This seems to me exactly what Cindy Sherman achieves in her series of 'Film Stills' and later 'Untitled' photographs. To present all those surfaces at once is such a superb way of flashing the images of 'Woman' back where they belong, in the recognition of the beholder. Sherman's pictures force upon the viewer that elision of image and identity which women experience all the time: as if the sexy black dress made you *be* a femme fatale, whereas 'femme fatale' is, precisely, an image; it needs a viewer to function at all. It's also just one splinter of the mirror, broken off from, for example, 'nice girl' or 'mother'. Cindy Sherman stretches this phenomenon in two directions at once – which makes the tension and sharpness of her work. *Within* each image, far from deconstructing the elision of image and identity, she very smartly leads the viewer to *construct* it; but by presenting a whole lexicon of feminine identities, all of them played by 'her', she undermines your little constructions as fast as you can build them up.

[. . .]

The stereotypes and assumptions necessary to 'get' each picture are found in our own heads. Yet, at the risk of being attacked as 'essentialist', I really do think the complicity of viewing is different for women and men. For women, I feel it shows us that we needn't buy the goods, or at least, we needn't buy them as being our 'true selves'. . . .

[W]hat we construct from the surface of each picture is an interior, a mixture of emotions. Each setting, pose and facial expression seems literally to express an almost immeasurable interior which is at once mysteriously deep, and totally impenetrable: a feminine identity. Obviously this is what acting is about, but these still images are like frozen moments of performance and so the sense of personality seems more trapped in the image itself. It is both so flat, and so full (it seems) of feeling. But what links the emotions portrayed in the pictures is that they are all emotional *responses*. The woman's expression is like an imprint of a situation, there is some action and her face registers a *reaction*. Certain photos make this very explicit: *Untitled No.96*, where a girl holds a scrap of newspaper in her hand, shows precisely the way that we read into her fundamentally 'unreadable' face some emotional response which is both very definite, and entirely ambiguous. She looks thoughtful, but whether she is happy or unhappy, worried or perfectly all right, we have no clue. She looks, exactly, uncertain. Yet between the newspaper cutting and her face there is an endless production of significance which seems inevitable (it's always already started) and almost clear in its vagueness. Another photo from the same group, *Untitled No.90*, shows a teenager lying, equally ambiguous in her expression, by a telephone. Is she happily dreaming, or anxiously awaiting a call? (It's just like the ads for home pregnancy testing kits which manage to get the model looking both as if she's hopefully waiting for the good news of having a baby, *and* as if she can't wait to be put out of her fear that she might be pregnant.) Either way, her expression is an index of something or someone else, something we don't know about but which everything in the frame points to. (In semiotic terms it literally is an index, as a footprint is to a foot – a relevant metaphor since so many Sherman women look as if they were trodden on by men, fate, or a B-movie plot.) With the cutting, the telephone, or the letter in *Untitled Film Still No.5* (where there seems to be a response to two things – the letter, and someone else off screen left), something is put in the image as a snippet to represent the unknown narrative; but these images simply make explicit what happens in all of them, which is that meaning is thrown endlessly back and forth between a 'woman' and a story. The cutting gives expression to the face, the face gives a story to the cutting.

This is exactly what happens in films, news-photos, adverts and media generally. An image of a woman's face in tears will be used by a paper or magazine to show by *impression* the tragedy of a war, or the intensity of, say, a wedding . . .

But the point is, the story is *her*. As we piece together, or guess, or assume, some meaning in the narrative, we find that the meaning is the woman. She appears to express the meaning of events. How like every narrative and photographic medium this is, and also how like actual life, the 'they've got it, she wears it' of personal relations. In tapping the relation between women and meaningfulness Sherman's work resonates through many other areas. Certainly it also illuminates the process of reading all still images, especially adverts, in the way objects, details, arrangements and settings construct a story and an identity simultaneously. Women are not always necessarily a part of this visual and ideological process. But in Sherman's work, what comes out of the imagined narratives is, specifically, femininity. It is not just a range of feminine expressions that are shown but the *process* of the 'feminine' as an effect, something acted upon.

[. . .]

[W]hat is crucial to the reading of Sherman's work is also the opposition between the images. 'Essentially feminine' as they all are, they are all different. This not only rules out the idea that any one of them *is* the 'essentially feminine', but also shows, since each *seems* to be it, that there can be no such thing . . .

Femininity is multiple, fractured, and yet each of its infinite surfaces gives the illusion of depth and wholeness. Realizing this means that we as women don't have to get trapped trying to 'be' the depth behind a *surface*, and men just might bang their heads up against it and stop believing in that reflected space. Sherman's work is more than either a witty parody of media images of women, or a series of self-portraits in a search for identity. The two are completely mixed up, as are the imagery and experience of femininity for all of us. Others might try to break open that web of mirrors, but Sherman's way of revealing it is just to keep on skilfully turning the kaleidoscope where a few fragments of fantasy go a long way.

Untitled Film Still No. 4, 1978

Untitled Film Still No. 40, 1979

Untitled Film Still No. 16, 1978

Untitled Film Still No. 63, 1980

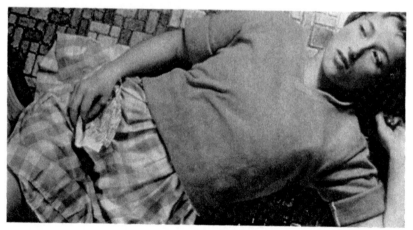

Untitled No. 96, 1981

Untitled No. 90, 1981

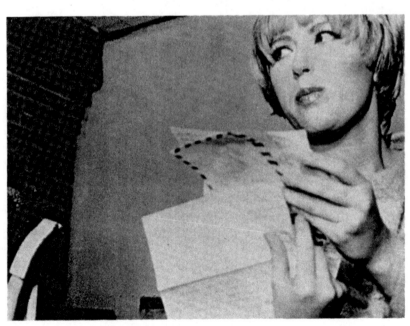

Untitled Film Still No. 5, 1978

Untitled Film Still No. 21, 1978

Untitled Film Still No. 46, 1979

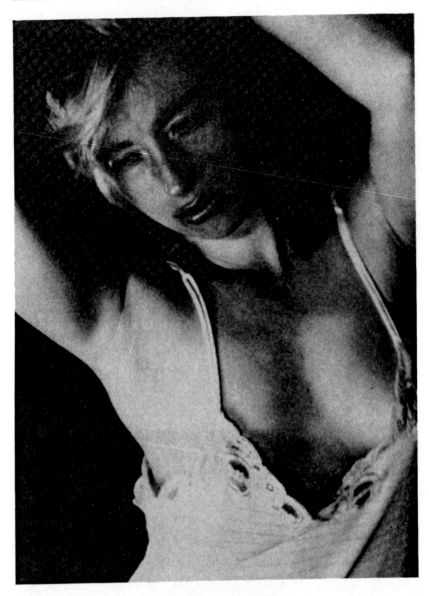

Untitled No. 103, 1982

Untitled No. 104, 1982

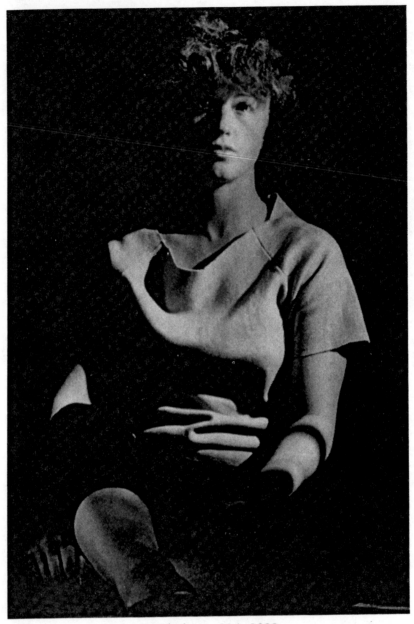

Untitled No. 116, 1982

Untitled No. 112, 1982

Untitled No. 110, 1982

6
SUBJECTIVITY AND IDENTITY

Feminist theories of subjectivity have been considerably influenced by Lacan's account of the subject. The idea that unconscious as well as conscious processes are involved in the construction of meaning helped in comprehending the way in which women were represented. Acknowledging the primary power of the mother and the symbolic power of the father also cast femininity and masculinity in a more complex light.

The Lacanian account of gender identity, however, had little to offer in terms of the possibilities for change. The idea that our status as subjects can only ever be achieved through acknowledging 'the law of the father' seems to close off any possibility for changing the relationship between masculinity and femininity. Thus, whilst feminism gained many insights from Lacan's theory, the theory also seemed to foreclose the project of feminism.

The question of change, however, was not just a problem for feminists attempting to use the Lacanian framework. It also constituted a difficulty for the theory itself. The problem resides in the way Lacanian theory analyses the subject as produced by the structure of the unconscious and the structure of language. In both, the operation of difference is paramount, creating as it does both meaning, and sexual identity, and the meaning of sexual identity. But this structuralist mode of analysing relationships between a set of necessary elements (for example, subject/object, mother/father, signifier/signified, male/female, conscious/unconscious) is very abstract. It tells the story of the subject without any reference to history, as if it were true for all time and historical change was of no consequence to the story. This is tantamount to suggesting that the construction of femininity in the Middle Ages, for example, was no different to that in the late twentieth century. At the level of the unconscious that may be true, but at the level of social meaning, it is clearly not the case. As far as Lacanian theory is concerned, this *historical* difference is of no consequence to the way we conceive the subject, whose meaning, along with that of sexual difference, is fixed within the unconscious. Although his account proposes a synthesis of social and psychic meaning, in the final analysis this synthesis is weighted towards the unconscious.

Lacan marginalizes questions of social process and historical change. Unconscious desire, however, is socially mediated and this means that its significance is historical and not just psychostructural. Language and the symbolic always include unconscious meaning, but they also convey historical meaning. Our subjectivities as women and men are formed not only by the unconscious, but also by the status and possibilities which socially define femininity and masculinity at particular historical periods. Contemporary feminism in particular has grappled with this political interface between the social definition of women and the subjective experience of femininity. Crucially, within this, the focus of feminism has been that of power and subordination.

FEMINISM AND FOUCAULT

In exploring the *politics* of subjectivity many feminists were influenced by the work of Foucault. As a post-structuralist, Foucault's philosophical starting-point is that meaning cannot be fixed because it is constructed relationally. In this radical insistence on the plurality and non-fixity of meaning, Foucault diverges from Lacan's account of meaning in one crucial way. He argues that meaning cannot be guaranteed by anything external to it and this includes Lacan's idea of the fixity of meaning within the unconscious. For Foucault the 'truth' of a discourse resides in the relations of power it sustains, not in empirical reality nor the reality of the unconscious. From this position within post-structuralism Foucault argues that the role of social criticism is to challenge dominant ideas and show the power and interests that such views of the world sustain.

Although no more preoccupied with the concerns of feminism than was Lacan, Foucault's analysis of power dovetails with that of feminism in that he is concerned with how the construction of subjectivity involves the operation of power. In Chapter 2 you encountered a feminist Foucauldian analysis of how ideologies of the body can structure feminine subjectivity. As that analysis makes clear, for Foucault power is neither positive nor negative. It is, to use Foucault's term, productive. Power is deployed in the production of meaning. It is consolidated through dominant ideas which, in sharing a common view of the world, make up a 'regime of truth'. Power is activated when people assume identities that are included within the prevailing views of the world. By occupying certain places within a discourse, the subject, according to Foucault, is empowered to act according to the identity prescribed by that discourse.

For Foucault, the discourses of femininity and masculinity do not repress or deny desire, but rather invoke it by proposing the means by which it can be satisfied. Thus power operates by regulating desire and thereby regulates society, but in a consensual way. Power is complied with through the many ways in which we attempt to give expression to desire by conforming to the dominant ideas as to how pleasure may best be achieved. In a further distancing from traditional conceptions of power, Foucault also argues that power is contested through counter-discourses which propose alternative accounts of subjectivity and social relations. This claim also has strong resonances with the directions of feminist theory.

THE DISCOURSE OF FOUCAULT

Central to Foucault's theoretical framework is his analysis of knowledge and truth, or how certain accounts of the world come to be accepted as expressing the essential truth about our social reality. Foucault argued that claims to the status of truth and knowledge could only be made from within a discourse, that we could only have an understanding of the world through our ideas about it. It is not possible, he suggests, to gain pure insight into the workings of society, simply because our perception is always structured by existing discursive arguments. This means that all knowledge is necessarily relative to the particular discursive frameworks which inform it and the criteria of truth underlying those discourses. Nonetheless theoretical discourses claim to represent the world 'as it is'. They claim to represent analytically true statements about social reality.

For Foucault, these knowledge claims represent a truth about social relations, not because they claim to be objective or scientific, but because they are accepted as true, and therefore people act as if they were true. When particular knowledges about the world are dominant, when they are broadly shared across social institutions, these discourses are true in the additional sense that they structure the world and exclude other interpretations of the world. In this way power and knowledge intersect to produce socially accepted conventions about knowledge and the nature of social reality.

Discourses, then, are not just ideas, they are also practices, ways of producing knowledge, and ways of shaping the world according to that knowledge. When challenging prevailing ideas about women's bodies and women's nature, feminism challenged not just the ideas but also those medical and scientific institutions which used these ideas to justify their exclusion of women. Feminists confronted both the ideas and the exclusionary practices they rationalized and through this political process ultimately challenged the status of truth such discourses claimed for themselves. This illustrates Foucault's point that the truth or falsity of knowledge is not something which can be established philosophically, nor by reference to 'the facts'. Discourses can be understood only in relation to other discourses. The discourse of sexual natures was challenged by that of sexual equality, not by empirical evidence refuting ideas of innate sexual characteristics.

Another illustration may make clearer precisely what Foucault means by the idea of empirical reality being unable to confirm knowledge. We cannot, for example, claim that women's mothering confirms the discourse of women's sexual natures and maternal instinct. The empirical reality of women's mothering is also seen within certain feminist discourses as the cornerstone of sexual subordination. Women caring for children can *prove* neither of these claims. This discourse of women's maternal nature, however, continues to be the more powerful and continues to represent the 'truth' about women, although this 'truth' is consistently being challenged by feminist discourses. It is the power of dominant discourses to define social identities which for Foucault constitutes the politics of truth. Equally it is the power of subjects to challenge discursive frameworks which constitutes the politics of resistance. For Foucault, both processes are given in the concepts of knowledge and power.

One difficulty with Foucault's account of discursive formations, however, is that it provides no way of analysing why we occupy certain subject positions and not others. In the first article in this chapter Hollway suggests that Foucault's theory of the subject involves a kind of discourse determinism. In other words, subjects are simply a product of, or constituted by, the various subject positions they have occupied since birth. The question Hollway raises is what motivates women and men to occupy the specific places they do within discourses?

Hollway suggests a synthesis of psychoanalytic and discourse theory to explain this process. She argues that the structure of femininity and masculinity ensures that we unconsciously invest in those discourses that affirm our sexuality, and in identifying with particular subject positions we re-produce that identity and the structure of unconscious desire which it involves. However, in challenging our identification with such a position, we can create another discursive position from which to mediate that unconscious desire. That, of course, is only the beginning of the story, not its end, for the process of transformation is neither immediate nor simple. What we gain though from this analytic framework is a way out of the impasse of the fixity of unconscious desire and the complicity of the symbolic in duplicating this. By focusing instead on discursive subjectification, we can analyse which unconscious desires and subject positions we are re-producing. In other words, we are not coincidentally trapped by discourse and the unconscious; it is possible to challenge and transform the terms and conditions of feminine desire, being mindful, however, of the resistance of the unconscious and the conservatism of the status quo.

In her account of Foucauldian criticism in the second article, Biddy Martin warns against being too easily seduced by discourse analysis. Her concern is with the political consequences of adopting a post-structuralist framework. Meaning, within the terms of post-structuralism, can only be understood through the method of its construction, that is, through the operation of difference. For the post-structuralists, 'woman' and 'women' are only social constructs and not categories grounded in either biological or psychosexual difference. Power is also seen as creating these fictitious entities of femininity and masculinity and the task therefore of social criticism is to deconstruct these constructions and expose the operation of power that is effected through them.

To some extent, as we have seen, feminism as a movement has already taken up this project, not because of any adherence to the post-structuralist methodological imperative, but because of the politics of feminism. From its initial starting-point of analysing all women as caught in the oppressive system of patriarchy, feminism was forced to recognize the differences between women, differences of race and ethnicity, of age, class and nationality, as well as the different sexualities of women. This in turn led to a recognition that women had to be analysed in terms of diversity and plurality and not through the fiction of a commonality of experience. This, however, was a formulation of difference and generality quite distinct from that proposed by post-structuralism. According to the latter, as Martin says, 'sexual difference, sexual identity, sexuality itself are fictions'. Any attempt by feminism to define the meaning of 'woman' or even 'women' is itself participating in relations of power. For post-structuralism, the task of feminism is that of vigilantly deconstructing the imagined unities of woman and women, thereby thwarting the operation of power. For feminism, however, there is an additional task of creating new meanings and new identities for women which embrace diversity and plurality.

Feminist theory is precisely concerned with the workings of power and the way in which power constitutes our subjectivity. However, the project of knowing women becomes a nonsense if we assume that women as such are only categories of meaning. The generality we share is a negative relation to social power which is not, as Foucault makes clear, to claim we are therefore powerless. Another commonality is our bodies. Perhaps Foucault is right to suggest that feminism, in displacing the edifice of discourses locating women as only ever sexual, has desexualized women. What remains to be understood is the potential of our historical identities as women defined not in terms of dominant discourses, but in terms of the feminist project for change.

Article 6.1
GENDER DIFFERENCE AND THE PRODUCTION OF SUBJECTIVITY

Wendy Hollway

INTRODUCTION

In this chapter I attempt to analyse the construction of subjectivity in a specific area: heterosexual relations. My framework depends on three conceptual positions . . .: the non-rational, non-unitary character of subjectivity; its social and historical production through signification; power relations and the re-production of systematic difference.

[. . .]

The material comes from dialogues and discussions conducted in the course of my PhD research (Hollway, 1982). Participants talked about relationships, sexuality and gender. I talked to them singly and in groups, and without using a structured format of questions. They were not chosen to represent a range of social differences. Rather, it was my intention to make detailed readings of their accounts, recognizing their specific social location and its effectivity in the re-production of gender difference in discourse and subjectivity through power and signification.

LIVING THE RECENT HISTORY OF GENDER DIFFERENCE

First I would like to illustrate the theme of gender difference, and the inseparability of subjectivity from the social domain by summarizing the contradictions of my own gender. What does it mean to be a woman in my class and culture? I have grown up in the 1950s and 1960s in a Western industrial society, in a middle-class home where education and the career possibilities it conferred were – in certain important respects – as available to me as they were to boys. Educational and job opportunity, unisex and permissiveness, were ideas which were, at least in principle, gender-blind. I went through university with as much money in my pocket as the men students (though I couldn't get such well-paid holiday jobs). The pill meant that I could have sexual relationships without becoming a mother.

Being as good as men

Early modern feminism (Greer, 1971; Firestone, 1972) was telling women like me that we were equal to men because we were the same as them. Certainly this fitted in with my pre-feminist assumptions that men represented all that was interesting, admirable, powerful and desirable. I was attracted to men, partly because I aspired to being like them.

I was keen to develop so-called masculine skills. For example, I learned to service my car, how to build houses and wire up electrical circuits. I disdained helping hands over gates and in general determined to walk, swim, run, drive – as far and as fast as my men companions.

Why was this a problem? Surely equality was desirable? To compete with men like this necessitated a negative definition of myself as woman, and it reproduced the signifier 'woman' unchanged. Women were a group I put myself outside of. When I made generalizations about women (almost always derogatory), I did not include myself in the group I was talking about.[1]

Differences as otherness

As my own recollections demonstrate, the difference between women and men was not just a neutral difference. It is based on the principle of 'otherness' (de Beauvoir, 1972). In many practices, to be like men I had to be not like women.[2] This is the crucial feature of gender differences. It also means that equality, in that earlier meaning of the term, produces contradictions, rather than simply offering additional and complementary possibilities. It is also more likely to produce reaction.

One of the participants in my research who changed sex to become a woman when she was in her twenties described how she felt at a very early age about being a boy:

Sheila: Yes it mostly wasn't a question of what I wanted to be, it was more a question of what one didn't want to be, what one didn't want to do. Because one was constantly faced with the things one was being told to do, one was taught to do, and that one was rejecting.

Whereas for boys and men the alternative gender-differentiated positions are clear-cut and appear mutually exclusive,[3] for girls and women it is easier to move among them. At a theoretical level it is quite easy to see why: 'man' and 'person' have been synonymous in Western, patriarchal thought, as is evidenced by the use of the terms 'man', 'mankind' and 'he/him' as universals. As women we can strive to be 'people' and 'women'. Logically there is no contradiction. However, because 'person' actually consists of all the attributes which are meant to be characteristic of men, there is an underlying contradiction.[4] I think I managed this contradiction by being (or trying to be) as good as men in the public world, and even competitive in my relationships with men. At the same time, by virtue of maintaining a heterosexual relationship, I preserved my feminine identity. Ever since I had grown up I had been in a couple relationship with a man, and however well I succeeded at doing things, they were always there – men who knew more than me, men whom I could learn from – to guarantee my femininity. Those qualities of men which 'guaranteed my femininity' demonstrate well that the differences which confer gender were not neutral in value. My position in relation to men demonstrates the nonunitary nature of my gendered subjectivity. I aspired to similarity in some spheres because of the value attached. At the same time I preserved my difference.

GENDER DIFFERENCE IN THREE DISCOURSES CONCERNING SEXUALITY

Foucault's use of the term discourse is historical and this is crucial to the analytic power of the concept. For my purposes the emphasis must be shifted in order to understand how at a specific moment several coexisting and potentially contradictory discourses concerning sexuality make available different positions and different powers for men and women. Thus the references to the histories of these discourses will be only in passing (but see Foucault, 1979a; Bland and Hollway, unpubl.; Heath, 1982). Given my objective of theorizing subjectivity as it is re-produced in discourses, it is personal genealogies which are a necessary part of the analysis . . .

In order to make a reading of the accounts I gathered concerning sexuality, I delineated three discourses: the male sexual drive discourse; the have/hold discourse; and the permissive discourse. I arrived at these three through a combination of my own knowledge and what was suggested by the data (an approach which Glaser and Strauss (1967) call 'grounded theory'). Clearly my own assumptions and those of research participants share a largely common historical production; they will also be recognizable to most readers. Some assumptions are more widespread than others (indeed, some would say that the discourse of male sexual drive was universal and that this supports a claim that it is based on the biological 'fact' of male sexuality). It would be relatively easy to identify more discourses, with different boundaries. For my purposes, however, what is more important is the use I make of these three in my analysis of the effects of gender difference in positioning subjects.

The male sexual drive discourse

This needs little introduction because it is so familiar – so hegemonic, or dominant – in the production of meanings concerning sexuality. A man friend of mine captured it succinctly: 'I want to fuck. I *need* to fuck. I've always needed and wanted to fuck. From my teenage years, I've always longed after fucking.' Its key tenet is that men's sexuality is directly produced by a biological drive, the function of which is to ensure reproduction of the species. The discourse is everywhere in common-sense assumptions and is reproduced and legitimized by experts, including psychologists. For example Anthony Storr asserts that,

> Male sexuality *because of the primitive necessity* of pursuit and penetration, does contain an important element of aggressiveness; an element which is both recognized and responded to by the female who yields and submits.
>
> (*quoted in* The Observer, *24 May 1981; my italics*)

A more recent example of the discourse being made respectable by experts through recourse to scientific explanations is Glenn Wilson's (1979) use of sociobiology to attack feminist accounts of sex differences which are based on social theories of women's oppression. The effect and intention of his argument is to represent women's position as biologically determined and therefore unchangeable . . .

The have/hold discourse

This has as its focus not sexuality directly, but the Christian ideals associated with monogamy, partnership and family life. The split between wife and mistress, virgin and whore, Mary and Eve, indicates how this and the male sexual drive discourse coexist in constructing men's sexual practices. In some aspects the discourses are consistent; for example both share assumptions about sexuality being linked to reproductivity, and also that sex is heterosexual. Yet the two recommend different and contradictory standards of conduct for men.

This contradiction is resolved for men by visiting it upon women. Either women are divided into two types (as above), or more recently a woman is expected to be both things. In effect we end up with a double standard (the widespread recognition and criticism of which has not wholly changed the practices): men's sexuality is understood through the male sexual drive discourse: they are expected to be sexually incontinent and out of control – 'it's only natural'.

The following letter from a man in *Spare Rib* (a British feminist magazine) demonstrates how these discourses can coexist in the beliefs of one person:

> As a mature male, I am in total support of the new 'women against violence against women' campaign, with the proviso that the supporters should realize that the majority of men are decent, of reasonably high principles and respect women as equal partners, and only a small proportion are grossly anti-social. But man being the animal he is, do you think that the answer to rape is well-ordered government-run brothels to

cater for the large section of single, sexually-frustrated men in our society?

(Spare Rib, *104, March 1981*)

The picture is more complicated for women. Underneath the insistence on our asexuality within this discourse is the belief that our sexuality is rabid and dangerous and must be controlled. This is far more explicit in Mediterranean cultures where women are traditionally seen as being in one of two categories: 'fallen' or 'not yet fallen' (Du Boulay, 1974). The implication is that women's sexuality is inevitable and dangerous. (It is not defined as a lack, as in post-Victorian northern Europe.) The only way to preserve the family honour is thus the total subservience of women to male control. Here men project onto women a rabid and ever-present sexuality, which leads to irrational jealousy (Moi, 1982). Later I shall approach the question in terms of men's 'desire for the Other' and the reasons for their projections, rather than falling into the assumption that this has something to do with women's sexuality.

According to the have/hold discourse, women's sexuality is seen as a lack, the possibility avoided by the stress on their relationship with husband and children. For example, Eustace Chesser, a liberal sexual reformer in the 1950s, argued that the sex act for women was only a prelude to satisfaction of the 'maternal instinct' and 'finding joy in family life' (quoted in Campbell, 1980).

Gender-differentiated positions

Before going on to comment on the permissive discourse, I will indicate the main implication of the coexistence of these two discourses for gender difference. It is not that women's sexuality is not constructed in the male sexual drive discourse. Rather woman is seen as its object. The position for a woman in this set of meanings is as the object that precipitates men's natural sexual urges:

Will: Well certainly in adolescence I felt that there was a very impersonal sexuality. But it wasn't anything particularly that women did. It was my need – as it were – that did it to me. That meant that any woman would be doing it to me – in a sense – even if she hadn't noticed my existence. And that's what I mean by feeling *quite enslaved* to an abstract impersonal sexuality.

However, in the practices of courtship and sexual activity, women are not just the hapless victims of this male sexual drive. Angela McRobbie in her work on adolescent working-class girls concludes that 'their goal is to attract and keep a man' (McRobbie, 1978). Commonly accepted practices of femininity take it for granted that there is status and power attached to being attractive to men. In order to attract them, women can take up the object position in the male sexual drive discourse. Women are often seen as 'trapping' men by their powers of sexual attraction. But sex can also derive its meaning from the have/hold discourse. For example:

Dot: The one time I did fuck with Charles, it felt really good, like there was an awful lot that was important going on. But I didn't have an orgasm . . . maybe the tension was too great or something. I don't know, I was very *turned on*. It was the idea of fucking with him rather than with someone else. The image I get makes me physically shudder with excitement. That reinforces my hunch that it's what's invested in the *idea*. I was in love with him. It's not fucking itself, it's something to do with the rights it gave me to see myself as having a relationship with him. I didn't have any of course.

Despite positioning herself in the permissive discourse (see below) by saying 'of course' she didn't have any rights to a relationship, Dot's reading of this one-off sexual encounter, and even her physical sexual response, were constructed through the set of meanings associated with the have/hold discourse. In another epoch, 'keeping a man' would have meant marriage. Here it is expressed as wanting a relationship. It entails positioning the woman as subject of the have/hold discourse. Although nothing was said on that matter between Dot and Charles, those meanings were an inalienable feature of her feelings. We don't know whether Charles positioned Dot through the have/hold discourse. When this is the case, in complementary fashion, the man is positioned as object of this discourse. This constructs the meanings, and affects the practices, of some men. For example Jim avoided casual sexual encounters because of what it might mean about commitment. Not specified, but a basic assumption in the following extract, is that a relationship was what the woman would want. The complementary position (that he does not) is also quite clear:

Jim: Feeling that sex was kind of dangerous. If you had sex, it meant that you were committed in some way and I didn't want that. Also that if you *just* had sex without a relationship, it was a pretty shitty thing to do to have one part of it without the other.

The permissive discourse

The sexual practices of the participants in my study (aged on average around 30 in 1980) cannot be understood without recourse to a third discourse: the 'permissive' discourse. In this, the principle of monogamy is explicitly challenged, as is illustrated by this comment from the Student Christian Movement in 1966 speaking, predictably, from within the have/hold discourse: 'The teaching of the Christian church that sexual intercourse should be confined to marriage is frequently attacked as a theory and ignored in practice' (Sex and Morality, p. 4). In assuming that sexuality is entirely natural and therefore should not be repressed, the permissive discourse is the offspring of the male sexual drive discourse. Similarly it takes the individual as the locus of sexuality, rather than looking at it in terms of a relationship.[5] In one important respect it differs from the male sexual drive discourse: it applies the same assumptions to women as to men. In other words it was – in principle at least – gender-blind. In 1968, a reviewer of Vance Packard's book *The Sexual Wilderness* summed up the characteristics of the permissive society in the following terms: 'On the whole the young of *both sexes* believe that they have a right to express their sexuality in any way they choose so long as nobody is hurt' (my italics). Women could now be subjects of a discourse in a way which meant active initiation of a sexual relationship based on the idea that our natural sexual drives were equal to (or the same as) men's. However, gender difference in sexuality was not suddenly transformed. That this was not the case demonstrates the importance of recognizing the historically specific nature of discourses, their relation to what has gone before and how practices – such as the one-night stands of the permissive era – are not the pure products of a single discourse.

The differences between men's and women's positions in the traditional discourses were never banished in permissive practices. Beatrix Campbell sums up what is commonly recognized now by women in the women's movement (many of whom were believers in the equality of sex in permissive practices at the time):

> [the permissive era] permitted sex for women too. What it did not do was defend women against the differential effects of permissiveness on men and women . . . It was about affirmation of young men's sexuality and promiscuity; it was indiscriminate, [so long as she was a woman]. The very affirmation of sexuality was a celebration of *masculine* sexuality.
>
> (Campbell, 1980, pp. 1–2)

In the following extract Jo describes why permissive sex was alienating for her:

Jo: I've fantasized it [the quickie] yes, but it's never functioned like that – even when that person was a complete stranger. Afterwards I just looked at that stranger and felt completely alienated from what I'd just done with him. I mean, really uncomfortable in the extreme. Why did I do it? I think in that situation I'd almost never come, because I'd just be too guarded. You know, there was too much, which I'm just not going to let go – with a complete stranger . . .

Colin: Isn't that just the point? – Why the attraction? It's the fact that it's a stranger. It's nothing to do with the rest of your life. There's no damage that can be caused, you know, and all that kind of thing.

Piera: Yes, you don't have to have a relationship with that person.

Jo: But I don't think I can have sex without having a relationship. So if I haven't got one, it feels alienated, because to me, sex is expressing whatever the relationship is, and is going to be, and what can be built and how I feel with that person, and if it doesn't I really do feel awful. I do feel that if all I want is a quickie – that is some sexual tension released – then I'm much happier masturbating.

Colin: I don't think that's the nature of a quickie, though.

The meanings of sex for Jo are inconsistent with the permissive discourse and therefore the practice which it promoted felt wrong. In contrast Colin's statements emanate from the assumptions of the permissive discourse. His account of the attraction of the quickie casts light on what Jim said above. In contrast to the have/hold discourse, the permissive discourse did not imply any commitment or responsibility. Had Jim been able to position himself by means of the permissive discourse rather than the have/hold discourse, sex would not have seemed so dangerous. However, as I shall argue in the fourth part of this chapter, the meanings of sex are more contradictory than that.[6]

The practices that a discourse re-produces are not neutral. The liberating effects of the permissive discourse were particularly contradictory for women. Certainly the discourse enhanced men's powers (men's 'rights') to a heterosexual practice without emotional bonds. Later I shall return to the question of why men had more invested in this than women.

Summary and restatement of the approach

My treatment of these three discourses makes several points which are theoretically significant for the use of a discourse analysis to understand the relation of gender difference, subjectivity and change.

1   Discourses make available positions for subjects to take up. These positions are in relation to other people. Like the subject and object[7] of a sentence (and indeed expressed through such a grammar), women and men are placed in relation to each other through the

meanings which a particular discourse makes available: 'the female who yields and submits' to the man (Storr, quoted above).

2   Because traditional discourses concerning sexuality are gender-differentiated, taking up subject or object positions is not equally available to men and women. (Try out Storr's formulation in reverse: 'the man who yields and submits to the woman's aggressive pursuit'.) The same applies to practices understandable in terms of gender-differentiated discourses. For example it's virtually imposs-ible for women to put themselves in the position of subjects in the male sexual drive discourse when it comes to practices such as bottom-pinching or wolf-whistling.

3   The positions are specified for the category 'man' or 'woman' in general. None the less particular men and women fill these positions. Their practices in relation to each other are rendered meaningful according to gender-differentiated discourses.

4   Practices and meanings have histories, developed through the lives of the people concerned. These histories are not the product of a single discourse (though, depending on the hegemony of one discourse, meanings may be more or less homogeneous).

5   Because discourses do not exist independently of their re-production through the practices and meanings of particular women and men, we must account for changes in the dominance of certain discourses, and the development of new ones (for example those being articulated by feminists) by taking account of men's and women's subjectivity. Why do men 'choose' to position themselves as subjects of the discourse of male sexual drive? Why do women continue to position themselves as its objects? What meanings might this have for women? How do the contradictions between the have/hold and male sexual drive discourses produce the practices of a particular heterosexual relationship? Do the practices signify differently for women and men, because they are being read through different discourses? Why and under what past and present circumstances are women more likely to read a sexual relationship through the have/hold discourse than men?

6   By posing such questions, it is possible to avoid an analysis which sees discourses as mechanically repeating themselves – an analysis which cannot account for change. By showing how subjects' investments, as well as the available positions offered by discourses, are socially constituted and constitutive of subjectivity, it is possible to avoid this deterministic analysis of action and change.

How can we understand gender difference in a way which can account for changes? If we do not ask this question the change of paradigm from a biologistic to a discourse theory of gender difference does not constitute much of an advance. If the concept of discourses is just a replacement for the notion of ideology, then we are left with one of two possibilities. Either the account sees discourses as mechanically repeating themselves, or – and this is the tendency of materialist theory of ideology – changes in ideology follow from changes in material conditions. According to such a use of discourse theory people are the victims of certain systems of ideas which are outside of them. Discourse determinism comes up against the old problem of agency typical of all sorts of social determinisms.

Foucault's genealogies – because they are based on empirical historical data – do not register the stasis of discourses, but rather their changes. However, there is a gap in the theory which he uses to account for such changes. He stresses the mutually constitutive relation between power and knowledge: how each constitutes the other to produce the truths of a particular epoch ... Rather than power being equated with oppression and seen as a negative thing, which can be got rid of come the revolution, power is seen as productive, inherently neither positive nor negative: productive of knowledges, meanings and values, and of certain practices as opposed to others. He still does not account for how people are constituted as a result of certain truths being current rather than others. The advantage of the idea that current at any one time are competing, potentially contradictory discourses (concerning for example sexuality) rather than a single patriarchal ideology, is that we can then pose the question, how is it that people take up positions in one discourse rather than another? If the process is not a mechanical positioning, why is it that men take up the subject position in the discourse of male sexual drive? What's in it for them? Under what conditions do men cease to do this? What accounts for the differences between some men and others? These questions require that attention is paid to the histories of individuals in order to see the recursive positioning in certain positions in discourses. It also requires a question concerning the *investment* in that position.

I have had considerable difficulty finding a good term here. 'Motivation' connotes biologically determined drives or alternatively individual needs ... 'Drive' gets its meaning from psychoanalytic theory and reduces to 'instinct'. The terms all express concepts which are subject to the weaknesses of dualism. They are also subject to the related problem of accounts of agency. For when the forces propelling people's actions have not been theorized as reducing to biology or society, they have been seen as a product of rational decision-making. Yet, following our critique of the rational subject, a term like 'choice' does not convey the complexity of causes for action. I have chosen 'investment' because it appears to avoid most of these problems. In addition it was the German word for 'investment', *Besetzung*, which Freud chose to refer to what in English has been translated as 'cathexis'. As the two uses share some important emphases, it is a potentially productive meeting of paradigms. By claiming that people have investments (in this case gender-specific) in taking up certain positions in discourses, and consequently in relation to each other, I mean that there will be some satisfaction or pay-off or reward (these terms involve the same problem) for that person. The satisfaction may well in in contradiction with other resultant feelings. It is not necessarily conscious or rational. But there is a reason. In what follows, I theorize the reason for this investment in terms of power and the way it is historically inserted into individuals' subjectivity . . .

BOYS' AND GIRLS' ENTRY INTO MASCULINITY AND FEMININITY

In this part I will try to give an account – albeit schematic – of boys' and girls' developing relation to sexuality through the available discourses. Any analysis which focuses on subjective positioning in discourses requires an account of the investment that a person has in taking up one position rather than another in a different discourse. Of course some discourses are more hegemonic and thus carry all the weight of social approval. But successful positioning in these discourses is not automatic, else there would be no variations. But to assume the mechanical reproduction of discourse requires asking how it got to be like that in the first place. And that question is in danger of throwing theory back into answers according to the terms of biological, Oedipal, or social and economic determinisms . . .

The point that I have been at pains to stress is that discourses coexist and have mutual effects and that meanings are multiple. This produces choice, though it may not be simple or conscious. Consequently we have to account for what investments a boy or girl has in taking up a particular position in discourses by relating in certain ways with the other.[8] What accounts for the different investments produced historically in people of the same gender? Clearly other major dimensions of social difference such as class, race and age intersect with gender to favour or disfavour certain positions. However, as well as recognizing cultural regularities it is also necessary – without resorting to essentialism – to account for the uniqueness of individuals. Lacanian theory does so by stressing the somewhat anarchic character of desire: desire as a motive force or process is common to all significations (although it is contentious whether it is universal). Although the significations which it occupies may be quite idiosyncratic, I try to show that they are not arbitrary. Significations are a product of a person's history, and what is expressed or suppressed in signification is made possible by the availability and hegemony of discourses. Positions available in gender-differentiated discourses confer relative power by enabling the suppression of significations which would be undermining of power.

Growing up properly for a boy

For Jim girls were essential to 'growing up properly':

Jim: I remember very young – before twelve – feeling a pressure to have a girlfriend and not having a clue. I remember hanging around a local cinema thinking that might be how something happened. But it was like an abstract pressure – I just felt that I should in order to show I was growing up properly. It didn't have any connection with the rest of my life, it was just something that I felt I should take on.

What did having a girlfriend mean that it signified 'growing up properly'? It positioned Jim as a 'proper man'; in other words it afforded him a gender-appropriate position:

Jim: I did feel the onus always to actually be pushy, to see how far it was possible to go with somebody, to see how far they were actually *into* me.

Wendy: What did you want?

Jim: Well just an obvious sign of . . . as a way of showing I was into them – well in a way showing I was a proper man.

The sexual (or protosexual) practices he engaged in enabled him to be positioned as subject in the male sexual drive discourse ('being pushy'). He was not the victim of a natural drive (though the girl concerned probably read it that way). His interest was to do with gender not sex. His successful masculine positioning depended on a girl being 'into him' and the proof of this would be that she let him get sexual with her.

'Being attractive' for a girl

The same principle is illustrated in Clare's account of her adolescent feelings about boys. The available positions are different however. Where Jim had to be pushy, Clare had to be attractive. There is a chain of assumptions running through the account: being attractive . . . (means) . . . being attractive to boys . . . (means) . . . engaging in sex (or protosex) with boys . . . (means) . . . having a boyfriend.

Clare: I can see from the photographs that I went from being a child who was quite pretty to an early adolescent who – I felt myself to be fat and ugly, and desperately lacking in confidence. I suspect I lacked confidence because I had had ways of dealing with people, which were to do with being an attractive child. They didn't work any more, because I wasn't one. When I was fourteen or fifteen I went on a diet – and I went down from being quite big to seven stone. It was an absolutely wonderful thing. It had a lot for me, to do with sexuality. I remember I thought I would be more confident, I thought I would be more attractive to boys.

Wendy: Were you more confident?

Clare: In a way, yes. I was quite good at school, though but certainly – when I lost weight, it seemed like the resolution of a set of contradictions. Having lost weight, I was no longer destined to be the 'ugly, clever type'. It would be alright because I was actually quite attractive as well. The more I dig deep, the more I think of the hurt – there's a hell of a lot of hurt around not being attractive enough and particularly about not having boyfriends. I remember, kind of, going out with anybody who asked me. I was so pleased to be asked, that I would have gone with anybody.

Wendy: When you did go out with them, what did you think of them?

Clare: Not a lot. I thought it was all a bit of a joke. Most of them were fools.

Adolescent girls' sexual practices gain them the reputation of being either slags or drags (Cowie and Lees, 1981) – a contradiction which is a logical product of women's contradictory positions in the male sexual drive and have/hold discourses. Yet girls do not on the whole feel free to forego relationships with boys, for the reasons that Clare illuminates. Her identity as an attractive girl is at stake. According to McRobbie (1978) adolescent girls' main goal is 'to attract and keep a boy'. There are ostensibly few pay-offs and plenty of risks: the danger of being called 'slags' (Cowie and Lees, 1981), no enjoyment of the kind of sex that boys practise, the experience that the boys are fools anyway. Their investment is in their own identities. Boys are necessary simply because in the only discourse in which being attractive can be understood, being attractive means being attractive to the opposite sex.

Attractiveness and femininity

It is within the practices of gender-differentiated discourses concerning sexuality that girls' and women's gender identity is re-produced. In the following quote, Clare explores why she felt in a weak position later on when she did get involved in a long-term relationship with a man:

Clare: I mean, with Phil he was very loud and domineering, and I was very quiet and weak. He was strong, and I was weak. I think that was the main thing. And I was more feminine.

Wendy: What did that involve?

Clare: Looking pretty. I think it relates back to when I said that when I was little I was the good, pretty little girl. It's to do with – the fear – being frightened of not being attractive enough.

Wendy: To keep him?

Clare: Mmmm.

Attracting a man is the defining feature of Clare's femininity. Keeping him, according to the male sexual drive discourse, means continuing to be attractive to him. This is the crucial recurrent interest in Clare's take-up of the object position in the male sexual drive discourse. In order to feel herself as gender-appropriate, she thus feels driven to be in a couple relationship with a man. These practices re-produce certain sexual and couple practices, and re-produce both gender difference and the inequality of women's position in the dominant discourses concerning sexuality.

I have shown that the practice of heterosexual couple relations (including sexual relations) is a site where different discourses concerning sexuality are available to produce different knowledges or meanings through which practices are mediated. Within this general usage of discourse analysis what is of particular significance is how the gender-differentiated nature of these discourses affects women's and men's powers and therefore the investment they have in taking up gender-appropriate positions and practices. Girls and women actively engage in certain heterosexual practices in order to re-produce their gender identity.

Heterosexual practice and the construction of women's sexuality

However, the investments of those participating in sexual relations are no more unitary than the powers conferred on them through their positions in discourses. In the following extract, Clare indicates that her sexuality was completely subordinated to the need to be attractive:

Clare: I think my understanding of my own sexuality when I was an adolescent was about zero. I mean it felt like doing this thing which meant you had to attract boys – to be attractive to them. There wasn't anything else. But even later, when I began fucking men, it was actually an extension of that.

That this need to be attractive produced her as passive in heterosexual sex is illustrated below. Clare and I discover the similarities in the way that our sexuality and gender was reproduced in the practices which were a product of the male sexual drive. The take-up of a position as object in the discourse of male sexual drive, motivated by the interest in being attractive, constructs the practice of heterosexual sex:

Clare: Well, I don't know, the term 'sexuality' means something quite different now. I don't think I felt I had a sexuality.

Wendy: I was never actually aware of having a spontaneous desire, that somehow seemed to be initiated by me, which I could then act out.

Clare: Right, yes. That's it.

Wendy: . . .Except the desire to attract a man, and follow it through.

Clare: Right. It was that which was powerful for me.

Wendy: Although, if I was attracted to a boy, and we went out together, or something, I was always – y'know, wanting kisses and cuddles, and fumbles, and . . . I don't know – the kind of things that would signify that it was getting more intense.

Clare: Yes, but I think that was because of what it signified, rather than because I actually liked it.

Wendy: Yes, and even that had a kind of genital goal. Because even though I didn't know at that point what we did, I knew that that was the most risky place.

Clare: Yes – I knew that. But I can't say that I enjoyed it. But then I didn't enjoy screwing very much either. I didn't know that I didn't, even. I feel very ashamed – I feel it's an awful admission. I actually had my first orgasm with Ken. I mean, I was sleeping with men for that long, and I never had one. I mean, I didn't think I was, and I wasn't sure, and for the life of me I wouldn't ask. It took me a long time to realize – well that I had masturbated and reached orgasm. I didn't know it was the same thing. I just thought it was something rather peculiar. I did masturbate when I was younger but I associated it – not one iota – with sex. I suppose later it was a certain kind of confidence which I had, which meant that I was more determined to get what I wanted. Even though I wasn't quite sure what that was. I mean, I think I was probably very passive.

Wendy: That passivity thing – I think is tied up with confidence. Er, with me, in short relationships, where I didn't actually . . . know a man very well, I never trusted the man enough for me to be active. Or, another way of putting it would be – to show myself as someone who had . . . desires.

Clare: I think that's right – for me. I was passive – because I didn't know how to express myself and also because I didn't know what to do. And because I felt judgements were being made of my sexual competence. And I had no idea, whether or not I was doing it right.

Wendy: The criterion that I evolved – of doing it right or not, was . . . um . . . ministering right to a man's needs, to what turned him on. If he seemed to enjoy it. And it was all about his sexuality.

Clare: Yes. Right.

Wendy: . . . I mean, that's how I learned to be sexual.

Clare: . . . Doing things that men liked. Yes.

Wendy: And in that sense I was quite active – I took initiatives.

THE SUPPRESSED IN DISCOURSE AND THE MULTIPLE SIGNIFICATIONS OF SEX

So far it might appear that men and women are so positioned by these different discourses that gender difference is well established and successful in producing men and women whose subjectivity is a unitary product of them. Is it not rather surprising, then, that men often stay in couple relationships – even hang on to them when the woman wants out – and find immediate replacements when a relationship ends? (I'm not saying women don't too, but this is consistent with women's positioning in discourses and inconsistent with men's.)

The meaning of sex is no more unitary than the discourses which compete to define the practice of sex. In this section I want to show how suppressed significations coexist with those expressed. Rather than seeing what is suppressed as something which is directly reducible to the Oedipus complex, or as invisible in the sense that the suppressed meanings have no effects (that is tantamount to the suppressed being non-existent and meaning being unitary), I will show how for men there are continued investments – to do with power – in defining women as subjects of the have/hold discourse, thereby suppressing their own wishes to have and to hold. One participant in my research wrote the following about the man she was in a relationship with:

> If he's saying he has no expectations, no needs, then I can't let him down. If I can't let him down, he has more power. He has the power to hurt me, but I don't have the power to hurt him.

Her observation is a beautifully clear recognition of the relation between knowledge (discourses) and power. As long as she and not he is positioned as the subject of the have/hold discourse, unequal power is the consequence.

What does a man want?

. . .One of the men who participated in my research expresses needs more in keeping with women's as they are articulated in the have/hold discourse, at the same time as being aware of the contradictions:

Sam: The thing that has caused me the most pain, and the most hope is the idea of actually living with Jane. And that's in the context of having tried to live with three other women before. And each time the relationship's been full of possibility. I don't want to live on my own. There's too many things all wrapped up in coupling. There's too many needs it potentially meets, and there are too many things it frustrates. I do want to have a close, a central-person relationship, but in the past, the negative aspects outweighed the positive aspects dramatically. Or my inability to work through them has led me to run.

What happens to men's needs for a 'close central-person relationship' as Sam put it? The negative aspects, which occupy the other side of Sam's contradiction, are not to do with free sexuality (although in the extract below he specifically refers to that discourse in order to gainsay it):

Sam: I'm very frightened of getting in deep – and then not being able to cope with the demands that the relationship's making. You see, a lot of these things aren't really to do with sexuality. They're to do with responsibility.

In this quotation from Sam, there is an elision between getting in deep[9] and responsibility. This occurs through the lack of clarity about whether Sam was frightened of getting in deep himself, or of the women doing so. In the following extract from Sam, the effect of the woman's position in the have/hold discourse is to protect Sam's own deep feelings. It is a further illustration of the relation between power and knowledge – the effect of discourse in action. It shows the idea of women requiring commitment being reproduced as a result of men's projected fears.

Sam: I'll tell you something – which I don't know what it means but I'll say it anyway. When I say to somebody, who I'm making love to – I'm close to, when I say, 'I love you, I love you' it's a word that symbolizes letting go. The night before Carol went away, she was saying it, and then I started saying it to her, when we were making love. What frightens me is that word, it's an act of commitment. Somebody suddenly, expects something of me. They've said something, that's the first word in a long rotten line towards marriage. That when you fall in love, you're caught up in the institution. And it's been an act of principle for me, that I can love somebody, and feel loved, without feeling any responsibility. That I can be free to say that I love somebody if I love them. Be free to feel. I can feel it quite unpredictably. It can hit me quite unexpectedly. And I think I worry about it because I can be quite sentimental.

The power of the meaning 'I love you' for Sam was that he felt close to someone and it was a 'letting go' of his emotions. This is dangerous because of the power it confers on someone else; the other in the sexual relationship. As soon as Sam has said this, the signifier 'letting go' is suppressed by its capture in the discourse which positions women as requiring commitment. The fear which is generated because this can 'hit me quite unexpectedly' is sufficient to produce its repression, its falling to the level of the signified. Thus gender difference in the discourse 'women requiring commitment' is reproduced.

However, there is a contradiction which remains: men still have needs for the intimacy of a heterosexual relationship. A man writing in *Achilles Heel* (an anti-sexist men's magazine) suggests that this is the only place where men can get these needs met:

> For men (heterosexual) sex works out as a trap because it's the only place where men can really get tenderness and warmth. But they have no skills to evoke these things because there is nothing in the rest of our lives that trains us to do this. So we come into this where we want warmth and intimacy and we don't know how to get it. But it's the only place it exists so there's this tremendous tension for men, getting into bed with women.
>
> (Achilles Heel, 2, 1979, p. 9)

This quotation again illustrates that sex can be a cover for men's need for intimacy to be met. The reproduction of women as subjects of a discourse concerning the desire for intimate and secure relationships protects men from the risk associated with their own need (and the consequent power it would give women). Their own simultaneous position as object of the have/hold discourse and subject of the male sexual drive discourse enables them to engage in the practice of sex, and thus get what they want without recognizing those needs or risking exposure. 'Sex' as male drive therefore covers for the suppressed signification of 'sex' as intimacy and closeness. Because the practice itself does not require verbalization, the suppressed signification is not necessarily recognized. These significations (not necessarily conscious) are completely woven in to the practices of sex, suppressed as they are with the aid of the male sexual drive discourse. This is illustrated by Sam's immediate association when asked how a woman makes him feel: 'It's a closeness, isn't it . . . going to sleep, cuddling close. Feeling – I mean, I don't worry about burglars. I think I feel a lot more secure.'

Unlike a reply from within the discourse of male sexual drive, such as 'it turns me on', Sam's response captures significations normally suppressed through projection: closeness and security.

A man's fear of 'getting in deep' requires theorization in its own right. What are the strong feelings that are evoked by women with whom they have – or want – sexual relationships, which are invested in suppressing their own emotions and projecting them on to women?

Desire for the Other, power relations and subjectivity

In the following extract, Martin describes forcefully what happens to him when he feels a little attracted to a woman.[10] The account imposes on my analysis the question of the irrational in couple relations.

Martin: People's needs for others are systematically denied in ordinary relationships. And in a love relationship you make the most fundamental admission about yourself – that you want somebody else. It seems to me that that is the greatest need, and the need which, in relationship to its power, is most strongly hidden and repressed. Once you've shown the other person that you need them, then you've made yourself incredibly vulnerable.

Wendy: Yes, I agree. But I think there's a question about – how much you show yourself to be vulnerable.

Martin: But you do, just by showing that you're soft on somebody. It seems to me when you've revealed that need, you put yourself in an incredibly insecure state. You've before managed by not showing anyone what you're like. By showing them only what is publicly acceptable. And as soon as you've shown that there is this terrible hole in you – that you want somebody else – then you're in an absolute state of insecurity. And you need much more than the empirical evidence that somebody likes you . . . You become neurotically worried that you're not accepted. Now you've let them see a little bit that's you. It'll be rejected. It's not so bad when a false exterior is rejected. The insecurity gives someone else power. I don't mean any viable self-exposure. I just mean any little indication that you like the other person.

Martin's experience of attraction leaves us with a pressing question: what is it that provides us with the irrational charge in sexual attraction? It is the quality of this experience which precipitates Martin's vulnerability and resistance. I call this experience 'desire for the Other',[11] and by the use of this concept, link in to psychoanalytic theory for an explanation: desire for the mother is repressed but never extinguished. It reasserts itself in adult sexual relations.[12]

I want to stress the effects of this subjective experience. Martin's 'desire for the Other' produces a feeling of intense vulnerability which in turn motivates him to exercise whatever powers he can muster in relation to women to whom he feels attracted. Sexist discourses serve this precise function. By reading himself as object of the have/hold discourse he can suppress the recognition of his dependence on a relationship with a woman. As long as he reads the woman as subject of the have/hold discourse he can camouflage his desire. If he succeeds, he can sustain the relationship and meet some of his needs while both remain unaware of them. That this has power effects, even when its suppression is not total, is illustrated in the following account by Martha, the woman with whom Martin has a relationship:

Martha: All these things that we've been talking about hand such power to people. Martin and I go up and down like a see-saw. There are days when he's in another city, and needing me, and suddenly I'm powerful and can dictate terms. We're back here, and I'm wanting a close, reciprocal, warm, working-out relationship, and suddenly he's powerful, because he doesn't want to give it. It really is dynamite . . . every day of our lives. It really is working less and less well. This business of having needs is so humiliating, because it makes one vulnerable.

Wendy: And shifts the power.

Martha: And shifts the power – exactly.

Her experience of the effects again bears witness to the way sexist discourse is productive of power – for men.

In the following extract Martha refers to the more general oppressive effects of Martin's resistance to the power he experiences her having in the relationship:

Martha: I put up with it, rather than saying, 'No, this is not the way I want to be treated'. I want to be treated as a complete person, someone who has feelings and ideas and intuitions that are actually worth taking notice of. No room is allowed for me to be myself, fully, because it might be too powerful an intrusion on his actions. To be accepted one hundred per cent means that the other person has to be strong enough . . . to keep their own integrity in the face of you being one hundred per cent yourself. It's so hard to find men who might be committed to taking those risks.

Her moving testimony to the effects on her of Martin's power is a specific example of the experience of gender difference: it points to the psychological characteristics which are consistent with – and reproduce – sexist discourses where woman is the inferior 'other'.

Misrecognition of men

When men behave warily and defensively, women do not necessarily read it as stemming from their vulnerability or dependence. This is because women too are subject to the production of meanings through dominant discourses. The available assumptions about men are that they are, for example, powerful, rational, autonomous, in control and self-confident. These features are, by definition, positively valued in sexist discourses. The effect is to foreground men's qualities and conceal their weaknesses and to do the opposite for women. Positioned within such discourses women misread themselves as easily as men. Clare's account of her relationship exemplifies this misrecognition:

Clare: That guy, I didn't even know he was so dependent on me.

Wendy: That's so often the way men play it. But it's also so often the way that women read it.

Clare: Oh, it's two-way. Precisely. His behaviour was very stereotypical, really. I thought he was a competent person – but he didn't think he was at all. He was outwardly confident – domineering – which actually made me feel incredibly oppressed.

Wendy: How long did it take you to realize that?

Clare: Oh, a long time. I didn't realize he was dependent on me, till I left him, I had no idea. That's the extent we both managed to keep this from each other. And when I look back on it, I realize that I should have known. It's always the same set of signs that I misread. The very signs that I took to signify confidence, were, for him – well, he actually used it as displays of confidence, but they were, actually, exactly the signs of his lack of confidence, like – talking too much . . . being opinionated and things that I couldn't bear. And when I read it back as lack of confidence, I could see . . . He was so insecure inside – and I didn't know. Quite a lot of things changed in our relationship. When I first met him, he had a Degree, and I had a Certificate and I wanted a Degree and he encouraged me. But I mean, not only did I do that . . . but I actually got far higher qualifications than he did. So that also made him feel unconfident. And I hadn't realized that either. We did things like . . . both applying for Open University teaching. I got it, and he didn't. It didn't occur to me it was a problem. Of course it was a problem for him.

It was possible for Clare to understand this as misrecognition because the process was uncovered when she left him. However, it is relevant to point out that this kind of misrecognition does not simply cease to operate through a rational process of learning by experience. The irrationality of women's desire for the Other also demands analysis:

Wendy: What you said – about not being able to read his dependence on you – I think that's true of you and Ken.

Clare: Um, yes, I've been told that before, but I still don't know how to know it.

Wendy: Yes, it's the kind of thing, y'know, when like, somebody kind of breaks, and expresses themselves on a different level. Like Phil did when you left – like Jeremy did when I left. He actually felt like a different person.

Clare: Yeah. Phil felt like a different person. Why is it then that I can't get hold of that knowledge about Ken? Why can't I see it? 'Cause I can't. Um . . . it's very silly 'cause I know where my power lies.

Desire and the signifier 'woman'

Misrecognition of the Other of desire, when it is an opposite-sexed Other, is not explicable simply by the existence of gender-differentiated discourses. I will argue, through analysing Jim's account, that the way in which 'woman' signifies for him has a history going back to his desire for the mother. The argument is an illustration of Lacan's slogan 'the desire for the Other is the desire for the mother' (Lacan, 1977, p. 286).

Like Sam, Jim is aware that he is frightened by strong emotions. Again like Sam, there is an elision between his own and the woman's emotions:

Wendy: And was it that the girls wanted to be more intimate?

Jim: Yeah – I was frightened of making that kind of commitment, that kind of involvement, 'cause I thought I'd be let down, because of what happened the first time, when I was so unreserved about how I felt. I think that really affected my life incredibly, that first time I fell in love.

Wendy: Why was having a relationship with her such a burden?

Jim: She was very strong and very emotional – that's pejorative, but I mean she had strong reactions, so that I didn't actually feel safe that I wasn't going to be knocked out, or sucked in by her.

It transpires that Jim's fear of her strong emotions was a projected fear of his own.[13] He feared them because it felt unsafe to feel so strongly for a woman. As many men experience with their first sexual relationship – particularly if it is with an older woman – their lack of defences leaves them painfully hurt when the relationship ends. As I have argued above, this constitutes the investment in reading the woman as the subject of the have/hold discourse.

What does Jim want that he's so afraid of losing that he can't have it in case he loses it?

Wendy: What was it that you wanted out of a stable relationship with Jeanette?

Jim: Well, I think support. Knowing that there was somebody who was going to be on my side, that I could talk about things that were affecting me and they would more or less automatically be important to her. And that she would be able to give me strength in that way. Very classic. Like my parents' relationship. But it was me who set the agenda, and she fitted in, and in a way that's what I wanted. Someone who wouldn't actually challenge me. There's a gaze of uncritical, totally accepting love that I find really attractive. 'I'll love you forever, whatever,' – is really a powerful gaze. And that's a mother's gaze.

I have considered in greater detail elsewhere (Hollway, 1982) the implications and theorization of this mother/Other link. Here I will give one further instance of the way that seemingly unimportant day-to-day relationships are suffused with meanings which must be explicated in terms of 'desire for the Other' and how the woman of the relationship is linked to the mother. Another woman Jim had a relationship with said:

I was feeling preoccupied with other things, so I suppose not paying him much attention. Jim got at me twice – about tiny things, in a way that felt antagonistic. When I pointed it out we tried to do some work on it. Blank. Then he came up with the word 'oranges', as if from nowhere. When he thought about it a bit he said it had something to do with his relations with women. If a woman peeled an orange for him, it showed that they cared for him. Then he said that his mother used to do it for him, even when he could do it for himself.

Desire has a history through its occupancy of certain significations – in this case, who peeled oranges. It does not express itself through the rationally accessible layer of meaning – it couldn't be included in the definition of oranges. But when it comes up in the practice of peeling oranges this meaning is there as a presence. For Jim it is part of a wider set of significations around proof of loving and caring through women doing things for him. It is consistent with the common experience of women in relationships with men that men get them to do things for them when they are 'objectively' unnecessary. The suppressed signification is 'I'll do it for you because I love you'. The signifying chain from mother to Other is historically unbroken for men, although, according to Freudian theory, savagely repressed.[14]

[. . .]

SPLITTING THE DIFFERENCES

The following introductory extract describes splitting between a gender-differentiated pair of characteristics: expressing feelings and giving support. The exclusion, through projection, of one 'side' of this pair is made possible by the way their meaning already contains a specification of what is gender-appropriate. The difference is re-produced in the subjectivities of each member of the heterosexual couple.

Jim: The thing got specialized, as it were polarized, where one person does the feeling. My relationship with Jeanette, who I lived with for many years, developed in such a way that she was responsible for doing the feelings – she was the one that got upset, and I was the one who was coping, providing support, kindness, et cetera. And so what that meant was that I didn't get to express any feelings and she didn't get to express any support. And so what that means is that both sides are completely prevented from experiencing what the other person's 'job' is. Which means that you get a completely shrivelled – a completely incomplete – idea of what's going on.

Two important points emerge from this comment. First – and most obviously – the content of the split is predictable from discourses specifying gender difference: it was the woman whose job it was to do the feeling.[15] Our common-sense experience of this split is through the naturalistic assumption that it is part of women's natural make-up. In consequence, this characteristic of their relationship was not read as a relational dynamic, it was read as aspects of their personalities. Jim said that at the time he firmly believed that he was just not a 'feeling person'. Whereas traditionally this would have been considered a positive characteristic, in the humanist and feminist climate of the post-1960s, he felt that it was a lack. None the less, the effect of the denial, through projection of these feelings, was experienced as part of his 'personality', that is as something fundamental and unchangeable. Clearly then, it is vital to understand the mechanisms whereby gender-differentiated characteristics – such as expressing feelings – are located in one member of a heterosexual couple. By focusing on the mechanisms, I am able to avoid seeing the effect as a once-and-for-all accomplishment of sex-role socialization. Instead I am seeing it as a dynamic which is constantly being re-produced in day-to-day couple relationships. I shall illustrate this in due course.

The second point emerges from the opposition which is implied between expressing feelings and giving support. This is not a logical pair of opposites, but you probably took it for granted when you read it (which illustrates the power of gender-differentiated discourses to construct our assumptions). The value which we are obliged to accept in order to make sense of this opposition is that people, usually women, who express feelings need support because expressing feelings is a weakness. 'Doing the feelings' is equated with 'getting upset'. Conversely the person, usually a man, who gives support is thus obliged to position himself as someone who is strong enough not to have feelings. The logic of the opposition is not contained in the meaning itself, but rather in the judgement attached to it. In our society, the judgement is a sexist one: expressing feelings is weak, feminine and in contradistinction to men's rationality. With the value – which is indeed inextricable from the meaning once it is seen as inserted into the discourse – comes power difference. Men can support women who are subject to the unfortunate bane of feeling and thus men are superior. As I have already argued, this constitutes a substantial investment in taking up such a position recurrently in relations. I have already shown how it can be the fear of their own feelings, signifying weakness, which is concealed by the manoeuvre. Now I shall show how splitting, through projection and introjection, operates as a defence. This accounts for the mechanism whereby gender-differentiated positions in discourses are reproduced.

This splitting is contradictory. Giving support implies not being able to ask for support, as I shall demonstrate in the example of Beverley and Will below. (Again there is not a logical opposition involved – support can in principle be mutual.) In this part I therefore want to clarify two issues raised by the idea of characteristics being split through gender difference into women and men. First, the interpersonal dynamic must be theorized – and this is where psychoanalytic theory's non-unitary, non-rational subject and the unconscious and its ability to theorize relations comes into play. Second, the space for movement in the gender-differentiated content of these splits must be specified. Here, the contradictory subject positions offered by coexisting and inconsistent discourses, and the consequent production of multiple meanings and powers, offer the necessary theoretical perspective.

Repression and rationality

How does this mechanism of splitting work? In the following extract, I look at an example in detail and link it to my concept of investment. Will is describing an occasion when he became aware of his feelings, and how they were related to a change in Beverley's position. One of the methodological (and theoretical) questions raised by the use of the concept of splitting is that – by definition – it is not observable while it is in operation. It feels like the natural state of affairs in a relationship, what personality psychology would deal with under the rubric of 'individual differences'. Here Will is able to describe it because for 'one and a half minutes' the splitting dynamic was ruptured:

Will: In a relationship for me, this 'frozenness' of certain feelings is really terrible. Much more of the time than I would like, we're doing this specialization job. There's maybe a split second in which I feel in touch with the set of feelings that I'm not normally responsible for, and that I don't particularly avow. And I don't even know if I feel them. And I think, 'Shit I actually felt that'. For two or three weeks I don't feel anything about it again, and I have to say, 'Well, at the moment I don't feel anything, but I do remember.' I mean at one stage, Beverley said [sighs], 'Well, maybe we should have an abortion,' and I suddenly burst into tears. Now it was very peculiar, because I'd actually been the person who'd been saying, 'You really should think about having an abortion,' you know, I was giving all the excellent reasons, 'cause normally – and this might be the Catholic thing – she has always said, 'No, an abortion is *terrible*.' And for me, it's just a matter of convenience. If she wants one. If it interferes with her studies, then we'll certainly wait two or three years. So I felt quite knowledgeable about it all, and there was no problem.

Wendy: Yes, this is Will, being the rational, reassuring side of the relationship.

Will: Yes, that's right. So it's my job to make her think about it. And then she actually thought about it, and she decided, maybe she would. And I burst into tears, which was completely unexpected for me. And I felt terribly depressed. And for that split second – it lasted about one and a half minutes – I knew that I actually did not want her to have an abortion. I mean, one of the things she's actually said to me is, 'I don't know whether you want to actually have this child or not' and I've said, 'Of course I want to have this child.' And at one level that's certainly true. But I didn't actually feel it in the same way. And I had to hold on to that feeling, because it went very quickly. A breakdown of that division or specialization is quite rare, and it's difficult to break out of that type of role – that division of labour. So I had to hold on to those moments of knowledge.

Wendy: What you said about Beverley saying, 'I don't know what you feel about having this baby' – at one level you knew that this was absurd: you'd said a hundred times, 'I'm into having this baby,' but you'd repressed a lot of the feelings – [*Will*: Mmmm] – for fear that you might be disappointed. So actually, she's right. Because apart from those moments, the feelings that you have about it aren't coming over and that's the information that is so lacking.

Will describes the rational arguments that he put forward in a way which exemplifies how they were devoid of his own desires. The experience of the issue is summarized by his comment, 'I felt quite knowledgeable about it all'. The effect is summed up as 'there was no problem'. His positon in relation to Beverley shows what he was not taking on himself: 'It's my job to make her think about it.' Will's account of what happened next illustrates the usefulness of the idea of positions in discourses. Beverley resisted the 'gender-appropriate' position. Rather than remaining the receptacle of all the non-rational feelings about abortion, Beverley adopted the position that Will had been occupying: 'She actually thought about it and she decided, maybe she would.' Will's ability to repress his feelings of wanting a baby were conditional on positioning Beverley so that she would want it (despite rational considerations, which he, not she, was representing). When this unconscious strategem failed, the effect was 'completely unexpected'. His defence against strong feelings that he wanted a baby – the mechanisms of projection – had broken down. It did not, however, break down for long. This demonstrates how the evanescence of feelings is the result of their repression by the defence mechanisms.

Defence mechanisms and social relations

The importance of this extract is that it illustrates the link between psychodynamics on the one hand, which affect (in this case) a man's experience of an issue and his understanding of his identity, and on the other the effects on social relations and gender difference. Will's repression was not just an intrapsychic matter. A theory of the unconscious is not just about personal well-being and individual treatment. Repression is a dynamic with social and political effects. However, the effects are not comprehensible if we stay within the framework of psychoanalytic theory. The latter has had a tendency to concentrate on processes and structures (the processes of splitting, defence mechanisms, identification and the structures of the unconscious, conscious and desire). Ignoring content, the conclusion – erroneous in my view – which psychoanalysis tends to draw is that the content of desire is inserted in infancy (most likely to be theorized as at the Oedipal stage). The political implications are thus not dissimilar from socialization theory: the continuous changes which characterize the social domain and are not linked to generational change are left out of the picture because there is no account of how these changes in content are produced in subjects' positions in multiple discourses; of what is suppressed and expressed; and of the content of splits. Discourse analysis provides a way of understanding the content of the split: what in this case Will calls 'being in charge of patriarchal reassurance' because 'somebody else's needs or fears or anxieties are greater than mine'.

Why did Will believe that he was the stronger of the two?[16] I have illustrated how the availability of a position in discourse which is positively valued and which confers power must be accompanied by a mechanism at the level of the psyche which provides the investment to take up this position. I have also argued that the investment in these positions is produced in the individual's history. Will's history is no exception:

Will: Women are developing strength, which is in a way what I wanted, because when I was at school – I mean, women were nothing and I hated it. Because I couldn't think of them as equals. I felt them as people with whom I could only have a false relationship. I felt really bad about that. And I used to read novels in which there were strong women, with whom I could talk because actually the women I found around were not like that.

Will experienced and positioned women through sexist discourses. He despised women for being weaker than him. The effect of the discourses was misogyny. Women were associated with weakness and consequently negatively valued. The following extract shows how these feelings about strength and weakness produce and are re-produced by Will's own contradictory subjectivity. He is responding to a woman who has been saying how she feels uneasy about being powerful with other women.

Will: Yeah but you feel that. Now you see I feel that in spades. If I fight, I fight from the wrong side. So I am constantly feeling like an elephant walking around with lots of eggshells, and I hate people for being eggshells. And I hate myself for being an elephant. I really fight feeling very kind to lots of people. When people were kind to me in that way, I used to lap it up, and hate me for needing it. And them.

Will's discomfort is with his own weakness: needing other people. If he can't accept this in himself, it is no wonder that he cannot accept it in women. In this respect he wanted women to be equally strong. There is a contradiction between this and the effects of splitting which means that he will position women as weaker because of his investment in being strong, the effect of which is to project the unwelcome feelings of weakness. The following extract illustrates this dynamic. Will is continuing the account of their decision whether to have a baby:

Will: We were having a conversation about something which at the moment I've repressed. Oh yes, it was about the small matter of pregnancy and having a child. I can't imagine how I forgot about that. [Laughs] And I was in a sort of reassuring mood. And what she said was she was very worried about it – it was at the end of quite a long conversation – and she'd been saying how she felt and I'd been doing my reassuring bit. It sounds so ludicrous but it wasn't at all. I said, 'In my mind, I'm prepared for every eventuality.' Right, and this was some way of saying, 'If you want an abortion, we'll have an abortion, and if you don't want an abortion, we won't have an abortion.' And she said quite sharply, and nastily, 'You mean we could have the child and then strangle it immediately afterwards!' And I burst into tears, because what her saying that meant was, 'You've been talking in a completely abstract way without any feeling whatsoever.' And that got me out of my reassuring general thing. I'd actually felt all that, yet I'd also felt quite distant. I felt I was the reassuring one, y'know, I was feeling anxious for myself, yes, but she was much more anxious and therefore I had to say we were prepared for every – blah blah. And that sharp remark – it just tore away that sheath over my emotions. That sheath of being in charge of patriarchal reassurance. The point is that if anything makes me feel – and it's incredibly easy for me to feel – that somebody else's needs or fears or anxieties are greater than mine I immediately shift into this caring thing.

Sarah: Yeah but, can you stop there a minute? Because do you really feel that theirs is greater than yours?

Will: I don't know whether it's true, I always tend to think that other people's needs to talk or needs to work things out are greater than my own. Because in a sense I have this fantasy of myself as quite strong.

Several important relational dynamics are illustrated in this part of the article.

1   The abstract mode is perfectly exemplified by Will's statement 'In my mind I'm prepared for every eventuality.' One important effect of this abstract mode of talking is that it purports to give people information, but the information it denies the other person is what really matters. It conceals value, importance, desire, the person's commitment to an issue or position. Beverley reflects this problem when she points out that despite the fact that Will says 'I want to have this child' her feeling is 'I don't know whether you want to have this child or not'. The effect of the abstract mode is that the information that comes over is not dependable: it leaves unsaid what is most important. In contrast, when Will burst into tears, Beverley told me that she got more information of the kind that she needed in order to make the decision than from Will's rational statements.

2   The abstract mode is not simply 'rational' (by implication, desirable). It is invested. The effect of not providing the information that counts is not an arbitrary by-product. It protects Will's vulnerability. Suppression of feelings enables Will to occupy a powerful position of not minding, disguising his strong wishes to have a baby and protecting him from the vulnerability which would follow due to the fact that Beverley might decide against it.

3   Repressed desires do not go away. The defence mechanisms of introjection and projection – the means through which they are expressed in displaced ways – are interpsychic, that is they are relational. This means that they are dependent on the participation of another. This other represents needs which are opposite, rather than just different. The opposition is a product of the principle that positive and negative value is imbricated in the meanings. What is projected onto another person represents the material which is unacceptable because of contradictions in the one who is doing the projecting. What is repressed is not just material whose repressed status is isolated from subjectivity. Freud maintained that repression was always related to a desire and vice versa, so that there is a principle of opposition. Repression of contradiction is thus a highly complementary mechanism to the principle of opposition which is fundamental to gender difference. Hence, Will suppresses his

feelings because of his vulnerability. They are more likely to be introjected by a woman because discourses have already conferred on her a position of doing the feelings.

4   The successful completion of the splitting still requires that Will can take up a position of rational reassurance (note that it is gendered: 'patriarchal reassurance'). The extract illustrates how this is made possible by the way he reads himself as stronger through sexist, gender-differentiated discourses. As he himself acknowledges, his deflection from his own feelings is through reading the other person as having greater needs, fears, anxieties than his. The discourse and the mechanism of projection work hand-in-glove: he is uncomfortable with his own needs. They don't go away. Rather he projects them. The moment he feels stronger than the other person, he can't help but shift into 'this caring thing'. His 'fantasy of himself as quite strong' is both the condition and effect of this dynamic condition because it invests him in that position (already differentially available to him as a man because of sexist discourses); effect because he can project his own weaknesses and thus his feelings of relative strength are reproduced. The continuity of Will's reproduction of his position as stronger requires a historical perspective: it is an investment which is inserted into his subjectivity.

5   Will's gendered subjectivity is articulated not in isolation but in relation to a woman: he wants her to be equally strong, not least because he can also get support and not take all the responsibility.[17] On the other hand, he ends up positioning himself as stronger because of suppression and projection of the negatively valued character of feelings of vulnerability. It is important to recognize such contradictions because they challenge the smooth reproduction of gender difference.

A complementary production of this contradiction is evident in many women in heterosexual relations who feel that they want a man to be stronger than they are. Consistent with their history of positioning they too reproduce themselves as needing support. Their investment, while not so clear cut as for men, is in getting looked after and being required to take little responsibility.[18] Yet because connotations of weakness and inferiority are carried along with their need for support, it contradicts their feelings of effectiveness and their experience of being strong enough to provide support.

The circle of reproduction of gender difference involves two people whose historical positioning, and the investments and powers this has inserted into subjectivity, complement each other. When there remain contradictions in each person's wants of the other, there is ground for an interruption of its reproduction. These contradictions are the products of social changes. It is through the kinds of social changes that I outlined at the beginning of this chapter that alternative discourses – for example feminist ones – can be produced and used by women in the struggle to redefine our positions in gender-differentiated practices, thus challenging sexist discourses still further. Changes don't automatically eradicate what went before – neither in structure nor in the way that practices, powers and meanings have been produced historically. Consciousness-changing is not accomplished by new discourses replacing old ones. It is accomplished as a result of the contradictions in our positionings, desires and practices – and thus in our subjectivities – which result from the coexistence of the old and the new. Every relation and every practice to some extent articulates such contradictions and therefore is a site of potential change as much as it is a site of reproduction.

Notes

1   The same phenomenon occurs with colonized peoples. For example, Gustav Jahoda (1961) quotes Ghanaian blacks generalizing in a derogatory manner about 'blacks', calling them superstitious, lazy, etc., in other words reproducing the racist discourses with which whites position them. Frantz Fanon (1968) addresses the same phenomenon in his analysis of black identity. He was one of the first to emphasize the importance of consciousness for political change and to use psychoanalytic theory alongside a radical political analysis of colonialism, to theorize the contradictions in the identities of black people in colonized countries.

2   Lewis Nkosi illustrates the same principle when talking about his experience of his Africanness in South Africa: 'I know that in my case I first discovered my Africanness the day I learned that I was not only black but non-white ... From that day onwards I began to regard this prefix *non* with absolute hostility. Everywhere I went in public places notices shouted at me 'non-whites only' and every time I read the message it vividly brought to mind the crude fact that in the eyes of the world my life represented something negative, something 'non'. In that small prefix put before the word *white* I saw the entire burden and consequence of European colonialism: its assault on the African personality; the very arrogance of this assumption' (Nkosi, 1983, pp. 44–5).

3   I think this partly accounts for why the vast majority of transsexuals are man to woman.

4   The classic and oft-quoted demonstration of this contradiction is the experiment by Broverman et al. (1970). Clinicians judged what was considered 'mentally healthy' for adults, for men and for women. Traits which represented a normally healthy male and a normally healthy adult were highly correlated. Traits characterizing a normally healthy female were significantly different and, predictably, not highly valued.

5   *Forum* magazine's emphasis on technique reflects this focus. The sexual partner is supposedly necessary 'to take part in reciprocal stimulation that will provide the maximum intensity of voluptuous sensations at coming off' (1971). The individualism of this discourse is characteristic of the epoch generally.

6   The contrast between Jim's and Colin's positions demonstrates that men's positions and thus the meanings of sexual practices, are not determined even for men of similar age and background.

7   By my use of 'subject' and 'object', I mean to emphasize the difference of position which is expressed in the grammatical differentiation between subject and object. In this use, subject is not equivalent to our general use of the term. Subjects occupy both positions in discourses, in that sense. Neither is object equivalent to the use made in some feminist theory, as in 'sex-object'. There it tends to imply that the position affords no agency and no power. As my analysis makes clear, I do not hold with this implication.

8   While a fair amount of feminist work has been done concerning girls (McRobbie, 1978; Nava, 1982; Cowie and Lees, 1981), it is difficult to find work on boys which challenges dominant assumptions. However, see Willis (1978) and Wood (1982) for descriptions of working-class boys' relations to girls.

9   This is the first instance of several sexual metaphors used by men in these accounts: getting in deep, letting go, soft on and sucked in. All refer to the danger of strong positive feelings for a woman and the metaphors all reflect a man's position in heterosexual sex. The unselfconscious use of these metaphors supports my argument that the significations of sex are closely bound up with the contradictions involved in 'desire for the Other'.

10   Martin does not speak of himself directly, but this is typical of his style and the phenomenon of protection that I am illustrating. Generalizing is a way of distancing oneself from the risk associated with what one is saying. As there is no commonly accessible discourse which says what he is expressing here, I am confident that Martin is speaking about his own experience.

11   See note 9.

12   The feelings are likely to be similar whether the person in receipt of them is same or 'opposite' sex. So the choice (compulsion might be a more accurate word) concerning the gender of the loved object is a very important phenomenon to account for. Psychoanalytic theory does provide an account which answers these questions about desire, love and the irrational. However, in its present form, it emphasizes desire as a process at the expense of the meanings it occupies (and thus the social content). Lacan's theorization of the metaphoric axis sees the chain of signifiers which desire has occupied as contained within the meaning of a word such as

'woman'. This historical chain runs from mother (the first Other) to woman/Other. The positions occupied in discourses in relation to a man – whether occupied by mother or woman – clarify how this historical chain of signification is produced.

13   This is not to claim that these feelings weren't the woman's as well. It is the fear of them which indicates his own projection. Another person is a suitable vehicle for a projection precisely when they are subject to the same feelings themselves.

14   The account of (heterosexual) women's desire for the Other represents a further theoretical problem: how and to what extent does the girl transfer her desire for the Other from mother, where it is originally located, to father and thence to a man? In the Freudian account, for the girl unconscious meanings (what Lacan would call the metaphoric axis) slip from wanting to 'be' the penis (that is on identification with the father and continuing desire for the mother) to wanting to 'have' it and give the father a gift of a baby. I cannot enter into a detailed critique here. However, if we see psychoanalytic theory as itself being subject to defence mechanisms operating in its (predominantly male) authors and reproducing sexist discourses, we can hypothesize that this formulation may be a reversal. The valorization of the penis would be a compensation for the power of the mother/woman to give birth and be reproduced through men's investment in this position in discourse. The process is similar to my analysis of Jim's and Sam's accounts who accomplished a reversal through projection.

15   In this context, Jim means that his coping and strength were in response to Jeanette getting upset. Jim equates 'doing the feeling' with getting upset. Clearly there are other feelings like anger which are more associated with men. However, the slippage in Jim's usage is a common one. The question of who 'gives support' in heterosexual couple relationships is a good deal more complicated than this and is traditionally divided into gender-appropriate areas. For example it was clear from the earlier extract from Jim that Jeanette provided a great deal of emotional support for him. Between Beverley and Will, another couple in my research, support was explicitly gender-differentiated: Beverley's was called 'mothering' and Will's 'patriarchal reassurance'.

16   It is particularly clear in Beverley's case that weakness is not a feature of who she 'is'. By this I mean a dynamic and a positioning which she unintentionally re-produces in new relationships and not her 'personality', as psychology might account for it. In a previous relationship she was not so positioned and her experience in this relationship is more recognizable as a relational dynamic: 'I feel like when I'm around you I lose all resolve. I feel completely weak and helpless. I don't know why it happens, why I let it happen.'

17   I have not developed or illustrated this claim here, but see Hollway (1982), chapter 7.

18   This may not be the case in practice, but if the investment has been inserted historically (a history of desire eventually linking back to the mother) it is not simply conditional on a rational view of the outcome. This is one reason why my use of investment in no way slides into a learning-theory explanation.

FEMINISM, CRITICISM AND FOUCAULT
Biddy Martin

In a lecture given on January 6, 1976, and later published in a collection of interviews entitled *Power/Knowledge*, Michel Foucault discusses his own work in terms of the discovery over the past fifteen years of 'a certain fragility in the bedrock of existence – even, and perhaps above all, in those aspects of it that are most familiar, most solid, and most intimately related to our bodies and our everyday behaviour' (1980a, p. 80). And he related this 'vulnerability to criticism' of aspects of knowledge and power that have long been obscured to a recognition of the inhibiting effects of 'global, *totalitarian theories.*' His polemics against systematizing, universalizing theories and their will to truth are clearly directed in part at scientific Marxism and its economism as well as to the 'laws' of psychoanalysis; and his *History of Sexuality* challenges various twentieth-century sexual liberationists' attempts to combine those two theories. Certainly, both his polemics and his methodological breaks with traditional social theory make him interesting for feminists, whose political and theoretical projects converge at important points with the provocations of Foucault.

[. . .]

Foucault's deconstructions of traditional conceptions of power provoke questions about the history, the consequences, and the validity of this kind of theorizing. In an interview with J.L. Brochier, Foucault describes his focus in this way: 'When I think of the mechanics of power, I think of its capillary form of existence, of the extent to which power seeps into the very grain of individuals, reaches right into their bodies, permeates their gestures, their posture, what they say, how they learn to live and work with other people' (quoted in Sheridan, 1980, p. 217). According to Foucault, power comes from below; it is induced in the body and produced in every social interaction. It is not exercised negatively from the outside, though negation and repression may be one of its effects. Power in the modern world is the relation between pleasures, knowledge and power as they are produced and disciplined. The state is not the origin, but an overall strategy and effect, 'a composite result made up of a multiplicity of centres and mechanisms' (ibid., p. 218). The same might be said of large-scale resistances or 'revolution'. Methodologically, then, the task set by Foucault could be described, as his translator Alan Sheridan has, thus: 'It is the task of a political anatomy to analyse the operation of these 'micro-powers', the relations that are made between them and their relations with the strategic aims of the state apparatus' (ibid., p. 219).

Foucault's elaborations of the relationship between desire–knowledge–power have opened up exciting critiques of both liberal and traditional Marxist approaches to questions of ideology, sexuality and power – approaches that we have taken over into our own work on feminist theory to varying degrees. His questions and hypotheses are part of a radical re-evaluation in post-structuralist thought of the classical humanist conceptual split between ideology and economics, sexuality and politics, the individual and the social, the subversive and the repressive. As such, they open up a space for feminist questions that have been obscured, marginalized and/or subsumed under the teleological projects of other theories. Of course, it is important to keep in mind that feminism has never assumed a place within 'avant-garde' theory or practice automatically or unproblematically. There are surprisingly few references in Foucault's writings or in interviews with him to feminist analyses or to the women's movement in spite of the fact that he has identified sexuality as a privileged object of analysis. The work of asserting and articulating the significance of post-structuralist thought for feminist inquiries, as well as the importance of feminism for post-structuralism, must be done by those who are committed to demonstrating rather than assuming harmonies in the two projects. It is essential that feminist thinkers not be seduced by the work of Foucault, that we not attempt to apply the hypotheses he articulates to the situation of women without careful attention to the implications of his work.

What seems crucial about the work of Foucault, particularly in the American context, is his break with classical theories of representation and power. His *History of Sexuality* states very clearly that discourses on sexuality, not sexual acts and their histories, are the essential place to grasp the workings of power in modern Western societies. As Alan Sheridan explains, Foucault's 'political anatomy – anatomy of the body politic in terms of an anatomy of the politicization of the body – is presented with Foucault's usual modesty as "another grid for deciphering history"' (1980, p. 217). In fact, Foucault's study is not really a history of sexuality in the conventional sense of that word, but a history of the discourses on sexuality and the various ways in which those discourses and the pleasures and powers they have produced have been deployed in the service of hierarchical relations in Western culture over the past three hundred years. Foucault describes the transformation in the nature of power in the seventeenth century in terms of a new power over life that evolved in two forms:

> One of these poles . . . centred on the body as a machine: its
> disciplining, the optimization of its capabilities, the extortion

of its forces, the parallel increase of its usefulness and its docility, its integration into systems of efficient and economic controls, all this was ensured by the procedures of power that characterized the *disciplines*: an *anatomo-politics of the human body*. The second . . . focused on the species body. Their supervision was effected through an entire series of inter-ventions and *regulatory controls: a biopolitics of the population*. *(1980b, p. 139)*

Foucault challenges the traditional notion of sex as an instinctual drive or force, intrinsically liberating for the individual when expressed, and apparently disruptive of a necessarily repressive state. His 'history' not only questions the validity of Freudian and Marxist approaches to sexual liberation from Reich to Marcuse, but goes so far as to ask whether those arguments have not been formulated from within the same discursive and strategic limitations as the power they would like to attack. The repressive hypothesis – the argument that the past two to three hundred years have been characterized by sexual repression and negation – has held up well. Foucault suggests that the coincidence of the emergence of capitalism with the supposed advent of the age of repression has given the belief in repression 'a solemn historical and political guarantee' (ibid., p. 5). And he points out that this conception of sex as essentially repressed within capitalism is gratifying because of the opportunity it affords us to 'speak out against the powers that be, to utter truths and promise bliss, to link together enlightenment, liberation, and manifold pleasures; to pronounce a discourse that combines the fervour of knowledge, the determination to change the laws, and the longing for the garden of earthly delights' (ibid., p. 7).

In fact, Western culture, far from having repressed sexuality, has actually produced it, multiplied it, spread it out as a particularly priviliged means of gaining access to the individual and the social bodies, as a way of 'policing' society through procedures of normalization rather than prohibition. Repression becomes one effect among many of this larger phenomenon. According to Foucault, the bourgeois class, long regarded as the class that introduced repression in order to enhance the productivity of its working class, actually applied its techniques first to itself in the process of distinguishing itself from the aristocracy and the working classes. It made its sexuality and the health of its 'bodies' a fundamental source of its own identity and its own discipline. As Sheridan points out, 'the nineteenth-century bourgeoisie became obsessed with biological, medical, eugenic doctrines of all kinds . . . The value placed on the body and its sexuality was bound up with establishment in society of bourgeois hegemony' (1980, p. 191).

What we have long accepted to be a natural but prohibited force constitutes, in fact, a construct, a systematization of pleasure in relation to the changing articulation and needs of power in our world. What we have believed to be the secret of ourselves and have felt compelled to tell in our search for redemption or liberation, or at the very least, health, amounts to our possible subjection to surveillance, to the intervention of experts in our lives, to discipline. The talk about sex, the obsession with it are part of the operations of power in contemporary society; they make normalization and control possible and invisible. To insist, then, on more and more sex and a greater freedom to speak it is to isolate sexuality and ourselves, to misunderstand 'sexuality' in ways that allow for a systematization and regulation of desire toward particular social and political ends.

Foucault insists that our subjectivity, our identity and our sexuality are intimately linked; they do not exist outside of or prior to language and representation, but are actually brought into play by discursive strategies and representational practices. The relationship between the body and discourse or power is not a negative one; power renders the body active and productive. Sexuality and identity can only be understood, then, in terms of the complicated and often paradoxical ways in which pleasures, knowledges and power are produced and disciplined in language, and institutionalized across multiple social fields. For Foucault, representation and discourses are themselves acts of power, acts of division and exclusion, which give themselves as knowledge. The body does not give knowledge that is then merely transmitted by an essentially neutral language and allowed or disallowed by a centralized form of prohibition. Discourse makes the body an object of knowledge and invests it with power. Our task, then, is not to search for the truth about sex, but to ask what is at stake in the historical question, in the compulsion to speak about the unspeakable. Foucault states it this way:

> This is the essential thing: that Western man [sic] has been drawn for three centuries to the task of telling everything concerning his sex; that since the classical age there has been a constant optimization and an increasing valorization of the discourse on sex; and that this carefully analytical discourse was meant to yield multiple effects of displacement, intensification, reorientation and modification of desire itself.
>
> (1980b, p. 23)

Foucault also challenges any easy division between a dominant and essentially repressive discourse and one oppositional, pure voice of liberation. He characterizes power as a multiplicity of force relations, the interplay of various discursive fields with their immanent necessities and developments. Power and authority are no longer vested in a central point, not in Foucault's analysis or in the actual workings of power in our world. Nor does resistance arise from a single point. For that reason, a very different form of political organization and struggle suggests itself, an alternative to the frontal attack on the state led by the One revolutionary subject, local struggles that undermine institutional power where it reveals itself in ideology under the mask of humanism, or as it operates in homes, schools, prisons, therapists' offices, and factories, wherever the work of normalization is carried on. What is crucial is the capacity to shift the terms of the struggle, the ability to see our position within existing structures but to respond from somewhere else. What Leftists have criticized in the women's movement as fragmentation, lack of organization, absence of a coherent and encompassing theory and the inability to mount a frontal attack may very well represent fundamentally more radical and effective responses to the deployment of power in our society than the centralization and abstraction that continue to plague Leftist thinking and strategy.

Beginning, then, at the level of discourse and the operations of power involved in the acquisition and distribution of knowledge, Foucault is able to deconstruct some of the last vestiges of the self-evident and apparently natural, exposing the workings of power in any will to or pretence at truth, finality or nature. All categories of the natural or the normal, as well as the unnatural or abnormal, are exposed as social constructs rather than distinctions given at the level of the body or individual psyche, categories that have been produced discursively and which function as mutually determining oppositions to normalize and to discipline. His methodological deconstructions explode the self-evidence of constituted meanings, defy the acceptance of received categories as exhaustive, and expose the cost at which such coherence and solidity are effected. The point from which Foucault deconstructs is off-centre, out of line, apparently unaligned. It is not the point of an imagined absolute otherness, but an 'alterity' that understands itself as an internal exclusion. From that perspective, it is possible to grasp and restructure the organization of our bodies, psyches and lives through discourse.

There are obvious convergences between Foucault's work and the interests of feminists, in terms of focus and methodology. Certainly, feminist analyses of the medical, psychiatric and educational institutions since the nineteenth century would support Foucault's suggestion that the intervention of experts and their knowledge of the female body have everything to do with the constitution of power in our world. Foucault has argued that the hysterization of the female body, a body now saturated with sex and inherently pathological, represented the production of knowledge and pleasures (in addition to the repression of those things) for the purpose of discipline and control of families and populations.

It is worth remembering that the first figure to be invested by the deployment of sexuality, one of the first to be 'sexualized', was the 'idle' woman. She inhabited the outer edge of the 'world', in which she always had to appear as a value, and of the family, where she was assigned a new destiny charged with conjugal and parental obligations.

(1980b, p. 121)

Health-care systems continue to monopolize 'scientific' knowledge and exercise control over individual bodies, families and the social body. And their operations are not the reflections of the needs of capital and/or the state in any simple sense; they are producing and reproducing as well as transforming the relations that are immanent and essential to their hierarchies and to the perpetuation of the status of their knowledges in society. Feminists have also voiced objections to classical liberationist approaches to questions of sexuality and power. The conception of a natural but repressed and inherently subversive female sexuality does run through feminist literature and theory both in the US and in Europe, and I would suggest that there is a level of historical and political necessity to those arguments in spite of their limitations. There is a related tendency to condemn male sexuality as naturally or intrinsically aggressive among some feminist thinkers who emphasize woman's passive victimization or internalization in relation to it. Again, this emphasis has its historical necessity as a response to the forms of violence against women that have been ignored or accepted by the society as self-evident for so long. However, the stress on victimization suffers strategic and theoretical limitations insofar as it reproduces, at least implicitly, the notion of women's passivity and suggests the presence of an essential and as yet undiscovered eroticism. It is an emphasis that does not get beyond the discursive limitations and manipulations of the object of its attacks.

In spite of the problems in certain formulations within feminist analyses and movement(s), it is legitimate to argue that feminist theorizing, taken as a whole, has gone beyond the male liberationists' focus on more and better sex to an understanding of sex as the structuring and regulating of desire toward socially and politically oppressive ends. Sexual expression, far from having liberated women, has historically often led to increased male access to women's bodies, allowing exploitation not just sexually but economically and politically as well. And feminists have long argued that to demand greater sexual freedom without formulating that demand in terms of a transformation of the social relations within which sexuality is organized and articulated is to invite an intensification of old constraints on women's desire. Traditionally, feminists have been labelled prudish by those liberationists who would force them into a position for or against sex; there is a sense of urgency within the women's movement now of the importance of developing our understanding of 'sexuality' so that we can move beyond these false alternatives and shift the focus of attention to the relations that have produced 'sexuality' as we know it.

Certainly, lesbian feminist theory has pushed the analysis of sexuality beyond the demand for the right to more sexual freedoms; the developing critique of the institutionalization of heterosexuality challenges the assumption of a natural sexual instinct and analyses the social configurations through which and as a result of which the apparatus of sexuality is constructed. The initial impulse of Adrienne Rich's article 'Compulsory heterosexuality' (1980) demonstrates from the point of view of excluded lesbian experience that heterosexuality is itself a compulsory set of relations produced not at the level of the body, but at the level of discourse and social practice, a compulsory sexuality that enables male dominance and refuses autonomy or solidarity among women. Turning the question back onto the discourse that has, in a sense, created 'homosexuality' and 'lesbianism' as we have come to know them effects what Foucault has called a methodological 'desexualization of the question'. According to Foucault,

> [T]he real strength of the women's liberation movements is not that of having laid claim to the specificity of their sexuality and the rights pertaining to it, but that they have actually departed from the discourse conducted within the apparatuses of sexuality. Ultimately, it is a veritable movement of desexualization, a displacement effected in relation to the sexual centering of the problem, formulating the demand for forms of culture, discourse, language and so on which are no longer part of that rigid assignation and pinning-down to their sex which they had initially in some sense been politically obliged to accept in order to make themselves heard.
>
> *(1980a, pp. 219–20)*

In a recent interview published in *Christopher Street*, Foucault makes similarly supportive statements about the implications of the gay (male) liberation movement, emphasizing its creation of supports for relationships other than those allowed within or by the heterosexual nuclear family structure. The creation of cultural and social supports for other relational forms goes far beyond the essentially liberal demand for homosexual or for women's rights. It has implications for the society as a whole as it facilitates different conceptions and possibilities for relating. Ultimately, such shifts threaten that 'bedrock of existence' of which Foucault has spoken elsewhere and undermine the structures on which contemporary power alignments and their solidity depend. In spite of what his critics have charged, Foucault's work does not negate the possibility of concrete political struggle and resistance. It does insist that we understand and take account of the ways in which we are implicated in power relations and the fact that we are never outside of power. He does not advocate *a* position; however, he is obviously aware of the necessity of taking position(s) and would insist that we remain aware of the possibilities for new pleasures and new forms of resistance created in every confrontation.

DESEXUALIZATION AND CULTURAL CRITICISM

In its most radical form, feminist criticism and practice can be a fundamentally deconstructive strategy that questions the possibility of universals or absolute meanings and exposes the constitution of power at stake in their assertion. Of course, both our humanist heritage and obvious historical and political necessities leave us with a conflict between a fundamentally deconstructive impulse and a need to construct the category woman and to search for truths, authenticity and universals. It is the necessity of a doubled strategy with respect to the question of the unity of woman and the value of 'desexualization' that I would like to address here.

Feminist criticism must be engaged in elaborating the extent to which the phallocentric meanings and truths of our culture have necessarily repressed multiplicity and the possibility of actual difference by appropriating difference, naming it opposition and subsuming it under the 'Identity of Man'. Feminism shares with post-structuralist criticism a critique of the hegemony of the identical and the desire for other forms of discourse. Unlike many of the male critics, feminists are quite consciously involved in systematically articulating the extent to which woman has been situated very differently with respect to the 'human', to 'Man', than has man; and feminist analyses demonstrate ever more convincingly that women's silence and exclusion from struggles over representation have been the condition of possibility for humanist thought: the position of woman has indeed been that of an internal exclusion within Western culture, a particularly well-suited point from which to expose the workings of power in the will to truth and identity.

If women have been marginal in the constitution of meaning and power in Western culture, the question of woman has been central, crucial to the discourse of man, situated as she is within the literary text, the critical text, the psychoanalytic situation, and social texts of all kinds as the riddle, the problem to be solved, the question to be answered. Foucault has not acknowledged the specificity of women's situation with respect to secrecy and truth; his analysis of the power struggles at stake in the humanist's pretence at truth makes it possible, however, to go beyond simply substituting new and more correct answers to the question of woman by insisting that we ask what is at stake in the question, what is involved in the articulation of the problem of sexual difference; how are discipline and power constituted at the moment at which woman is made the object of knowledge? Foucault's methodological work and our own insistence on a different approach to meaning and ideology allow us to question every text not so much in terms of what it presents, but in terms of what it does to obscure its own political bases. For Foucault, the question of the truth of one's sex, of one's self is not a self-evident question, and the answers that literature, medicine, psychiatry and religion provide are, in fact, a matter of rendering our bodies and pysches subject to control. Having created sex and gender as problems of a particular kind, the experts must necessarily intervene in our lives to provide solutions and to bind us within a particular identity, a subjectivity. Woman, as a category of meaning, and women have been subject to the gaze, the interventions, and the control of medical, psychoanalytic and aesthetic experts who do the work of limiting and regulating what it means to be a woman in line with the exigencies of their own discursive fields and legitimating truths.

Such an analysis of the question of woman as it has figured in male discourse allows and, in fact, insists that we examine our own formulations for potential reductions and prescriptions. The question for those of us engaged in the development of new forms of discourse is how to enter struggles over the meaning(s) of woman in ways that do not repress pluralities, without losing sight of the political necessity for fiction and unity. We are forced, when we ask the question of woman, to question the extent to which we make ourselves the riddle, establishing among us a new set of experts who will speak the truth of ourselves and our sex in categorical terms; we must question the extent to which our projects and our meanings subsume difference and possibility under the conceptual and strategic grasp of a unitary identity of woman, the extent to which we close our struggle around certain privileged meanings, naturalizing the construct woman once again. Is it possible to ask and not answer, or to avoid the certainties and limitations with which the question has been answered by those who would consolidate their power around their privileged position with respect to knowledge?

Some American radical feminist thought (the work, for example, of Mary Daly) is, for all its importance and contributions, particularly susceptible to a polemic against patriarchy that ultimately ontologizes woman in terms of an essential superiority and a privileged relationship to nature and truth. The tendency in such polemics is to counter what are considered to be male distortions of reality with what are held to be authentic female representations, and to correct male distortions with the authentic experience that can be read out of women's texts and lives. Unfortunately, this cultural criticism cannot go far beyond the assertion and documentation of a history of sexism, and our own cultural production is based on the premise that we as feminists can speak authentically, can speak the truth of ourselves for all women by virtue of our supposed exclusion from male culture and as a result of our rejection of their meanings. The tendency to place women outside culture, to define femininity in terms of an absolute exclusion and consequent innocence with respect to language and ideology reflects an overly simplistic understanding of the relationship between identity and discourse. It reproduces the classical split between the individual and the social formation, assuming that we can shed what is supposedly a false consciousness imposed and maintained from the outside, and begin to speak an authentic truth. The search for a more perfect self, for a truer, more natural sexuality, a more authentic 'I' too often represents a refusal to account for the position from which we speak, to ground ourselves materially and historically, to acknowledge and be vigilant of our own limitations and our own differences.

Foucault's deconstructive methodology provides an immanent critique of such a search for *the* authentic female voice or *the* sexuality, a warning against the commitment to any confessional mode as necessarily liberating, and a challenge to the notion that simply speaking or writing frees us in any simple way from patriarchy or phallocentrism. His analysis of the confessional mode in Western culture exposes the misconceptions in our definitions of truth:

> The obligation to confess is now relayed through so many different points, is so deeply ingrained in us, that we no longer perceive it as the effect of a power that constrains us; on the contrary, it seems to us that truth, lodged in our most secret nature, 'demands' only to surface; that if it fails to do so, this is because a constraint holds it in place, the violence of a power weighs it down, and it can finally be articulated only at the price of a kind of liberation. Confession frees, but power reduces one to silence; truth does not belong to the order of power, but shares an original affinity with freedom: traditional themes in philosophy, which a 'political history of truth' would have to overturn by showing that truth is not by nature free – nor error servile – but that its production is thoroughly imbued with relations of power. The confession is an example of this.
>
> (*Foucault, 1980b, p. 60*)

It is imperative that we understand and not abuse the need and/or the desire to speak and be heard, and that we question the structure of the communicative relations that is operating.

The insistence on analysing power in terms of its local, discursive and specific formations implies a critique of a polemics of patriarchy that conceives of exclusive and exhaustive divisions between oppressor and oppressed, between a dominant or false and a subversive or true discourse. What is useful for us is the suggestion to be read out of Foucault's work that we analyse the historically and discursively specific ways in which woman has figured as a constitutive absence. To totalize or universalize Otherness as an answer to the question of woman is to leave ourselves with no possibility for understanding or intervening in the processes through which meaning is produced, distributed and transformed in relation to the shifting articulation of power in our world.

On the other hand, it is imperative that we not dismiss the importance of the concepts patriarchy and oppression as they have been developed by radical feminist thinkers. The radical feminist articulation of the universality and totality of the oppression of women constitutes the condition of possibility for feminist deconstructive work. The assertion even of a fiction of the unity of woman and the globality of patriarchy has created a space for us from which to interpret as well as to speak. Our task is to deconstruct, to undo our own meanings and categories, the identities and the positions from which we intervene at any given point so as not to close the question of woman and discourse around new certainties and absolutes. We cannot afford to refuse to take a political stance 'which pins us to our sex' for the sake of an abstract theoretical correctness, but we can refuse to be content with fixed identities or to universalize ourselves as revolutionary subjects. Our deconstructions are neither identical nor synchronous with those of the male avant-garde in spite of the very significant points of convergence in our interests.

[. . .]

The struggle for control over representational and social practices through which and across which sex has been defined and organized has been a heterosexist struggle between and among men in which woman has figured as the object of knowledge and the metaphor for truths. Having achieved a position from which to enter the struggle over definition, we are confronted with the avant-garde's observations that sexual difference, sexual identity, sexuality itself are fictions, and that the perpetuation of those categories can only further enhance the workings of power. Men will no longer speak for mankind. Should women, by implication, no longer (i.e., never) speak as women? The question of woman, like all questions of meaning, must be particularized, localized, specified, and robbed of the mystical and ontological. However, if we fail now to assert the category woman from our own shifting and open-ended points of view, our oppression may easily be lost among the pluralities of new theories of ideology and power. There is the danger that Foucault's challenges to traditional categories, if taken to a 'logical' conclusion, if made into imperatives rather than left as hypotheses and/or methodological provocations, could make the question of women's oppression obsolete.

It seems clear that the intersection of post-structuralist, anti-humanist strategies with feminist analyses provides the possibility for a materialist critical practice and political struggle. In terms of cultural criticism, the convergences between the feminist and post-structuralist projects of Foucault make it possible for us to divest ourselves of the bourgeois heritage that has taught us to consider texts as the expressions of fixed meanings intended by an author, transparent to the educated critic, and approached quite passively by most other readers. As feminists we have based our critical practice on authorial intentionality and classical notions of language for too long. We have been engaged on the one hand in exposing sexism in male texts on the level of manifest content, condemning what we document to be a history of sexist images and preserving those images of women that seem to conform in isolation to a pre-given conception of a positive portrayal; and on the other hand, we have worked on creating a canon of women writers and developing an analysis of their writing that might unify woman as artist. Certainly, both projects have been crucial to the development of a feminist cultural criticism and alternative cultural sphere; however, they are limited by an approach to language and culture that interprets images as the more or less authentic reflection of a preconceived reality or truth, and assumes that women, by virtue of our powerlessness, can create new meanings without simultaneously engaging in a careful analysis of the processes through which meanings are negotiated across various discursive practices at any given historical moment.

A materialist cultural interpretive practice insists that we read not only individual texts but literary histories and critical discourse as well, not as reflections of a truth or lie with respect to a pre-given real, but as instruments for the exercise of power, as paradigmatic enactments of those struggles over meaning. For feminists, the task is to elaborate the ways in which sexual difference, the meaning of woman, figures in these processes by creating alternative points from which to approach traditionally accepted meanings. Feminism does, in fact, provide a context out of which we can pluralize meaning by opening apparently fixed constructs onto their social, economic and political determinacies.

7
EXPERIENCE AND
THE POLITICS OF IDENTITY

Paralleling the explorations of theories of the subject and subjectivity were the political developments within feminism around the politics of identity. The idea that the women's movement could represent the interests of all women was based on the notion that women shared a common experience of oppression and subordination. The slogan 'Sisterhood is Powerful' was adopted to represent both this communal experience and the political aspiration that women's solidaristic unity could bind the movement into a coherent force for change. As such, it was part of the tradition within political theory and practice which advocated the power of the collective to achieve the common good. The women's movement did not appropriate this tradition uncritically and one of its own political signatures became the rejection of ideas of hierarchical organization and selective leadership. From the outset the women's movement and feminist theory were acutely sensitive to the working of power and the way in which its operation inevitably meant some people being defined as inferior, or as 'other' to those holding power. However, when the power of the women's movement to speak on behalf of 'all' women was challenged by 'other' women, then the question of hierarchy and power – in particular, the power to define – had to be rethought. Such a challenge initiated a difficult and very often painful examination of the nature of feminism. As we shall see in this chapter, however, the rewards of this process have been great and have produced a profoundly different conception of political community.

Historically, the discussion of difference within feminism had been concerned with the difference between women and men, a polarization underwritten by essentialist discourses of sexual natures. It was through examining theories of the subject, particularly the coherent and unified subject of humanism, that feminism was able to break free from the tyranny of these fixed and oppositional identities. Much of this theoretical examination was motivated by political dynamics within feminism, particularly those involving the intervention of black feminists. As Razia Aziz argues in the first article in this chapter, in response to the call for women's liberation, black women demanded to know what such liberation was from, and how it applied to which women. These questions were important because they raised again the issue of experience, and pointedly and politically illustrated the difference between the experience of black women and white women. They also brought out the politics of the presumptions behind speaking for all women. The specificity of the position of black women did not include the conceit of universalizing their experience, although since in practice the liberation of black women would incorporate the demise of racism, it would entail far greater change than that which would be necessary to liberate white, middle-class women.

The presumed commonality of women's position were shattered by considerations of racism and imperialism, and this brought the complexity of women's identity to the fore. It posed new problems for feminism: how to analyse theoretically and recognize politically both power between women and the way in which all women, albeit differently, were implicated in dominant power relations. It dispelled once and for all the myth of women's innocence and brought a whole new focus on the question of women's agency – or the way we individually and collectively act in the world. Initially too it meant that the issue of essentialism had again to be broached. If there could be no essential feminine nature, neither could there be an essential identity for black women or white women; therefore the conditions of those differences had to be theorized. Moveover, as Aziz makes clear, it was not just a question of theorizing new polarities of difference, as this would simply suppress differences between black women and differences between white women. Rather the intervention of black women had put the complex heterogeneity of women on the agenda and necessitated what Aziz calls a feminism of difference.

The depth of this project is brought out in the article by Lata Mani. Her own research on colonial discourses on women in India brings other questions to bear on the subject. In particular she shows how discursive systems replicate historical forces and continue to reproduce traditional ideas of women. In much the same way as Hollway showed how ideas about women and men from the nineteenth century reverberate in contemporary relations between the sexes, Mani identifies how colonial ideas about 'traditional' societies are mobilized in contemporary debates about the position of women in the post-colonial era. In examining an incident of a widow burning in India in 1987, Mani is able to show how the discursive construction of different identities of 'woman' – whether as bound by traditionalism or modernity – actually represent the interests of particular social forces and their vying for power to define the nature of the society. She shows the way in which feminism is able to deconstruct these positions and thereby illuminate how definitions of gender are a very particular medium through which the identity of the society is articulated. Concern with women as women is expressed only by feminism, and by making clear the way in which the status of women in the debate on *sati* was representing the interests of distinct social forces other than those of women, feminist analysis is able to go beyond this, to deconstruct this process, and thereby to identify the particular interests and concerns of women.

This mode of analysis brought into stark relief the question of agency, the role of women themselves in the predicament of their existence. In this case the 'civilizing' discourse of the colonizers prided itself on the cultural and political superiority of its conception of the individual and individual responsibility. As one of the flagships of modernity, individualism proclaims its progressive disdain for traditionalism. As we have seen, however, the identity of women within this discourse has always been problematic and this is further compounded by discourses of the colonial and post-colonial subject. In this instance, to locate the self-immolation of a woman within the discourse of liberal individualism is to presume either complicity or selflessness or both, for it is incapable of specifying the material constraints on agency which led to the woman's death. Mani, however, is careful to stress that feminist analysis is not interested in invoking the status of women as victims, as somehow outside the domain of responsibility that contextualizes individual action. Feminist discourse is hardly yet a dominant ideological space in which women can critically negotiate their identity and from which they can strive towards new cultural locations. Immense social, political, ideological and material constraints continue to circumscribe women and the task of feminist analysis is to show how the constraints faced by women, including physical coercion, constitute sexual subordination.

What Mani's analysis makes clear is not only the discursive complexity of the fragmentary and contradictory nature of women's identity and subjectivity and the material forces which underpin these, but also the need to locate the question of agency not as an abstract property of 'the individual' but as the negotiation of an historical situation which often constitutes both the ideological and material denial of women as autonomous. What Lata Mani is suggesting is that there is no simple morality or political prescription from which we can understand women, only the imperative that we are aware of the position from which we speak and the need to recognize the politics of difference that constitute the voices of women. What is said and what is heard are never innocent and always require a commitment to analysing the specificity of relations between women.

This is echoed in the extract from Minnie Bruce Pratt's autobiographical narrative, *Identity: Skin Blood Heart*, which illustrates the very different conception of politics that has emerged within feminism from contemporary debates on experience, identity and subjectivity. Pratt's account of her own history problematizes the assumption that Western women are homogeneous and heirs to identities somehow outside the reality of colonialism, imperialism and racism. She shows that the very idea of unified subjects with stable continuous histories hides the reality of difference, power and domination and that biographical narratives uninterrupted by reference to these realities are stories abstracted from the social forces which shape our lives. In reviewing her own life through critical concepts of self, home and community, she displaces the familiar narrative of her life as a white, middle-class woman. She recognizes that she cannot in any simple sense escape her formation in, heritage of and continuing responsibility for her class of origin. She recognizes, too, that in leaving the 'home' of her class and the sense of self this gave her, she does so with a considerable sense of loss. She is critical of the idea that we can leave the illusory coherence of one identity such as that of a married, middle-class, white woman, and recreate it in the language of feminism – lesbian feminist activist. She insists the project of feminism is not about finding sanctuary in the politics of identity, precisely because such a position is exclusionary and creates negative positions of otherness for those who don't fit within the parameters of that identity. There is no easy, non-contradictory solution to the contradictory nature of women. Women are diverse and intersected by historical and political lines of difference. As feminists we have to refuse the status of home and occupy the critical space that is prepared always to acknowledge the configuration of forces that outline women in their specificity. This critical space is not pure and innocent but has its own discursive and material location, its own trajectory and origin which must be recognized. This is not an invitation to guilt but is rather an acknowledgment of the forces which have wrought our identities, for without such acknowledgment we are not in a position to recognize those of others. In this, Minnie Bruce Pratt is affirming some of the insights to emerge out of feminist theories of the subject and subjectivity, in particular the recognition that we are not discrete individuals but that our subjectivity and identity are always constituted relationally.

By stressing her own positionalities, the vantage points from which she speaks and acts, Minnie Bruce Pratt acknowledges the divisions of race, gender, class, ethnicity and sexualities in which, and through which, her own identity is constructed and through which she constructs the identities of others. Agency in the world can in a sense only be made more cumbersome by virtue of this acknowledgement of the full significance of social relationship, but – if nothing else – feminism has shown it is the only way to proceed if progress is to be secured without cost to others.

Article 7.1
FEMINISM AND THE CHALLENGE OF RACISM: DEVIANCE OR DIFFERENCE?

Razia Aziz

INTRODUCTION

In the long and uneven history of women's liberation in the West, its project has been frequently and seriously challenged by imperialism and racism. This is because – in combination with class – imperialism and racism have repeatedly posed the question of differences between women in the starkest terms. Slavery, conquest and colonialism created dominant and subject peoples within global structures of material exploitation and political subordination. They also involved the representation of the dominated peoples discursively – in language – as an inferior Other (as against the 'superior' white peoples of Europe and North America).[1] These processes – political, discursive and economic – provided the breeding ground for various racisms.

What has this to do with women's liberation? It indicates that women on different sides of these global processes have significantly different interests: most crucially, women oppressed and exploited by racism and/or by imperialism, have some interests in common with their menfolk, and in opposition to those of white Western men *and* women. In reality this maps out a vast area of complex solidarities, contradictions and struggles which women, seen globally, inhabit.

Thus both terms in the phrase 'women's liberation' have come under question and we are led to ask *which women?* or *what is a 'woman'?*; and *whose liberation?* or *liberation from what?* In 1852 a black woman, Sojourner Truth, delivered a speech that posed these questions forcefully:

> That man over there says that women need to be helped into carriages and lifted over ditches, and to have the best places . . . ain't I a woman? I have ploughed and planted, and gathered into barns, and no man could head me – and ain't I a woman? I could work as much as any man (when I could get it) and bear the lash as well – and ain't I a woman? I have borne five children and seen them most sold off into slavery, and when I cried out with grief, none but Jesus heard – and ain't I a woman?
>
> *(Bhavnani and Coulson, 1986, p. 83)*

Sojourner Truth's speech, delivered in 1852, still has political currency, '. . . but what sense has been made of them?' ask Bhavnani and Coulson (1986, p. 83). Very little, is their verdict. Why are Truth's words still so powerful? Arguably because rather than simply criticizing paternalistic male attitudes which depict 'women' as fragile and helpless, she asks *which* women?'. She is a woman, but is not afforded that luxury of fragility. Hers is a self-presentation of the lived experience of black/white difference in 1850s' Ohio, but she insists she is *no less woman* for this difference. In other words, she is no deviant, but one example of woman-ness.

Truth does not have to fight for the right to work but rather to survive compulsory work; she does not resist dependency on some man as much as struggle with social relations that bind her into poverty and punishing labour; the violence she speaks of is not perpetrated by a husband, father or male stranger but by the overseer's whip and the viciousness of slavery as a social system; her mother's grief is not of the kind that would pluck heart strings all over white Ohio. Yet her experience of slavery is a *woman's* experience.

The quote is rich in reference to sex, class and 'race'. But these are not spoken as abstract forces combining in some simple additive way in Truth's person. She does not live three separate forms of oppression and exploitation. What she utters is a complex reality from which these social relations may be abstracted, which is quite a different matter: in the very act of challenging her audience she defies them to see her as no more than a product and vicitim of racism–sexism–slavery.

Had what is understood as feminism been constructed from Sojourner Truth's perspective, how might its agenda have looked? What priorities would it have set for women's liberation? How would it have treated difference? These questions point to a critical space: the space marking the schism between black women's accounts of their history and experience on the one hand, and the 'sense' white feminists have made of them on the other.

The political context within which the British racism–and–feminism 'debate' has taken place continues to be one in which racism and imperialist domination figure strongly. In this context, black women's critiques frequently have a particular vibrancy derived from an insistence on placing the question of history centre-stage. This is more a political than an academic point. History is not given, it has to be made. In making a history that takes black women as its *subjects* and *agents*, not its *victims*, black women have challenged feminism with a project of the kind that is arguably dear to all feminists. Yet it is exacting in the demand that white women acknowledge and take responsibility for their own agency, witting or otherwise, as *oppressors* of black women *and* men.

In spite of a stormy relationship, feminism and its black women critics appear to have done each other a service: feminism by providing fertile ground for the analysis and politics of the Other in history; black women by injecting a much needed theoretical and political dynamism into feminism. For those who work for alliances among women, the schism may actually point to a potential for the creation of new forms of struggle, including what I call a *feminism of difference*. What I mean by this and why I think we need it will, I hope, become clear. I begin my argument with a discussion of 'race', racism and black struggle. Later, I look more closely at feminist debates in Britain.[2]

'RACE', RACISM AND BLACK STRUGGLE

Any racism relies on two assertions: the first is the 'self-evident truth' that different races exist in the world (determined in some way by biology); the second is that these races exist in a hierarchy of superiority and inferiority. In this article, I write of 'race', not race. I seek in doing this to problematize the concept, and ask you to consider what use it would serve if racism (or *race-ism*) did not exist. Put another way, what cause is furthered by the assertion that there exist in the world discrete and identifiably different 'races' (quite aside from whether it is factually correct)? As food for thought, I would like to give the word a health warning: 'If its meaning is treated as self-evident, this word may impede critical thought'!

The meaning of *black* varies *between* contexts; it is also contested *within* a context. I use it mostly to refer to people of African and Asian descent living in Britain.[3] Black people do not comprise a hermetically sealed or homogeneous category: skin colour, history and culture all play a part in their definition. Black-ness is a product of self-conscious political practice: its meaning has been given by, and has in turn affected the struggles of people in Britain who have identified themselves (and have been identified) as black. (The fact that many black people do not identify as black has continued to be a weakness in black strategy, and one to which I will return towards the end of this article.)

The term 'black' was appropriated in a movement involving those social groups who were the main targets of post-World War Two racism. Black *culture*, in this sense, is not the same as ethnicity: it acknowledges that migration and racism have not left so-called traditional cultures untouched; and that a *racialized* First World context demands more than a conservative defence of, for example, 'Muslim', 'Sikh' or 'Afro-Caribbean' cultures. Black political identification implies a complex understanding of the need for common strategies and visions.

At this point it is worth considering ethnicity – a concept as widely used as it is strongly criticized. In spite of their commonalities, different communities clearly differ in language, religion and other social practices. Ethnicity could be a way of theorizing this. But the term 'ethnic minorities' has some very odd qualities: who are the 'ethnic minorities'? None other than groups labelled 'Asians', 'Afro-Caribbeans', 'Greek Cypriots', 'Turkish Cypriots' etc., as if each of these were cohesive and self-explanatory as a social category. Why, then, is the ethnic label not extended to Australians, North Americans, Scots and even English? Because, I would argue, the definition of ethnicity is largely dictated by racism. None of the 'ethnic minorities' are uncontroversially white. Yet are there not linguistic, religious, regional and class differences in *white* people's cultures? Is *any* culture, in any case, a fact fixed in perpetuity or is it changeable and hybrid, beset by internal contradictions? Is culture, in other words, within or outside of history?

Culture is frequently important to people's sense of self, but both culture and ethnicity must be carefully defined to be analytically useful *and* politically appropriate. Cultural prejudice and misunderstanding form part of racism but alone cannot explain its violence, its preoccupation with colour, or its class dimension. The ethnicity issue continues to confound black politics partly because it is backed by the funding strategies of central and local government *and* positively regarded by (often the most conservative) elements of the said 'ethnic minorities'.[4] This can divert attention from racism, and from the really interesting question of how black people can negotiate the actual differences between them which find cultural expression.

Black refusal of shades of colour, ethnic or biologically racial bases for resistance has not always been easy to sustain,[5] but it has tended to undermine commonly held conceptions of 'race' and therefore – I would argue – racism itself. *It emphasizes that 'race' is a social category, not a natural one*, and that people acquire 'race' through their entry into historically specific and racist social relations, just as they acquire black political identity through historically specific practices. The creative appropriation of experiences of imperialism, colonialism and slavery, encourages common struggles across ethnic and class divisions. It does not mean that black identity is the same as Third World identity, but that identification with Third World struggles forms an important part of black politics.

Similarly, black people are not 'a class', but their common struggles respond to an important extent to local and global economic processes. They highlight the fact that the various labour migrations which brought black peoples to British shores were products of an imperialist international economic and political order. Migration, exploitation and class mobility are all prominent features of black histories. Compare these migrations (along with the forced migration of slaves) with the nature of the intimately related migrations of white peoples to North and South America, Africa, Asia and Australasia, and the global dimension of black/white difference becomes still clearer. *Anti-black racism is one of the great political facts of our time, in large part because of its relationship to immense wealth creation and appropriation on a global scale.*

In Britain, black resistance has emerged strongly in confrontations with the state and its representatives: over immigration controls that have explicitly institutionalized racism since the early 1960s, and which continue to divide black families; over police brutality towards black youth on the one hand, and their failure to take racist crimes seriously on the other; over the racism of the courts, schools, social services and the state as an employer; and in the inner-city riots, in combination with white people who suffered similar economic disadvantage, against the system as a whole. These struggles strongly inform black women's critiques of feminism.

However, black resistance is not just about state power and material goals. Identity and culture are integral to a struggle that responds to the complexity of racism, but goes far beyond the agenda it sets. In his pathbreaking book, *There Ain't No Black in the Union Jack*, Gilroy demonstrates the importance of culture both to the resilience of racism and to the process of resisting it. He alerts us to the prevalent cultural representations of black people as either 'problem' or 'victim' – both of them categories of deviance. This means that the representation (including self-presentation) in speech, writing, music and forms of political action of black people *outside these categories* – that is as the subjects of history and agents of historical change, as people who struggle, resist and live incredibly varied and complex lives – is in itself a weapon against racism (as it is against women's subordination).

Though subversive forms of representation in isolation cannot defeat racism, the *culture* of resistance is inseparable from the *goals* of liberation. An appropriation of history can establish black people as subjects of history, contemporary and past. To the extent that language, culture and discourse constitute reality, this process is pivotal. (The *denial* of history is, by contrast, a centrepiece of racism – as demonstrated, for instance, by the curious synonymity of 'black' and 'immigrant', and the portrayal of immigration as a national threat.) What needs to be placed at the heart of discourse about 'race' is a history which allows black people the complexity, passion, intelligence and contradictions of thought, action and word that white people are implicitly credited with when black people are seen as victims or problems. It is a history that 'sees' *difference* precisely because it insists on a fundamental human *commonality*, namely the capacity for agency.

The elements of such a history are present in the understanding of black-ness as *not defined by common oppression so much as a common context of struggle and resistance* (Mohanty, 1988, p. 67). That context, as I have tried to show, is infused with a historically specific blend of economic exploitation, cultural oppression and social subordination in which the state is prominent, and needs, furthermore, to be seen in an international perspective.

Racism requires a perspective of deviance. It speaks (implicitly or explicitly) from the position of the dominant white group. A racist perspective is composed of two elements: first, the failure to own the *particularity* of white-ness; second, the failure to acknowledge that, in a racist context, a 'white' voice stands in a relationship of authority to a 'black' voice. To 'see' deviance instead of difference means to take the experience of the dominant group as the implicit or explicit *universal* standard or norm.

Below I seek to take these observations and arguments into feminist territory. I look at the case for a perspective of difference contained in the critiques of feminism offered by black women, and at the nature of the challenge thus posed to feminism.

THE PROBLEM OF DIFFERENCE

Earlier in this article I underlined the existence of racial domination as a social fact that is negotiated and resisted by black women and men. Black women bring to feminism lived realities of a racism that has marginalized and victim-ized them in the wider world. In their writings (as with Truth) the bid for a feminism that 'sees' agency and struggle in black women's lives is explicit. This involves giving black women centre-stage, and refusing consignment to the role of exotic sideshow.

In attempting to shift the ground of feminist discourse, the adversary has at times appeared to be *white feminists* but is in fact, I would venture, White feminism – by which I expressly do *not* mean any feminism espoused by white feminists. I refer, rather, to any feminism which comes from a white perspective, *and* universalizes it.

I do not propose that White feminism is a clearly defined, coherent and internally consistent body of thought that feeds off conscious racist intentions. It is, rather, a way of seeing which, however inadvertent, leaves identifiable traces. It subsists through a failure to consider both the wider social and political context of power in which feminist utterances and actions take place, and the ability of feminism to influence that context.

Much of the black women's critique has highlighted the suppression within feminism of black/white *difference*. This can happen in one of two ways: the first is the denial of difference which is implicit in the assumption that all women have certain interests (rather than others) in common. On closer inspection, supposedly universal interests turn out to be those of a particular group of women. For instance, the pro-abortion feminist stance of the 1970s did not take into account the fact that many black women's reproductive struggles were around the right to keep and realize their fertility. For these women abortions, sterilizations and Depo Provera[6] were all-too-easily available, and were often administered without adequate consultation and/or under the shadow of poverty.[7] These are not experiences restricted to black women, but it was the intervention of black women which exposed the in fact narrow base of what seemed to some to be a universal demand, and transformed the campaign – which now focuses on choice and reproductive rights.

The second way in which it was claimed black/white difference has been suppressed in feminism is through its re-presentation as black deviance. The issue is that black women have been marginalized in feminist discourses, so that when they are depicted, it is as the exception. This problematizes the ways in which black women differ from White feminism's standard of Woman, rather than the general applicability of this standard.

To address this problem requires the prior recognition that black women's historical position as peripheral to the grand workings of power in society has precluded them hiding behind a mask of generality: too often the exception, the special case, the puzzling, more-oppressed or exotic anomaly (even within feminism), they have been largely denied the voice of authority by which white women appear to speak on behalf of the female sex as a whole. Black women's particularity is transparent because of racism; any failure of white women to recognize *their* own particularity continues that racism.

THE INSEPARABILITY OF BLACK AND WHITE EXPERIENCE

In keeping with the politics of black resistance, an appropriation of imperialist history has been integral to black women's political practice. In this way they have forged an identity deeply imbued with temporal and spatial solidarities: with their political and familial predecessors on the one hand, and with Third World liberation movements on the other. It is not my view that black women have a monopoly on internationalism, *or* that black women – in the First World – have an identity of interests with Third World women. Nevertheless, black women have frequently been left 'holding' the argument for the simultaneous consideration of class, 'race', imperialism and gender. This is not because only they can see it, but because they live it in a particularly acute way.

White women are as much part of social relations as black women are. Therefore, they must be as knowledgeable about the interactions of these structures of domination, albeit from a very different position. Racism, however, relies on a perspective of deviance which obscures white particularity. This masks the fact that white-ness is every bit as implicated as black-ness in the workings of racism. Thus, whether or not they are aware of it, *racism affects white women constantly.*

In articulating black women's experiences of the British state, the labour market, their families and their sexualities, black feminist writers have emphasized black/white difference (sometimes at the expense of other issues – see the next section). However, it is important to note that their's are not stories parallel to those of white women, but intricately intertwined with them. Black women cannot – even if they wanted to – speak of their struggles outside of the context of racism and resistance (if only because their colour is never 'invisible'); white feminists, on the other hand, can speak – and many do – as if that context did not exist.

The point is not, I would argue, that white women experience the state (to take one example) as patriarchal, whereas black women experience the state as racist *and* patriarchal: if the state is racist, it is racist to everyone; it is merely more difficult for white people to see this, because part of the racism of the state is to treat and promote white-ness as the norm.

THE ISSUE OF MEN

Another important contribution of black women has been to raise awareness about how racism undermines black *masculinity*, treating it as pathological in relation to white masculinity (another form of Other-ness). The myth of black men as rapists of white women, for example, justifies violence against these men and is an indication that not all men are equal – or equally favoured – in patriarchy. The failure to recognize these issues independently was only one example of the poor track record of British feminism where racism is concerned.[8] As Ramazanoglu pointed out: 'Racism divides feminists not because our attitudes, statistics or concepts need correcting (although, of course, they do), but because *black women have real political interests in common with black men*' (1986, p. 85; emphasis added). To which may be added: and because racism really does reside in relationships between white women on the one hand and black women and men on the other. These two claims demand much more from feminism than an adding on of the special concerns of black women. Racism is only one of many reasons why the oppression and exploitation of men matters to feminism (class is another). The thrust of black women's arguments was that the feminist project itself had to be re-evaluated.

What are the implications for feminism of these critiques? A key piece of the re-evaluation demanded by black women was that feminism should abandon the notion that all women automatically have common interests (and that men and women have opposing interests). The underlying logic is that common interests between women only emerge as a consequence of common appropriation of historical experiences of oppression, subordination and exploitation through the essentially political practices of solidarity, alliance and resistance.

In other words, feminism has been challenged to place itself in history, and to locate itself in relation to other forms of resistance such as black, Third World liberation and class struggles. As a consequence, it needs to work for its coherence as a political force, rather than assuming a ready-made, but false, coherence by placing itself outside history, and shirking the responsibilities attendant on its power as a social movement.

Many of the issues raised by black women – about who sets the political agenda, about marginalization in language and practice, in short about Other-ness – are familiar to white feminists from their own history of resistance. What has not been so easy to come to terms with is the need to acknowledge the uncomfortable dual position of oppressor and oppressed. In this way the 'debate', however acrimonious, provided feminism with a fresh opportunity to address its most troublesome weaknesses and to move on from them.

In the next section, I attempt to move beyond the 1980s by considering the limits of focusing on black/white difference. In order to do this, I look at the issues of class and culture; both implicated in the lived realities of difference amongst women.

BEYOND THE DEBATE

Black women are an immensely varied social group spanning different histories, classes, sexualities, languages and religions. What I have attempted to do is distil the recasting of the politics of history which *some* black women have brought to feminism. The works I have drawn upon do not constitute an internally consistent body of scholarship, much less unerringly espouse what I have termed a perspective of difference. In fact, I shall argue below that the strategy of highlighting black/white difference has involved certain tactics that undermine the move towards such a perspective. I am not suggesting that the strategy is entirely misguided (I have adopted it myself up till this point!). But it is also important to place it under scrutiny. In doing so, I make a point which is conceptually simple, but politically complex: namely that the energetic assertion of black/white (or any other) difference tends to create fixed and oppositional categories which can result in another version of the suppression of difference. Differences *within* categories – here black and white – are underplayed in order to establish it *between* them. Consequently, each category takes on a deceptive air of internal coherence, and similarities between women in the different categories are thus suppressed.[9]

These effects are not deliberate: in fact the writers I have 'drawn upon all note the heterogeneity of black women as a group. Having done so, however, they tend to leave this fact untheorized. The heterogeneity of *white* women as a group, on the other hand, goes almost unacknowledged. Here I concur with Martin and Mohanty's observation that critics of White (or Western) feminism have concentrated on its inadequacy in dealing with black women, but have left virtually unexamined the implicit assumption that it is '. . .*adequate* to the task of articulating the situation of white women' (Martin and Mohanty, 1986, p. 193).

In order to unravel the issues raised by stressing black/white difference, I will focus first on how issues of *class* are raised or ignored in order to emphasize that difference. I will then offer some comments on the strategy of black-ness as it relates to the problem of *culture* and identity.

The problem of class

There has been some acknowledgement by black women that white working-class women have also been marginalized in the feminist movement. Take, for instance, Amos and Parmar:

> In describing the women's movement as oppressive we refer to the experiences of Black and working-class women of the movement and the inability of feminist theory to speak to their experience in any meaningful way.
>
> *(1984, p. 4)*

However, this observation drops out of their argument. They were not alone in failing to engage with white working-class (or Irish) women's struggles, and – crucially – *how the existence of these struggles affects black/white difference and potential black/white solidarity.* Class often disappears in the desire to make a point against White feminism; for instance when Carby states that, '. . .Black people. . . have a solidarity around the fact of race, which white women of course do not need to have with white men' (1982, p. 213), she is clearly not thinking of white working-class struggles such as the 1984–5 miners' strike.

It is of course not only class, but also ethnic, religious and even imperialist differences among white women that are implicitly denied here. In the attempt to deliver a jolt to White feminist complacency, certain issues of political significance are neglected, with the effect of homogenizing white women. The significance of such omissions is that they de-emphasize the oppression of *white* women by other white women, leaving black women *apparently* the sole aspirants to that dubious accolade.

A different problem arises when we consider the *self-preservation* of black women. Here class has been used selectively in a way that seems to deny the diversity of black women. The most common manifestation of this is the majoritarian approach: since *most* black people are working class, it is okay to behave as if they *all* are. I am not attacking analyses of the exploitation of black people and the role of capitalism in producing it, only noting a tendency to *class*-ify black people – a social group that displays class diversity *and* mobility.

This tendency inadvertently supports the unexamined position demonstrated in the following quotes:

> All black people are subordinated by racial oppression, women are subordinated by sexual domination, and *black women are subordinated by both as well as class.*
>
> (*Foster-Carter, 1987, p. 46; emphasis added*)

> . . .black women are subjected to the *simultaneous* oppression of patriarchy, class and 'race'. . .
>
> (*Carby, 1982, p. 213*)

The effect of this is to represent black women as *homogeneously oppressed in almost every politically significant way.* In bringing this argument, I could (as a black middle-class woman) be accused of special pleading; which is precisely my point: unless black identity *is* class identity, black middle-class people cannot be considered a 'special', or deviant, case.

Black people are an extremely heterogeneous group, and racism does not affect them all in the same ways. (Some of us – thanks to factors such as a university education – manage to publish articles and speak, in spite – and because[10] – of racism, with the voice of authority afforded by class privilege!) Many black struggles have focused on the issue of survival with dignity in the face of violence, poverty and humiliation, but black identity is not built on that alone.

The problem of culture and identity

The tendency to homogenize the oppression of black people comes from an understandable desire to find common ground and to resist the power of racism to divide black people from one another. However, it remains the case that perhaps more than half the people who may be labelled 'black' do not identify as such: I refer, of course, to the majority of British people of South Asian descent.

In spite of the criticisms of the 'ethnicity' approach which I offered earlier, there is a real political and experiential issue to be answered which is not just about divisive strategies of *racism* but about actual historical differences in the nature of colonialism, imperialism, racism and representation – and in how these are appropriated.

The growth of anit-Muslim racism and the Islamization of Muslim communities in Britain during and since the Rushdie Affair is only one particularly acute example of why cultural *identity* matters. This example is of interest to all black women because of the profound consequences for Muslim *women* (many of whom identify with Islam) of the move towards fundamentalism (which is, of course, not confined to Muslim communities). The strategy of underplaying inter-black difference has never been equal to this challenge of *subjectivity*: at a time like this, it can appear at best politically naive, and at worst irresponsible.

Any line of argument chosen to emphasize black/white difference will tend to deny the complexity of both black and white experience. This may be unavoidable, but unless it is explicitly acknowledged a racial essentialism can emerge through the back door of fixed and oppositional identities. If alliances are seriously sought, the strategy of stressing one difference is limited. The dilemma is clear, even if its solution is not: in order for difference to be taken seriously it has to be established in debate and action; but it is important to take a broad view of the political consequences of this process, otherwise there is a risk of again detaching difference from history.

The issue of identity is one which best crystallizes this dilemma. Rooted as it is in complex layers of struggles and contexts, identity is not neat and coherent, but fluid and fragmented. Yet attempts to assert it seem to undermine potential solidarities between specific groups of women. In the final section, I address the question of identity more directly. I ask what post-modernist thinking can offer feminists seeking to progress on the issues raised by racism. In doing so, I attempt to locate a space in which a feminism of difference might take root.

Locating a feminism of difference

Recent years have seen the demise of grand (or modernist) theories; namely those which claim to establish *a fundamental determinant* of history (such as class or patriarchy). This demise is very closely related to the inability of such theories to respond to the complexities of difference and power. Socialist-feminists have attempted to juggle the grand structures of 'race', class and gender without giving one of them overall primacy. This strategy has not, however, been totally successful. It has become increasingly apparent that the attempt to combine (and so 'democratize') grand theories of 'race', class and gender may be unworkable. The endeavour tends to produce and multiply unwieldy and static categories without much analytical power (such as 'the white, middle-class male') as the list of oppressions became as long as the range of political struggles was multitudinous.

This 'democratization' of oppressions can be seen in retrospect as an attempt to push grand theory to its limits. It was accompanied by the growth of a phenomenon often labelled 'identity politics'. Oppressions tended to be increasingly regarded as 'relative', with attached identities that tended to be elevated above criticism. This can lead to an inward-looking identity politics where oppressions are added and subtracted. The capacity to analyse the *interrelations* between identities and social relations, and to establish political priorities, is thereby seriously weakened.

Identity politics ceases to be progressive when it sees the assertion of identity *as an end in itself*. Jenny Bourne (1983) urges us to ask what identity *does* in relation to the politics of resistance? Does identity politics promote or does it divert resistance by providing a sanctuary for people who do not want to acknowledge that they are oppressors? Bourne laments the analytical and political loss of privilege of the *material* (particularly the economic) as a determining factor separate from and somehow more real than language, culture and representation. Yet this dethroning need not take the ahistorical route Bourne criticizes. The view that language is constitutive of reality can, instead, open the field for historically aware analyses of the relationship between, for example, 'race', class and culture.

A focus on representation as a social *act* allows us to understand the ways in which the historical, the biological and the material are given a reality and meaning through language. It offers us a more complex conception of power as exercised in all manner of social interactions. Crucially, it allows us to see competing discourses – for instance those of dominant racism, of ethnicity and of black resistance – as *intrinsic to* the exercise of power in society.

This paradigmatic shift is rightly labelled *post-modernist* as it is a response to – and an attempt to move beyond – the weaknesses of grand theory. At its heart is an entirely different treatment of *subjectivity* – or the way in which people live and understand their selves and identities.

Post-modernism is *deconstructive*: it sees subjectivity as a *product* of power rather than its author; and agency as power's way of acting through the individual. Power, in this understanding, is exercised in historically specific discourses (or ideologies) and practices: in contrast to the modernist conception, it is not unitary and zero-sum, but diffuse, constantly changing and plural. Post-modernism is therefore antithetical to essentialism of any kind – racial, sexual or human.[11] It proposes that the selves we think are fixed and unitary are actually unstable, fragmented and contradictory. It can thus potentially help us look at changes and tensions (such as that of oppressor/oppressed) in who we understand ourselves as being.

Such a perspective can save identity from 'mummifying' by challenging us self-consciously to deconstruct our identities. This act of deconstruction is *political*, as it exposes the intricate operations of power that constitute subjectivity. Thus the particular deconstruction of the identity 'woman' that black women have achieved can be seen as exposing the link between racism at large and its subjective articulation. Nor is black identity somehow privileged (as I have tried to show): the cost of a 'home' in any identity is the exercise of a power to include the chosen and exclude the Other.

I may appear at this point to be espousing contradictory positions – am I *for* or *against* the assertion of identity? – in response to which I simply re-state the question: 'What is identity for?'

In providing us with self-presentations of black women as subjects of history, black women have established their identity as an influential political fact. An anti-humanist insistence on always *de*-constructing subjectivity ignores political context and the importance of identity in resistance. The assertion of identity is a process people can relate to because it reclaims agency and makes them feel power-ful. The importance of this cannot be underestimated. Furthermore, any focus on language and subjectivity which divorces them from material forces (such as the current crisis and restructuring of capitalism) also divorces theory from some of the things that affect people most severely.

Post-modernism does not immunize us from the responsibility to locate ourselves relative to the political movements of our time: as a discourse, it is part of – and is implicated in – the very power relations in society that we analyse and aim to change. If a feminism of difference is to compete with reactionary forces for the spaces caused by political schisms, it needs to incorporate *both* the deconstruction of subjectivity *and* the political necessity of asserting identity. Additionally, its recognition of the fact that language and culture constitute reality needs to coexist with a recognition of the unmitigated realities of violence, economic exploitation and poverty. For a feminism of difference, these questions need to be answered in relation to the imperatives of each historical moment. This requires a degree of self-consciousness and responsibility of thought, utterance and action from our oppressed and oppressor selves alike which is nowhere near prevalent as yet. But the potential for alliance between and among black and white women depends upon it.

Acknowledgement
I am indebted to Jo Beall and Jane Rostren for reading and commenting on drafts of this article.

Notes

1   See the excellent essay, *Orientalism*, by E. W. Said (1979), in which he critically investigates the process by which this has occurred.

2   It is important to note that neither feminism nor black politics in Britain can be entirely understood in isolation from debates and struggles internationally. See Lorde (1984), Moraga and Anzaldua (1981) and Bulbeck (1988).

3   The strongest competing definition of 'black' (and the most prevalent) confines it to people of the African diaspora only.

4   This means that different black communities are effectively pitched in competition with each other for scarce resources, so the 'ethnic minority' approach, dressed up as an attempt to encourage racial harmony, in fact divides and separates black communities.

5   Black people of all kinds experience allegiances based on one or more of these characteristics, which some would argue is partly because of what racism has done to us – a view with which I concur.

6   A long-acting, injectible contraceptive banned in the United States because of disturbing side-effects.

7   Angela Davis, in *Women, Race and Class* (1981), informs us that the US-backed sterilization campaign in Puerto Rico in the 1970s claimed the fertility of 35% of all women of reproductive age.

8   See Amos and Parmar (1984) for other examples.

9   See Phoenix (1988) for a good, short study which challenges this tendency.

10   By this I mean that being black made it far more likely that I would be asked to write this kind of article.

11   In other words it is anti-*humanist*, rejecting the idea of an essential human-ness shared by all human individuals.

Article 7.2
MULTIPLE MEDIATIONS: FEMINIST SCHOLARSHIP IN THE AGE OF MULTINATIONAL RECEPTION

Lata Mani

'Unusual knowing', a cognitive practice, a form of consciousness that is not primordial, universal, or coextensive with human thought. [. . .] but historically determined and yet subjectively and politically assumed.

(de Lauretis, March 1990)

On the acupuncturist's table, Berkeley, California, July 1988:

I am lying in wait for the complex verbal negotiation that attends each visit to my acupuncturist. I want a diagnosis – a definable illness, a definite cure. He is disdainful of this desire for clarity and resolution and insists on treating my body as a zone in which energies rise and fall, sometimes rebelliously, at other times gracefully and once even, as he put it, 'stroppily'. As I ponder the frustrating untranslatability of his idiom, he asks the dreaded question: 'Well, what is your PhD thesis about?'

I stare at the infra-red lamp and wonder which version to present. The various responses I have elicited over the years race through my mind like a film running at high speed. My usual strategy is to assess the cultural politics of those addressing me (such as I can discern them), the tenor of the question (is this a serious inquiry or merely a polite one?) and my frame of mind at the time (do I want to educate, be patronized or try to avoid both by being vague, but thereby risking the impression that I know not what I am doing?). I did not, however, have time for such musings. I was trapped under the beady eye of my white American doctor of needles who, having taken my pulse, was awaiting a reply. So I blurted out what I consider my minimalist 'no-nonsense' description: 'I am working on the debate between colonial officials, missionaries and the indigenous male élite on *sati* (widow burning) in colonial India.'

I felt weak, as though it had been a confession extorted from me after intense cross-examination. I sighed inwardly. Meanwhile, my declaration had provoked what turned out to be a half-hour lecture on the dilemmas of cross-cultural understanding. He said that such practices would always be difficult for Westerners to comprehend, hastily adding that it was important none the less not to impose alien values and that *sati* probably had a particular significance within Indian culture which it would be enlightening to know. At this point he turned away from my foot, into which he had just finished inserting needles, and asked, 'So how do *you* understand widow burning?'

I felt myself stiffen. He had thrown me a challenge that would require a command performance in colonial and post-colonial history and discourse, one that I did not feel equal to at the time. So I said evasively, 'It's a long story and I'm trying to sort it out.'

'Good', said the genial man in the white coat tapping my arm. Not waiting for a response, he continued. 'Of course, you are Westernized and your ideas have probably changed from living here. I wonder what women in India feel about it?' So saying, he left the room.

I was furious. I had not interrupted his liberal, relativist, patronizing discourse, and was as a result caught in its pincer movement: an apparent but ultimately repressive tolerance, a desire for 'true' knowledge, and a demand for authenticity that was impossible for me to meet, given that any agreement between us, however fragile and superficial, would immediately make me 'Westernized': not like 'them' but like 'him'. I wished for the millionth time that I had been working on a less contentious topic, one that, unlike *sati*, had not served as metonym for Indian society itself . . . or had had the panache to wag my finger like him and say, 'Read my book and you'll find out'.

THE EMERGENCE OF A POLITICS OF LOCATION

This paper explores questions of positionality and location and their relation to the production of knowledge as well as its reception. These issues have animated feminism from its inception. Here they are approached through a set of interconnected reflections, on the processes that shaped my study of debates on *sati* under British colonialism, and on the different ways in which this analysis has been received in Britain and in India. Such alternative readings thematize the politics of intellectual work in neo/post-colonial contexts, and the difficulties of achieving an international feminism sensitive to the complex and diverse articulations of the local and the global.

Contemporary theory in feminism and in the humanities has brought a critical self-consciousness to bear both on the place and mode of enunciation (who speaks and how) and that of its reception (how it is interpreted and why). As claims to universality and objectivity have been shown to be the alibis of a largely masculinist, heterosexual and white Western subject, both readers and writers have had to confront their particularity and history. Gender, race, class, sexuality and historical experience specify hitherto unmarked bodies, deeply compromising the fictions of unified subjects and disinterested knowledges.

Such developments, or should I say acknowledgements, require attentiveness to the theoretical and political impulses that shape our projects, and an openness to the inevitable fact that different agendas may govern their reception. Needless to say, there have always been multiple investments and diverse audiences. Our accounting of these phenomena today simply attests to the successful struggles for discursive spaces of those overlapping and hitherto marginalized groups, women, Third World people, gays and lesbians. Institutional concessions to the heterogeneity of the social landscape have prompted the emergence of new fields of study within US universities, for instance ethnic studies and women's studies. It has also given new momentum to interdisciplinary work. The current mobilization of talents and energies around culture studies is a case in point.[1]

The revolt of the particular against that masquerading as the general, of what Donna Haraway has called 'situated' as against 'disembodied knowledges' (Haraway, 1988), has brought to the fore theoretical and political questions regarding positionality and identity. This issue has probably been most fully developed within feminism, in part in debates about the relationship between experience and knowledge. One locus of such discussion in the Euro-American context has been the related struggles over racism and white-centredness of dominant feminism (Moraga and Anzaldua, 1981; hooks, 1981, Amos et al., 1984; Bhavnani and Coulson, 1986, among others) and its replication of elements of colonial discourse (Spivak, 1981; Mohanty, 1984; Minh-ha 1986/7; Lazreg, 1988). Feminists have called for a revised politics of location – 'revised' because, unlike its initial articulation, the relation between experience and knowledge is now seen to be one not of correspondence, but fraught with history, contingency and struggle. (In addition to the authors already cited, see Bulkin et al., 1984; Segrest, 1985; Rich, 1986; de Lauretis, 1986; Kaplan, 1987.)[2] These terms powerfully suggest some of the problems of positionality as they confront me: a post-colonial Third World feminist working on India in the United States.

Chandra Talpade Mohanty argues that developing a politics of location requires exploration of 'the historical, geographic, cultural, psychic and imaginative boundaries which provide the ground for political definition and self-definition' (Mohanty, 1987, p. 31). Location, in her terms, is not a fixed point but a 'temporality of struggle' (p. 40), characterized by multiple locations and non-synchronous processes of movement 'between cultures, languages, and complex configurations of meaning and power' (p. 42). These processes, in Mohanty's view, enable 'a paradoxical continuity of self, mapping and . . . political location . . . [M]y location forces and enables specific modes of reading and knowing the dominant. The struggles I choose to engage in are then the intensification of these modes of knowing' (p. 42). This definition of the space of politics very nicely illuminates the dynamics of how my conception of a project on the debate on *sati* in colonial India bears the traces of movement between cultures and configurations of meaning, multiple locations and specific modes of knowing.

My research examines colonial official, missionary and indigenous élite discourses on *sati* in Britain and India in the late eighteenth and early nineteenth centuries. I investigate the conditions of production and the burden of each of these discourses, the intersections, differences and tensions between them, and the competing and overlapping ways in which they were deployed. Among other things, I argue that a specifically colonial discourse on India framed the debate on *sati*, producing troubling consequences for how 'the woman's question' in India was to be posed thereafter, whether by Indian nationalists, or Western feminists (Mani, 1989).

One of the things that has prompted and sustained my energy through hours of plodding through archival documents and reels of dizzying microfilm has been a conviction of the importance of the contemporary ideological and political legacy of such debates about women and culture. I have always been aware that this legacy has had a differential trajectory in India and in, for example, the US or Britain: that the relation of this earlier discourse to contemporary knowledges, popular and specialist, about India in the West, was different from its relation to the contemporary self-knowledge of Indians. It is the contours of this difference that this [article] will now explore.

The following section reflects on the experience of presenting my work (Mani, 1987) to groups in the US, Britain and India and discovering that the audiences in these places seized on entirely different aspects of my work as politically significant. These responses in turn have caused me to reflect on how moving between different 'configurations of meaning and power' can prompt different 'modes of knowing'. The experience has also required me squarely to confront a problem not adequately theorized in discussions of positionality or of the function of theory and criticism: the politics of simultaneously negotiating not multiple but discrepant audiences, different 'temporalities of struggle.'[3]

BACK TO THE FUTURE: THE AFTER-LIVES OF COLONIAL DISCOURSES

'Colonial' or Eurocentric discourses on India, and on the Third World more generally, have an abiding presence in the USA and Britain, the two Western countries with which I am most familiar. Television documentaries, scholarly writing and popular wisdom circulate such notions as the centrality of religion – whether framed as the essential 'spirituality' of the East or as the dominance of caste (Inden, 1986; Appadurai, 1988) – the antiquity of Indian 'culture', and the victimization of women. These ideas 'hail' those of us living here with a systematicity that, over time, makes them truly oppressive. As a Marxist-feminist who had come to feminism in India, I initially responded to the predominance of culturalist understandings of Indian society with surprise and bemusement at the ignorance they betrayed. I assumed that such ignorance must also account for my having so often to explain the supposed anomaly of being an Indian feminist.

The repetition of such incidents as my encounter with the acupuncturist, the dynamics of which I would barely have been able to fathom when I first arrived in the US, compelled me to think seriously about the prehistory of such knowledges about India and Indian women. I brought this new sensibility to bear on reading the debate on *sati*. It has been, I believe, by and large productive. For although I have read many of the same documents as other historians, Indian and non-Indian, an alertness to how British colonialism may have shaped knowledge about colonized society has turned up unexpected disjunctures, contests and determinations, for instance, over what constitutes 'tradition'. Given a context in which elements of this nineteenth-century discourse continue to circulate, on occasion virtually unreconstructed, in the service of British racism and US cultural imperialism, I consider excavation of the colonial prehistory of such ideas to be a political gesture.

By and large, most discussions that followed presentations of my work in the US or Britain tended to focus on the contemporary replications, resonances or rearticulations of what I had sketched. In Britain, for instance, we explored how the British state manipulates women's 'oppression' in Indian and Pakistani 'culture' to legitimate virginity tests, immigration controls and policing of Asian marriages and family life. This 'civilizing' racist British state has placed black feminists in Britain in a position analogous to that of nineteenth-century Indian male social reformers, who defended 'culture' and 'women' in a similarly overdetermined context (Parmar, 1982; Amos et al., 1984; Grewal et al., 1988). The significant difference between then and now is that black feminists (unlike many male nationalists) have insisted on keeping women at the centre of the struggle, refusing to let themselves become mere pawns in a contest between the state and community. They have charted a complex strategy. On the one hand, they have challenged the self-serving appropriation of 'women's issues' by a racist British state. Simultaneously, they have resisted both the 'protection' of men in the black community when it has come with a defence of practices oppressive to women, and white feminist attempts to rescue them from patriarchy. In short, black feminists in Britain have refused 'salvation', whether by the state in the name of civilized modernity, by black men on behalf of tradition and community integrity, or by white feminists in the interest of ethnocentric versions of women's liberation. In this context, discussions after my presentations explored, among other things, questions of rhetoric and strategy: how to argue for women's rights in ways that were not complicit in any way with patriarchal, racist or ethnocentric formulations of the issues. Thus, given that the British state draws on key elements of nineteenth-century discourses on India to further its own current projects, my delineation of the colonial dimension of these discourses was seen to have an explicitly political character.

In India, however, this dimension of my project was interpreted quite differently, primarily as an academic and historical argument. To some extent this is not surprising. Notions of 'timeless textual traditions' or the essential spirituality of Indian society have a different afterlife in the Indian public domain. Quite simply, they are not, as in Britain, critical to the elaboration of hegemony. Certainly, development policies explicitly embrace the logic of modernity, brahmanical texts have come to represent quintessential Hinduism, and the colonial legacy of making religious scriptures the basis of civil law has enormously complicated feminist projects of legal reform. However, notions like 'timeless traditions' function most often to inspire literature from the Indian Tourist Development Corporation or to feed the fantasy life of petit-bourgeois middle- and high-caste Indians regarding the glory of ancient India (read, 'of their own lineage'). Except in the case of Government of India documentaries on tribal peoples, or sometimes in relation to remote rural areas, there does not exist a serious convention of representing Indian citizens as lacking agency, inhabiting a timeless zone, and immobilized by 'tradition'. Indeed, this kind of analysis would be difficult to sustain, given that the authority of the Indian state has been continually challenged since independence, and is bolstered today not by a democratic consensus but through a brutal and increasingly unashamed use of violence.

The Indian context thus presents a sharp contrast to the West; naming something 'colonial' in India has, accordingly, a different import. It becomes a question of periodization, rather than a crucial move in developing an oppositional, anti-imperialist critical practice. Such a reading is further comprehensible because, in a palpable, existential sense, when one is in India, colonialism does indeed seem like a thing long past. Despite India's economically dependent status in the world economy and its wilful exploitation by multinationals and agencies like the World Bank, 'the West' as ideological and political presence articulates with such a density of indigenous institutions, discourses, histories and practices that its identity as 'Western' is refracted and not always salient. This is not to say that Indians are naive about the impact of the West. (There was, for example, little confusion about the ultimate culpability of the US-based corporation Union Carbide, in the Bhopal industrial disaster.) What I am suggesting is that, unlike, for example, many nations in the Caribbean or in Central America, in India it is not the boot of imperialism that is felt as an identifiable weight upon one's neck. The pressure one feels compelled to resist is rather that of the nation state, dominant social and political institutions, and religious 'fundamentalisms' of various kinds. No doubt, the activities of the nation state are themselves related in complex ways to regional and global geopolitical trends, but it is the local face of this international phenomenon against which one is moved to struggle.

It comes as no surprise, then, that in India, the 'political' dimension of my work is seen to be expressed primarily in my engagement with nationalism, the limited parameters within which nationalists posed the question of women's status, the marginality of women to nineteenth-century discussions supposedly about them, and the legacy of colonialism in contemporary discussion of women's issues. This last point was made in my presentation in relation to the recent controversy over reform of Islamic law provoked by the 'Shahbano case'. The case was one in which the Supreme Court had upheld the application of a Muslim woman, Shahbano, for lifelong maintenance from her ex-husband. The Supreme Court's verdict became a rallying point for many Muslims who felt that the court had (contrary to its claims) violated Islamic law and thus undermined the only legal protection Indian Muslims enjoyed as a religious minority (Punwani, 1985; Kishwar, 1986; Engineer, 1987; Pathak and Sunder Rajan, 1989). In analysing the case, it was possible to point out how, in this as in many instances in the nineteenth century, contests over women's rights were being debated as contests over scriptural interpretation, and as struggles over a community's autonomy and right to self-determination. While these terms do not exhaust the arguments made in relation to the case, they point to significant parallels between nineteenth- and twentieth-century debates on women (Mani, 1987, pp. 153–6). My interest in such continuities was in the ways in which they constrained the form and content of contemporary discussions. I did not assume that the persistence of certain discursive elements implied unchanged significance, meanings or effects; ideas are potentially available for different kinds of appropriation by different social forces. Suffice it to say that the case, more than any theoretical argument about 'colonial discourse', served to convey some of the political impulses of my project. Even here, however, the 'colonial' dimension was of academic interest. The burden of the discussion, not inappropriately, fell to the practical problems of building coalitions between Hindu and Muslim women in the wake of the divisiveness produced by the Shahbano case and the growth of communalism in Indian politics.

SITUATING OUR INTERVENTIONS

These differing receptions of my work in Britain and India raise questions regarding the relationship between 'experience' and 'theory', one's geographical location and the formulation of one's projects. It seems to me that travelling to the US and living under its regimes of truth regarding India and the Third World more generally have intensified for me certain 'modes of knowing'. The disjunctions between how I saw myself and the kinds of knowledge about me that I kept bumping into in the West, opened up new questions for social and political inquiry.

Reading Edward Said's *Orientalism* in this context was enormously productive and energizing (Said, 1979). It contextualized the phenomena, discourses and attitudes I was encountering and helped me in the task of situating personal experiences within a historical problematic. It quickened my impulse to take more seriously than I had previously been inclined to, colonial official and missionary discourses on India. My interest in these was not merely that of a historian of ideas, but of someone curious about the history of the present. I can only wonder at how my project might have been fashioned in the absence of this experience of travel to a different economy of power and knowledge. In this regard, I find it significant that an Indian friend of mine once remarked that the full force of Said's argument in *Orientalism* had come home to her only after spending time in Europe. Prior to this she had believed, and this is a fairly common perception in India, that Said was perhaps overstating his case, stretching a point.[4]

It seems to me that the politics and epistemology of differing readings such as these dramatizes the dilemma of post-colonial intellectuals working on the Third World in the West. One diagnosis of this situation accuses such intellectuals of inauthenticity or ideological contamination by the West. This charge may be levelled by First World intellectuals demanding a spurious authenticity of their Third World colleagues. It often works to challenge the latter groups' credibility, by implying that their politics are exceptional and ungeneralizable. This analysis may, however, also be shared by Third World intellectuals working in the Third World. The criticism in this instance may be rooted in the assumption, not always unwarranted, that intellectuals abroad are, so to speak, 'selling out'. It is, however, ultimately simplistic because it over-generalizes, and one does not, of course, have to leave home to sell out. Alternatively, assertions about ideological contamination are often shorthand allusions to genuine issues, such as asymmetries in the material conditions of scholarship in metropolitan and Third World contexts. Such problems are, however, not clarified by a moralistic formulation of the issue in terms of purity or pollution.

In the face of this discourse of authenticity, some Third World intellectuals working in the First World have reterritorialized themselves as hybrid. This strategy is compelling when such a demonstration of hybridity becomes, as in Gloria Anzaldua's *Borderlands* (1987) an enabling moment for the possibility of a collective politics attentive to difference and contradiction. When, however, the elaboration of hybridity becomes an end in itself, serving only to undo binary oppositions, it runs the risk of dodging entirely the question of location. To this one must say, 'necessary but insufficient'.

Finally, for those intellectuals from the geographical Third World who have an elsewhere to return to, there is the possibility of adopting a tactic which would separate projects into what is deemed appropriate or inappropriate to do 'while one is in the West'. Here again we have a prescription which may make sense in specific instances, for political and practical reasons. On the other hand this strategy also has the potential for side-stepping the issue. It implicitly conceives of the West and non-West as autonomous spaces and thereby evades the thorny issue of their intersections and mutual implications (Mohanty, 1989).

How, then, would I proceed to delineate, in my own case, the potential and limits of my location, working on the Third World in the belly of the First? For one thing, it seems to me that the mode of knowing enabled by the experience of existing between discursive systems makes it difficult for me to isolate colonialism as a distinct historical period with little claim on the present. Consequently, I have tried to train myself to look for discontinuities in apparently smooth surfaces, and continuities across the dominant and oppositional. Secondly, the deadening essentialism of much historical and contemporary Western representation of the Third World has confirmed for me, albeit in a different way, a lesson learnt earlier from Marxism: an abiding suspicion of primarily cultural explanations of social phenomena. At the same time, perhaps not paradoxically, experiences of such a persistent privileging of 'culture' have in turn compelled me to take very seriously the domain designated by it. What counts as 'culture'? How is it conceived and represented? With what consequences? In short, I have been persuaded of the need to open to critical reflection the vexed and complex issue of the relationship between colonialism and questions of culture.

This is a problem that is, to my mind, yet to be adequately thematized in the literature on colonialism in India. Historiography on nineteenth-century India, for instance, has produced sophisticated analysis of the impact of colonialism on India's economy and politics, but has paid comparatively little attention to its impact on culture or on conceptions of it. Perhaps the ways in which I may be tempted to frame the problem will be marked by the fact that it became an issue for me as a result of my experience of Britain and the US. It may be that I accent the colonial rather more heavily than my imagined counterpart, the feminist writing in India. But as I reflect on what moves me, I also need to be aware that I now inescapably participate in multiple conversations, not all of which overlap. As for the gains of being situated in the interstices, only time will tell. In the meantime, it seems to me that my attempt to specify location might also be fruitfully undertaken in dialogue with feminists in India. After all, the dangers of reading the local as global are potentially present both in India and in the West: in the former through minimizing colonialism, in the latter through aggrandizing it.

PRIORITIES REDETERMINED: THE AFTERMATH OF ROOP KANWAR'S BURNING

The difficulties of straddling different temporalities of struggle cannot, however, always be resolved through listening for and talking about our specificities. There are political moments which pose limits to the possibility of conceiving of international feminist exchanges (whether between First and Third World women in the West or between Third World women cross-nationally) as negotiated dialogues which, while they may alternately diverge and intersect, are ultimately benign and noncontradictory.

On 22 September 1987, Roop Kanwar died on the funeral pyre of her husband in Deorala, Rajasthan. The incident has sparked off a nationwide controversy on *sati* in India, unearthed the information that there have been at least thirty-eight widow immolations in Rajasthan since independence, and dragged out of the closet vociferous supporters of the practice. In this recent case, the government of India vacillated in taking action against family members found to have coerced Roop. State officials were present along with an estimated 300,000 others at an event 'honouring' the episode thirteen days after the burning, and when the state finally banned glorification of *sati*, the response was too little, too late.

Meanwhile, a massive debate on *sati* had been set in motion, with opponents and defenders staking out their claims in terms that were in many ways remarkably reminiscent of the nineteenth-century controversy which is the subject of my own research. As in the colonial period, issues of scriptural interpretation, the so-called 'traditional' nature of *sati*, its barbarity, the role of the state, women's social conditioning and the question of the widow's consent, all emerged as key items in the debate.

Four positions were discernible in the discussions that followed upon Roop Kanwar's death. Each of these is more elaborate than my characterization of it suggests, but my purpose here is merely to sketch in broad strokes the discursive space that was constituted, referring readers to others who have analysed them more thoroughly (Patel and Kumar, 1988; Sangari, 1988, among others). There was firstly, a 'liberal' position, critical of *sati* as 'traditional', 'religious' and barbaric and arguing that the incident represented the failure of the project of modernization. Secondly, and opposed to this, was the conservative, pro-*sati* lobby. This valorized *sati*'s 'traditional' and 'religious' status and argued that the rationality of the practice was necessarily inaccessible to Westernized, urban Indians.

Ostensibly critical of both these positions, although reserving the burden of its critique for the former and ultimately aligning itself with the latter, was a third stance (Nandy, 1987, 1988a, 1988b). Ashis Nandy, a trenchant critic of the philosophies of modernization and development, castigated liberal condemnation of *sati* as the response of a rootless, decultured urban bourgeoisie, unable, if not unwilling, to comprehend the masses. We may agree with Nandy that the incomprehension of *sati* expressed by the liberal media required examination and critique: after all, *sati* is only one among many practices exploitative of women. In a sense, contemporary liberal incomprehension parallels nineteenth-century colonial horror. Both cast *sati* simultaneously as an exceptional practice *and* one that is emblematic of society as a whole. The sense of its exceptionalism emerges in analyses of *sati* which treat it in isolation from women's subordination in general, while its emblematic status is dramatized in the way in which the incident has provoked anxiety about the nature and extent of India's social progress.

This, however, is not the direction in which Nandy develops his argument. Nandy's ire is directed mainly at what he perceives as the 'Western' modes of denouncing *sati* reproduced by 'modernists'. Nandy's stand on *sati* has drawn sharp criticism from feminists (Qadeer and Hasan, 1987; Patel and Kumar, 1988, Sangari, 1988; Philipose and Setalvad, 1988) whom he scorns as modernist, overlooking thereby important distinctions between feminist and liberal critiques of the practice (Nandy, 1988b). What is even more curious, however, is that Nandy's critique of the colonial mentality of these modernists itself reproduces three key moves of colonial discourse. He reaffirms the 'tradition'/'modernity' dichotomy in analysing the practice, and replicates the colonial oppositions, 'glorious past/degraded present' and 'authentic/inauthentic *sati*'. The latter two are brought together in his positive evaluation of the original, mythological *sati*, said to express women's sacred and magical powers, as against his negative description of contemporary widow burning which, he claims, is merely the product of a dehumanized market morality.

The fourth, and to my mind, genuinely anti-imperialist position (even though, unlike Nandy's it was not articulated as such) was that taken by feminists. Not surprisingly, concern for women's lives was very much at the centre of feminist discourse. Feminists insisted that Roop Kanwar's death should be understood in the context of the general subordination of women in Indian society, challenged attempts to frame the issue as one of tradition or religion and located the Deorala incident within post-independent political and economic developments in Rajasthan (Kishwar and Vanita, 1987; Bhasin and Menon, 1988; Vaid, 1988, among others). Feminists also pointed to the modernity of the incident and to the character of the pro-*sati* lobby, whose members were urban, educated men in their twenties and thirties. For example, Madhu Kishwar and Ruth Vanita argued that Deorala was not a rural backwater, but rather a prosperous town with electricity, tap water and a 70 per cent literacy rate (Kishwar and Vanita, 1987). Further, they pointed out that Roop Kanwar was a city-educated woman while her husband had a degree in science and her father-in-law, one of the abettors, was employed as a school teacher. In addition to the insufficiency of derisively analysing *sati* as 'traditional', feminists argued that such a ploy would play into the hands of pro-*sati* 'traditionalists'. Religious arguments were similarly exposed as serving to legitimate the oppression of women. Again, Kishwar and Vanita described how the daily rituals around the spot where the burning had taken place resembled victory celebrations, not religious devotion. In arguing that cries of 'religion' could not absolve anyone of murder, Indira Jaising put it thus: 'just as the personal is political, the religious is secular where women are concerned' (Jaising, 1987).

But all feminists warned against the danger of demanding more stringent laws and greater state intervention, the recurring pleas of liberal opponents of *sati*. They highlighted the appalling lack of will demonstrated by the state in prosecuting Roop's in-laws, and the possibility that the state would merely abuse the greater powers that would accrue to it. These fears have largely been realized. Local police have used their powers to harass journalists and others investigating the case and, despite the law against abetting and glorifying *sati*, an estimated 8,000 people gathered at Deorala in September 1988 to 'celebrate' the one year anniversary of the burning of Roop Kanwar (Pachauri, 1988). And perhaps worst of all, one of the provisions of the legislative act on *sati* makes its victims liable to punishment: women who attempt *sati* are hereafter to be subject to fine or imprisonment!

The events that have followed Roop Kanwar's burning have radically changed the Indian context for my work. Widow burning is no longer, as it had been when I began, a 'historical' problem, but very much a charged and explosive contemporary issue. Although my own discussion here has focused most on feminist arguments, they are, alas, marginal to the current debate. The discursive space is principally being defined by conservatives and liberals. The former are more active in mobilizing a constituency and have had the support of political parties more wedded to securing votes than to fundamental rights of any kind. This context has made it imperative to contextualize and frame in particular ways some of the arguments I develop in my thesis.

How, for instance, might my critique of the civilizing mission be appropriated in the current situation? Part of my argument has been to show, in some detail, what is occluded in the following statement which represents a dominant story about colonialism and the question of woman: 'we came, we saw, we were horrified, we intervened'. Taking the instance of *sati*, whose abolition by the British in 1829 supposedly illuminates, *par excellence*, the legitimacy of this account, I have tried to suggest that the story is much more complicated. Among other things, I point out that legislative prohibition of *sati* was preceded by its legalization, a procedure that involved British officials in determining and enforcing a colonial version of the practice deemed traditional and authentic; that intervention in *sati* provided grounds for intervention in civil society; and that a fundamental ambivalence to *sati* structured colonial attitudes to the practice (Mani, 1987). I argue that missionary involvement in *sati* was similarly complex and ambivalent, with horror being reserved primarily for fundraising material produced for a British public. My point is that ultimately, for both officials and missionaries, women were not really at issue. Women rather provided ground for the development of other agendas.

I make a related argument about nineteenth-century indigenous discourses on *sati*. I argue that these developed within the constraints of a discourse on Indian society privileged by the British, that ambivalence to the practice is discernible even among those passionately opposed to *sati*, and that here too, concern for women seems secondary to concern for 'tradition' or for the general good of society. Women thus appear as obstacles to societal reform, and as individuals who must be trained to take up the duties of modern life with its own requirements of good wife and mother. My argument, then, has called into question the overly positive evaluation of the civilizing impulses of colonialism and the modernizing desires of proto-nationalism and nationalism: not because women did not gain from them, but because neither seemed to me to be selfless and benign in their espousal of women's rights, nor even centrally concerned with them.

How will such a critique of colonialist and nationalist arguments against *sati* resonate in India today? Is there any danger that my critique of the *terms* of these arguments will be read reductively as support for *sati*? Authorial intention, it is generally conceded, guarantees nothing. Considerable care will be necessary in framing my discussion in such a way that only a deliberate misreading can appropriate my arguments to reactionary ends. In addition, perhaps in my discussion of the nineteenth-century debate on *sati* I should also explicitly engage the contemporary moment so as to clarify how once again, with the signal exception of feminists and some progressives, arguments about women's rights have provided the basis for a further entrenchment of patriarchy in the name of 'tradition' (a point made by many Indian feminists) and for the arrogation of greater powers to the state in the name of 'modernity'.

I was lucky to be in India in the aftermath of Deorala. Lucky, because, in and of themselves, newspaper clippings and magazine articles could not have conveyed to me the political temperature there. Grasping the situation required the cumulative experience of countless conversations with friends, family members and neighbours, chance encounters on buses and trains, reports from feminists and civil libertarians who had travelled to Deorala, public meetings, and accounts of group discussions held in schools, colleges, political and community organizations. Much of this would obviously have been unavailable in print. My combined impressions strongly suggest that great care will have to be exercised in making arguments such as a critique of the Western civilizing mission.

The possible implications of other issues, such as exploration of the question of women's agency, appear to be even more treacherous. The problem of women's agency occupies a paradoxical position in feminist thinking in that, despite being a central concern, it remains poorly theorized. This is equally true of post-structuralist theory which, while being critical of the bourgeois conception of agency as the free will of an autonomous self, has yet to produce an adequate alternative formulation.

The widow's will has been a recurring theme in both the nineteenth- and twentieth-century debates on *sati*. Here, discussion of agency is framed around the limited and analytically unhelpful binary terms, coercion and consent. Those defending *sati* have, then as now, made claims about the 'voluntary' nature of the act. Against this, opponents of *sati* have emphasized coercion, and questioned the meaning of consent. In the earlier debate, consent was sometimes conceived as impossible by definition: women were simply deemed incapable of it. At other times, the issue was formulated more broadly in terms of women's social position and of the meagre alternatives available to them. For instance, it was pointed out that one could hardly speak of consent when widowhood imposed its own regimes of misery. By and large, those against *sati* today have developed this latter argument, feminists far more consistently than liberals. In the colonial situation, this dualistic conception of agency led to legislation requiring women to be cross-examined at the pyre and being permitted to burn if their action was declared to be voluntary. A static conception of agency intersected with the assumption of religious hegemony to marginalize the ways in which women actively negotiated and struggled against the social and familial constraints upon them. Nowhere is this more evident than in colonial eyewitness accounts of *sati*, which consistently effaced signs of women's agency in struggle, resistance and coercion (Mani, 1989).

I have long felt anxious about how a broader consideration of women's agency is foreclosed by its reductive translation into an issue of whether or not the widow went willingly. Limiting discussion of women's agency in this way makes it difficult to engage simultaneously women's systematic subordination *and* the ways in which they negotiate oppressive, even determining, social conditions. (Ong, 1987 and Gordon, 1989 develop such complex analyses of women's agency.) I know that part of my own concern with these questions comes from a sense of the extent to which Third World peoples are consistently represented in Eurocentric discourses as lacking agency. I also know that it comes from a conviction that structures of domination are best understood if we can grasp how we remain agents even in the moments in which we are being intimately, viciously oppressed.

The discourse of woman as victim has been invaluable to feminism in pointing to the systematic character of gender domination. But if it is not employed with care, or in conjunction with a dynamic conception of agency, it leaves us with reductive representations of women as primarily beings who are passive and acted upon. In other words we are left with that common figure of Eurocentric feminist discourse: the Third World woman as 'always, already victim' (Mohanty, 1984). What is forsaken here is the notion of women's oppression as a multifaceted and contradictory social process. It is crucial to stress in this regard, however, that when Indian feminists speak of woman as victim it is in a complex material sense. It is also important to note that in emphasizing women's systematic subordination rather than debating questions of agency, Indian feminists are specifically attempting to counter right-wing discourse that falsely proposes women's total freedom.[5]

Questions of agency provoke issues at the heart of feminism. But in raising them in the current Indian context, one walks a tightrope. Firstly, given the dominant discourse on *sati*, to claim that women are agents even in their coercion is to court the possibility of misappropriation by the right wing. Secondly, current legislation on *sati*, by making women attempting *sati* liable to punishment, implicitly conceives of them as 'free agents'. The law states that any such punishment must take account of the circumstances in which the woman's decision was taken. But given that legal and political institutions routinely punish victims instead of perpetrators, why should we trust that this proviso will not work against women? In the short term, then, it seems safest to counter the notion of woman as free agent by emphasizing her victimization. However, unless we include in this a complex sense of agency, we run the risk of producing a discourse which sets women up to be saved. This would situate women within feminist analysis in ways that are similar to their positioning within colonialist or nationalist discourse.

The example of women's agency is a particularly good instance of the dilemmas confronted in simultaneously attempting to speak within different historical moments and to discrepant audiences. What might be a valuable pushing of the limits of current rethinking of agency in Anglo-American feminism, may, if not done with extreme care, be an unhelpful, if not disastrous move in the Indian context. If criticism is to be 'worldly' (Said, 1983, pp. 1–30) or 'situated' (Haraway, 1988), or engaged, it must take account of the worlds in which it speaks. Perhaps to Bruce Robbins' suggestion that theory is a 'when' not a 'what' (Robbins, 1987/8, p. 5), we should also add the notion of a 'where'.

Acknowledgements

Kum-Kum Bhavnani, Vivek Dhareshwar, Ruth Frankenberg, Mary John and Kamala Visweswaran have left the imprint of their critical readings on the final version of this paper. I am also indebted to Indian feminists and progressives whose political insight and imaginative interventions in the contemporary debate on widow burning have been inspiring and instructive. An earlier version of this paper appeared in *Inscriptions*, No. 5, University of California, Santa Cruz, 1989.

Notes

1   The relative rapidity with which the concept of 'culture studies' has found institutional support in the US academy compared to ethnic or women's studies should give us pause. bell hooks (Gloria Watkins) (1989) and Gayatri C. Spivak (1989) have recently mapped out what is at stake intellectually and politically in the kinds of theoretical and curricular agendas being privileged and excluded in the institutionalization of 'Third World' or 'culture studies'.

2   As a whole, however, as Norma Alarcon (1991), Aida Hurtado (1989) and Chela Sandoval (forthcoming) have recently argued, the critique of US white feminism has been taken up very unevenly and has failed fundamentally to transform dominant feminist thinking.

3   Edward Said (1986) raises the problem of discrepant experiences and constituencies but develops instead a case for foregrounding the *shared* intellectual and political terrain produced by colonialism. See also Said (1983, pp. 226–47).

4   There may be many reasons for a critique of Said's *Orientalism*, some more persuasive than others (Mani and Frankenberg, 1985). There is firstly the theoretical resistance of those working within an objectivist paradigm to his social constructionist approach. Then there is the question of the scope of his argument. Many Indian readers, for example, felt that the book's value for them was seriously limited by its primary focus on the West and its lack of analysis of internal class and power relations in colonized territories. My point here, then, is not that there are no grounds to criticize *Orientalism*: rather that, in India, the political and ideological impetus of Said's project has generally not been apprehended as compelling, a response tied to both geographical location and historical experience.

5   Rajeswari Sunder Rajan is approaching the problem of the widow's subjectivity in *sati* from a different perspective. She argues that the 'methodological impasse' generated by the 'coercion-consent' framework can be avoided if the question of the widow's subjectivity is engaged via an exploration of 'both the phenomenonology of pain and a politics that recognizes pain as constitutive of the subject' (forthcoming).

Article 7.3
IDENTITY: SKIN BLOOD HEART

Minnie Bruce Pratt

I live in a part of Washington, DC, that white suburbanites called 'the jungle' during the uprising of the '60s – perhaps still do, for all I know. When I walk the two-and-a-half blocks to H St NE, to stop in at the bank, to leave my boots off at the shoe-repair-and-lock shop, I am most usually the only white person in sight. I've seen two other whites, women, in the year I've lived here. (This does not count white folks in cars, passing through. In official language, H St NE, is known as 'The H Street Corridor', as in something to be passed through quickly, going from your place, on the way to elsewhere.)

When I walk three blocks in a slightly different direction down Maryland Avenue, to go to my lover's house, I pass the yards of Black folks: the yard of the lady who keeps children, with its blue-and-red windmill, its roses-of-sharon; the yard of the man who delivers vegetables with its stacked slatted crates; the yard of the people next to the Righteous Branch Commandment Church-of-God (Seventh Day) with its tomatoes in the summer, its collards in the fall. In the summer, folks sit out on their porches or steps or sidewalks; when I walk by, if I lift my head and look toward them and speak, 'Hey,' they may speak, say, 'Hey' or 'How you doing?' or perhaps just nod. In the spring, I was afraid to smile when I spoke, because that might be too familiar, but by the end of summer I had walked back and forth so often, I was familiar, so sometimes we shared comments about the mean weather.

I am comforted by any of these speakings for, to tell you the truth, they make me feel at home. I am living far from where I was born; it has been twenty years since I have lived in that place where folks, Black and white, spoke to each other when they met on the street or in the road. So when two Black men dispute country matters, calling across the corners of 8th St – 'Hey, Roland, did you ever see a hog catch a rat?' – 'I seen a hog catch a *snake*' – 'How about a rat? Ever see one catch a *rat*?' – I am grateful to be living within sound of their voices, to hear a joking that reminds me, with a startled pain, of my father, putting on his tales for his friends, the white men gathered at the drug-store.

The pain, of course, is the other side of this speaking, and the sorrow: when I have only to turn two corners to go back in the basement door of my building, to meet Mr Boone, the janitor, who doesn't raise his eyes to mine, or his head, when we speak. He is a dark red-brown man from the Yemassee in South Carolina – that swampy land of Indian resistance and armed communities of fugitive slaves, that marshy land at the headwaters of the Combahee, once site of enormous rice plantations and location of Harriet Tubman's successful military action that freed many slaves. When we meet in the hall or on the elevator, even though I may have just heard him speaking in his own voice to another man, he 'yes ma'am's' me in a sing-song: I hear my voice replying in the horrid cheerful accents of a white lady: and I hate my white womanhood that drags between us the long bitter history of our region.

I think how I just want to feel at home, where people know me; instead I remember, when I meet Mr Boone, that home was a place of forced subservience, and I know that my wish is that of an adult wanting to stay a child: to be known by others, but to know nothing, to feel no responsibility.

Instead, when I walk out in my neighbourhood, each speaking-to another person has become fraught, for me, with the history of race and sex and class; as I walk I have a constant interior discussion with myself, questioning how I acknowledge the presence of another, what I know or don't know about them, and what it means how they acknowledge me. It is an exhausting process, this moving from the experience of the 'unknowing majority' (as Maya Angelou called it) into consciousness. It would be a lie to say this process is comforting.

[. . .]

Where does the need come from, the inner push to walk into change, if by skin colour, ethnicity, birth culture, we are women who are in a position of material advantage, where we gain at the expense of others, of other women? A place where *we* can have a degree of safety, comfort, familiarity, just by staying put. Where is our *need* to change what we were born into? What do we have to gain?

When I try to think of this, I think of my father: of how, when I was about eight years old, he took me up the front marble steps of the courthouse in my town. He took me inside, up the worn wooden steps, stooped under the feet of folks who had gone up and down to be judged, or to gawk at others being judged, up past the courtroom where my grandfather had leaned back in his chair and judged for over forty years, up to the attic, to some narrow steps that went to the roof, to the clock tower with a walled ledge.

What I would have seen at the top: on the streets around the courthouse square, the Methodist church, the limestone building with the county Health Department, Board of Education, Welfare Department (my mother worked there), the yellow brick Baptist church, the Gulf station, the pool hall (no women allowed), Cleveland's grocery, Ward's shoestore: then all in a line, connected, the bank, the post office, Dr Nicholson's office, one door for whites, one for Blacks: then separate, the Presbyterian church, the newspaper office, the yellow brick jail, same brick as the Baptist church, and as the courthouse.

What I could not have seen from the top: the sawmill, or Four Points where the white mill folks lived, or the houses of Blacks in Veneer Mill quarters.

This is what I would and would not have seen, or so I think: for I never got to the top. When he told me to go up the steps in front of him, I tried to, crawling on hands and knees, but I was terribly afraid. I couldn't, or wouldn't, do it. He let me crawl down: he was disgusted with me, I thought. I think now that he wanted to show me a place he had climbed to as a boy, a view that had been his father's and his, and would be mine. But I was *not* him: I had not learned to take that height, that being set apart as my own: a white girl, not a boy.

Yet I was shaped by my relation to those buildings and to the people in the buildings, by ideas of who should be working in the Board of Education, of who should be in the bank handling money, of who should have the guns and the keys to the jail, of who should be *in* the jail; and I was shaped by what I didn't see, or didn't notice, on those streets.

Not the way your town was laid out, you say? True, perhaps, but each of us carries around those growing-up places, the institutions, a sort of back-drop, a stage-set. So often we act out the present against a back-drop of the past, within a frame of perception that is so familiar, so safe that it is terrifying to risk changing it even when we know our perceptions are distorted, limited, constricted by that old view.

So this is one gain for me as I change: I learn a way of looking at the world that is more accurate, complex, multi-layered, multi-dimensioned, more truthful: to see the world of overlapping circles, like movement on the millpond after a fish has jumped, instead of the courthouse square with me at the middle, even if I *am* on the ground. I feel the *need* to look differently because I've learned that what is presented to me as an accurate view of the world is frequently a lie: so that to look through an anthology of women's studies that has little or no work by women of colour is to be up on that ledge about the town and be thinking that I see the town, without realizing how many lives have been pushed out of sight, beside unpaved roads. I'm learning that what I think that I *know* is an accurate view of the world is frequently a lie: as when I was in a discussion about the Women's Pentagon Action with several women, four of us Christian-raised, one Jewish. In describing the march through Arlington Cemetery, one of the four mentioned the rows of crosses. I had marched for a long time through that cemetery; I nodded to myself, visualized rows of crosses. No, said the Jewish woman, they were headstones with crosses or stars-of-David engraved above the names. We four objected; we all had seen crosses. The Jewish woman had some photographs of the march through the cemetery, laid them on the table. We saw rows and rows and rows of rectangular gravestones, and in the foreground, clearly visible, one inscribed with a name and a star-of-David.

So I gain truth when I expand my constricted eye, an eye that has only let in what I have been taught to see. But there have been other constrictions: the clutch of fear around my heart when I must deal with the *fact* of folks who exist, with their own lives, in other places besides the narrow circle I was raised in. I have learned that my fear is kin to a terror that has been in my birth culture for years, for centuries: the terror of a people who have set themselves apart and *above*, who have wronged others, and feel they are about to be found out and punished. It is the terror that in my culture has been expressed in lies about dirty Jews who kill for blood, sly Arab hordes who murder, brutal Indians who massacre, animal Blacks who rise in rebellion in the middle of the night and slaughter. It is the terror that has *caused* the slaughter of all those peoples. It is the terror that was my father, with his stack of John Birch newspapers, his belief in a Communist-Jewish-Black conspiracy. It is the desperate terror, the knowledge that something is *wrong*, and tries to end fear by attack.

When I am trying to understand myself in relation to folks different from me, when there are discussions, conflicts about anti-Semitism and racism among women, criticisms, criticism of me, and I get afraid: when, for instance, in a group discussion about race and class, I say I feel we have talked too much about race, not enough about class, and a woman of colour asks me in anger and pain if I don't think her skin has something to do with class, and I get afraid; when, for instance, I say carelessly to my Jewish lover that there were no Jews where I grew up, and she begins to ask me: how do I know? do I hear what I'm saying? and I get afraid; when I feel my racing heart, breath, the tightening of my skin around me, literally defences to protect my narrow circle, I try to say to myself:

Yes, that fear is there, but I will try to be at the edge between my fear and outside, on the edge at my skin, listening, asking what new thing will I hear, will I see, will I let myself feel, beyond the fear. I try to say to myself: To acknowledge the complexity of another's existence is not to deny my own. I try to say: When I acknowledge what my people, what those who are like me, have done to people with less power and less safety in the world, I can make a place for things to be different, a place where I can feel grief, sorrow, not to be sorry *for* the others, but to mourn, to expand my circle of self, follow my need to loosen the constrictions of fear, be a break in the cycle of fear and attack. When I can do this, that is a second gain.

To be caught within the narrow circle of the self is not just a fearful thing, it is a *lonely* thing. When I could not climb the steps that day with my father, it marked the last time I can remember us doing something together, just the two of us; thereafter, I knew on some level that my place was with women, not with him, not with men; later I knew more clearly that I did not want his view of the world. I have felt this more and more strongly since my coming out as a lesbian. Yet so much has separated me from other women, ways in which my culture set me apart by race, by ethnicity, by class. I understood abruptly one day how lonely this made me when a friend, a Black woman, spoke to me casually in our shared office: and I heard how she said my name, the drawn-out accent: so much like how my name is said at home.

Yet I knew enough of her history and mine to know how much separated us: the chasm of murders, rapes, lynchings, the years of daily humiliations done by my people to hers. I went and stood in the hallway and cried, thinking of how she said my name like home, and how divided our lives were. It is a pain I come to over and over again, the more I understand the ways in which I have been kept from other women, and how I keep myself from them. The pain, when, for instance, I realize how *habitually* I think of my culture, my ethics, my morality, as the culmination of history, as the logical extension of what has gone before; the kind of thinking represented by my use, in the past, of the word *Judeo-Christian*, as if Jewish history and lives have existed only to culminate in Christian culture, the kind of thinking that the US government is using now to promote Armageddon in the Middle East; the kind of thinking that I did until recently about Indian lives and culture in my region, as if Indian peoples have existed only in museums since white folks came to this continent in the 1500s; the kind of thinking that separates me from women in cultures different from mine, makes their experience less central, less important than mine. It is painful to keep understanding this separation within myself and in the world. Sometimes this pain feels only like despair: yet I have felt it also to be another kind of pain, where the need to be with other women can be the breaking through the shell around me, painful, but a coming through into a new place, where with understanding and change, the loneliness won't be necessary. And when this happens, then I feel a third gain.

[. . .]

I was not at all accustomed to thinking of myself as belonging to an *oppressed* group. The last time I had conceptualized myself as belonging to a specific class of people was when I was a teenager. At the height of Black civil rights demonstrations in Alabama, and of the brutality of white police and citizens, I received a request from a German penpal for my views on what was going on: and wrote what my mother remembers as an eloquent justification of white superiority and supremacy. Though I'd read *The Diary of Anne Frank* I did not reflect on what repetition of history, what cries of Nazi/Aryan superiority and Jewish inferiority were in my words. Sliding aside the polite lie that 'Here we just treat everyone as individuals', I justified how we were treating folks: us the superior class, me in the group *white*.

By the time I was mid-way through college, I had slipped into being unselfconscious of myself as white; this happened as I became liberal. This meant that I looked on with my Philosophy class as a few students demonstrated while Gov. Lurleen Wallace, in a jeep, reviewed the ROTC troops, the students getting trained to defend Alabama from 'outsiders': all the white boys saluted under the white dogwoods flowering on the quad, while we debated the usefulness of protest. A year later, the night of Dr King's death, I drove with my husband and a friend into Birmingham, curfewed after a day of violence, drove in to look around the empty downtown streets in the spring rain, looking for I don't know what, and not finding it, went to the Tutwiler for drinks, not thinking of ourselves as white, of course, nor in any way out of place on the streets that night, because we were intellectuals, not at all like James Earl Ray or any white person who did violence.

I slipped from thinking of myself as white, to thinking of myself as *married*, without much regard for other categories in the meantime, except for a few startling moments. I felt *gentile* (though I didn't know the word) when the Jewish man I was dating called it off because I was 'too much like a girl he might marry'. I was baffled by this: I thought of Jewishness as a state of being defined by Christianity, a category changeable by conversion or association with Christians: I couldn't understand why this was something he didn't seem to want to do.

Going through the negotiations to marry a Catholic-raised man, I had some longer moments of feeling *Protestant*: as debates went on between my husband-to-be and the priest who was counselling us under the new guidelines of Vatican II, I puzzled over the need for an intricate resolution between *them* about what kind of birth control I would, or would not, use.

After the wedding, I was relieved to be myself: a non-religious, thinking person. I tried not to think of myself as *woman*, a reality that bulged outside the safe bounds of *wife*, a reality that had shaken and terrified me with my two unplanned pregnancies. Walking to my classes at graduate school, I put the width of the sidewalk between me and the woman sitting at the literature table in front of the library. The pamphlets and the 2c newsletters –

Research Triangle Women's Liberation Newsletter, August 11, 1969 – were loose on the cardboard table and were not *in* the library. At the other edge of the sidewalk, I tried to separate myself from the new ideas about what it meant to be a woman. I rushed away slowly through the humid air, weighted by my unborn second child, who sat like a four-month-old rock in my stomach.

During the last months of my pregnancy, I shared a class with Elizabeth, the woman from the lit table. The class was 'Shakespeare's History Plays'. Elizabeth analysed men and power, fathers and sons in *Henry IV*; the other students thought she was crazy; I was afraid she was. One evening, as I carried my enormous heavy belly from the seminar table to my car, she told me that she thought I was brave to stay in school, unlike so many other married women with children, and she wished me well. The men in my department had begun to joke that they would get stuck with me in the elevator, and I'd go into labour. That evening I cried the ten miles home: she had spoken to me as *a woman*, and I'd been so lonely, without knowing it: her speaking to me changed how I thought of myself and my life.

[. . .]

The place that I missed sometimes seemed like a memory of childhood, though it was not a childish place. It was a place of mutuality, companionship, creativity, sensuousness, easiness in the body, curiosity in what new things might be making in the world, hope from that curiosity, safety, and love.

It was like a memory of July: the slash of morning sun on my face as I walked with my cousin Annie down to the gravelpit, through the maze of small canyons with clay walls: the place where I put my face against the clay, the sweat of cool water in the heat, the flesh of the earth. We would stay all day there, get cleanly dirty, dig clay, shape pots, retreat to the cool, then out in the heat again in a place we knew was ancient because of the fossil rocks we found, ancient and serenely a home.

It was a place I had been to with my father, who took me to the woods, not to hunt (for he was not a hunter) but to walk, he with a double-bladed axe that he raised to trim dead branches, with his silence except to name the trees (black-jack oak, sweet bay) and to say how to step (high over logs where copperheads liked to rest cool): his silence that may have been his prayer to the trees that he counted on weekdays at the sawmill as dead board feet (but he is dead now, and I will never know what went on in his mind: his silence that taught me to listen to the life rushing through the veins of the animal world).

It was a place I had been in recently, just before my move to the market town, when with a few other women I had begun the talking about the forbidden that was called consciousness-raising:

making a place where I had said the word *masturbation* outloud for the first time. In the startled silence of the other women, I felt that I had abruptly created a new world out of the stuffy plastic apartment where we were meeting.

In the market town I began to try, steadily, to make a place like the memory, yet that would last longer than a morning or an evening: it was to be a place where I could live without the painful and deadly violence, without the domination: a place where I could live free, *liberated*, with other women. I began doing some political work, organized another consciousness-raising group. Then I fell in love with another woman, after she told a secret to the group. I thought I had come again to the place of intense curiosity, powerful creativity. It was March, it was April, wisteria, dogwood, pink tulip magnolia. I began to dream my husband was trying to kill me, that I was running away with my children on Greyhound buses through Mississippi. I began to dream that I was crossing a river with my children; women on the other side, but no welcome for me with my boys.

The place I wanted to reach was not a childish place, but my understanding of it was childish. I had not admitted that the safety of much of my childhood was because Laura Cates, Black and a servant, was responsible for me; that I had the walks with my father because the woods were 'ours' by systematic economic exploitation, instigated, at that time, by his White Citizens' Council; that I was allowed one evening a month with woman friends because I was a wife who would come home at night. Raised to believe that I could be where I wanted and have what I wanted, as a grown woman I thought I could simply claim what I wanted, even the making of a new place to live with other women. I had no understanding of the limits that I lived within, nor of how much my memory and my experience of a safe space to be was based on places secured by omission, exclusion or violence, and on my submitting to the limits of that place.

I should have remembered, from my childhood, Viola Liuzzo, who was trying to reach the place by another way, shot down in Lowndes County, Alabama, while driving demonstrators during the Selma-to-Montgomery march. Her death was justified by Klan leader Robert Shelton on the grounds that she 'had five children by four different husbands', 'her husband hadn't seen her in two, three months', 'she was living with two nigger men in Selma', 'she was a *fat* slob with crud . . . all over her body', 'she was bra-less'. Liuzzo, Italian, white-but-not-white, gone over to the other side, damned, dead.

[. . .]

If I have come to the point of consciousness where I have begun to understand that I am entrapped *as* a woman, not just by the sexual fear of the men of my group, but also by their racial and religious terrors; if I have begun to understand that when they condemn me as a lesbian and a free woman for being 'dirty', 'unholy', 'perverted', 'immoral', it is a judgement that has been called down on people of colour and Jews throughout history by the men of my culture, as they have shifted their justification for hatred according to their desires of the moment; if I have begun to understand something of the deep connection between my oppression and that of other folks, what is it that keeps me from acting, sometimes even from speaking out, against anti-Semitism and racism? What is it that keeps me from declaring against and rejecting this 'protection' at every level?

The image from my childhood, from Poe's story, returns to me: the woman who escapes with superhuman effort, from a coffin whose lid is fastened down by screws, from a vault with iron doors of immense weight: she may free herself, but then she dies violently, carrying with her the home and her kin: catastrophe. Melodramatic: yet twenty years after I first read the story, when I began to admit to myself how I had been buried by my culture, coffined heart and body, and how this was connected to my sex, my race, my class, my religion, my 'morality'; when I began to push through all this, I felt like my life was cracking around me.

I think this is what happens, to a more or less extreme degree, every time we expand our limited being: it is upheaval, not catastrophe: more like a snake shedding its skin than like death: the old constriction is sloughed off with difficulty, but there is an expansion: not a change in basic shape or colour, but an expansion, some growth, and some reward for struggle and curiosity. Yet, if we are women who have gained privilege by our white skin *or* our Christian culture, but who are trying to free ourselves *as* women in a more complex way, we can experience this change as loss. Because it is: the old lies and ways of living, habitual, familiar, comfortable, fitting us like our skin, were *ours*.

Our fear of the losses can keep us from changing. What is it, exactly, that we are afraid to lose?

As I try to strip away the layers of deceit that I have been taught, it is hard not to be afraid that these are like wrappings of a shroud and that what I will ultimately come to in myself is a disintegrating, rotting *nothing*: that the values that I have at my core, from my culture, will only be those of negativity, exclusion, fear, death. And my feeling *is* based in the reality that the group identity of my culture has been defined, often, not by positive qualities, but by negative characteristics: by the *absence of*: 'no dogs, Negroes, or Jews'; we have gotten our jobs, bought our houses, borne and educated our children by the negatives: no niggers, no kikes, no wops, no dagos, no spics, no A-rabs, no gooks, no queers.

331

We have learned this early, and so well. Every spring, almost, when I was in grammar school, our field trip would be an expedition to Moundville State Park, where part of our education was to file into a building erected over a 'prehistoric' Indian burial ground; and stand overlooking the excavated clay, dug out so that small canyons ran between each body, the bundles of people's bones, separating each from each, as if water had eroded, except it was the hands of a probably white, probably Christian archaeologist from the university, meticulously breaking into the sacred ground. Floodlights exposed people curled or stretched in the final vulnerability of death, while we stood in the safe darkness of the balconies, looking down.

It has taken a long time for me to understand that this place was sacred not because it had been set aside for death, but because it was a place where spiritual and physical life returned to life, bones and bodies as seeds in the fertile darkness of the earth. It took me so long because so much in my culture is based on the principle that we are *not* all connected to each other, that folk who seem different should be excluded, or killed, and their living culture treated as dead objects.

No wonder, then, that if we have been raised up this way, when we begin to struggle with the reality of our anti-Semitism and racism, we may simply want to leave our culture behind, disassociate ourselves from it. In order to feel positively about ourselves, we may end up wanting not to *be* ourselves, and may start pretending to be someone else. Especially this may happen when we start learning about the strong traditions of resistance and affirmation sustained for centuries by the very folks *our* folks were trying to kill.

Without a knowledge of this struggle for social justice in our own culture, we may end up clothing our naked, negative selves with something from the positive traditions of identity which have served in part to help folks survive our people. We may justify this 'cultural impersonation' by our admiration and our need for heroines, as did one woman at an evening of shared spirituality which I attended: a Euro-American woman, very fair-haired and fair-complexioned, renamed herself in a ritual during which she took three women's names, each from a different tribe of native American people; she explicitly stated that the names represented powers and gifts she desired, those of healing, leadership, love, qualities she felt she was lacking in. We may justify taking the identity of another as our own by stating a shared victimization, as I have heard from some Christian-raised women when they have mentioned that they have 'always felt like a Jew' because of how they have felt exclusion and pain in their lives: sometimes they have then used this feeling to assert that they were Jews and to justify a conversion to Judaism.

Sometimes the impersonation comes because we are afraid we'll be divided from someone we love if we are ourselves. This can take very subtle forms: as when I wrote a poem for my lover, whom I'd been dealing with about issues of Jewish-gentile differences; anxious, without admitting it to myself, about the separation that opened at times between us, I blurred our difference in the poem by using images and phrases from a Jewish women's spiritual tradition as if they were from my *own*, using them to imply that she and I were in the same affirming tradition.

Sometimes we don't pretend to *be* the other, but we take something made by the other and use it for our own: as I did for years when I listened to Black folk singing church songs, hymns, gospels and spirituals, the songs of suffering, enduring and triumph. Always I would cry, baffled as to why I was so moved; I understood myself only after I read a passage in Mary Boykin Chesnutt's diary in which she described weeping bitterly at a slave prayer meeting where the Black driver shouted 'like a trumpet': she said, 'I would very much have liked to shout too.' Then I understood that I was using Black people to weep for me, to express *my* sorrow at my responsibility, and that of my people, for their oppression: and I was mourning because I felt they had something I didn't, a closeness, a hope, that I and my folks had lost because we had tried to shut other people out of our hearts and lives.

Finally I understood that I could feel sorrow during their music, and yet not confuse their sorrow with mine, or use their resistance for mine. *I needed to do my own work*: express my sorrow and my responsibility myself, in my own words, by my own actions. I could hear their songs like a trumpet to me: a startling, an awakening, a reminder, a challenge: as were the struggles and resistance of other folk: but not take them as replacement for my own work.

8
THE AIMS AND ACHIEVEMENTS OF FEMINIST THEORY

In this book, we have critically examined a wide range of mainstream theories, generally neither accepting nor rejecting them in their entirety. For we had often first to reformulate them, sometimes almost beyond recognition, to remove their male-centredness. For example, despite being critical of Freud's own biologistic account of femininity, we saw how psychoanalytic theory could provide insights into the workings of the unconscious, which were important in understanding the cultural and symbolic significance of femininity. Similarly, although Foucault's own account is surprisingly blind to considerations of gender, his analysis of how discourse is imbued with power provided invaluable insights into the non-material constraints that can operate on women. Although we made use of these theories – or rather of some feminist appropriations of parts of them – we had in both cases first to uncover the original male bias. And in these two examples, the feminist critiques were different: in Freud's case, the criticism concerned not his lack of attention to women, but the way he fitted their psychosexual development around that of men; in Foucault's case, the critique was of the complete absence of any reference to gender when exploring an area – sexuality – in which gender would appear to be fundamental.

So we have examined both how to criticize theories and how to use them to illuminate women's experience. But we have not yet examined what our aim in all this should be – a question we raised in the Introduction to this book and to which we now return in its final chapter. Are we attempting to build some new overarching understanding of the gendered world in which we live, that is more objective and more encompassing than the theories we have been criticizing? Is our aim in removing male bias, however it slipped in, to replace it by a theory which is unbiased in its understanding both of gender and of the biasing effects gender has?

If so, how deep do we have to go to do this? Have the social scientists of patriarchy simply got their facts wrong, so that the theories they have developed misrepresent women's lives? If this is the case, as feminists we must do the empirical work better, collect the facts more thoroughly, so that we can develop better theories. Existing scientific methodology is not, then, the problem, it is just that the scientists were not following it properly, perhaps because they were blinkered by sexism. The advent of feminism gives us the chance to lift the blinkers to reveal to everyone the biases which ignored and distorted women's experiences, so that we all – men as well as women – will in future be able to do better scientific work.

But if scientists, just like everyone else, work in society and are subject to its values, perhaps it is not just a case of correcting the sexist biases of individual scientists; rather the whole scientific enterprise may be irremediably flawed. Are the social sciences, and perhaps the natural sciences too, so embued with sexism that they are impossible to reform? The argument that this is the case is a methodological one, that so-called 'scientific methodology' in its search for objectivity and rationality, necessarily excludes women and much that women's lives are centred around. In particular, the aim of making a separation between rationality and emotion in the pursuit of value-free knowledge, this argument claims, is a peculiarly masculine aim, neither desired by nor possible for women.

And if we come to this conclusion, what should be done about it? Should feminism be attempting to build a new 'successor' science, free of the problems of existing masculinist science? Such a successor science would be based on the deeper understanding that women have through their experience of oppression and the wide range of work that they do. It should therefore be able to produce a more objective and universal theory, of use to everyone.

Or is this a misguided aim? Should theory aspire to be objective and universal? Must any theory always reflect the standpoint from which it originated? In which case, the feminist aim should be to produce a woman-centred understanding of the world for ourselves alone, which can demonstrate the falseness of male-centred theories' claims to universality and objectivity, but must then refrain from making a similar claim for itself. And if we do this, we need not claim a single standpoint for all women, for the diversity of women's experience of oppression implies an equal diversity of standpoints, giving no one the right to claim to know *the* truth.

Feminists are not, of course, the first to raise these questions. For centuries, the questions of how we acquire knowledge and what claims it is legitimate to make for such knowledge have been the subject of debate, with all the above positions being taken, though not in these particular gendered forms. This long-running epistemological debate among philosophers has rarely impinged on the work of scientists or social theorists, who have tended, except at particular moments of crisis, to pursue the process of trying to understand their objects of study, without worrying too much about the status of the theory being produced.

And this was also true of feminist theory initially. However, as feminist criticism proliferated and reached deeper into the methodology as well as the content of mainstream theory, it seemed to matter more and more that the theories being criticized had, on the whole, been produced by men and that the alternatives were being developed by women. In other words, the historical circumstances in which feminist theory was being developed seemed to be impinging directly on the process of theorizing itself, not just on the subject matter of the theory. However, any epistemology – any theory of knowledge – which makes a total separation between the theorist and the theory, as distinct subject and object, would have to reject the significance of these observations. If feminism was to accept and explain the political nature of its own theories, that it did matter that they were produced by and for women, then feminism had to engage with epistemologies that make that separation.

Further, feminists' burgeoning interest in theories of the subject and subjectivity raised questions about the claims to knowledge of all theories. For the analysis of subjectivity demonstrated that how knowledge and its subjects are constituted is a social question, and a question in which the operation of power is central. This was one of the ideas that feminism took and modified from Foucault: that the creation of knowledge is imbued with power, the power to define 'reality' for others. This means that an alternative feminist knowledge also has to grapple with the issues of its own power and who it represents.

Post-modernist discourses, both feminist and non-feminist, have rejected all attempts to impose a conceptual structure on the world as exercises in power, arguing that it is only in so far as the perspective of one group dismisses that of all others that 'reality' can appear to have a unified structure; such theoretical structures are just attempts to police thought. Post-modernist feminists therefore argue that we should give up the attempt to exercise power in this way, and not claim that a feminist standpoint provides a superior methodology that will produce greater truth. But to those who argue for a feminist standpoint, this is to abdicate all responsibility for talking about the world as it now is; having developed the ability to criticize the male-centredness of mainstream theory, it is then nonsense *not* to claim that our own theories are superior. To do so is a political as well as a theoretical responsibility.

Sandra Harding, in the first of the two articles for this section, takes up these epistemological issues. She explores whether male-centredness is a characteristic only of 'bad science' or whether it applies to all 'science as usual'. Deciding that the criticisms which focus on 'bad science' actually undercut the basis on which 'science as usual' is supposed to operate, she then turns to the issue of whether feminism should be seeking to build a successor science or should share the post-modernist scepticism of that project. On this issue, she refuses to come down on one side or the other, insisting that even if we recognize that knowledge is inevitably bound up with power in the world today, we have to accept the political responsibilities of using knowledge to create a world in which thought no longer needs policing. That such dilemmas cannot be resolved in today's world means that, what she calls 'conceptual instabilities', uncertainties about the epistemological coherence of what we are engaged in, remain an inevitable, but productive, characteristic of feminist theorizing.

In the second article, Elizabeth Gross, writing from within a more clearly post-modernist framework, is concerned with the political history and potential of feminist theorizing. She sees the movement of feminist thought away from patriarchal epistemologies as a movement towards autonomy, parallel to the movement which rejected equality with men as the standard by which political progress should be measured. Feminist theory, she argues, must recognize its own perspective, that it is being written from a particular point of view with partisan aims, and must therefore be seen not as an attempt to produce new universal or objective truths, but as a political intervention.

Article 8.1
THE INSTABILITY OF THE ANALYTICAL CATEGORIES OF FEMINIST THEORY

Sandra Harding

Feminist theory began by trying to extend and reinterpret the categories of various theoretical discourses so that women's activities and social relations could become analytically visible within the traditions of intellectual discourse. If women's natures and activities are as fully social as are men's, then our theoretical discourses should reveal women's lives with just as much clarity and detail as we presume the traditional approaches reveal men's lives. We had thought that we could make the categories and concepts of the traditional approaches objective or Archimedean where they were not already.

As we all have come to understand, these attempts revealed that neither women's activities nor gender relations (both inter- and intra-gender relations) can be added to these theoretical discourses without distorting the discourses and our subject matters. The problem here is not a simple one, because liberal political theory and its empiricist epistemology, Marxism, critical theory, psychoanalysis, functionalism, structuralism, deconstructionism, hermeneutics and the other theoretical frameworks we have explored both do and do not apply to women and to gender relations. On the one hand, we have been able to use aspects or components of each of these discourses to illuminate our subject matters. We have stretched the intended domains of these theories, reinterpreted their central claims, or borrowed their concepts and categories to make visible women's lives and feminist views of gender relations. After our labours, these theories often do not much resemble what their non-feminist creators and users had in mind, to put the point mildly. (Think of the many creative uses to which feminists have put Marxist or psychoanalytic concepts and categories; of how subversive these revised theories are of fundamental tendencies in Marxism and Freudianism.) On the other hand, it has never been women's experiences that have provided the grounding for any of the theories from which we borrow. It is not women's experiences that have generated the problems these theories attempt to resolve, nor have women's experiences served as the test of the adequacy of these theories. When we begin inquiries with women's experiences instead of men's, we quickly encounter phenomena (such as emotional labour or the positive aspects of 'relational' personality structures) that were made invisible by the concepts and categories of these theories. The recognition of such phenomena undermines the legitimacy of the central analytical structures of these theories, leading us to wonder if we are not continuing to distort women's and men's lives by our extensions and reinterpretations. Moreover, the very fact that we borrow from these theories often has the unfortunate consequence of diverting our energies into endless disputes with the non-feminist defenders of these theories: we end up speaking not to other women but to patriarchs.

Furthermore, once we understand the destructively mythical character of the essential and universal 'man' which was the subject and paradigmatic object of non-feminist theories, so too do we begin to doubt the usefulness of analysis that has essential, universal woman as its subject or object – as its thinker or the object of its thought. We have come to understand that whatever we have found useful from the perspective of the social experience of Western, bourgeois, heterosexual, white women is especially suspect when we begin our analyses with the social experiences of any other women. The patriarchal theories we try to extend and reinterpret were created to explain not men's experience but only the experience of those men who are Western, bourgeois, white and heterosexual. Feminist theorists also come primarily from these categories – not through conspiracy but through the historically common pattern that it is people in these categories who have had the time and resources to theorize, and who – among women – can be heard at all. In trying to develop theories that provide the one, true (feminist) story of human expereince, feminism risks replicating in theory and public policy the tendency in the patriarchal theories to police thought by assuming that only the problems of *some* women are human problems and that solutions for them are the only reasonable ones. Feminism has played an important role in showing that there are not now and never have been any generic 'men' at all – only gendered men and women. Once essential and universal man dissolves, so does his hidden companion, woman. We have, instead, myriads of women living in elaborate historical complexes of class, race and culture.

I want to talk here about some challenges for theorizing itself at this moment in history and, in particular, for feminist theorizings. Each has to do with how to use our theories actively to transform ourselves and our social relations, while we and our theories – the agents and visions of reconstruction – are themselves under transformation. Consider, for instance, the way in which we focus on some particular inadequate sexist or earlier feminist analysis and show its shortcomings – often with brilliance and eloquence. In doing so, we speak from the assumptions of some other discourse feminism has adopted or invented. These assumptions always include the belief that we can, in principle, construct or arrive at the perspective from which nature and social life can be seen as they really are. After all, we argue that sexist (or earlier feminist) analyses are wrong, inadequate or distorting – not that they are equal in scientific or rational grouding to our criticisms.

However, we sometimes claim that theorizing itself is suspiciously patriarchal, for it assumes separations between the knower and the known, subject and object, and the possibility of some powerful transcendental, Archimedean standpoint from which nature and social life fall into what we think is their proper perspective. We fear replicating – to the detriment of women whose experiences have not yet been fully voiced within feminist theory – what we perceive as a patriarchal association between knowledge and power.[1] Our ability to detect androcentrism in traditional analyses has escalated from finding it in the content of knowledge claims to locating it in the forms and goals of traditional knowledge seeking. The voice making *this* proposal is itself super-Archimedean, speaking from some 'higher' plane, such that Archimedes' followers in contemporary intellectual life are heard as simply part of the inevitable flux and imperfectly understood flow of human history. (And this is true even when the voice marks its own historical particularity, its femininity.) When it is unreflective, this kind of post-modernism – a kind of absolute relativism – itself takes a definitive stand from yet further outside the political and intellectual needs that guide our day-to-day thinking and social practices. In reaction we wonder how we can not want to say *the way things really are* to 'our rulers' as well as to ourselves, in order to voice opposition to the silences and lies emanating from the patriarchal discourses and our own partially brainwashed consciousnesses. On the other hand, there is good reason to agree with a feminist post-modernist suspicion of the relationship between accepted definitions of 'reality' and socially legitimated power.

How then are we to construct adequate feminist theory, or even *theories* – whether post-modern or not? Where are we to find the analytical concepts and categories that are free of the patriarchal flaws? What are the analytical categories for the absent, the invisible, the silenced that do not simply replicate in mirror-image fashion the distorting and mystifying categories and projects of the dominant discourses? Again, there are two ways to look at this situation. On the one hand, we can use the liberal powers of reason and the will, shaped by the insights gained through engaging in continuing political struggles, to piece what we see before our eyes in contemporary social life and history into a clear and coherent conceptual form, borrowing from one androcentric discourse here, another one there, patching in between in innovative and often illuminating ways, and revising our theoretical frameworks week by week as we continue to detect yet further androcentrisms in the concepts and categories we are using. We can then worry about the instability of the analytical categories and the lack of a persisting framework from which we continue to build our accounts. (After all, there should be some progress toward a 'normal' discourse in our explanations if we are to create a coherent guide to understanding and action.) On the other hand, we can learn how to embrace the instability of the analytical categories; to find in the instability itself the desired theoretical reflection of certain aspects of the political reality in which we live and think; to use these instabilities as a resource for our thinking and practices. No 'normal science' for us.[2] I recommend we take the second course, an uncomfortable goal, for the following reason.

The social life that is our object of study and within which our analytical categories are formed and tested is in exuberant transformation. Reason, will power, reconsidering the material – even political struggle – will not slow these changes in ways over which our feminisms should rejoice. It would be a delusion for feminism to arrive at a master theory, at a 'normal science' paradigm with conceptual and methodological assumptions that we presume all feminists accept. Feminist analytical categories *should* be unstable – consistent and coherent theories in an unstable and incoherent world are obstacles to both our understanding and our social practices.

We need to learn how to see our theorizing projects as illuminating 'riffing' between and over the beats of patriarchal theories, rather than as rewriting the tunes of any particular one (Marxism, psychoanalysis, empiricism, hermeneutics, deconstructionism, to name a few) so that it perfectly expresses *what we think at the moment we want to say*. The problem is that we do not know and should not know just what we want to say about a number of conceptual choices with which we are presented – except that the choices themselves create no-win dilemmas for our feminisms.

In the field in which I have been working – feminist challenges to science and epistemology – this situation makes the present moment an exciting one in which to live and think, but a difficult one in which to conceptualize a definitive overview. That is, the arguments between those of us who are criticizing science and epistemology are unresolvable within the frameworks in which we have been posing them. We need to begin to see these disputes not as a process of naming issues to be resolved but instead as opportunities to come up with better problems than those with which we started. The destabilization of thought often has advanced understanding more effectively than restabilizations, and the feminist criticisms of science point to a particularly fruitful arena in which the categories of Western thought need destabilization. Though these criticisms began by raising what appeared to be politically contentious but theoretically innocuous questions about discrimination against women in the social structure of science, misuses of technology, and androcentric bias in the social sciences and biology, they have quickly escalated into ones that question the most fundamental assumptions of modern, Western thought. They therefore implicitly challenge the theoretical constructs within which the original questions were formulated and might be answered.

Feminisms are totalizing theories. Because women and gender relations are everywhere, the subject matters of feminist theories are not containable within any single disciplinary framework or any set of them. 'The scientific world-view' has also taken itself to be a totalizing theory – anything and everything worth understanding can be explained or interpreted within the assumptions of modern science. Of course there is another world – the world of emotions, feelings, political values, of the individual and collective unconscious, of social and historical particularity explored in novels, drama, poetry, music and art, and the world within which we all live most of our waking and dreaming hours under constant threat of its increasing reorganization by scientific rationality.[3] One of the projects of feminist theorists is to reveal the relationships between these two worlds – how each shapes and informs the other. In examining feminist criticisms of science, then, we must consider all that science does not, the reasons for these exclusions, how these shape science precisely through their absences – both acknowledged and unacknowledged.

Instead of fidelity to the assumption that coherent theory is a desirable end in itself and the only reliable guide to action, we can take as our standard fidelity to *parameters* of dissonance within and between assumptions of patriarchal discourses. This approach to theorizing captures what some take to be a distinctively women's emphasis on contextual thinking and decision-making and on the processes necessary for gaining understanding in a world not of our own making – that is, a world that does not encourage us to fantasize about how we could order reality into the forms we desire. It locates the ways in which a valuably 'alienated consciousness', 'bifurcated consciousness', 'oppositional consciousness' might function at the level of active theory-making – as well as at the level of scepticism and rebellion. We need to be able to cherish certain kinds of intellectual, political and psychic discomforts, to see as inappropriate and even self-defeating certain kinds of clear solutions to the problems we have been posing.

'BAD SCIENCE' OR 'SCIENCE AS USUAL'?

Are sexist assumptions in substantive scientific research the result of 'bad science' or simply 'science as usual'? The first alternative offers hopes of reforming the kind of science we have; the second appears to deny this possibility.

It is clear that feminist criticisms of the natural and social sciences have identified and described science badly practised – that is, science distorted by masculine bias in problematics, theories, concepts, methods of inquiry, observations and interpretations of results of research. There are facts of the matter, these critics claim, but androcentric science cannot locate them. By identifying and eliminating masculine bias through more rigorous adherence to scientific methods, we can get an objective, de-gendered (and in that sense, value-free) picture of nature and social life. Feminist inquiry represents not a substitution of one gender loyalty for the other – one subjectivism for another – but the transcendence of gender which thereby increases objectivity.

In this argument, we use empiricist epistemology because its ends are the same as ours: objective, value-neutral results of research. This feminist empiricism argues that sexism and androcentrism are social biases. Movements for social liberation 'make it possible for people to see the world in an enlarged perspective because they remove the covers and blinders that obscure knowledge and observation' (Millman and Kanter, 1975, p. *vii*). Thus the women's movement creates the opportunity for such an enlarged perspective – just as did the bourgeois revolution of the fifteenth to seventeenth centuries, the proletarian revolution of the nineteenth century, and the revolutions overthrowing European and US colonialism in recent decades. Furthermore, the women's movement creates more women scientists and more feminist scientists (men as well as women), who are more likely than non-feminist men to notice androcentric bias.

Feminist empiricism offers a powerful explanation – though a misleading one – for the greater empirical adequacy of so much of feminist research. It has the virtue of answering the question of how a political movement such as feminism could be contributing to the growth of objective scientific knowledge. In making this argument, however, we avert our eyes from the fact that this appeal to empiricism in fact subverts empiricism in three ways. (1) For empiricism, the social identity of the observer is supposed to be irrelevant to the quality of research results. Feminist empiricism argues that women (or feminists, men and women) as a group are more likely to produce unbiased, objective results of inquiry than are men (or non-feminists) as a group. (2) We claim that a key origin of androcentric bias lies in the selection of problems for inquiry and in the definition of what is problematic about them. Empiricism insists that its methodological norms are meant to apply only to the context of justification and not to the context of discovery where problematics are identified and defined. Hence we have shown the inadequacy, the impotence, of scientific methods to achieve their goals. (3) We often point out that it is exactly following the logical and sociological norms of inquiry which results in androcentric results of research – appealing to the already existing (Western, bourgeois, homophobic, white, sexist) scientific community for confirmation of the results of research; generalizing to all humans from observations only of males. Our empiricist criticisms of 'bad science' in fact subvert the very understandings of science they are meant to reinforce.

These problems suggest that the most fundamental categories of scientific thought are male biased. Many of the critics of 'bad science' also make this second criticism though it undercuts the assumptions of the first. Here they point to historians' descriptions of how sexual politics have shaped science, and science, in turn, has played a significant role in advancing sexual politics. Each has provided a moral and political resource for the other. Furthermore, they show that 'pure science' – inquiry immune from the technological and social needs of the larger culture – exists only in the unreflective mental life of some individual scientists and in the rhetoric of science apologists. That is, one does not have to impugn the motives of individual physicists, chemists or sociologists in order to make a convincing case that the scientific enterprise is structurally and symbolically part and parcel of the value systems of those cultures that maintain it. This argument poses difficulties for us, nonetheless, since if the very concepts of nature, of dispassionate, value-free, objective inquiry, and of transcendental knowledge are androcentric, white, bourgeois and Western, then no amount of more rigorous adherence to scientific method will eliminate such bias, for the methods themselves reproduce the perspectives generated by these hierarchies and thus distort our understandings.

While these new understandings of the history of science and sexuality expand our understanding immensely, they do not tell us whether a science apparently so inextricably intertwined with the history of sexual politics can be pried loose to serve more inclusive human ends – or whether it is strategically worthwhile to try to do so. Is history destiny? Would the complete elimination of androcentrisms from science leave no science at all? But isn't it important to try to degender science as much as we can in a world where scientific claims are *the* model of knowledge? How can we afford to choose between redeeming science or dismissing it altogether when neither choice is in our best interest?

SUCCESSOR SCIENCE OR POST-MODERNISM

The dilemma that arises in criticisms of 'bad science' and of 'science as usual' reappears at a metalevel in feminist theory's conflicting tendencies toward post-modernism and what I shall call the feminist successor science projects. Feminist empiricism explains (albeit subversively) the achievements of feminist inquiry – of that purported contradiction in terms: a politicized scientific inquiry – by appeal to the familiar empiricist assumptions. In contrast, the feminist standpoint epistemologies articulate an understanding of scientific knowledge seeking that replaces, as successor to, the Enlightenment vision captured by empiricism. Both the standpoint and post-modern tendencies within feminist theory place feminism in an uneasy and ambivalent relationship to patriarchal discourses and projects (just as did feminist empiricism). There are good reasons to think of both as imperfect and converging tendencies toward a post-modernist reality, but there are also good reasons to nourish the tendencies in each which conflict.

The feminist standpoint epistemologies use for feminist ends the Marxist vision in which science can reflect 'the way the world is' and contribute to human emancipation. Feminist research claims in the natural and social sciences do appear to be truer to the world, and thus more objective than the sexist claims they replace. They provide an understanding of nature and social life that transcends gender loyalties and does not substitute one gender-loyal understanding for another. Furthermore, these feminist appeals to truth and objectivity trust that reason will play a role in the eventual triumph of feminism, that feminism correctly will be perceived as more than a power politic – though it is that, too. The successor science tendencies aim to provide more complete, less false, less distorting, less defensive, less perverse, less rationalizing understandings of the natural and social worlds.

This is already a radical project, for the Enlightenment vision explicitly denied that women possessed the reason and powers of dispassionate, objective observation required by scientific thinking. Women could be objects of (masculine) reason and observation but never the subjects, never the reflecting and universalizing human minds. Only men were in fact envisioned as ideal knowers, for only men (of the appropriate class, race and culture) possessed the innate capacities for socially transcendent observation and reason. The ends and purposes of such a science turned out to be far from emancipatory for anyone.

Marxism reformulated this Enlightenment vision so that the proletariat, guided by Marxist theory and by class struggle, became the ideal knowers, the group capable of using observation and reason to grasp the true form of social relations, including our relations with nature (Engels, 1972; Lukács, 1968). This Marxist successor to bourgeois science was, like its predecessor, to provide one social group – here, the proletariat – with the knowledge and power to lead the rest of the species toward emancipation. Marxism's epistemology is grounded in a theory of labour rather than a theory of innate (masculine) faculties; so just as not all human faculties are equal in the bourgeois version, here not all labour is equal. It was through struggle in the workplace that the proletariat would generate knowledge. In neither socialist practice nor Marxist theory were any women ever conceptualized as fundamentally defined by their relation to the means of production, regardless of their work force participation. They were never thought of as full-fledged members of the proletariat who could reason and thus know how the world is constructed. Women's distinctive reproductive labour, emotional labour, 'mediating' labour thus disappeared within the conceptual framework of Marxist theory, leaving women invisible as a class or social group of agents of knowledge. (Other forms of non-wage or non-industrial labour similarly disappeared from the centre of this conceptual scheme, mystifying the knowing available to slaves and colonized peoples.)

This standpoint tendency in feminist epistemology is grounded in a successor theory of labour or, rather, of distinctively human activity, and seeks to substitute women or feminists (the accounts differ) for the proletariat as the potentially ideal agents of knowledge. Men's (sexists') perceptions of themselves, others, nature, and the relations between all three are characteristically not only partial but also perverse.[5] Men's characteristic social experience, like that of the bourgeoisie, hides from them the politically imposed nature of the social relations they see as natural. Dominant patterns in Western thought justify women's subjugation as necessary for the progress of culture, and men's partial and perverse views as uniquely and admirably human. Women are able to use political struggle and analysis to provide a less partial, less defensive, less perverse understanding of human social relations – including our relations with nature. The standpoint theorists argue that this analysis, not feminist empiricism, accounts for the achievements of feminist theory and research because it is politically engaged theory and research from the perspective of the social experience of the subjugated sex/gender.

The second line of thought, one that can be found within many of these very same writings, expresses a profound skepticism toward the Enlightenment vision of the power of 'the' human mind to reflect perfectly a ready-made world that is out there for the reflecting. Many feminists share a rejection of the value of the forms of rationality, of dispassionate objectivity, of the Archimedean perspective, which were to be the means to knowledge. Here they are ambivalently related to such other sceptics of modernism as

Nietzsche, Wittgenstein, Derrida, Foucault, Lacan, Feyerabend, Rorty, Gadamer, and the discourses of semiotics, psychoanalysis, structuralism and deconstructionism.[6] What is striking is how the successor science idea and the post-modern scepticism of science are both embraced by these theorists, though the concepts are diametrically opposed in the non-feminist discourses.

From the perspective of this post-modern tendency in feminist thinking, the feminist successor science project can appear still too firmly rooted in distinctively masculine modes of being in the world. As one theorist puts the issue, 'Perhaps "reality" can have "a" structure only from the falsely universalizing perspective of the master. That is, only to the extent that one person or group can dominate the whole, can "reality" appear to be governed by one set of rules or be constituted by one privileged set of social relations' (Flax, 1983, p. 17). How can feminism radically redefine the relationship between knowledge and power if it creates yet another epistemology, yet another set of rules for the policing of thought?

However, this post-modern project can appear viciously Utopian from the perspective of the successor science tendency.[7] It seems to challenge the legitimacy of trying to describe the way the world is from a distinctively feminist perspective. It can appear of a piece with masculine and bourgeois desire to justify one's activities by denying one's social, embodied location in history; to attempt to transcend one's objective location in politics by appeal to a *mea culpa*, all-understanding, bird's-eye view (the transcendental ego in naturalistic garb) of the frailty of mere humans. That is, in its uneasy affiliation with non-feminist post-modernism, the feminist post-modernist tendency appears to support an inappropriate relativist stance by the subjugated groups, one that conflicts with feminism's perception that the realities of sexual politics in our world demand engaged political struggle. It appears to support an equally regressive relativism for those mildly estranged members of the subjugating groups with doubts about the legitimacy of their own objective privilege and power (see list above of non-feminist sceptics of modernism). It is worth keeping in mind that the articulation of relativism as an intellectual position emerges historically only as an attempt to dissolve challenges to the legitimacy of purportedly universal beliefs and ways of life. It is an objective problem, or a solution to a problem, only *from the perspective of the dominating groups*. Reality may indeed appear to have many different structures from the perspectives of our different locations in social relations, but some of those appearances are ideologies in the strong sense of the term: they are not only false and 'interested' beliefs but also ones that are used to structure social relations for the rest of us. For subjugated groups, a relativist stance expresses a false consciousness. It accepts the dominant group's insistence that their right to hold distorted views (and, of course, to make policy for all of us on the basis of those views) is intellectually legitimate.

Are not the policing of thought in the service of political power and the retreat to purportedly politically innocent, relativistic, mere interpretations of the world the two sides of the Enlightenment and bourgeois coin to which feminism is opposed? Is it not true – as these theorists all argue in different ways – that men's and women's different kinds of interactions with nature and social life (different 'labour') provide women with distinctive and privileged scientific and epistemological standpoints? How can feminism afford to give up a successor science project if it is to empower all women in a world where socially legitimated knowledge and the political power associated with it are firmly lodged in white, Western, bourgeois, compulsorily heterosexual, men's hands? Yet how can we give up our distrust of the historic links between this legitimated knowledge and political power?

One way to see these two tendencies in feminist theory is as converging approaches to a post-modernist world – a world that will not exist until both (conflicting) tendencies achieve their goals. From this perspective, at its best post-modernism envisions epistemology in a world where thought does not need policing. It recognizes the existence today of far less than the ideal speech situation, but disregards (or fails to acknowledge) the political struggles necessary to bring about change. The standpoint tendency attempts to move us toward that ideal world by legitimating and empowering the 'subjugated knowledges' of women, without which that post-modern epistemological situation cannot come into existence. It fails nonetheless to challenge the modernist intimacies between knowledge and power, or the legitimacy of assuming there can be a single, feminist story of reality. Whether or not this is a useful way to see the relationship between the two tendencies, I am arguing that we must resist the temptation to explain away the problems each addresses and to choose one to the exclusion of the other.

THE FEMINIST STANDPOINT AND OTHER 'OTHERS'

Feminist successor science projects stand in an uneasy relation to other emancipatory epistemologies insofar as the former seek to ground a uniquely legitimate and distinctive science and epistemology on the shared characteristics of women's activity. Hilary Rose (1983) locates these grounds in the way women's labour unifies mental, manual and caring labour. Nancy Hartsock (1983a,b) focuses on the deeper opposition to the dualities of mental versus manual labour to be found in women's daily, concrete activities both in domestic life and wage labour. Jane Flax (1983) identifies the relatively more reciprocal sense of self women bring to all their activities. She suggests that the small gap between men's and women's concepts of self, others and nature prefigures the possible larger gap between the defensively dualistic knowledge characteristic of male-dominant social orders and the relational and contextual knowledge possible in a future society of 'reciprocal selves'. Dorothy Smith (1974) argues that women's social labour is concrete rather than abstract, that it cannot be articulated to either administrative forms of ruling or the categories of social science, and that it has been socially invisible – combining to create a valuably alienated and bifurcated consciousness in women. However, other emancipatory perspectives claim as resources for their politics and epistemologies similar aspects of their own activity.

On the one hand, of course, feminism is right to identify women and men as classes in opposition at this moment in history. Everywhere in the world we find these two classes, and virtually everywhere the men subjugate the women in one way or another.[8] Furthermore, even male feminists receive benefits from an institutionalized sexism they actively struggle to eliminate. Objectively, no individual men can succeed in renouncing sexist privilege any more than individual whites can succeed in renouncing racist privilege – the benefits of gender and race accrue regardless of the wishes of the individuals who bear them. Gender, like race and class, is not a voluntarily disposable individual characteristic. After all, fundamentally our feminisms address the extraction and transfer of social benefits from women to men *as groups* of humans, on a worldwide scale. Thus the standpoint theorists, in identifying the common aspects of women's social experience cross-culturally, contribute something important to our work.

On the other hand, the distinctive characteristics of women's activities that Rose, Hartsock, Flax and Smith identify for our culture are probably to be found also in the labour and social experience of other subjugated groups. There are suggestions in the literature on Native Americans, Africans and Asians that what feminists call feminine versus masculine personalities, ontologies, ethics, epistemologies and world-views may be what these other liberation movements call non-Western versus Western personalities and world-views.[9] Thus, should there not also be Native American, African and Asian sciences and epistemologies, based on the distinctive historical and social experience of these peoples? Would not such successor sciences and epistemologies provide similar analyses to those of the standpoint theorists? (I set aside the crucial and fatal complication for this way of thinking – the facts that one-half of these peoples are women and that most women are not Western.) On what grounds would the feminist sciences and epistemologies be superior to these others? What is and should be the relationship of the feminist projects to these other emancipatory knowledge-seeking projects?

It is a vast over-generalization to presume that all Africans, let alone all colonized peoples, share distinctive personalities, ontologies, ethics, epistemologies or world-views. But is it any worse than the presumption that there are commonalities to be detected in *all women's* social experiences or world-views? Let us note that we are thinking here about perspectives as inclusive as those referred to in such phrases as the 'feudal world-view', the 'modern world-view', or the 'scientific world-view'. Moreover, we women also claim an identity we were taught to despise (Cliff, 1980); around the globe we insist on the importance of our social experience as *women*, not just as gender-invisible members of class, race or cultural groups. Similarly, Third World peoples claim their colonized social experience as the grounding for a shared identity and as a common source of alternative understandings. Why is it not reasonable to explore how the experience of colonization itself shapes personalities and world-views? How can white Western women insist on the legitimacy of what we think we share with all women and not acknowledge the equal legitimacy of what colonized peoples think they share with each other? In short, we cannot resolve this problem for the feminist standpoint by insisting on the cultural particularity of individuals in other cultures while at the same time arguing for the gender similarities of women cross-culturally.

One resolution of this dilemma for the standpoint tendency would be to say that feminist science and epistemology will be valuable in their own right alongside and as a part of these other possible sciences and epistemologies – not superior to them. With this strategy we have relinquished the totalizing, 'master theory' character of our theory-making which is at least an implicit goal of much feminist theorizing, and we have broken away from the Marxist assumptions that informed the feminist successor science projects. This response to the issue has managed to retain the categories of feminist theory (unstable though they be) and simply set them alongside the categories of the theory-making of other subjugated groups. Instead of the 'dual systems' theory with which socialist feminists wrestle (Young, 1981), this response gives us multisystems theory. Of course, it leaves bifurcated (and perhaps even more finely divided) the identities of all except ruling-class, white, Western women. There is a fundamental incoherence in this way of thinking about the grounds for feminist approaches to knowledge.

Another solution would be to renounce the goal of unity around shared social experiences in favour of solidarity around those goals that can be shared. From this perspective, each standpoint epistemology – feminist, Third World, gay, working class – names the historical conditions producing the political and conceptual oppositions to be overcome but does not thereby generate universal concepts and political goals. Because gender is also a class and racial category in cultures stratified by class and race as well as by gender, no particular women's experience can uniquely generate the groundings for the visions and politics that will emancipate us from gender hierarchy. A variety of social groups are currently struggling against the hegemony of the Western, white, bourgeois, homophobic, androcentric world-view and the politics it both generates and justifies. Our internal racial, sexual and class struggles, and the differences in our cultural histories which define for us who we are as social beings, prevent our federating around our shared goals. It is history that will resolve or dissolve this problem, not our analytic efforts. Nevertheless, white, Western, bourgeois feminists should attend to the need for a more active theoretical and political struggle against our own racism, classism and cultural centrism as forces that insure the continued subjugation of women around the world.

CULTURE VERSUS NATURE
AND GENDER VERSUS SEX

Historians and anthropologists show that the way contemporary Western society draws the borders between culture and nature is clearly both modern and culture bound.[10] The culture versus nature dichotomy reappears in complex and ambiguous ways in a number of other oppositions central to modern, Western thinking: reason versus the passions and emotions; objectivity versus subjectivity; mind versus the body and physical matter; abstract versus concrete; public versus private – to name a few. In our culture, and in science, masculinity is identified with culture and femininity with nature in all of these dichotomies. In each case, the latter is perceived as an immensely powerful threat that will rise up and overwhelm the former unless the former exerts severe controls over the latter.

This series of associated dualisms has been one of the primary targets of feminist criticisms of the conceptual scheme of modern science. It is less often recognized, however, how the dualism reappears in feminist thinking about gender, sex or the sex/gender system. In preceding sections, I have talked about eliminating gender as if the social could be cleanly separated from the biological aspects of our sexual identities, practices and desires. In feminist discourses, this mode of conceptualizing sexuality is clearly an advance over the biological determinist assumption that gender differences simply follow from sex differences. Since biological determinism is alive and flourishing in sociobiology, endocrinology, ethology, anthropology and, indeed, most non-feminist discourses, I do not want to devalue the powerful analytical strategy of insisting on a clean separation between the known (and knowable) effects of biology and of culture. Nevertheless, a very different picture of sexual identities, practices and desires emerges from recent research in biology, history, anthropology and psychology. Surprisingly, it could also be called biological determinism, though what is determined on this account is the plasticity rather than the rigidity of sexual identity, practice and desire. Our species is doomed to freedom from biological constraints in these respects, as existentialists would put the issue.

The problem for feminist theory and practice here is twofold. In the first place, we stress that humans are *embodied* creatures – not Cartesian minds that happen to be located in biological matter in motion. Female embodiment is different from male embodiment. Therefore we want to know the implications for social relations and intellectual life of that different embodiment. Menstruation, vaginal penetration, lesbian sexual practices, birthing, nursing and menopause are bodily experiences men cannot have. Contemporary feminism does not embrace the goal of treating women 'just like men' in public policy. So we need to articulate what these differences are. However, we fear that doing so feeds into sexual biological determinism (consider the problems we have had articulating a feminist perspective on premenstrual syndrome and work-related reproductive hazards in ways that do not victimize women). The problem is compounded when it is racial differences between women we want to articulate (Reid, 1975). How can we choose between maintaining that our biological differences ought to be recognized by public policy and insisting that biology is not destiny for either women or men?

In the second place, we have trouble conceptualizing the fact that the culture versus nature dichotomy and its siblings are not simply figments of thought to be packed up in the attic of outmoded ideas. The tendency toward this kind of dualism is an ideology in the strongest sense of the term, and such tendencies cannot be shucked off by mental hygiene and will power alone. The culture/nature dichotomy structures public policy, institutional and individual social practices, the organization of the disciplines (the social *v.* the natural sciences), indeed the very way we see the world around us. Consequently, until our dualistic practices are changed (divisions of social experience into mental *v.* manual, into abstract *v.* concrete, into emotional *v.* emotion denying), we are forced to think and exist within the very dichotomizing we criticize. Perhaps we can shift the assumption that the natural is hard to change and that the cultural is more easily changed, as we see ecological disasters and medical technologies on the one hand, and the history of sexism, classism and racism on the other (Raymond, 1979). Nonetheless, we should continue insisting on the distinction between culture and nature, between gender and sex (especially in the face of biological determinist backlash), even as we analytically and experientially notice how inextricably they are intertwined in individuals and in cultures. These dichotomies are empirically false, but we cannot afford to dismiss them as irrelevant as long as they structure our lives and our consciousnesses.

[. . .]

[This article has discussed] some of the central conceptual instabilities that emerge in considering the feminist criticism of science. Several of them arise in feminist theorizing more generally. I have been arguing that we cannot resolve these dilemmas in the terms in which we have been posing them and that instead we should learn how to regard the instabilities themselves as valuable resources. If we can learn how to use them, we can match Archimedes' greatest achievement – his inventiveness in creating a new kind of theorizing.

Acknowledgement

My thinking about these issues has been greatly improved by the commens of Margaret Anderson and the anonymous reviewers for *Signs: Journal of Women in Culture and Society*, as well as by discussions over the last several years with many of the feminist science critics cited in this paper. This research is part of a larger project: see *The Science Question in Feminism* (Ithaca, NY: Cornell University Press, 1986).

Notes

1   See, for example, Lugones and Spelman (1983); many of the selections in Marks and de Courtivron (1981); Jane Flax (1986); Haraway (1983).

2   See, Kuhn (1970). 'Normal science' was Kuhn's term for a 'mature science', one where conceptual and methodological assumptions are shared by the inquirers in a field.

3   Milan Kundera, in the article 'The novel and Europe' (1984), asks if it is an accident that the novel and the hegemony of scientific rationality arose simultaneously.

4   Important formulations of the epistemology for a feminist 'successor science' have been provided by, Flax (1983); Hartsock (1983a,b); Rose (1983,1984); Smith (1974,1979).

5   Hartsock, especially, discusses the perversity of the androcentric vision (note 4 above). I shall subsequently refer to the men vs. women dichotomy since that is the way most of these standpoint theorists put the issue. However, I think these categories are inadequate even for the standpoint projects: it is feminists vs. nonfeminists (sexists) we should be discussing here.

6   Jane Flax (1986) discusses this post-modern strain in feminist theory.

7   Flax appears to be unaware of this problem. Engels (1972) distinguishes Utopian and scientific socialisms.

8   'Virtually everywhere' to give the benefit of the doubt to the anthropologists' claims about 'egalitarian virtues'. See, for example, Leacock (1981).

9   I have discussed this situation more fully in Harding (1986b) and in Chapter 7 of Harding (1986a).

10   See especially the responses to Sherry Ortner (1974) in MacCormack and Strathern (1980).

Article 8.2
WHAT IS FEMINIST THEORY?
Elizabeth Gross

> If we continue to speak this sameness, if we speak to
> each other as men have spoken for centuries, as they
> have taught us to speak, we will fail each other. Again
> . . . words will pass through our bodies, above our heads,
> disappear, make us disappear.
>
> (*Irigaray, 1980, p. 69*)

In the sixties, feminists began to question various images, representations, ideas and presumptions traditional theories developed about
women and the feminine. To begin with, feminists directed their
theoretical attention to patriarchal discourses, those which were
either openly hostile to and aggressive about women and the
feminine, or those which had nothing at all to say about women.
Feminists seemed largely preoccupied with the inclusion of women
in those spheres from which they had been excluded, that is, with
creating representations which would enable women to be regarded
as men's *equals*. Instead of being ignored by and excluded
from theory, women were to be *included* as possible objects of
investigation. Issues of direct relevance to women's lives – the
family, sexuality, the 'private' or domestic sphere, interpersonal
relations – were to be included, in some instances for the first time,
as a relevant and worthy object of intellectual concern. Generally,
feminists continued to rely on the methods, techniques, concepts
and frameworks of traditional patriarchal theories, especially in
leftist or radical form, using them to develop accounts of women's
oppression. Some of the relevant names circulating in feminist
discourses at the time included Marx, Reich, Marcuse, McLuhan,
Laing, Cooper, Sartre, Fanon, Masters and Johnson. Women
attempted to include women as the equals of men in the sphere of
theoretical analysis, developing out of various theories of (class or
race) oppression by modifying and adjusting their details in order
to account for women's specific oppression.

Among the relevant features or characteristics describing this
phase in the development of feminist theory could be the following:

1   Women and the feminine become worthwhile objects of theory
    and research. Having been neglected, or denied value in
    patriarchal terms, women become focal points of empirical and
    theoretical investigation.

2   Women and the feminine, as excluded or neglected objects in
    traditional theoretical terms, are now conceptualized as men's

equals – as the same as men in relevant socio-economic and intellectual terms.

3   While elements or components of patriarchal discourses may be criticized, questions about their more basic framework and assumptions, whether ontological, epistemological or political, remain unasked.

4   While remaining critical toward the attitude of patriarchal discourses to the position of women, feminist theory is largely concerned with 'women's issues', those which directly affect women's lives, leaving other, 'broader' or more 'public' issues uncriticized.

5   Patriarchal discourses were subjected to an either/or decision: either they were considered thoroughly infiltrated with patriarchal values and thus need to be rejected; or they are capable of 'rectification' so that women can now be included. Patriarchal discourses, in other words, were either rejected outright or were more or less wholeheartedly accepted (with 'minor adjustments').

However, within a short period it became clear that the aim of including women as men's equals within patriarchal theory contained a number of problems not anticipated at the outset. Perhaps most strikingly, it became increasingly clear that it was not possible simply to include women in those theories where they had previously been excluded, for this exclusion forms a fundamental structuring principle and key presumption of patriarchal discourses. Many patriarchal discourses were *incapable* of being broadened or extended to include women without major upheavals and transformations. There was no space within the confines of these discourses to accommodate women's inclusion and equal participation. Moreover, even if women were incorporated into patriarchal discourses, at best they could only be regarded as variations of a basic humanity. The project of women's equal inclusion meant that only women's *sameness to men*, only women's *humanity* and not their *womanliness* could be discussed. Further, while women could not be included as the objects of theoretical speculation, their positions as the subjects or producers of knowledge was not raised. In other words, in adopting the role of the (male) subjects of knowledge, women began to assume the role of surrogate men.

As subjects of knowledge, women were faced with a dilemma. They could either remain detached from the 'objects' of their theoretical investigations (where these objects are women or femininity), in which case women may be considered to retain their 'objectivity' and 'neutrality'; or women could maintain a closeness to and identification with their 'objects'. In the first case, such women, while gaining the approval of their male colleagues and possibly some position of respect within academic communities, must nevertheless disavow their own positions as women. In the second case, by their self-inclusion within the category of objects investigated, many women lose the detachment needed to be considered 'scientific' or 'objective', resulting, perhaps, in ridicule or some form of academic secondariness. Yet such women, through the risks they thus take in questioning the most general assumptions and *givens* of intellectual inquiry, retain some possibility of maintaining identities as women. In the long run this may have led to questioning the use and value of the distinction between subject and object, transforming the very grounds of current debate.

In abandoning such attempts to include women where theory excluded them, many feminists came to realize that the project of women's inclusion as men's equals could not succeed. This was because it was not simply the range and scope of objects that required transformation: more profoundly, and threateningly, the very questions posed and the methods used to answer them, basic assumptions about methodology, criteria of validity and merit, all needed to be seriously questioned. The political, ontological and epistemological commitments underlying patriarchal discourses, as well as their theoretical contents required re-evaluation from feminist perspectives, as it became increasingly clear that women could only be included in patriarchal texts as deviant or duplicate men: the a priori assumptions of sameness or interchangeability, sexual neutrality or indifference, the complete neglect of women's specificities and differences, could not be accommodated in traditional theoretical terms. The whole social, political, scientific and metaphysical underpinning of patriarchal theoretical systems needed to be shaken up.

While problematic and ultimately impossible, the aspiration towards an equality between men and women was nevertheless politically and historically necessary. Without such attempts, women could not question the naturalness or seeming inevitability of women's second-class status as citizens, subjects, sexual beings etc. This aim of equality served as a political, and perhaps as an experiential, prerequisite to the more far-reaching struggles directed towards female *autonomy* – that is, to women's right to political, social, economic and intellectual self-determination. This seems probably the most striking shift in feminist politics since its revival in the sixties.

This basic shift from a politics of equality to a politics of autonomy may have created an uneasy tension within feminist circles, for these two commitments are not necessarily compatible. Autonomy implies the right to see oneself in whatever terms one chooses – which may imply an integration or alliance with other groups and individuals or may not. Equality, on the other hand, implies a measurement according to a given standard . . . Equality is the equivalence of two (or more) terms, one of which takes the role of norm or model in unquestionable ways. Autonomy, by contrast, implies the right to accept or reject such norms or standards according to their appropriateness to one's self-definition. Struggles for equality . . . imply an acceptance of given standards and a conformity to their expectations and requirements. Struggles for autonomy, on the other hand, imply the right to reject such standards and create new ones.

Feminists concerned with questions surrounding women's autonomy and self-determination are, ironically, no less concerned with the work of male or masculinist theory than their equality-oriented counterparts, although the male proper names have changed significantly over the twenty-year period of feminism's existence as a self-consciously political intervention into theory. The names of Freud, Lacan, Nietzsche, Derrida, Deleuze, Althusser, Foucault in France, and Richard Rorty, Anthony Wilden, Frederic Jameson, Stephen Heath, Terry Eagleton, Paul de Man etc. in [the UK] and North America constitute just some of the 'names' with which contemporary feminist theory has engaged. But what has dramatically changed is the feminist attitude towards and use of patriarchal discourses. Instead of these discourses and their methods and assumptions providing uncriticized tools and frameworks by which women could be analysed as objects, now these discourses become the objects of critical feminist scrutiny. Such discourses and methods are now *tactically used* without necessarily retaining general commitment to their frameworks and presumptions. Feminists do not seem so eager to slot women into pre-existing patriarchal categories and theoretical spaces; instead, it is women's lives, and experiences, that provide criteria by which patriarchal texts can be judged. Basic, unspoken assumptions of patriarchal theories, the ways in which they develop and gain precedence, their use of criteria and methods of inclusion and exclusion are all beginning to be analysed from feminist perspectives . . . Women asserted themselves not as objects but as subjects of knowledge with particular perspectives and points of view often systematically different from men's. Such perspectives or viewpoints are not simply 'subjective' in the sense of individual, personal or idiosyncratic positions – 'subjectivity' being seen as an *interference* with the 'objective' procedures of knowledge in just the same way that men's theoretical productions are a function of their lived positions in the world. The production of discourse is, for the first time, being examined as a process of *sexual division* and exclusion.

Feminists of autonomy can be contrasted with feminists committed to struggles of equality on at least the following points:

1   Women become both the subjects as well as the objects of knowledge; but, in occupying the position of subject, feminists do not continue to produce knowledge as if they were men, as if knowledge were sexually indifferent. Women's femininity is asserted as a theoretical undertaking, with a number of consequences, among them:

2   In assuming the positions of knower or subject, the methods, procedures, presumptions and techniques of theory are all put into question.

3   Feminists develop perspectives not just *on* or *about* women and 'women's issues' but about *any* object at all – including other theories, systems of representation etc., etc.

4   Feminists don't simply assert the either/or alternative, based on 'expelling unsound' or patriarchal elements or wholesale adoption of theoretical viewpoints. Instead, while attempting to 'work through' patriarchal texts, understanding how they work and how they exert their dominances, feminists attempt to use what they can of these theories – often against themselves! No longer simply condemning or accepting certain discourses, now they are analysed, examined and questioned – actively engaged with and challenged in their operations.

5   Feminist theory challenged both the content and the frameworks of discourses, disciplines and institutions, attempting to present alternatives or develop them where they did not yet exist.

These interventions and interrogations may have produced one of the most subversive challenges to patriarchal theory that this century, or epoch, has seen: 'It is a major historical event which holds the promise of enabling a more complete challenge to domination than has yet been possible' (Finn and Miles, 1982, p. 10).

In the diverse disciplines constituting the social sciences and humanities, in which most feminist theorists received their training, many matured from a position akin to apprenticeship (where women learned the skills of prevailing (masculine) forms of scholarship and research) to a position of relative self-determination (where women are able to use the techniques and skills they have acquired against the very disciplines in which they were trained). These disciplines, and the specific texts and practices associated with them, have become the objects of feminist analysis and criticism. Theory, rather than 'Woman', is now the terrain of contestation between feminists and non- or anti-feminists.

Feminist struggles for autonomy, self-determination and a viable place which women can occupy as women in the theoretical and socio-political universe have developed into a two-pronged or dual-faceted form. On the one hand, feminist theory has radically questioned and attempted to undermine the presumptions, methods and frameworks of phallocentric or patriarchal discourses and disciplines. On the other hand, feminist theory has simultaneously attempted to explore and develop alternatives to these phallocentric systems, bringing into being new, hitherto unarticulated, feminine perspectives on the world. In other words, today feminist theory is involved in both an *anti-sexist* project, which involves challenging and deconstructing phallocentric discourses; and in a positive project of constructing and developing alternative models, methods, procedures, discourses etc.

The anti-sexist project clearly implies a thorough knowledge of and familiarity with prevailing theoretical paradigms and their histories. Such an endeavour means working with, understanding and reflecting on those theoretical systems which comprise women's history and their contemporary situation, and participating in women's oppression. Yet anti-sexism is largely negative and reactive, aiming to challenge what currently exists, what is presently dominant and responsible for women's phallocentric position in theoretical representation. Such a critical, reactive project is necessary if feminist theory is to avoid the intellectual perils of abstraction, idealization or irrelevance. It risks projecting an ideal or Utopian future for women which is unanchored in or unrelated to what exists here and now. It risks a series of commitments it may wish, on reflection, to reject. It risks repeating problems of the past without recognizing them as problems or learning from them. The critical, anti-sexist project is directed against the methods, assumptions and procedures by which patriarchal discourses reduce women to a necessary dependence on men as well as against more insidious, structural expressions of misogyny, which, rather than making sexist pronouncements about women instead present perspectives on the world from a masculine point of view as if such a position were sexually neutral.

If, however, feminist theory remains *simply* reactive, *merely* a critique, paradoxically it affirms the very paradigms it seeks to contest. It remains on the very grounds it wishes to question and transform. To criticize prevailing theoretical systems *without posing viable alternatives* is to affirm such theoretical systems as necessary. Although feminist theory must retain a familiarity with these systems, it must also establish a theoretical distance from too close an adherence to them. If feminist theory does not extend beyond the terms of anti-sexism, it remains bound up with a politics of sameness or equality even while criticizing it. The limited but strategically necessary aim of destabilizing and dismantling patriarchal discourses is only the first stage or prerequisite for a more encompassing and threatening challenge to patriarchal domination – the struggle for autonomy, implying struggles for the right to different paradigms, theoretical tools, and possibly even a reconceptualization of the entire system of knowledges and acceptable theoretical methods.

Coupled with the anti-sexist project, feminism must thus also be involved in the positive task of experimenting with and creating alternatives to patriarchal theoretical norms. Feminist theory can no longer be content with adapting patriarchal theories so that they are capable of analysing woman – which in itself is a phallocentric endeavour, for it reduces women to theories and categories appropriate for and developed from masculine points of view. The positive components question and displace the very foundations upon which traditional theories are based.

It cannot be specified in advance what an autonomous feminist theory would involve, for this contradicts the very idea of autonomy, the right to choose and define the world for oneself. In their diversity and multiplicity, women claim the right to define their own aims and goals. Although it cannot be specified using one or many models, feminist theory can nevertheless be outlined negatively, for it seems clear that there are a number of theoretical assumptions it would not wish to reproduce. It cannot be regarded, for example, as the reverse or opposite of patriarchal texts, transforming their objects but not their underlying assumptions. On the contrary, it attempts to move beyond them, their frameworks and their limits.

In other words, feminist theory cannot be accurately regarded as a *competing* or rival account, diverging from patriarchal texts over what counts as true. It is not a true discourse, nor a mere objective or scientific account. It could be appropriately seen, rather, as a *strategy*, a local, specific, concrete intervention with definite political, even if provisional, aims and goals. In the 1980s, feminist theory no longer seems to seek the status of unchangeable, trans-historical and trans-geographic truth in its hypotheses and propositions. Rather, it seeks effective forms of intervention into systems of power in order to subvert them and replace them with others more preferable. Strategy implies a recognition of the current situation, in both its general, structural features (macrolithic power alignments), and its specific, detailed, regionalized forms (microlithic power investments). It needs to know the spaces and strategies of its adversaries in order to undermine their positions within an overall system. It must thus be aware of the kinds of counter-strategy or tactics used by phallocentric discourses to deploy in order to seek the points of vulnerability. All forms of strategy, in short, involve recognizing what *is* in order to move on to what *should* be. Strategy always involves short-term aims, seen as necessary for the achievement of longer-term ideals, which themselves are capable of being modified and transformed during the processes of struggle. As a form of strategy, feminist theory needs to use whatever means are available to it, whether these are 'patriarchal' or not. Phallocentric insights, concepts and theoretical tools are evaluated in terms of their usefulness, their functioning in particular contexts, rather than in terms of an ideal but impossible purity. As strategy, it is necessarily implicated in the systems it wishes to challenge. Aspirations to a theoretical purity, a position 'untainted' by patriarchal impingements, that is, forms of theoretical separatism where patriarchal terms and practices are rejected, seem naive. They are unable to struggle with, or thus move beyond the patriarchal terms that return to haunt them. In order to challenge and move beyond patriarchal models, feminists must be able to use whatever means are at hand, including those of the very systems it challenges.

As a series of strategic interventions into patriarchal texts, feminist theory does not simply aim to reveal what is 'wrong' with, or false about, patriarchal theories – to replacing one 'truth' with another. It aims to render patriarchal systems, methods and presumptions unable to function, unable to retain their dominance and power. It aims to make clear how such a dominance has been possible; and to make it no longer viable. Since feminist theory lacks the means to directly confront a sophisticated patriarchal theoretical regime in creating alternatives, feminists have had to resort to forms of intellectual guerilla warfare, striking out at the points of patriarchy's greatest weakness, its blindspots (see Irigaray, 1985: Part 1). The grounds and terrain upon which patriarchy develops its arguments reveals their partial and partisan instead of universal or representative position. Patriarchal intellectual systems are unlikely to allow such attempts at political subversion to proceed uncontested. In fact, it is clear that traditional discourses and the positions they support have developed a series of counter-strategies and tactical response to the incursions of feminism, and indeed, women, into its fields of operation. These range from more or less personal or petty tactics to more serious, far-ranging threats – from personal ridicule, ignorance, stereotyping, to forms of counter-attack including wilful misrepresentation, being refused access to professional status and/or a livelihood or having one's work co-opted or neutralized. Such counter-attacks are by no means mutually exclusive and are exercised with greater or lesser strength according to the degree of threat feminist theories and objections pose. Without at least some awareness of the range and ferocity of these counter-attacks, feminism may be unable to effect the wide-ranging subversions it seeks. It need not be committed to patriarchal discourses and their values, yet without understanding them in detail, feminists will be unable to move beyond them.

In summary, feminist theory involves, first, a recognition of the overt and covert forms of misogyny in which discourses participate. This means developing the skills of recognizing what makes these discourses patriarchal – including their explicit pronouncements about men and women, and their respective values, as well as the capacity to see how such theories divide up the world according to masculine interests. Second, it involves an ability to recognize patriarchal discourses in terms of their absences, gaps, lacunae, around the question of women and the feminine, understanding how these silences function to structure and make patriarchal discourses possible. Third, feminist theory must be capable of articulating the role that these silences and masculinist representations play in the suppression of femininity, and of affirming the possibility of other, alternative, perspectives, making patriarchal texts unable to assert their hegemony; and fourth, it must develop viable methods for superseding phallocentric systems of representation even if this means relying on patriarchal methods, using them as a starting-point for new directions in theoretical research. By its very existence, such forms of feminist theory demonstrate that patriarchal discourses are *not* neutral, universal or unquestionable models, but are the effects of the specific (political) positions occupied by men.

On the basis of . . . works by a number of . . . feminists within social and political theory . . . feminist theory can be provisionally located at the interface of the negative, anti-sexist project and a more positive, speculative, project. It is the refusal of a number of central values, concepts and operations necessary for the functioning of patriarchal theory, and an affirmation of the alternatives to these given forms of discourse. Among the central concepts and values questioned by feminist theory is a core of assumptions shared by most, if not all of the social sciences. In particular, it has seriously questioned patriarchal adherences to the following theoretical commitments:

1   Commitment to a singular or universal concept of truth and methods for verifying (or falsifying) truth. Few theories aspiring to the status of scientific objectivity and truth, conventionally understood, accept their own historicity and the effects that context, environment and particular circumstances have on the production and evaluation of theory. In particular, such theoretical aspirations cannot acknowledge the costs (the silences, exclusions and invalidations) on which they are founded: in seeking the status of truth, they seek a position beyond history and outside power.

2   Its commitments to objectivity, observer-neutrality and the context-independence as unquestioned theoretical values. These are

closely related to the over-evaluation of science and truth as models for knowledge. Objectivity is considered as a form of interchangeability or substitutability of observers or experimenters, as a check against individual bias. This ideal of interchangeability is based on the assumption of a similarity of viewpoint and position between observers – who must be 'appropriately trained'. This assumption is necessarily blind to the different structural positions men and women occupy, their different degrees of access to suitable training, and their (possibly) different relations to their disciplines. The neutrality and universality of many patriarchal discourses presumed in the social sciences is thus sex-blind – unable to acknowledge the different social positions of men and women in presuming a neutral, interchangeable subject.

3   The commitment to a universal subject of knowledge, a subject presumed to have certain qualities and features: the ability to separate *him*self from feelings, emotions, passions, personal interests and motives, socio-economic and political factors, the past, one's aspirations for the future etc. This subject of knowledge is capable of achieving a distance from the object known, thus being able to reflect on it. It is, however, a subject incapable of accepting its own limits, its materiality and historicity, its immersion in socio-economic and political values. The subject is conceived as disembodied, rational sexually indifferent subject – a mind unlocated in space, time or constitutive interrelations with others (a status normally only attributed to angels! cf. Irigaray, 1984).

4   The commitment to a fixed, static truth, an immutable, given reality, a guaranteed knowledge of Being and access to Reason. Such an ahistorical view cannot account for the variability and historical nature of what counts as true except in terms of a greater and greater access to and knowledge of the truth, that is, except in terms of historical views being *false* views. It refuses to endorse the possibility of a 'politics of truth', of the political investments in truth (cf. Foucault, 1980b). Truth, as a correspondence or veridical reflection of reality, is a *perspectiveless* knowledge, a knowledge without a point of view – or, what amounts to the same thing, a truth claiming a universal perspective.

5   The commitment to the intertranslatability of concepts, terms, truths, propositions and discourses. As embodied in a propositional form, knowledge 'is not regarded as dependent on its particular modes of formulation, but on the underlying thoughts it is presumed to express. Language is considered a vehicle for the communication of pre-existent thoughts or ideas. It is seen merely as a medium, a dispensable tool for the transmission of thought, rather than being seen as thought's necessary condition. In denying the materiality of language, prevailing discourses can avoid recognizing their dependence on and debt to tropes, figures of speech, images,

metaphors etc. evoking the feminine, women or maternity. Patriarchal discourses ignore the complicity of discursive systems with oppressive social structures, and the dependence of discourses on particular positions established by particular modes of language.

There are, of course, many positive features that can be briefly sketched out in general ways which do not pre-empt women's various attempts at self-determination. Included among them are:

1   Intellectual commitments, not to truth, objectivity and neutrality, but to theoretical positions openly acknowledged as observer and context-specific. Rather than deny its spatio-temporal conditions and limits, feminist theory accepts and affirms them, for they are its raison d'être. Following Nietzsche, it seems prepared to avow its own perspectivism, its specific position of enunciation, its being written from a particular point of view, with specific aims and goals.

2   In acknowledging its conditions of production, feminist theory seems prepared to question the value of the criteria of objectivity and scientificity so rigidly and imperialistically accepted by intellectual orthodoxies. This is not, however, an admission of any 'subjective bias'. The very distinction between objective (knowledge) and subjective (opinion) is put into question. Feminists seem prepared to accept that the knower always occupies a position, spatially, temporally, sexually and politically. This is a corollary of its perspectivism. It is neither subjective nor objective, neither absolute nor relative. These alternatives, for one thing, cannot explain the productive investments of power in the production of knowledges. This does not, however, mean that feminist theory used no criteria of evaluation or self-reflection. Rather, its norms of judgement are developed from *intersubjective*, shared effects and functions; and in terms of a discourse's *intertextual* functions, its capacity to either undermine or affirm various dominant systems and structures.

3   Instead of presuming a space or gulf between the rational, knowing subject and the object known, feminist theory acknowledges the contiguity between them. Prevailing views of the rational subject posit a subject artificially and arbitrarily separated from its context. This creates a distance required for its separation from the emotions, passions, bodily interferences, relations with others and the socio-political world. Feminist theory seems openly prepared to accept the constitutive interrelations of the subject, its social position and its mediated relation to the object. For feminists (in so far as they uphold such a notion) the rational subject is *not* free of personal, social and political interests, but is necessarily implicated in them. Theories are seen as sexualized, as occupying a position in relation to the qualities and values associated with the two sexes, or the attributes of masculinity and femininity. But to claim a sexualization

of discourses and knowledges is not to equate the discourse's position with that of its author or producer; there is no (direct) correspondence between feminine or feminist texts and female authors, or between phallocentric texts and male authors. The sexual 'position of the text' can only be discerned contextually and in terms of the position which the speaking subject (the implicit or explict 'I' of the text) speaks from; the kind of subject (implicitly) presumed as the subject *spoken to* (or audience), and the kind of subject *spoken about* (or object). As well as the range of various subjects posited in any or all texts, the text's position also depends on the *kind of relations* asserted between these different subjects (cf. Benveniste, 1961, Chs 19–20). In the case of feminist theory, the subject, object and audience are not dichotomously divided into mutually exclusive and mutually exhaustive categories (subject/object, knower-master/ignorant-disciple, teacher/pupil, self/other etc.; cf. Jay (1981)) but may be defined more in terms of continuities and/or differences. The speaking subject, the subject spoken to and the subject spoken about may be equated; but in any case, there is a constitutive interrelatedness presumed between all three terms. This means, for example and to take a concrete case, that men do not speak with greater objectivity about women's oppression, as some male academics recently asserted with great sincerity. Men too are necessarily implicated in and part of women's oppression. It is of course clear that their relations to such oppression must be very different from women's. In short, particular interests are served by every theoretical position and in any textual or discursive system. The politics or 'power' of the text (cf. Foucault, 1972) cannot, however, be automatically read off from what the text overtly *says*, but, more frequently, from *how* it says it, what is invoked, and what is thus effected. Feminist theory has the merit over prevailing discursive systems of being able not only to accept but to actively affirm its own political position(s) and aspirations, to accept that, far from being objective in the sense of 'disinterested' and 'unmotivated', it is highly motivated by the goals and strategies involved in creating an autonomy for women. Such motivation or purposiveness, however, does not invalidate feminist theory, but is its acknowledged function, its rationale.

4   Because it refuses to accept the pre-given values of truth, objectivity, universality, neutrality and an abstract reason, feminist theory – along with some contemporary male theorists – is not committed to or motivated by these values. It sees itself in terms of a critical and constructive strategy. It is neither abstraction, blueprint nor handbook for action, nor a distanced form of reflection. These views, for one thing, imply a theory outside or beyond practice. In questioning the dichotomous conceptualization of the relation between theory and practice, feminist theory considers itself both a 'theoretical practice' – a practice at the

level of theory itself, a practice bound up with yet critical of the institutional frameworks within which the production of theoretical discourses usually occurs, a practice involving writing, reading, teaching, learning, assessment, and numerous other rituals and procedures; as well, it is a 'practical theory' – a theory openly seen as a part of practice, a tool or tactic playing a major part in the subversive, often dangerous assault on one particular site of the functioning of patriarchal power relations – the sphere of knowledge, which provides patriarchy with rationalizations and justifications for its ever-expanding control. Feminist theory is an interweaving of strands that are simultaneously theoretical and practical. It is a site where dominant discourses, subjugated discourses, voices hitherto silenced or excluded . . ., forms of coercion and control as well as concerted forms of resistance are able to be worked through in relation to each other. It is a threshold for the intervention of theories within concrete practices, and the restructuring of theory by the imperatives of experience and practice, a kind of hinge or doorway between the two domains. In aiming at a destruction of misogynistic theory and its fundamental assumptions and at establishing a positive influence on day-to-day and structural interactions between the sexes, it is neither a prelude to practice, nor a reflection on practice because it is already a form of practice within a specific region of patriarchy's operations.

5   Feminist theory, similarly, cannot be conceived in terms of the categories of rationality or irrationality. Since at least the seventeenth century, if not long before, reason has been understood in dichotomous terms, being characterized oppositionally and gaining its internal coherence only by the exclusion of its 'others' – the passions, the body, the emotions, nature, faith, materiality, dreaming, experience, perception, madness or many other terms (cf. Jay; Lloyd, 1984; Irigaray, 1984). In questioning this binary mode of categorization, feminists demonstrated that reason is a concept associated with the norms and values of masculinity, and its opposites, or 'others', with femininity. Feminist theory today is not simply interested in reversing the values of rational/irrational or in affirming what has been hierarchically subordinated, but more significantly, in questioning the very structure of binary categories. In short, feminist theory seeks to transform and extend the concept of reason so that instead of excluding concepts like experience, the body, history, etc., these are included within it or acknowledged as necessary for reason to function. In taking women's experiences and lives as a starting-point for the development of theory, feminism attempts to develop alternatives to the rigid, hierarchical and exclusive concept of reason. It seeks a rationality not divided from experience, from oppression, from particularity or specificity; a reason, on the contrary, that includes them is a rationality not beyond or above experience but based upon it.

6   In challenging phallocentrism, feminist theory must also challenge the evasion of history and materiality so marked in theoretical traditions in the West. In conceiving of itself as a rational, private, individual activity and struggle towards truth and knowledge, a pure, intellectual activity, it must also deny its status as a historical and political product. Predominant theoretical traditions refuse to accept their dependence on the materiality of writing, on practices involved in training, producing, publishing and promoting certain methods, viewpoints and representatives, on struggles for authority and domination. In opposition to these prevailing theoretical ideals, feminist theory openly acknowledges its own materiality as the materiality of language (language being seen as a weapon of political struggle, domination and resistance), of desire (desire as the will to achieve certain arrangements of potentially satisfying 'objects' – the desire for an identity, a sexuality and a recognized place in culture being the most clear-cut and uncontentious among feminists) and of power (power not just as a force visible in the acts, events and processes within political and public life, but also as a series of tactical alignments between institutions, knowledges, practices involved with the control and supervision of individuals and groups); in more particular terms, the alignments of male socio-economic domination with the forms of learning, training, knowledge and theory.

7   In rejecting leading models of intellectual inquiry (among them, the requirements of formal logic, the structuring of concepts according to binary oppositional structures, the use of grammar and syntax for creating singular, clear, unambiguous, precise modes of articulation and many other assumed textual values), and its acceptance of the idea of its materiality as theory, feminist theory is involved in continuing explorations of and experimentation with new forms of writing, new methods of analysis, new positions of enunciation, new kinds of discourse.

No one method, form of writing, speaking position, mode of argument can act as representative, model or ideal for feminist theory. Instead of attempting to establish a new theoretical norm, feminist theory seeks a new *discursive space*, a space where women can write, read and think *as women*. This space will encourage a proliferation of voices, instead of an hierarchical structuring of them, a plurality of perspectives and interests instead of the monopoly of the one – new kinds of questions and different kinds of answer. No one form would be privileged as *the* truth, the correct interpretation, the right method; rather, knowledges, methods, interpretations can be judged and used according to their appropriateness to a given context, a specific strategy and particular effects.

Feminist theory is capable of locating itself historically, materially, enunciatively and politically in relation to patriarchal structures. During its development over the last twenty-five years, it has emerged as a capacity to look at women in new, hitherto unexplored ways by refusing to reduce and explain women's specificity to terms that are inherently masculine; it has developed the ability to look at any object from the point of view of perspectives and interests of women, of understanding and going beyond phallocentrism in developing different kinds of theory and practice. This description may sound like an idealized or Utopian version of what a self-conscious and politically committed, active and informed theoretical practice should involve. Perhaps. It is not yet clear how far along this Utopian path feminist discourses have come. But . . . feminist theory is in the process of developing along these diverse trajectories. It is in the process of reassessing the theoretical heritage it needs to supersede in order to claim a future for itself. This future may initiate a new theoretical epoch, one capable of accepting the full implications of acknowledging sexual difference. Theory in the future would be seen as sexual, textual, political and historical production. Although this may threaten those who adhere to the values of phallocentrism, it may open up hitherto unimagined sites, sources and tools for theoretical exploration. An autonomous femininity may introduce, for the first time in our recorded history, the possibility of dialogue with an 'alien voice', the voice of woman.

> Sexual difference would constitute the horizon of worlds of a still unknown fecundity . . . Fecundity of birth and regenerescence for amorous partners, but still production of a new epoch of thought, art, poetry, language . . . Creation of a new *poietics*.
>
> (*Irigaray, 1984, p. 1*)

REFERENCES

ALARCON, N. (1991) 'The theoretical subject(s) of *This Bridge Called My Back* and Anglo-American feminism', in Calderon, H. and Saldivar, J. D. (eds) *Criticism in the Borderlands: studies in Chicano literature, culture and ideology*, Durham, NC, Duke University Press.

ALLEN, J. (1983) 'Marxism and the man question: some implications of the patriarchy debate', in Allen, J. and Patton, P. (eds) *Beyond Marxism*, Sydney, Intervention Publications, pp. 99–102.

AMOS, V. AND PARMAR, P. (1984) 'Challenging Imperial feminism', *Feminist Review*, No.17, pp. 3–20.

AMOS, V., LEWIS, G., MAMA, A. AND PARMAR, P. (1984) (eds) 'Many voices, one chant: black feminist perspectives', *Feminist Review*, No. 17.

ANZALDUA, G. (1987) *Borderlands/La Frontera: The New Mestisa*, San Francisco, CA, Spinsters/Aunt Lute.

APPADURAI, A. (1988) 'Putting hierarchy in its place', *Cultural Anthropology*, Vol. 3, No. 1.

BALINT, A. (1939) 'Love for the mother and mother love', in Balint, M. (ed.) (1952) *Primary Love and Psychoanalytic Technique*, London, Tavistock.

BALINT, M. (1935) 'Critical notes on the theory of the pre-genital organizations of the libido', pp. 37–58 in Balint, M. (1965).

BALINT, M. (1956a) 'Perversions and genitality', in Balint, M. (1965).

BALINT, M. (1956b) 'Pleasure, object and libido: some reflections on Fairbairn's modifications on psychoanalytic theory', *British Journal of Medical Psychology*, Vol. 29, No. 2, pp. 162–7.

BALINT, M. (1965) *Primary Love and Psychoanalytic Technique*, London, Tavistock (New York, Liveright Publishing).

BALINT, M. (1968) *The Basic Fault*, London, Tavistock.

BANNER, L. (1983) *American Beauty*, Chicago, IL, University of Chicago Press.

BARASH, D. (1977) *Sociobiology and Behavior*, New York, Elsevier.

BARBACH, L.G. (1975) *For Yourself: the fulfilment of female sexuality*, London, Signet.

BARDWICK, J. (1980) *Women in Transition*, Brighton, Harvester.

BENEDEK, T. (1959) 'Parenthood as a developmental phase: a contribution to the libido theory', *Journal of the American Psychoanalytic Association*, Vol. 7, No. 3, pp. 389–417.

BENVENISTE, E. (1961) *Problems in General Linguistics*, Miami, FL, University of Miami Press.

BHASIN, K. AND MENIN, R. (1988) 'The problem', *Seminar*, No. 342, Special Issue on *sati*.

BHAVNANI, K. AND COULSON, M. (1986) 'Transforming socialist–feminism: the challenge of racism', *Feminist Review*, No. 23, pp. 81–92.

BIBRING, G. (1953) 'On the "passing of the Oedipus complex" in a matriarchal family setting', pp. 278–84 in Loewenstein, R.M. (ed.) *Drives, Affects and Behavior: essays in honor of Marie Bonaparte*, New York, International Universities Press.

BINSWANGER, L. (1958) 'The case of Ellen West', in May, R. (ed.) *Existence*, New York, Simon and Schuster.

BIRKE, L. (1986) *Women, Feminism and Biology*, Brighton, Wheatsheaf.

BIRKE, L. (1991) 'Science, feminism and animal natures: extending the boundaries', *Woman's Studies International Forum*, in press.

BLAND, L. AND HOLLWAY, W. (n.d.) 'Turning off what turns you on? The problem for feminism of biological accounts of sexuality and sexual desire', unpublished manuscript.

BOOTH, A. (1972) 'Sex and social participation', *American Sociological Review*, Vol. 37, pp. 183–93.

BOTT, E. (1957) *Family and Social Network: roles, norms and external relationships in ordinary urban families*, London, Tavistock.

BOURNE, J. (1983) 'Towards an anti-racist feminism', *Race and Class*, Vol. XXV, No. 1.

BRAIDOTTI, R. (1989) 'The politics of ontological difference', in Brennan, T. (ed.).

BRENNAN, T. (ed.) (1989) *Between Feminism and Psychoanalysis*, London, Routledge.

BROVERMAN, I. *et al.* (1970) 'Sex role stereotypes and clinical judgments of mental health', *Journal of Consulting and Clinical Psychology*, Vol. 34, No. 17.

BRUCH, H. (1973) *Eating Disorders*, New York, Basic Books.

BRUCH, H. (1979) *The Golden Cage: the enigma of anorexia nervosa*, New York, Vintage.

BRUNSWICK, R. M. (1940) 'The pre-Oedipal phase of the libido development', in Fliess, R. (ed.) (1969) pp. 23–47.

BULBECK, C. (1988) *One World Women's Movement*, London, Pluto Press.

BULKIN, E., PRATT, M. BRUCE AND SMITH, B. (1984) *Yours in Struggle: feminist perspectives on racism and anti-semitism*, Ithaca, NY, Firebrand Books.

CALDECOTT, L. AND LELAND, S. (eds) (1983) *Reclaim the Earth*, London, The Women's Press.

CAMPBELL, B. (1980) 'A feminist sexual politics: now you see it, now you don't', *Feminist Review*, No. 5, pp. 1–18.

CARBY, H. V. (1982) 'White woman listen! Black feminism and the boundaries of sisterhood', pp. 212–35 in Centre for Contemporary Cultural Studies (ed.).

CENTRE FOR CONTEMPORARY CULTURAL STUDIES (ed.) (1982) *The Empire Strikes Back: race and racism in 1970s' Britain*, London, Hutchinson.

CHASSEGUET-SMIRGEL, J. (1964) 'Feminine quilt and the Oedipus complex', pp. 94–134 in Chasseguet-Smirgel J. (ed.) (1970).

CHASSEGUET-SMIRGEL, J. (ed.) (1970) *Female Sexuality*, Ann Arbor, MI, University of Michigan Press.

CHERNIN, K. (1981) *The Obsession: reflections on the tyranny of slenderness*, New York, Harper and Row. (Published as *Womansize: the tyranny of slenderness*, London, The Women's Press, 1983).

CHERNIN, K. (1985) *The Hungry Self*, New York, Harper and Row.

CHODOROW, N. (1978) *The Reproduction of Mothering*, Berkeley, CA, University of California Press.

CIXOUS, H. (1980) 'The laugh of the Medusa', in Marks, E. and de Courtivron, I. (eds) (1981).

CLIFF, M. (1980) *Claiming an Identity They Taught Me to Despise*, Watertown, MA, Persephone Press.

COLLINS, P. HILL (1990) *Black Feminist Thought*, London, Unwin Hyman.

COOTE, A. AND CAMPBELL, B. (1982) *Sweet Freedom*, London, Picador.

COWIE, C. AND LEES, S. (1981) 'Slags or drags', *Feminist Review*, No. 9, pp. 17–32.

DAVIS, A. (1981) *Women, Race and Class*, London, The Women's Press.

DAVIS, M. AND WALLBRIDGE, D. (1983) *Boundary and Space: an introduction to the work of D. W. Winnicott*, Harmondsworth, Penguin Books.

DE BEAUVOIR, S. (1953) *The Second Sex*, London, Jonathan Cape (Harmondsworth, Penguin Books, 1972). (First published in France in 1949.)

DE LAURETIS T. (1990) 'Eccentric subjects: feminist theory and historical consciousness', *Feminist Studies*, Vol. 16, No. 1, pp. 115–50.

DE LAURETIS, T. (ed.) (1986) *Feminist Studies/Critical Studies*, Bloomington, IN, Indiana University Press (Basingstoke, Macmillan, 1988).

DE RIENCOURT, A. (1974) *Sex and Power in History*, New York, David McKay.

DERRIDA, J. (1978) *Writing and Difference*, London, Routledge and Kegan Paul.

DEUTSCH, H. (1925) 'The psychology of woman in relation to the functions of reproduction', pp. 165–79 in Fliess, R. (ed.) (1969).

DEUTSCH, H. (1944 and 1945) *The Psychology of Women*, Vols. 1 and 2, New York, Grune and Stratton.

DINNERSTEIN, D. (1970) *Mermaid and the Minotaur*, New York, Harper and Row.

DREYFUS, D. L. AND RABINOW, P. (1983) *Michel Foucault: beyond structuralism and hermeneutics*, Chicago, IL, University of Chicago Press.

DU BOULAY, J. (1974) *Portrait of a Greek Mountain Village*, Oxford, Clarendon Press.

DWORKIN, A. (1972) *Woman Hating*, New York, E. P. Dutton.

EASLEA, B. (1980) *Witch-hunting, Magic and the New Philosophy*, Atlantic Highlands, NJ, Humanities Press.

EHRENREICH, B. AND ENGLISH, D. (1979) *For Her Own Good*, Garden City, NY, Doubleday.

EICHENBAUM, L. AND ORBACH, S. (1982) *Outside In. . . Inside Out*, Harmondsworth, Penguin Books.

EICHENBAUM, L. AND ORBACH, S. (1983) *Understanding Women: a feminist psychoanalytic approach*, New York, Basic Books.

EISENSTEIN, H. (1984) *Contemporary Feminist Thought*, London, Unwin.

EL DAREER, A. (1982) *Women, Why Do You Weep? Circumcision and its consequences*, London, Zed Press.

EL SADAAWI, N. (1983) *Woman at Point Zero*, London and Atlantic Highlands, NJ, Zed Books.

ENGELS, F. (1972) 'Socialism: Utopian and scientific', in Tucker, R. (ed.) *The Marx and Engels Reader*, New York, W. W. Norton.

ENGINEER, A. A. (1987) *The Shahbano Controversy*, Bombay, Orient Longman.

FAIRBAIRN, W. R. D. (1952) *An Object-Relations Theory of the Personality*, New York, Basic Books.

FANON, F. (1968) *Black Skin, White Masks*, London, Paladin.

FAUSTO-STERLING, A. (1985) *Myths of Gender*, New York, Basic Books.

FEMINIST REVIEW (1984) 'Many voices, one chant: black feminist perspectives', *Feminist Review* Special Issue, No. 17.

FERENCZI, S. (1924) *Thalassa: a theory of genitality*, New York, W. W. Norton.

FINN, G. AND MILES A. (eds) (1982) *Feminism in Canada: from pressure to politics*, Montreal, Black Rose Books.

FIRESTONE, S. (1970) *The Dialectic of Sex: the case for feminist revolution*, New York, William Morrow (London, Paladin, 1972).

FLAX, J. (1983) 'Political philosophy and the patriarchal unconscious: a psychoanalytic perspective on epistemology and metaphysics', in Harding, S. and Hintikka, M. B. (eds.).

FLAX, J. (1986) 'Gender as a social problem: in and for feminist theory', *American Studies/Amerika Studien*, June.

FLIESS, R. (ed.) (1969) *The Psychoanalytic Reader: an anthology of essential papers with critical introductions*, New York, International Universities Press.

FOSTER-CARTER, O. (1987) 'Ethnicity: the fourth burden of Black women - political action', *Critical Social Policy*, No. 20, pp. 46–56.

FOUCAULT, M. (1972) *The Archaeology of Knowledge*, New York, Harper and Row.

FOUCAULT, M. (1979) *Discipline and Punish*, New York, Vintage Books.

FOUCAULT, M. (1980a) *Power/Knowledge: selected interviews and other writings*, ed. Gordon, C., New York, Pantheon.

FOUCAULT, M. (1980b) *The History of Sexuality*, Vol. 1: *An Introduction*, trans. Hurley, R., New York, Vintage Books (Paris, Gallimard, 1976; London, Allen Lane, 1979).

FOUCAULT, M. AND SENNETT, R. (1981) 'Sexuality and solitude', *London Review of Books*, Vol. 3, No.9.

FREIRE, P. (1970) *The Pedagogy of the Oppressed*, New York, Seabury Press.

FREUD, S. (1931) 'Female sexuality', *Standard Edition of the Complete Psychological Works of Sigmund Freud*, Vol. 21, pp. 223–43, London, Hogarth Press and Institute of Psychoanalysis.

FREUD, S. (1933) 'New introductory lectures on psychoanalysis', *Standard Edition of the Complete Psychological Works of Sigmund Freud*, Vol. 22, pp. 3–182, London, Hogarth Press and Institute of Psychoanalysis.

FREUD, S. (1963) 'Introductory lectures on psychoanalysis', *Standard Edition of the Complete Psychological Works of Sigmund Freud*, Vol. 26, London, Hogarth Press and Institute of Psychoanalysis.

FREUD, S. (1973) *The Pelican Freud Library*, Harmondswoth, Penguin Books.

FRIEDAN, B. (1963) *The Feminine Mystique*, London, Victor Gollancz.

GAINES, C. AND BUTLER, G. (1983) 'Iron sisters', *Psychology Today*, November.

GANS, H. (1967) *The Levittowners*, New York, Vintage Books.

GARFINKEL, P. AND GARNER, D. (1982) *Anorexia Nervosa: a multidimensional perspective*, New York, Brunner/Mazel.

GAY, P. (1984) *The Bourgeois Experience*, Vol. 1: *Education of the Senses*, New York, Oxford University Press.

GENOVA, J. (1989) 'Women and the mismeasure of thought', in Tuana, N. (ed.) *Feminism and Science*, Bloomington IN, Indiana Unversity Press.

GILROY, P. (1987) *There Ain't No Black in the Union Jack*, London, Hutchinson.

GLASER, B. G. AND STRAUSS, A. L. (1967) *Grounded Theory: strategies for qualitative research*, Chicago, IL, Aldine.

GOLDBERG, S. (1974) *The Inevitability of Patriarchy*, London, Temple Smith.

GORDON, L. (1986) 'What's new in women's history?', in de Lauretis, T. (ed.).

GORDON, L. (1989) *Heroes of their Own Lives: the politics and history of family violence*, New York, Penguin.

GREEN, J. (1982) *A Dictionary of Contemporary Quotations*, London, Pan Books.

GREER, G. (1971) *The Female Eunuch*, London, Paladin.

GREWAL, S., KAY, J., LANDOR, L., LEWIS, G. AND PARMAR, P. (eds) (1988) *Charting the Journey: writings by black and third world women*, London, Sheba.

GRIFFIN, S. (1984a) *The Roaring Inside Her*, London, The Women's Press.

GRIFFIN, S. (1984b) *Woman and Nature*, London, The Women's Press.

GRUNBERGER, B. (1964) 'Outline for a study of narcissism in female sexuality', pp. 68–83 in Chasseguet-Smirgel, J. (ed.).

GUNTRIP, H. (1961) *Personality Structure and Human Interaction*, New York, International Universities Press (London, The Women's Press).

HAMBLIN, A. (1974) 'The suppressed power of female sexuality', in Allen, S. *et al.* (eds) *Conditions of Illusion*, London, Feminist Books.

HARAWAY, D. (1983) 'A manifesto for cyborgs: science, technology, and socialist feminism in the 1980s', *Socialist Review*, No. 80, pp. 65–107.

HARAWAY, D. (1988) 'Situated knowledges: the science question in feminism and the privilege of partial perspective', *Feminist Studies*, Vol. 14, No. 3, pp. 575–99.

HARDING, S. (1986a) *The Science Question in Feminism*, Ithaca, NY, Cornell University Press.

HARDING, S. (1986b) 'The curious coincidence of African and feminine moralities', in Meyers, D. and Kittay, E. (eds) *Women and Moral Theory*, Totowa, NJ, Rowman and Allenheld.

HARDING, S. AND HINTIKKA, M. B. (eds) (1983) *Discovering Reality: feminist perspectives on epistemology, metaphysics, methodology and philosophy of science*, Dordrecht, The Netherlands, D. Reidel Publishing Company (now Kluwer Academic).

HARTSOCK, N. (1983a) 'The feminist standpoint: developing the ground for a specifically feminist historical materialism', in Harding, S. and Hintikka, M. (eds).

HARTSOCK, N. (1983b) *Money, Sex and Power*, Boston, MA, Northeastern University Press.

HEATH, S. (1982) *The Sexual Fix*, London, Macmillan.

HENRY, J. (1963) *Culture Against Man*, New York, Knopf.

HITE, S. (1976) *The Hite Report*, London, Dell (New York, MacMillan).

HMSO (1974) *Equality for Women*, Cmnd 5724, London, Her Majesty's Stationery Office.

HOGGETT, P. AND HOLLAND, S. (1978) 'People's Aid and Action Centre', *Humpty Dumpty*, No. 8.

HOLLWAY, W. (1982) *Identity and Gender Difference in Adult Social Relations*, unpublished PhD thesis, University of London.

HOOKS, B. (1981) *Ain't I A Woman?: Black women and feminism*, Boston, MA, South End Press.

HOOKS, B. (1989) 'Critical integration: talking race, resisting racism', paper at Conference on Feminisms and Cultural Imperialism: The Politics of Difference, Ithaca, NY, Cornell University, 22-3 April.

HURTADO, A. (1989) 'Relating to privilege: seduction and rejection in the subordination of white women and women of color', *Signs*, Vol. 14, No. 4, pp. 833–55.

INDEN, R. (1986) 'Orientalist constructions of India, *Modern Asian Studies*, Vol. 20, No. 3.

IRIGARAY, L. (1980) 'When our two lips speak together', *Signs*, Vol. 6, No. 1, pp. 69–79.

IRIGARAY, L. (1984) *L'Ethique de la Différence Sexuelle*, Paris, Minuit.

IRIGARAY, L. (1985) *Speculum of the Other Woman*, Ithaca, NY, Cornell University Press.

JAHODA, G. (1981) *White Man: a study of the attitudes of Africans to Europeans in Ghana before Independence*, London, Oxford University Press.

JAISING, I. (1987) 'Women, religion and the law', *The Lawyers Collective*, Vol. 2, No. 11.

JANUS, BESS AND SALTERS (1976) *A Sexual Profile of Men in Power*, Hemel Hempstead, Prentice-Hall.

JAY, N. (1981) 'Gender and dichotomy', *Feminist Studies*, Vol. 7, No. 1, pp. 38–56.

JONES, E. (1956) *Sigmund Freud: Life and Work*, Vol. 1, London, Hogarth Press.

JOURNARD, S. AND SECORD, P. (1955) 'Body cathexis and the ideal female figure', *Journal of Abnormal and Social Psychology*, Vol. 50, pp. 243–6.

KAPLAN, C. (1987) 'Deterritorializations: the rewriting of home and exile in Western feminist discourse', *Cultural Critique*, No. 6.

KATZ, J. (1976) *Gay American History*, New York, Thomas Y. Crowell.

KATZ, J. (1983) *Gay/Lesbian Almanac*, New York, Harper and Row.

KINSEY, A.C. *et al.* (1953) *Sexual Behavior in the Human Female*, Philadelphia, PA, Saunders.

KISHWAR, M. (1986) 'Pro-woman or anti-Muslim? The Shahbano controversy', *Manushi*, No. 32.

KISHWAR, M. AND VANITA, R. (1987) 'The burning of Roop Kanwar', *Manushi*, No. 42–43.

KLEIN, M. (1937) 'Love, guilt and reparation', in Klein, M. and Riviere, J. (eds) (1964) *Love, Hate and Reparation*, New York, W. W. Norton.

KOMAROVSKY, M. (1962) *Blue-collar Marriage*, New York, Vintage Books.

KOMAROVSKY, M. (1974) 'Patterns of self-disclosure of male undergraduates', *Journal of Marriage and Family*, Vol. 36, No. 4, pp. 677–86.

KOSO-THOMAS, O. (1987) *The Circumcision of Women: a strategy for eradication*, London, Zed Press.

KOVEL, J. (1978) *A Complete Guide to Therapy: from psychoanalysis to behaviour modification*, Harmondsworth, Penguin Books.

KOVEL, J. (1988) *White racism: a psychohistory*, London, Free Association Books.

KRISTEVA, J. (1980) *Desire in Language*, New York, Columbia University Press.

KUHN, T. S. (1970) *The Structure of Scientific Revolutions*, Chicago, IL, University of Chicago Press.

KUNDERA, M. (1984) 'The novel and Europe', *New York Review of Books*, Vol. 31, No. 12, 19 July.

LACAN, J. (1977) *Écrits: a selection*, London, Tavistock.

LACAN, J. (1982) *Feminine Sexuality: Jacques Lacan and the École Freudienne*, Mitchell, J. and Rose, J. (eds), Basingstoke, Macmillan.

LAKOFF, R. (1975) *Language and Woman's Place*, New York, Harper and Row.

LASCH, C. (1979) *The Culture of Narcissism*, New York, Warner Books.

LAZREG, M. (1988) 'Feminism and difference: the perils of writing as a woman on women in Algeria', *Feminist Studies*, Vol. 14, No. 1, pp. 81–107.

LEACOCK, E. (1981) *Myths of Male Dominance*, New York, Monthly Review Press.

LIU, A. (1979) *Solitaire*, New York, Harper and Row.

LLOYD, G. (1984) *The Man of Reason: 'male' and 'female' in Western philosophy*, London, Methuen.

LORDE, A. (1984) *Sister Outsider*, Trumansburg, NY, The Crossing Press.

LUGONES, M. C. AND SPELMAN, E. V. (1983) 'Have we got a theory for you! Feminist theory, cultural imperialism and the demand for the "women's voice"', *Hypatia: A Journal of Feminist Philosophy* (special issue of *Women's Studies International Forum*) Vol. 6, No. 6, pp. 573–82.

LUKÁCS, G. (1968) 'Reification and the consciousness of the proletariat', in *History and Class Consciousness*, Cambridge, MA, MIT Press.

MACCORMACK, C. AND STRATHERN, C. (eds) (1980) *Nature, Culture and Gender*, Cambridge and New York, Cambridge University Press.

MACDONALD, B. (1984) 'Barbara's Introduction', in Macdonald, B. and Rich, C. (1984).

MACDONALD, B. AND RICH, C. (1984) *Look Me in the Eye*, London, The Women's Press.

MANI, L. (1987) 'Contentious traditions: the debate on *sati* in colonial India', *Cultural Critique*, No. 7; also published in Sangari, K. K. and Vaid, S. (eds) (1989) *Recasting Women: essays on colonial history*, New Delhi, Kali.

MANI, L. (1989) *Contentious traditions: the debate on sati in colonial India, 1780-1833*, PhD dissertation, University of California, Santa Cruz.

MANI, L. AND FRANKENBERG, R. (1985) 'The challenge of *Orientalism*', *Economy and Society*, Vol. 14, No. 2, pp. 174–92.

MARCUS, M. (1981) *A Taste for Pain*, London, Souvenir Press.

MARKS, E. AND DE COURTIVRON, I. (eds) (1981) *New French Feminisms*, New York, Schocken Books (Brighton, Harvester Press).

MARTIN, B. AND MOHANTY, C. T. (1986) 'Feminist politics: what's home got to do with it?', pp. 191–212 in de Lauretis, T. (ed.).

MASTERS, W. AND JOHNSON, V. (1966) *The Human Sexual Response*, Boston, MA, Little, Brown & Co (New York, Bantam).

MATTHEWS, S. (1979) *The Social World of Old Women*, Beverly Hills, CA, Sage.

MCINTOSH, M. (1968) 'The homosexual role', *Social Problems*, Vol. 16, pp. 182–91. Reprinted in Plummer, K. (ed.) (1981) *The Making of the Modern Homosexual*, London, Hutchinson.

MCKINNON, C. (1987) *Feminist Unmodified: discourses on life and law*, Cambridge, MA, Harvard University Press.

MCROBBIE, A. (1978) *'Jackie*: an ideology of adolescent femininity', *Working Papers in Cultural Studies*, SP53, Birmingham Centre for Contemporary Cultural Studies.

MEULENBELT, A. (1981) *For Ourselves*, London, Sheba.

MILLER, J. BAKER (1978) *Towards a New Psychology of Women*, Harmondsworth, Penguin Books.

MILLETT, K. (1976) *Sita*, London, Ballantine Books.

MILLMAN, M. AND KANTER, R. MOSS (1975) 'Editorial introduction', in *Another Voice: feminist perspectives on social life and social science*, New York, Anchor Books.

MINH-HA, TRIHN, T. (ed) (1986/7) 'She the inappropriate/d Other', *Discourse*, No. 8.

MITCHELL, J. (1971) *Woman's Estate*, Harmondsworth, Penguin Books.

MOHANTY, C. T. (1984) 'Under Western eyes: feminist scholarship and colonial discourses', *Boundary 2*, Spring/Fall, Vol. 12, No. 3/Vol. 13, No. 1. (Revised 1988, *Feminist Review*, No. 30, pp. 61–88.)

MOHANTY, C. T. (1987) 'Feminist encounters, locating the politics of experience', *Copyright*, Vol. 1, No. 1.

MOHANTY, S. P. (1989) 'Us and them: on the philosophical bases of political criticism', *Yale Journal of Criticism*, Vol. 2, No. 2.

MOI, T. (1982) 'Jealousy and sexual difference', *Feminist Review*, No. 11, pp. 53–69.

MOI, T. (1989) 'Patriarchal thought and the drive for knowledge', in Brennan, T. (ed.).

MOIR, A. AND JESSEL, D. (1989) *Brain Sex: the real difference between men and women*, London, Michael Joseph.

MONEY, J. AND EHRHARDT, A. (1972) *Man and Woman, Boy and Girl: the differentiation and dimorphism of gender identity from conception to maturity*, Baltimore, MD, Johns Hopkins University Press.

MORAGA, C. AND ANZALDUA, G. (eds) (1981) *This Bridge Called My Back: writings by radical women of color*, Latham, NY, Kitchen Table/Women of Color Press.

NANDY, A. (1987) 'The sociology of *sati*', *Indian Express*, 5 October.

NANDY, A. (1988a) 'The human factor', *The Illustrated Weekly of India*, 17 January.

NANDY, A. (1988b) 'Sati in Kaliyuga', Economic and Political Weekly, 17 September.

NAVA, M. (1982) '"Everybody's views were just broadened": a girls' project and some responses to lesbianism', Feminist Review, No. 10, pp. 37–60.

NKOSI, L. (1983) Home and Exile, 2nd edn, Oxford, Blackwell.

OAKLEY, A. (1972) Sex, Gender and Society, London, Temple Smith.

ONG, A. (1987) Spirits of Resistance and Capitalist Resistance: factory women in Malaysia, Albany, NY, SUNY Press.

ORBACH, S. (1978) Fat is a Feminist Issue, New York, Berkley.

ORBACH, S. (1986) Hunger Strike, New York, W. W. Norton.

ORTNER, S. B. (1974) 'Is female to male as nature is to culture?' in Rosaldo, M. Z. and Lamphere, L. (eds).

PACHAURI, P. (1988) 'Turning a blind eye: glorification of sati continues despite the law', India Today, 15 October.

PACKARD, V. (1968) The Sexual Wilderness, London, Pan.

PAIGE, K. (1973) 'Women learn to sing the menstrual blues', Psychology Today, September, pp. 41–6.

PALMERI, A. (n.d.) 'Feminist materialism: on the possibilities and power of the nature/culture distinction', unpublished ms.

PARMAR, P. (1982) 'Gender, race and class: Asian women in resistance', in Centre for Contemporary Cultural Studies (ed.).

PATEL, S. AND KUMAR, K. (1988) 'Defenders of sati', Economic and Political Weekly, 23 January.

PATHAK, Z. AND SUNDER RAJAN, R. (1989) '"Shahbano"', Signs, Vol. 14, No. 3, pp. 558–82.

PEARSON, D. AND SHAW, S. (1982) Life Extension, New York, Warner.

PERSON, E. (1980) 'Sexuality as the mainstay of identity: psychoanalytic perspectives', in Stimpson, C. R. and Person, E. S. (eds) Women: sex and sexuality, Chicago, IL, University of Chicago Press.

PHILIPOSE, P. AND SETALVAD, T. (1988) 'Demystifying sati', The Illustrated Weekly of India, 13 March.

PHOENIX, A. (1988) 'Narrow definitions of culture: the case of early motherhood', in Westwood, S. and Bhachu, P. (eds) (1988) Enterprising Women: ethnicity, economy and gender relations, London, Routledge.

PIERCY, M. (1972) Woman on the Edge of Time, New York, Fawcett.

PUNWANI, J. (1985) 'The strange case of Shahbano', The Sunday Observer, 24 November.

PUTNAM, H. (1964) 'Robots: machines and artificially created life?', Journal of Philosophy, Vol. 61, November, pp. 668–91.

QADEER, I. AND HASAM, Z. (1987) 'Deadly politics of the state and its apologists', *Economic and Political Weekly*, 14 November.

RAMAZANOGLU, C. (1986) 'Ethnocentrism and socialist-feminist theory: a response to Barrett and McIntosh', *Feminist Review*, No. 22, pp. 83–6.

RAYMOND, J. (1976) *The Transsexual Empire: the making of the she-male*, Boston, MA, Beacon Press.

RAYMOND, J. (1979) 'Transsexualixm: an issue of sex-role stereotyping', in Tobach, E. and Rosoff, B. (eds) (1979) *Genes and Gender II*, New York, Gordian Press.

REID, I. SMITH (1975) 'Science, politics and race', *Signs*, Vol. 1, No. 2, pp. 397–422.

RICH, A. (1976) *Of Woman Born: motherhood as experience and institution*, New York, W. W. Norton.

RICH, A. (1977) *Of Woman Born*, London, Virago.

RICH, A. (1986) 'Notes toward a politics of location (1984)', in *Blood Bread and Poetry*, New York, W. W. Norton.

RICH, C. (1980) 'Compulsory heterosexuality and lesbian existence', *Signs*, No. 5, Summer, pp. 631–60.

ROBBINS, B. (1987/88) 'The politics of theory', *Social Text*, No. 18.

ROSALDO, M. ZIMBALIST AND LAMPHERE, L. (eds) (1974) *Woman, Culture and Society*, Stanford, CA, Stanford University Press.

ROSE, H. (1983) 'Hand, brain and heart: a feminist epistemology for the natural sciences' *Signs*, Vol. 9, No. 1, pp. 73–90.

ROSE, H. (1984) 'Is a feminist science possible?', paper presented at MIT, Cambridge, MA.

ROSE, S., KAMIN, L. AND LEWONTIN, R. (1984) *Not in Our Genes*, Harmondsworth, Penguin Books.

ROSEN, T. (1983) *Strong and Sexy*, New York, Puritan.

ROSSI, A. (1969) 'Sex equality: the beginning of ideology', *The Humanist*, Vol. xxix, No. 5. (Reprinted in Roszak, B. and Roszak, T. (eds), pp. 173–86.)

ROSZAK, B. AND ROSZAK, T. (eds) *Masculine/Feminine*, New York, Harper and Row.

RUBIN, G. (1984) 'Thinking sex', pp. 267–319 in Vance, C. S. (ed.) *Pleasure and Danger: exploiting female sexuality*, London, Routledge and Kegan Paul.

SAID, E. (1979) *Orientalism*, New York, Vintage.

SAID, E. (1983) *The World, The Text and the Critic*, Cambridge, MA, Harvard University Press.

SAID, E. (1986) 'Intellectuals in the post-colonial world', *Salmagundi*, No. 70–1.

SALAAM, K. Y. (1980) 'Rape: a radical analysis – an African-American perspective', *Black Books Bulletin*, Vol. 6, No. 4.

SANDAY, P. REEVE (1981) *Female Power and Male Dominance*, Cambridge, Cambridge University Press.

SANDOVAL, C. (forthcoming) 'US Third World feminism: the theory and method of oppositional consciousness', in *Oppositional consciousness in the post-modern world*, Doctoral dissertation in progress, University of California, Santa Cruz.

SANGARI, K. K. (1988) 'Perpetuating the myth', *Seminar*, No. 342, Special Issue on *sati*.

SAYERS, J. (1982) *Biological Politics*, London, Tavistock.

SCRUTON, R. (1983) 'The case against feminism', *The Observer*, 22 May, p.27.

SEGAL, H. (1979) *Klein*, Glasgow, Collins-Fontana Modern Masters.

SEGAL, L. (1987) *Is the Future Female?* London, Virago.

SEGREST, M. (1985) *My Mama's Dead Squirrel: lesbian essays on southern culture*, Ithaca, NY, Firebrand Books.

SHANDALL, A. ABU-EL-FUTUH (1967) 'Circumcision and infibulation of females: a general consideration of the problem and a clinical study of the complications in Sudanese women', *Sudan Medical Journal*, Vol. 5, pp. 178–207.

SHERIDAN, A. (1980) *Michel Foucault: the will to truth*, New York, Tavistock Publications.

SLATER, P. E. (1961) 'Toward a dualistic theory of identification', *Merrill-Palmer Quarterly of Behavior and Development*, Vol. 7, No. 2, pp. 28–128.

SMITH, B. (ed.) (1983) *Home Girls: a black feminist anthology*, Latham, NY, Kitchen Table/Women of Color Press.

SMITH, D. (1974) 'Women's perspective as a radical critique of sociology', *Sociological Inquiry*, Vol. 44, No. 1, pp. 7–13.

SMITH, D. (1979) 'A sociology for women', in Sherman, J. and Beck, E. T. (eds) *The Prism of Sex: essays in the sociology of knowledge*, Madison, WI, University of Wisconsin Press.

SMITH, D. (1984) 'The new Puritans', *New York*, 11 June.

SNITOW, A. B. (1979) 'Mass market romance: pornography for women is different', *Radical History Review*, No. 20.

SNITOW, A. B. (1980) 'The front line: notes on sex in novels by women, 1969-79', *Signs*, Vol. 5, No. 4.

SPELMAN, E. V. (1982) 'Woman as body: ancient and contemporary views', *Feminist Studies*, Vol. 8, No. 1, pp. 109–31.

SPELMAN, E. V. (1988) *Inessential Woman: problems of exclusion in feminist thought*, Boston, MA, Beacon Press (London, The Women's Press, 1990).

SPELMAN, E. V. (n.d.) 'Bodies and their persons', unpublished ms.

SPENDER, D. (1980) *Man Made Language*, London, Routledge and Kegan Paul.

SPIVAK, G. C. (1981) 'French feminism in an international frame', *Yale French Studies*, No. 62.

SPIVAK, G. C. (1989) 'Post-coloniality and the field of value', paper at Conference on Feminisms and Cultural Imperialism: The Politics of Difference, Ithaca, NY, Cornell University, 22-3 April.

STACK, C. B. (1974) *All Our Kin*, New York, Harper and Row.

STEPHENS, E. (1975) 'The moon within your reach: a feminist approach to female orgasm', *Spare Rib*, No. 42, December.

STOLLER, R. (1975) *Perversion: the erotic form of hatred*, New York, Delta.

STORR, A. (1971) *Human Aggression*, Harmondsworth, Penguin Books (quoted in *The Observer*, 24 May 1981).

STRATHERN, M. (1980) 'No nature, no culture: the Hagen case', in MacCormack, C. and Strathern, M. (eds).

SUNDER RAJAN, R. (forthcoming) 'The subject of *sati*: pain and death in the contemporary discourse on *sati*', *Yale Journal of Criticism*.

SYDIE, R. (1987) *Natural Woman, Cultured Man*, Milton Keynes, Open University Press.

VAID, S. (1988) 'Politics of widow immolation', *Seminar*, No. 342, Special Issue on *sati*.

WHITING, J. W. M. (1971) 'Causes and consequences of the amount of body contact between mother and infant', paper presented to the American Anthropological Association Meetings, New York.

WHITING, P. (1972) 'Female sexuality: its political implications', in Wandor, M. (ed.) *The Body Politic*, London, Stage One.

WILLIS, P. (1978) *Learning to Labour: how working-class kids get working-class jobs*, London, Saxon House.

WILSON, G. (1979) 'The sociobiology of sex differences', *Bulletin of the British Psychological Society*, Vol. 32, pp. 350–3.

WILSON, E. O. (1978) *On Human Nature*, Cambridge MA, Harvard University Press (New York, Bantam, 1980).

WINNICOTT, D. W. (1965) *The Family and Individual Development*, New York, Basic Books.

WITTIG, M. (1979) 'One is not born a woman', *Proceedings of the Second Sex Conference*, New York, New York Institute for the Humanities.

WOLFF, C. (1971) *Love Between Women*, London, Duckworth (New York, Harper and Row).

WOLGAST, E. H. (1980) *Equality and the Rights of Woman*, Ithaca, NY, and London, Cornell University Press.

WOLLSTONECRAFT, M. (1792) *A Vindication of the Rights of Women*, (Harmondsworth, Penguin Books, 1972).

WOOD, J. (1982) 'Adolescents', *New Socialist*, No. 5, pp. 41–3.

WOODS, J. (1981) 'I was starving myself to death', *Mademoiselle*, May.

WOOLEY, O., WOOLEY, S. AND DYRENFORTH, S. (1979) 'Obesity and women: a neglected feminist topic', *Woman's Studies Institute Quarterly*, No. 2, pp. 61–92.

YOUNG, I. (1981) 'Beyond the unhappy marriage: a critique of the dual systems theory', in Sargent, L. (ed.) *Women and Revolution*, Boston, South End Press.

YOUNG, I. (1981) 'Woman and political philosophy', *Teaching Philosophy*, Vol. 4, No. 2, pp. 183–9.

YOUNG, M. AND WILLMOTT, P. (1957) *Family and Kinship in East London*, Harmondsworth, Penguin Books.

SOURCE LIST OF ARTICLES

Article 1.1 Age, race, class and sex: women redefining difference
Audre Lorde from Lorde, A. (1984) *Sister Outsider*, Trumansburg, NY, The
Crossing Press (pp. 14–23).

Article 1.2 Ageing, ageism and feminist avoidance   Cynthia Rich
from MacDonald, B. and Rich, C. (1984) *Look Me In The Eye*, London, The
Women's Press (pp. 9–10, 'Cynthia's Introduction', and pp. 55–6).

Article 2.1 Transforming biology   Lynda Birke
Commissioned article.

Article 2.2 Human biology in feminist theory: sexual equality
reconsidered   Alison M. Jaggar
from Gould, C. (ed.) (1983) *Human Biology in Feminist Theory: sexual
equality revisited*, Totowa, NJ, Rowman and Allanheld (pp. 21–41).

Article 2.3 Anorexia nervosa: psychopathology as the crystallization of
culture   Susan Bordo
from Diamond, I. and Quinby, L. (eds) (1988) *Feminism and Foucault:
reflections on resistance*, Boston, MA, Northeastern University Press
(pp. 87–109).

Article 3.1 Sexuality   Catharine McKinnon
from McKinnon, C. (1987) *Feminism Unmodified: discourses on life and law*,
Cambridge, MA, Harvard University Press.

Article 3.2 Sensual uncertainty, or why the clitoris is not enough
Lynne Segal
from Cartledge, S. and Ryan, J. (eds) (1983) *Sex and Love*, London, The
Women's Press, Chapter 3 (pp. 30–47).

Article 3.3 Social construction theory: problems in the history of
sexuality   Carole S. Vance
from Altman, D. *et al.* (eds) (1989) *Homosexuality, Which Homosexuality?:
Essays from the International Scientific Conference on Gay and Lesbian
Studies*, Amsterdam, Schorer/London, GMP Publishers (pp. 13–34).

Article 4.1 The psychodynamics of the family   Nancy Chodorow
from Chodorow, N. (1978) *The Reproduction of Mothering: psychoanalysis
and the sociology of gender*, Los Angeles, University of California Press,
Chapter 12 (pp. 191–209).

Article 4.2 Psychoanalysis and women loving women   Joanna Ryan
from Cartledge, S. and Ryan, J. (eds) (1983) *Sex and Love*, London, The
Women's Press, Chapter 13 (pp. 196–208).

Article 5.1 Lacan   Rosalind Minsky
Commissioned article.

Article 5.2 Sitting up and lying down: experiences of psychotherapy
and psychoanalysis   Sarah Maguire
Commissioned article.

Article 5.3 Images of 'woman': the photography of Cindy Sherman
Judith Williamson
from *Screen*, Vol. 24, No. 6, pp. 102–6 (Nov–Dec 1983).

Article 6.1 Gender difference and the production of subjectivity
Wendy Hollway
from Henriques, J., Hollway, W., Urwin, C., Venn, C. and Walkerdine, V.
(eds) (1984) *Changing the Subject: psychology, social regulation and
subjectivity*, London, Methuen, Chapter 5 (pp. 227–63).

Article 6.2 Feminism, criticism and Foucault   Biddy Martin
from Diamond, I. and Quinby, L. (eds) (1988) *Feminism and Foucault:
reflections on resistance*, Boston, MA, Northeastern University Press.

Article 7.1 Feminism and the challenge of racism: deviance or
difference   Razia Aziz
Commissioned article.

Article 7.2 Multiple mediations: feminist scholarship in the age of
multinational reception   Lata Mani
from *Feminist Review*, No. 35, pp. 24–41 (Summer 1990).

Article 7.3 Identity: skin blood heart   Minnie Bruce Pratt
from Bulkin, E., Pratt, M. Bruce and Smith, B. (1988) *Yours in Struggle:
three feminist perspectives on anti-semitism and racism*, Ithaca, NY,
Firebrand Books (pp. 11–41).

Article 8.1 The instability of the analytical categories of feminist
theory   Sandra Harding
from *Signs*, Vol. 11, No. 4, pp. 645–62 (1986).

Article 8.2 What is feminist theory? Elizabeth Gross
from Pateman, C. and Gross, E. (eds) (1987) *Feminist Challenges: social and
political theory*, Boston, MA, Northeastern University Press (pp. 190–204).

ACKNOWLEDGEMENTS

Grateful acknowledgement is made to the following sources for permission to reproduce material in this book:

Text

Chapter 1: Miller J.B. (1978) *Toward a New Psychology of Women,* pp. 6-8 & 87-93, Penguin Books, copyright © Jean Baker Miller. Reproduced by permission of Beacon Press; Bardwick, Judith M. (1980) *In Transition.* Copyright © 1979 by Holt, Rinehart and Winston Inc., New York. Reproduced by permission of the publisher; Rich, A. (1977) *Of Woman Born,* Virago Press. Reproduced by permission of W.W. Norton and Co.; Segal, L. (1987) *Is The Future Female?,* Virago Press; Gordon, L. (1987) 'What's new in women's history?' in de Lauretis, T., *Feminist Studies/Critical Studies,* Center for Twentieth Century Studies, University of Wisconsin; de Beauvoir, S. (1953) *The Second Sex,* Jonathan Cape. From The *Second Sex* by S. de Beauvoir, trans. and ed., H.M. Parshley. Copyright © 1952 by Alfred A. Knopf, Inc. Reprinted by permission of the publisher; Lorde, A. (1984) *Sister Outsider,* The Crossing Press, © 1984 Audre Lorde; MacDonald, B. and Rich, C. (1984) *Look Me In The Eye: old women, aging and agism,* London, The Women's Press Limited.

Chapter 2: Jaggar, A.M. (1983) 'Human biology in feminist theory: sexual equality reconsidered', in Gould, C. (ed.), *Beyond Domination: new perspectives on women and philosophy,* Rowman and Littlefield, © 1982 by Alison M. Jaggar; Bordo, S. (1988) 'Anorexia nervosa: psychopathology as the crystallization of culture', first published in *The Philosophical Forum,* Vol. XVII, No. 2, Winter 1985-86.

Chapter 3: Reprinted by permission of the publishers from *Feminism Unmodified: discourses on life and law* by C. McKinnon, Cambridge, Mass., Harvard University Press, Copyright © 1987 by the President and Fellows of Harvard College; Segal, L. (1983) 'Sensual uncertainty, or why the clitoris is not enough', in Cartledge, S. and Ryan, J. (eds), *Sex & Love,* The Women's Press Limited; Vance, C. S. (1989) 'Social construction theory: problems in the history of sexuality', in Altman, D. et al. (eds) *Homosexuality, Which Homosexuality? Essays from The International Scientific Conference on Gay and Lesbian Studies,* Amsterdam, Schorer, 1989.

Chapter 4: Nancy Chodorow (1978) The *Reproduction of Mothering: psychoanalysis and the sociology of gender,* University of California Press, Copyright © 1978 The Regents of the University of California; Ryan J. (1983) 'Psychoanalysis and women loving women', in Cartledge, S. and Ryan, J. (eds), *Sex & Love,* The Women's Press Limited.

Chapter 5: Williamson, J. (1983) 'Images of "Woman"', *Screen,* Vol. 24, No. 6, Nov-Dec 1983, Oxford University Press. Reproduced by permission.

Chapter 6: Hollway, W. (1984) 'Gender difference and the production of subjectivity', in Henriques, J., Hollway, W., Urwin, C., Venn, C. and Walkerdine, V. (eds), *Changing the Subject: psychology, social regulation and subjectivity,* Methuen and Co; Martin, B. (1988) 'Feminism, criticism and Foucault', in *From Feminism and Foucault: reflections on resistance,* edited by Irene Diamond and Lee Quinby. Copyright © 1988 by Irene Diamond and Lee Quinby. Reprinted with the permission of Northeastern University Press, Boston.

Chapter 7: Mani, L. (1990) 'Multiple mediations: feminist scholarship in the age of multinational reception', *Feminist Review*, No. 35, Summer 1990; Bruce Pratt, M. (1988) 'Identity: skin blood heart', in Bulkin, E., Bruce Pratt, M. and Smith, B. (eds), *Yours in Struggle: three feminist perspectives on anti-semitism and racism*, Firebrand Books, Ithaca, New York, USA.

Chapter 8: Harding, S. (1987) 'The instability of the analytical categories of feminist theory', *Signs*, Vol. 2, No. 4, 1986. Reproduced by permission of the University of Chicago Press; Gross, E. (1987) 'What is feminist theory?', in Pateman, C. and Gross, E. (eds), *Feminist Challenges*, Allen and Unwin, NSW, Australia.

Illustrations

p. 13: cartoon by Lesley Ruda from Thompson, J. (compiler) (1980) *Equality for Some: a tape-study pack for women*, Cambridge, National Extension College; *p. 59*: cartoon by Deirdre Janson-Smith from Brighton Women and Science Group, *Alice through the Microscope*, London, Virago; *p. 131*: © Ellen Levine 1972. Reproduced from Anne Koedt, Ellen Levine and Anita Rapone (eds) *Radical Feminism*, 1973, New York, Quadrangle Books; *p. 145*: front cover design by Phyllis Mahon for *Sex & Love: new thoughts on old contradictions*, edited by Sue Cartledge and Joanna Ryan, 1983, London, The Women's Press Limited; *p. 169*: Mary Kelly, *Corpus*, 1985, reproduced by permission of Mary Kelly; *p. 204*: Reproduced with permission from Ros Asquith, *Baby*, 1988, Macdonald Optima, p. 46; *pp. 225-34:* photographs by Cindy Sherman. Reproduced by permission of Cindy Sherman and Metro Pictures, New York: *p. 225*: Untitled Film Still No. 4, 1978, black and white photograph, 8" x 10" and Untitled Film Still No. 40, 1979, black and white photograph, 8" x 10"; *p. 226*: Untitled Film Still No. 16, 1978, black and white photograph, 8" x 10"; *p. 227*: Untitled Film Still No. 63, 1980, black and white photograph, 8" x 10" and Untitled Film Still No. 96, 1981, colour photograph, 24" x 48"; *p. 228*: Untitled Film Still No. 90, 1981, colour photograph, 24" x 48" and Untitled Film Still No. 5, 1978, black and white photograph, 8" x 10"; *p. 229*: Untitled Film Still No. 21, 1978, black and white photograph, 8" x 10" and Untitled Film Still No. 46, 1978, black and white photograph, 8" x 10"; *p. 230*: Untitled Film Still No. 103, 1982, colour photograph, 30" x 19.75"; *p. 231*: Untitled Film Still No. 104, 1982, colour photograph, 30" x 19.75"; *p. 232*: Untitled Film Still No. 116, 1982, colour photograph, 45.25" x 30"; *p. 233*: Untitled Film Still No. 112, 1982, colour photograph, 45.25" x 30"; *p. 234*: Untitled Film Still No. 110, 1982, colour photograph, 45.25" x 30".

INDEX

(Note: Page numbers in bold indicate articles by these authors.)